SHAKESPEARE: THE CRITICAL HERITAGE
VOLUME I 1623–1692

THE CRITICAL HERITAGE SERIES

GENERAL EDITOR: B. C. SOUTHAM, M.A., B. LITT. (OXON.)
Formerly Department of English, Westfield College, University of London

For a list of books in the series see the back end paper

SHAKESPEARE

THE CRITICAL HERITAGE

VOLUME 1   1623–1692

Edited by
BRIAN VICKERS
Professor of English, University of Zürich

ROUTLEDGE & KEGAN PAUL : LONDON AND BOSTON

First published in 1974
by Routledge & Kegan Paul Ltd
Broadway House, 68–74 Carter Lane,
London EC4V 5EL and
9 Park Street,
Boston, Mass. 02108, U.S.A.
© Brian Vickers 1974
No part of this book may be reproduced in
any form without permission from the
publisher, except for the quotation of brief
passages in criticism
ISBN 0 7100 7716 5
Library of Congress Catalog No. 73–85430

Printed in Great Britain by
Richard Clay (The Chaucer Press) Ltd
Bungay, Suffolk

General Editor's Preface

The reception given to a writer by his contemporaries and near-contemporaries is evidence of considerable value to the student of literature. On one side we learn a great deal about the state of criticism at large and in particular about the development of critical attitudes towards a single writer; at the same time, through private comments in letters, journals or marginalia, we gain an insight upon the tastes and literary thought of individual readers of the period. Evidence of this kind helps us to understand the writer's historical situation, the nature of his immediate reading-public, and his response to these pressures.

The separate volumes in the *Critical Heritage Series* present a record of this early criticism. Clearly, for many of the highly productive and lengthily reviewed nineteenth- and twentieth-century writers, there exists an enormous body of material; and in these cases the volume editors have made a selection of the most important views, significant for their intrinsic critical worth or for their representative quality—perhaps even registering incomprehension!

For earlier writers, notably pre-eighteenth century, the materials are much scarcer and the historical period has been extended, sometimes far beyond the writer's lifetime, in order to show the inception and growth of critical views which were initially slow to appear.

Shakespeare is, in every sense, a special case, and Professor Vickers is presenting the course of his reception and reputation extensively, over a span of three centuries, in a sequence of six volumes, each of which will document a specific period.

In each volume the documents are headed by an Introduction, discussing the material assembled and relating the early stages of the author's reception to what we have come to identify as the critical tradition. The volumes will make available much material which would otherwise be difficult of access and it is hoped that the modern reader will be thereby helped towards an informed understanding of the ways in which literature has been read and judged.

B.C.S.

Contents

CONTENTS

Preface

This is the first of six volumes in the *Critical Heritage Series* to be devoted to Shakespeare, and it differs from its companions in a number of ways. For one thing, I print no contemporary allusions in the text proper, since it seems to me that none of these amount to sustained criticism of any great value. For another, it would have been a falsification of the total picture to limit the selections to formal criticism. Having taken stock of the various courses taken by the reaction to Shakespeare, I decided to include, in addition to regular critical essays, and poems to or about Shakespeare, items in the following categories: the adaptations of Shakespeare's plays, of which over a hundred appeared in the period 1660–1820; theatre criticism, dealing with performances of both the original plays and the adaptations; notes and comments from the editions of Shakespeare. I intend to offer a more detailed account of the progress of Shakespeare criticism once these volumes have been completed.

For the present volume only the first of these additional categories was relevant: I have chosen excerpts from all the major adaptations. The demands on space were strong, and although I would have liked to include several of these in their entirety I had to settle for selections, as generous as possible. If the reader has a copy of Shakespeare open he will be able to follow the most important of the transformations in plot, character and language. The Select Bibliography lists some detailed studies of these versions.

It only remains for me to thank the libraries which have made this collection possible: the Folger Library, Washington; the British Museum; the Bodleian; Cambridge University Library, and King's College Library. For assistance in checking the manuscript I am indebted to Mr Albert Freiling and to Mr Wilhelm Schmid.

B.W.V.

Introduction

The evaluation of Shakespeare made by his contemporaries was generous but not searching. If we read the three hundred pages of *The Shakespeare Allusion-Book*[1] devoted to references prior to the publication of the First Folio edition of his plays in 1623 we will find him praised for his industry, his eloquence, or his pleasant personal qualities. Henry Chettle, writing in 1592 an apology for the attack on Shakespeare made by Greene in his death-bed pamphlet *Green's Groats-Worth of Wit* (1592), regretted having helped publish Greene's work because he himself had seen Shakespeare's 'demeanor no lesse civill than he exelent in the qualities he professes: Besides, divers of worship have reported his uprightnes of dealing, which argues his honesty, and his facetious grace in writing, that approoves his Art' (*Sh. A.B.*, I, 4). In 1612 Webster praised 'the right happy and copious industry of *M. Shakespeare*', Dekker and Heywood (I, 233), and '*copious* Shakespeare' was the formulation of Francis Kirkman in 1652 (II, 24). In the testimony of his fellow-actors and sharers, Heminge and Condell, who collected his plays together for the First Folio, Shakespeare's fluency became almost legendary:

Who, as he was a happie imitator of Nature, was a most gentle expresser of it. His mind and hand went together: And what he thought, he uttered with that easinesse, that wee have scarse received from him a blot in his papers. (I, 316)

'Neatness' is a relative term, of course: by the standards of Elizabethan playhouse manuscripts Shakespeare's papers may have been tidier than others, but that does not seem to have helped editors much. And Ben Jonson (No. 1a below) took exception to this panegyric in terms of the classical conception of 'the Art to blot'. Reactions to Jonson's criticism form one of the centres of the Art–Nature controversy over the next two hundred years.

The epithet 'Gentle' used by Jonson and in Heminge and Condell's tribute was echoed by others (I, 407), and collectively such references build up a flattering picture: '*Friendly* Shakespeare' (I, 133), with 'his cunning braine' (I, 365) or 'that nimble *Mercury* [his] braine' (I, 245), 'Ingenious *Shakespeare*' (I, 280). Of tribute there is no shortage, but discrimination does not extend much beyond varying an accepted praise-term. The quality most often attributed to Shakespeare (largely, it must be noted, on the strength of his early Ovidian poems *Venus and Adonis* and *The Rape of Lucrece*) was that of eloquence, usually expressed in the word 'sweet'. In his *Polimanteia* (1595) W. Covell added a marginal note to his praise of Samuel Daniel: 'All praise worthy. Lucrecia Sweet Shakespeare' (I, 23). In Jonson's poem in the First Folio (No. 1a below) we have the famous 'sweet Swan of Avon' (echoed in 1647: I, 503), while in *L'Allegro* Milton went one better:

> ... sweetest *Shakespeare*, Fancy's child,
> Warble his native wood-notes wild. (I, 372)

The phrase 'sweet Shakespeare' occurs so often in the *Parnassus* plays, those trendy Cambridge satires of the 1600s (cf. I, 67, 68 (twice), 69, 102) that one suspects a parody of a stock response. Variations on it abound: 'Honie-tong'd *Shakespeare*' is John Weever's address to the poet in 1595, and he goes on to celebrate some of his favourite creations—*Adonis, Lucrece, Romeo, Richard*—with their 'sugred tongues' (I, 24); 'hony-flowing Vaine' is Richard Barnfield's version three years later (I, 51); 'mellifluous' says Heywood in 1635 (I, 393), and in 1639 Thomas Bancroft adores 'Thy Muses sugred dainties' (I, 439). George Lynn praised 'Smooth *Shakespeare*' in 1640 (I, 451), a year which saw the publication of the *Poems* by John Benson. In his address to the reader Benson promised that:

in your perusall you shall finde them Seren, cleere and eligantly plaine, such gentle straines as shall recreate and not perplexe your braine, no intricate or cloudy stuffe to puzzell intellect, but perfect eloquence. ... (I, 454)

After the energies expended on the *Sonnets* by modern critics that assurance seems over-confident, but Benson is merely subscribing to the accepted evaluation of Shakespeare: so an anonymous poem appended to the volume celebrates these 'smooth Rhimes' (I, 422). The definitive expression of this established view is the effusive, indeed cloying encomium of Francis Meres in his *Palladis Tamia. Wits Treasury* (1598):

As the soule of *Euphorbus* was thought to live in *Pythagoras*; so the sweete wittie soule of *Ovid* lives in mellifluous & hony-tongued *Shakespeare*, witnes his *Venus* and *Adonis*, his *Lucrece*, his sugred Sonnets among his private friends, &c. . . .

As *Epius Stolo* said, that the Muses would speake with *Plautus* tongue, if they would speak Latin: so I say that the Muses would speak with *Shakespeares* fine filed phrase, if they would speake English. (I, 46)

Our respect for Meres's independent testimony is bound to be reduced by D. C. Allen's discovery that he 'borrowed' the form and much of the content of his work from the *Officina* (1520) by J. Ravisius Textor and, so to speak, merely inserted English names in the gaps.[2] Yet it is an accurate summing-up of the dominant tone of contemporary allusions, generous but facile.

Reading through the allusions after 1623 one does not discover a sudden access of penetration. The celebration becomes more ecstatic: Richard Flecknoe admires

> inimitable *Shakespeare*'s way,
> *Promethian-like*, to animate a Play (II, 163)

while other writers become idolatrous: '*Godlike* Shakespeare', 'Divine', 'immortal' (II, 338, 259, 264, 339), although we occasionally find the traditional and more moderate epithets: 'gentle' (II, 71), 'sweet' (II, 277). But these miscellaneous references are sometimes a useful guide to the changes of taste that were overtaking the mid-seventeenth century. As early as 1647 Thomas Cartwright, in the Folio collection of Beaumont and Fletcher, elevated Fletcher since his wit was more up-to-date:

> *Shakespeare* to thee was dull, whose best jest lyes
> I'th Ladies questions, and the Fooles replyes,
> Old fashion'd wit, which walkt from town to town
> In turn'd Hose, which our fathers call'd the Clown,
> Whose wit our nice times would obsceanness call,
> And which made Bawdry pass for Comicall:
> Nature was all his Art, thy veine was free
> As his, but without his scurility. (I, 511)

The rather self-conscious refinement of the Restoration stage can be seen again in a prologue to Shirley's *Love Tricks*, republished in 1667:

> In our Old Plays, the humour Love and Passion
> Like Doublet, Hose, and Cloak, are out of fashion:
> That which the World call'd Wit in *Shakespeare*'s age,
> Is laught at, as improper for our Stage. (II, 138)

3

One immediate modernisation was in costume: Catherine Philips, in a letter dated 3 December 1662, recorded how 'only the other day, when *Othello* was play'd, the Doge of Venice and all his Senators came upon the Stage with Feathers in their Hats, which was like to have chang'd the Tragedy into a Comedy, but that the Moor and Desdemona acted their Parts well'.[3] Another and more important updating also involved *Othello* on the first occasion, recorded in Thomas Jordan's 'Prologue to introduce the first Woman that came to Act on the Stage in the Tragedy, call'd *The Moor of Venice*':

> . . . In this reforming age
> We have intents to civilize the Stage.
> Our woman are defective, and so siz'd
> You'd think they were some of the Guard disguiz'd;
> For (to speak truth) men act, that are between
> Forty and fifty, Wenches of fifteen;
> With bone so large, and nerve so incomplyant,
> When you call *Desdemona*, enter Giant. (II, 87)

This happy event seems to have taken place in 1660.

The impact on English culture of the return of a King and court from France has been duly noted by literary historians. For the reception of Shakespeare it soon produced a tension between an idolatry for our greatest dramatist and the highly developed critical concepts of rules, decorum, propriety, the unities and so on—that amalgam of Aristotle and Horace borrowed from the French seventeenth century (who had themselves borrowed it from the Italian sixteenth century), which was to determine neoclassical attitudes to Shakespeare for several generations. The diarist John Evelyn noted the new trend very early, writing on 26 November 1661: 'I saw *Hamlet* Prince of Denmark played: but now the old playe began to disgust this refined age: since his Majestie being so long abroad.'[4] According to the canons of refinement Shakespeare left much to be desired, yet it was still open for the critic to maintain a balance between the demands of the present and idolatry for the past. Such a balance was effected by Edward Phillips in 1675, in the Preface to his *Theatrum Poetarum*, refurbishing the traditional distinction between 'Wit, Ingenuity . . . Learning, even Elegancy' in verse on the one hand, and, on the other, 'True Native Poetry', which has an 'Air and Spirit' of its own, not to be reached by study, industry, or the observance of the rules:

this Poetic *Energie* . . . would be required to give life to all the rest, which shines through the roughest most unpolish't and antiquated Language, and may happly be wanting, in the most polite and reformed. . . . [So] *Shakespeare*, in spight of all his unfiled expressions, his rambling and indigested Fancys, the laughter of the *Critical*, yet must be confess't a *Poet* above many that go beyond him in Literature some degrees. (II, 221)

II

That balance could be struck by the critic, since he was involved in the evaluation of a finished output, a settled canon. But to those in the theatre, concerned with Shakespeare as a living force and as a way of life—the 'refined' and 'reforming' attitudes which were disgusted by the 'Old fashion'd wit' of the Elizabethans—the tension could only be resolved by changing the poet rather than the taste of the age. Part of the explanation for the need to adapt is social, to do with the size of the audience and the number of theatres. Whereas in Shakespeare's London there were from five to eight theatres open at any one time, and a weekly audience of some 18,000 to 24,000,[5] in November, 1660 only two companies were licensed by the crown: the Duke's Men, managed by Sir William D'Avenant, and the King's Men, run by Thomas Killigrew. Indeed in 1682, due largely, it seems, to a decline in the status and quality of actors available, and hence of audiences attracted, the two companies amalgamated into one (though they returned to two in 1695). The theatres were much smaller than the open-air public theatres of Shakespeare's day; they accommodated about four hundred people, at much higher prices, in late afternoon and evening performances. Although there are enough references to rowdyism and violence within the Restoration theatres for us not to make the mistake of equating them with a decorous court-theatre or the kind of intimate circle which Gibbon records around Voltaire, it is nonetheless true that by comparison with Shakespeare's this was a more socially select audience, of fashionable or would-be-fashionable people, their hangers-on and their servants. Since the available audience was small, a company would get through its repertoire quickly, and unless many new plays were forthcoming they would be in constant need of material. It was evidently with this in mind that in the winter of 1660 D'Avenant 'humbly presented . . . a proposition of reformeinge some of the most ancient Playes that were played at Blackfriers and of makeinge them, fitt.'[6] D'Avenant obtained the rights for a number of plays by Shakespeare, and others by Jonson, Shirley, Beaumont and Fletcher, while Killigrew's troupe received a similar dispensation. The companies' dependence on the old plays in the period 1660–1700 can be seen from the fact that out of the 959 performances of which we have records, 486 were of old plays, 473 of new.[7]

The adaptations themselves constitute a unique document: there is no comparable instance of the work of a major artist being altered in such a sweeping fashion in order to conform to the aesthetic demand or expectations of a new age. In the prefaces and prologues the adapters give their reasons for altering Shakespeare's plays, often speaking as if they had rendered him and the public some great service in rescuing a few worthwhile parts from an otherwise obsolete and useless work. Some of their ostensible reasons can be listed:

(a) to make a more attractive theatrical vehicle;
(b) to remove metaphors and those instances of 'figurative language' which either seemed too bold for current critical theory or could create difficulties in comprehension;
(c) to remove violations of the unities of place, time and action;
(d) to remove violations of the decorum of action, such as violence or deaths on stage;
(e) to remove violations of the decorum of social position, such as low-life characters being involved in serious plots, or heroes who speak in prose;
(f) to remove violations of the decorum of genre, such as intro-ducing comic characters or incidents into tragedy;
(g) to remove violations of poetic justice.

Instances of all these motivations can be found in the statements of intent included below: see especially Nos 9 (Dryden and D'Avenant), 18 (Ravenscroft), 19 (Dryden), 20 (Otway), 21, 23 and 24 (all by Tate).

The processes can be observed in the remarkable freedom with which the adapters worked. For *The Law Against Lovers* D'Avenant con-flated *Measure for Measure* with *Much Ado About Nothing*, and the result seems to a modern reader like a bad dream, in which his brain is simultaneously present at performances of both plays. Lucio is changed from the lower-plot villain to a gentleman, and Angelo is changed from the upper-plot villain to a character who, as he explains, did not *really* want Isabella's virginity or Claudio's life but was merely testing her fortitude. The neoclassical critics ran into some confusion over the concept of 'good' characters. Instead of being 'good in their kind',

6

i.e., villainous villains, evil kings or good kings, they understood 'morally good': all kings should be just and humane, all women chaste and modest, all soldiers irascible and warlike. If D'Avenant suppresses the unpleasant aspects of Lucio and Angelo, Tate performs the same operation on Richard II, carefully removing all the unpleasant traits which Shakespeare, faithful to history, had given him. This desire to avoid evil and suffering is seen most sharply in Tate's *Lear*, where neither Lear nor Cordelia dies, and Edgar marries Cordelia; since Tate also omits the Fool, it could be said that he has cut both comedy and tragedy from the play.

Yet the actual evidence of the adaptations shows many divergences from the declared principles. Tate adds more comedy to *Coriolanus*, making Valeria an exercise in Restoration satire; Shadwell does the same thing to Melissa in his *Timon of Athens*. Although both characterisations are well-observed, and enjoyable in themselves, they hardly square with neoclassical tenets. Unity of plot was another criterion for having failed to observe which Shakespeare was often criticised: yet the Dryden–D'Avenant *Tempest* adds a whole gallery of subsidiary characters who act out a matching plot[8] (another woman who has never seen a man; a man who has never seen a woman—as one critic has observed, it is surprising that they omitted to give Prospero a wife). Similarly in his *Macbeth* D'Avenant expands the character of Lady Macduff until she is the exact anti-type of Lady Macbeth, and then expands Lady Macbeth's part until it provides a more sustained balance. Violence and bloodshed onstage were unanimously deplored by both critics and adapters, as in Tate's reason for changing the end of *King Lear*: 'Otherwise I must have incumbered the Stage with dead Bodies, which Conduct makes many Tragedies conclude with unseasonable Jests'. Yet few stages are cluttered with corpses as quickly as in the final scene of Dryden's *Troilus and Cressida*, while the last act of Ravenscroft's *Titus Andronicus*, including as it does an onstage torture scene, is far more gruesome than anything in Shakespeare. In fact, violence was fashionable on the Restoration stage: for his *Empress of Morocco* in 1673 Elkanah Settle had prepared an elaborate and realistic backcloth (duly reproduced in the Quarto text) which showed dead and dying bodies racked and torn in a torture chamber.[9] In both his *Lear* and *Coriolanus* adaptations Tate included an attempted rape scene, and was imitated with more gusto by D'Urfey for his *Cymbeline*.

Another area in which the adapters' work could hardly be defended by appeal to critical principle was the increased spectacles and shows which were added as theatrical attractions. *Macbeth* was altered by D'Avenant to include greater opportunities for flying witches, singing, dancing and stage tricks. The great spectacular was of course the Dryden–D'Avenant *Tempest* in its operatic version by Shadwell, all the stage directions from which are included here. Writing of the opening direction ('The Front of the Stage is open'd, and the Band of 24 Violin's [i.e., stringed instruments of all kinds], with the Harpsicals and Theorbo's which accompany the Voices, are plac'd between the Pit and the Stage') Edward J. Dent observed the greater importance attached to the music, in that the orchestra was double its usual size and was placed in the pit, instead of in the gallery over the stage, the usual place.[10] Music plays a greater part in many of the adaptations included here: the song for the prison scene in Tate's *Richard 2*, the dance with castanets and the quartet for voices in D'Avenant's *Law Against Lovers*, the masque in Shadwell's *Timon of Athens*. By the time of *The Fairy Queen* (1692) the masque is more important than the play: this heavily cut version of *A Midsummer Night's Dream* acts as a kind of interlude to the masque, as the normal relationship is reversed. Yet one should not take the masque as providing a tableau ending; as Dent observed,

in no case does the act end with the end of the music. On every occasion there is a certain amount of spoken dialogue after the music is over. This is no doubt due to the habit then prevailing of keeping the curtain up during the whole of the play. . . . There was then no attempt to make a 'situation' or 'tableau' at the end of an act, since an effect of this kind depends essentially on the sudden obliteration of the picture by the closing curtain. (*Op. cit.*, p. 229)

Yet the music and spectacle were undeniably a major attraction, as the long history of eighteenth-century theatre will show.

If modern readers are disturbed by the spectacular effects inserted into Shakespeare's plays they are likely to be even more upset by what happened to his language. All the adapters took a free rein in changing details of style, above all metaphor. A useful example of the kinds of 'improvement' is D'Avenant's *Hamlet*, in which he made a great number of small-scale alterations (which made it unsuitable for excerpting here). Hazelton Spencer's analysis (in what is still the best book on the adaptations in the period 1660 to 1710) finds over three hundred alterations.[11] Decorum seems to be the operating principle: 'O villain, villain, smiling [damned] villain' (1.5.106) is cut altogether; 'The Divell take thy soule' (5.1.246) becomes 'Perdition catch thee'.

'Vulgar', or physical words are toned down: 'To *grunt* and sweat under a weary life' (3.1.77) becomes 'groan and sweat'; '*In hugger mugger* to inter him' (4.5.80) is revised as 'Obscurely'; 'I do not set my life at a pin's fee' becomes 'I do not value my life'. (Pins, like blankets and knives, were not thought appropriate to the high style of tragedy). Strong metaphors become weak: 'here Affront Ophelia' (3.1.30 f.) becomes 'meet Ophelia here'; 'Is sicklied ore with the pale cast of thought' (3.1.85) is refined to 'Shews sick and pale with Thought'; 'And wants not *buzzers* to infect his ear' (4.5.86) is scaled down to 'whispers'. The two most striking instances of this translating of Shakespeare into a cooler, more polite language, are D'Avenant's *Macbeth* and Tate's *Lear*, where a line-by-line comparison with the original will reveal a continuity between theatrical taste and critical opinion, for on no issue were the Augustan critics between Dryden and Dr Johnson more unified than in their reservations about Shakespeare's lawless poetry.

What, in general, are we to make of these adaptations? Not all of their contemporaries were pleased with the adapters' work. In a squib called *Sir William Davenant's Voyage to the Other World* (1668) Richard Flecknoe visualised his hero's discomfiture in that place: 'Nay even Shakespeare, whom he thought to have found his greatest Friend, was as much offended with him as any of the rest for so spoiling and mangling of his Plays' (pp. 8–9).[12] An anonymous poet writing in a collection called *Epilogue to the Ordinary* (1673) mocked the triumph of spectacle:

> Now empty shows must want of sense supply,
> Angels shall dance and *Macbeth's* Witches fly (p. 167)

while the notorious vigour with which Dryden and D'Avenant's seamen imitated their shipwreck called forth this analogy in the anonymous poem *The Country Club*:

> Such noise, such stink, such smoke there was, you'd swear
> The *Tempest* surely had been acted there.

But these are minor objections compared to the outrage expressed by nineteenth- and twentieth-century critics:

... it is impossible not to feel how false was the taste upon which [the adaptations] were built.[13]

[On Tate's *Lear*]: this shameless, this execrable piece of dementation.[14]

9

[On the operatic *Tempest*]: an object-lesson of prime importance . . . no imagination, derived from a mere description, can adequately depict its monstrosity,—to be fully hated it must be fully seen.[15]

[On the Dryden –D'Avenant *Tempest*] I doubt if sillier stuff was ever written by two poets, laureate or other . . . this capital offence.[16]

[On the same]: a licentious farce. Everything that the authors lay their hands on is defiled.[17]

Yet a new generation of scholars, who specialise in these adaptations, has recently arisen to defend them.[18] Unfortunately a certain degree of special pleading seems necessary. Professor C. Spencer advises us to treat the adaptations as if they were new plays, for 'if we are in the proper mood, we can enjoy a play containing two women who have never seen a man, a man who has never seen a woman, brother and sister monsters, and male and female spirits' (*Five Restoration Adaptations*, p. 9); had Shakespeare written in the Restoration climate he might well have 'included a love story in *King Lear*' (p. 10). In any case Shakespeare can stand some improvements: 'one does not expect a tight structure in Shakespeare', thus Cibber rightly omitted 'quantities of unnecessary material' in *Richard III* and Granville understandably 'prunes much of the expansive material . . . from *The Merchant of Venice*', while Dryden and Davenant actually improved the plot-structure of *The Tempest*. 'The resulting plays are more tightly coherent and are primarily *social*: they emphasise permanent patterns of human relationships with less attention to the depths of individual experience' (p. 12). In *King Lear*, indeed, 'The Fool is quite properly omitted; he would have no function in Tate's version, and he occupies time needed for the love story' (p. 23).

It would be possible to argue that Professor Spencer does not understand Shakespeare's plot-structures or style or dramatic meaning, and it is to be regretted that both parties—those who have defended the adaptations and those who have attacked them—have seen fit to denigrate Shakespeare in comparison.[19] However, it seems more fruitful to concentrate on the plays themselves, and to analyse in a less partisan manner quite what model of theatrical effect they were designed to satisfy. And further—a task as yet little attempted—we ought to see to what extent the alterations reflect contemporary critical attitudes. I hope that the full coverage given to the adaptations in this collection will assist study of the interrelation of criticism and drama.

III

Some of the areas in which these volumes take a necessarily different course do not in fact get under way in the period covered by this first instalment. There is little theatrical criticism, other than the rather special case of Pepys (No. 4). For near-contemporary histories of the theatre we have to wait until John Downes in 1708 (Volume 2) and Colley Cibber in 1740 (Volume 3). There is little scholarship, but the pioneering study of sources by Langbaine (No. 27) was to hold the field for a long time. Although there were three re-issues of the Folio in this period (F2: 1632, F3: 1663, F4: 1685), and although these underwent some corrections (albeit of a kind which sometimes introduced more errors than it corrected)[20] it is too early to speak of 'editing' Shakespeare, if by that we mean a systematic review of the text and the authorities for it, with an attempt to gloss and explain words or usages which are unfamiliar or liable to be misunderstood.

We are left with literary criticism as such. One of the major issues has already been touched on, the question of Shakespeare's Art, that is, his demonstrated knowledge of classical languages, models and critical canons. Not surprisingly, given his own learning, Jonson pronounced Shakespeare innocent of any extensive knowledge of Latin and Greek. In his conversations with William Drummond in 1619 'his Censure of the English Poets was this . . . That Shakespeare wanted Arte',[21] but in the First Folio verses he qualified Shakespeare's alignment with Nature:

> Yet must I not give Nature all: Thy Art,
> My gentle *Shakespeare*, must enjoy a part. (cf. No. 1a)

That qualification was little heeded, though: we have seen Milton's celebration of Shakespeare as 'Fancy's child,/warbling his native wood-notes wild' and in Leonard Digges's tribute Shakespeare appears to be wholly ignorant of Art:

> Next Nature onely helpt him, for looke thorow
> This whole Booke, thou shalt find he doth not borrow,
> One phrase from Greekes, nor Latines imitate,
> Nor once from vulgar Languages Translate. . . . (cf. No. 2)

Although incorrect to a remarkable degree, this soon became the established *topos*: 'thy natural braine' is how Drayton addresses him in 1627 (*Sh. A.B.*, I, 334), and in his *History of the Worthies of England*

(1662) Thomas Fuller added further authority to the tradition. Having stressed Shakespeare's affiliation with Ovid ('the most *natural* and *witty* of all Poets') he gives this account of Shakespeare:

He was an eminent instance of the truth of that Rule, *Poeta non fit, sed nascitur*; one is not *made*, but *born* a Poet. Indeed his Learning was very little, so that, as *Cornish diamonds* are not polished by any Lapidary, but are pointed and smoothed even as they are taken out of the Earth, so *nature* it self was all the *art* which was used upon him. (I, 483)

As with many aspects of criticism, in time the founding viewpoints were not only taken literally but were exaggerated. Thus a writer in the memorial volume for Jonson in 1638 takes it for granted that '*Shakespeare* scarce could understand' Latin (I, 417). Aptly enough a tradition soon established itself of juxtaposing Jonson with Shakespeare.[22] Sir John Denham seems to have inaugurated it in the 1647 Fletcher Folio, dubbing Fletcher, Shakespeare and Jonson 'the Triumvirate of wit' and, predictably enough, giving Fletcher the palm:

> Yet what from JONSON's oyle and sweat did flow,
> Or what more easie nature did bestow
> On SHAKESPEARE's gentler Muse, in thee full growne
> Their Graces both appeare. . . . (I, 504)

Twenty years later Denham shifts his ground slightly:

> Old Mother Wit, and Nature gave
> *Shakespeare* and *Fletcher* all they have;
> In *Spenser*, and in *Jonson*, Art
> Of slower Nature got the start. (II, 159)

In 1675 Edward Phillips could write that each of 'the happy *Triumvirate* . . . excelled in his peculiar way: *Ben Jonson* in his elaborate pains and knowledge of Authors, *Shakespeare* in his pure vein of wit, and natural Poetic heighth; *Fletcher* in a courtly Elegance, and gentle familiarity of style . . .' (II, 222). This critical tradition can be seen operating in the texts below: in Flecknoe (No. 7), Dryden (No. 10), in the unsigned prologue to *Julius Caesar* (No. 11), in Robert Gould's satire *The Play-House* (No. 26). And in 1686 we find Nahum Tate praising a poet for having a muse which could '*temper* Shakespeare's *Flame with* Jonson's *Art*' (II, 317).

There are occasional attempts in this period to show that Shakespeare did have a knowledge of the classics (as in Tate's praise of the authenticity of his Romans: No. 22) or of the modern languages, as by Langbaine (No. 27). But a more characteristic reaction was to accept his ignorance and then celebrate his achievements none the less. In an Oxford miscellany of 1685 an anonymous poet assures us that

> Shakespeare, tho rude, yet his immortal Wit
> Shall never to the stroke of time submit (II, 313)

and a preface to William Mountford's play *The Successful Strangers* (1690) describes how Shakespeare,

> . . . to th' amaze of the more Letter'd men,
> Minted such thoughts from his own Natural Brain,
> As the great Readers, since could ne'ere attain,
> Though daily they the stock of Learning drain. (II, 341)

The most intense variation on this theme comes from Edward Phillips in his *Theatrum Poetarum* of 1675:

> . . . from an Actor of Tragedies and Comedies, he became a *Maker*; and such a Maker, that though some others may perhaps pretend to a more exact *Decorum* and *oeconomie*, especially in Tragedy, never any express'd a more lofty and Tragic heighth; never any represented nature more purely to the life, and where the polishments of Art are most wanting, as probably his Learning was not extraordinary, he pleaseth with a certain wild and native Elegance; and in all his Writings hath an unvulgar style. . . . (II, 222–3)

That might seem the ultimate stage in this form of praise, yet it gave rise to a further development which was to be much invoked in the eighteenth century, the idea that Nature and Art are not merely separate but mutually exclusive. In his essay 'Upon the Ancient and Modern Learning' published in his *Miscellanea*, part 2 (1690) Sir William Temple speculated: 'who can tell whether Learning may not even weaken Invention in a man that has great Advantages from Nature and Birth, whether the weight and number of so many other mens thoughts and notions may not suppress his own, or hinder the motion and agitation of them from which all Invention arises'.[23] Shakespeare's flame could burn more brightly since it was not smothered with wood—that is the implication, as John Dryden Junior quickly saw, writing in the dedication to his play *The Husband His own Cuckold* (1696) that

Shakespeare among all the Writers of our Nation may stand by himself as a Phoenix, the first and last of his Order; in whom bounteous Nature wonderfully supply'd all the parts of a great Poet, and Excellent Oratour; and of whom alone one may venture boldly to say, that had he had more Learning, perhaps he might have been less a Poet (Sig A$_2$v).[24]

O felix culpa!

In this way Shakespeare's deficiencies were turned to his advantage, and a general current of praise built up which, although not yet bardolatrous, was certainly reverent. Thus John Aubrey: 'His Comoedies will remaine witt as long as the English tongue is understood, for that he handles *mores hominum*. Now our present writers reflect so much on particular persons and coxcombeities that twenty years hence they will not be understood.'[25] At about the same time the anonymous translator of Scudéry's *Amaryllis to Tityrus* (1681) prefixed to that novel an 'Essay on Dramatic Poetry' in which he wrote:

I can't, without infinite ingratitude to the Memory of those excellent persons, omit the first Famous Masters in't, of our Nation, Venerable *Shakespeare* and the great *Ben Jonson*: I have had a particular kindness always for most of *Shakespeare*'s Tragedies, and for many of his Comedies, and I can't but say that I can never enough admire his Stile (considering the time he writ in and the great alteration that has been in the Refineinge of our Language since) for he has expressed himself so very well in't 'tis generally approv'd of still; and for maintaining of the Characters of the persons, design'd, I think none ever exceeded him. (II, 274)

If we turn now from this general climate to the criticism selected here we will find some continuities. On the issue of decorum of character Margaret Cavendish embarks on a defence of Shakespeare's wit precisely in terms of this neoclassic category (No. 6); Abraham Wright's praise of the parts of Othello and Iago, and his reservations about Hamlet (No. 3) are all couched in the form of dramatic roles (rogue, jealous husband, madman) and their consistency. Similarly with Dryden's praise of Caliban (No. 19).

Yet given the general praise of Shakespeare it will come as a surprise to confront the two major critics of this age, Dryden and Rymer. The full course of Dryden's references to Shakespeare is a curious sequence of ups and downs, as the reader of the selections which follow will discover, or as we can see by considering some of the briefer allusions, which were not substantial enough to be included in the body of the text below. In these passing references it is striking how little Dryden—or his contemporaries—knew about the history of English drama or the facts about Shakespeare as a dramatist (an ignorance which permitted some odd critical judgments). Thus in the preface to his *Rival Ladies* (1664) Dryden wrote that '*Shakespeare* (who, with some Errors not to be avoided in that Age, had, undoubtedly a larger Soul of Poesie than ever any of our Nation) was the first, who to shun the pains of continual Rhyming, invented that kind of Writing, which we call Blanck Verse . . .' (Sig. A₃ᵛ). In an equally unguarded moment (the preface to *An Evening's Love, or the Mock-Astrologer*, 1671) he claimed that 'Most of *Shakespeare's* Playes, I mean the Stories of them, are to be found in the *Hecatommuthi*, or hundred Novels of *Cinthio*. I have, my self, read in his *Italian*, that of *Romeo and Juliet*, the *Moor of Venice*, and many others of them'. (*Sh. A.B.*, II, 170–1; see Langbaine below, No. 27). In his prologue to D'Avenant's *Circe* (1684) he made a wild guess about chronology:

> *Shakespeare's* own Muse her *Pericles* first bore,
> The Prince of *Tyre* was elder than the *Moore.* (II, 303)

Mistakes such as these, or Dryden's remarkably influential pronouncement that Shakespeare lived in an age of barbarism and merely inherited the vices of his times (No. 12) show how extremely tenuous our literary history was in this period.

Yet if unsure of his facts Dryden was in no doubt as to his opinions. That is to say, no doubt as to an opinion at the time when he uttered it, even though he subsequently could maintain the exact opposite. In these smaller allusions we find effusive praise of Shakespeare, as in the 'Prologue, to the University of Oxford, 1674', renewing the 'fame' of the dramatists of the last age (II, 205), or in the lines on '*Shakespeare's* Picture drawn by Sir *Godfrey Kneller*, and given to the Author' (1694):

> *Shakespeare*, thy Gift, I place before my sight;
> With awe, I ask his Blessing ere I write;
> With Reverence look on his Majestick Face;
> Proud to be less; but of his Godlike Race. (II, 394)

Shakespeare's 'greater Genius still prevail'd' over 'great *Jonson's* learning' (II, 374); Shakespeare 'excell'd the Ancients in . . . Tragedy' (II, 180 and again: II, 393); 'honest *Shakespeare*' is invoked as a precedent for not keeping to the Unities (II, 178) and praised for his imaginative creation of fairies and magic in *The Tempest* and *A Midsummer Night's Dream* (177). In the prologue to his *Aureng-Zebe* (1676) Dryden offered the supreme compliment:

> But spite of all his pride a secret shame,
> Invades his breast at *Shakespeare's* sacred name:
> Aw'd when he hears his God-like *Romans* rage,
> He, in a just despair, would quit the Stage. (II, 227)

Yet simultaneously with those allusions we find him resentfully attacking 'custome, which cozen'd us so long: we thought, because *Shakespeare* and *Fletcher* went no farther, that there the Pillars of Poetry were to be erected. That, because they excellently describ'd Passion without Rhyme, therefore Rhyme was not capable of describing it; but time has now convinced most men of that Error' (II, 171). Dryden gives slighting praise to Shakespeare for having 'created the Stage among us' but for having written 'happily'—that is, accidentally well— '[rather] than knowingly and justly' (II, 393). Or he criticises Shakespeare and Fletcher for their 'superfluity and wast of wit', and pronounces: 'I would have the characters well chosen, and kept distant from interfering with each other; which is more than *Fletcher* or *Shakespeare* did' (II, 170). With a similar invocation of the concept of decorum Dryden pronounces that 'the Persons of a *Play*, whatsoever is said or done by any of them, must be consistent with the manners which the *Poet* has given them distinctly: and even the Habits must be proper to the degrees, and humours of the Persons as well as in a *Picture*. He who enter'd in the first Act, a Young man like Pericles Prince of *Tyre*, must not be in danger in the fifth Act, of committing Incest with his Daughter . . .' (II, 403).

If we read the four major essays in which Shakespeare figures (Nos 10, 12, 16 and 19 below) we will find that, discussing Shakespeare's plots, characterisation or language, Dryden can praise or blame him according to the needs of the moment. One would like to be able to accept the praise as a considered judgment, were it not for the equally confident attacks on aspects previously celebrated. This oscillation makes one doubt the sincerity of the praise-reflex. I find it difficult to accept David Nichol Smith's claim that Dryden 'is the father of Shakespearian criticism' (surely Ben Jonson earned that title) nor his supporting argument that though Dryden 'disguised the veneration at times, he expressed his true faith when he wrote, deliberately, the fervent estimate in the *Essay of Dramatic Poesy*', that 'magnificent eulogy of Shakespeare', what Smith described elsewhere as 'this great passage'.[26] A much more accurate assessment is that of Hazelton Spencer:[27]

It is true that Dryden and other critics not infrequently compliment Shakespeare in terms scarcely less ardent than their gratulatory epistles and addresses to each other. But their eulogies are commonly couched in the vaguest and most general terms. Dryden's famous characterization of Shakespeare as the man 'who of all modern and perhaps ancient, poets had the largest and most comprehensive soul' is a striking and sonorous saying; but it means little, especially when compared with Dryden's other utterances. When he and his colleagues turn from phrase-making to detailed examination and criticism, there is much more of objection than of praise.

Dryden's legacy is a distinctly ambivalent one.

By contrast Rymer is utterly consistent: neoclassical principles are observed throughout, whatever the consequences. I have included a few excerpts from Rymer's *Tragedies of the Last Age* (No. 15) as from Dryden's essay on 'The Grounds of Criticism in Tragedy' so that the reader could see the theoretical foundations from which Rymer's attack on *Othello* (to be included in the next volume) grew, and also as examples of the neoclassic mixture of Aristotelian and Horatian precepts. For the next century Shakespeare criticism was to be dominated by the neo-Aristotelian categories of which Dryden's outline is as good as any: the action, the persons, probability, instruction and delight, the moral, the manners, decorum, the characters, the proper nature of a hero and king, the passions, the thoughts, the words. Innumerable critics work through that scheme, often in just that order, and evaluate Shakespeare under each of those heads, one by one.

Rymer uses this scheme too, indeed he had translated one of the most influential expressions of it, Rapin's *Reflections on Aristotle's Treatise of Poesie*, in 1674. Where Rymer differs from his contemporaries is in the ferocity with which he applies the system. In his hands criticism becomes mandatory, indeed exclusive, as some excerpts from the index to this first attack on English tragedy will show:

Action, the *unity* must be observ'd, or else the *conduct* will be all at random. . . .

Action, where [the unity is] observ'd, the Poet cannot easily transgress in the *unities* of time and place. . . .

Argument, Plot or Fable for a Tragedy ought to be taken from History; ought to be more accurate and Philosophical than History; ought to represent persons better than the life. . . .

So far these may seem to be the orthodox injunctions, but Rymer steps up the pressure:

Evil design to be represented in its fall but not in its advances. . . .

Kings are all in Poetry presumptive Heroes; not to be sway'd by evil Ministers; cannot be accessary to a crime. . . .

Man's life not to be taken away without a just account. . . .

Manners to be reform'd by Poetry. . . .

Passion allows no long speeches; no comparisons; no parenthesis. . . .

Poets . . . must take care that the Criminal sin not too far, and are not to be trusted for an Hell behind the Scenes. . . .

Who and who may kill one another with decency.

Wilful murder not to be suffer'd in Tragedy.

Wicked persons not to be brought on the stage.

Women . . . Are not to suffer any cruelties from man.

With its forbidding prohibitions ('not to be trusted', 'not allowed', 'not to be suffer'd', 'not to be brought on') Rymer's critical decalogue had a considerable impact on his contemporaries. Dryden sketched the main topics for a reply to him (No. 16) but did not publish it; instead he made several approving endorsements of Rymer (No. 19). Even in the 'Heads of an Answer' we can sense some unease as Dryden attempts to argue from first principles, and a greater confidence when he uses the simple empirical appeal: the example of Shakespeare would refute the theory. That was an argument which was to become extremely important in its implications, as subsequent volumes will show.

NOTES

1 *The Shakespeare Allusion-Book: A Collection of Allusions to Shakespeare From 1591 to 1700.* . . . ed. J. Munro (1909), and re-issued with a preface by E. K. Chambers, 2 vols (1932). Subsequently referred to as *Sh. A.B.,* with volume and page numbers.

2 See D. C. Allen's edition, *Frances Meres's treatise 'Poetrie'* (Urbana, Ill., 1933).

3 *Letters from Orinda to Poliarchus* (1705), p. 96; *cit.* in [G. Thorn-Drury], *More Seventeenth Century Allusions to Shakespeare* (1924) p. 4.

4 *The Diary of John Evelyn,* ed. E. S. de Beer (London, 1959) p. 431.

5 For the size of the Elizabethan audience I rely on A. Harbage, *Shakespeare and the Rival Traditions* (New York, 1952, 1968) pp. 24-5, 45-7.

6 Allardyce Nicoll, *A History of Restoration Drama 1660-1700* (Cambridge, 1923) pp. 352-3.

7 Gunnar Sorelius, *'The Giant Race Before The Flood'. Pre-Restoration Drama on the Stage and in the Criticism of the Restoration* (Uppsala, 1966) pp. 71-4.

8 On structural balance in the adaptations see G. C. D. Odell, *Shakespeare*

From Betterton to Irving (New York, 1920) i, pp. 26–33 and Hazelton Spencer, *Shakespeare Improved. The Restoration Versions in Quarto and on the Stage* (Cambridge, Mass., 1927) pp. 158–9, 163, 193 ff.

9 On violence see, e.g., E. Rothstein, *Restoration Tragedy: Form and the Process of Change* (Wisconsin, 1967) and A. Nicoll, *op. cit.* pp. 24 (on incest), 119–20 (onstage mutilation, impaling and spiking of bodies). Settle's gruesome engraving is reproduced in *The London Stage, 1660–1800. Part I: 1660–1700*, ed. W. Van Lennep (Carbondale, Ill., 1965) at pp. 64–5.

10 Dent, *Foundations of English Opera. A Study of Musical Drama In England During the Seventeenth Century* (Cambridge, 1928) p. 140.

11 H. Spencer, *op. cit.* pp. 178 ff.

12 This and the next two allusions are from G. Thorn-Drury, *op. cit.* pp. 15, 17, 24.

13 Charles Knight, 'A History of Opinion on the Writings of Shakespeare', *The Pictorial Edition of the Works of Shakespeare*, revised ed. (1867) vii, p. 348.

14 H. N. Hudson, *Lectures on Shakespeare*, ii (New York, 1848) pp. 277–8; *cit.* C. Spencer, in his *Five Restoration Adaptations*, p. 8.

15 H. H. Furness, *A New Variorum Shakespeare: The Tempest* (Philadelphia, 1897) p. viii.

16 Odell, *op. cit.*, i, p. 32.

17 H. Spencer, *op. cit.* p. 203.

18. See, e.g., C. Spencer, 'A Word for Tate's *King Lear*', *Studies in English Literature 1500–1900* iii (1963) pp. 241–51, and his edition already cited; Lucyle Hook, 'Shakespeare Improv'd, or A Case for the Affirmative', *Shakespeare Quarterly* iv (1953) pp. 289–99.

19 G. C. Odell, for instance, could not be too concerned over Ravenscroft's adaptation 'since no one, I suppose, regards Shakespeare's Titus with veneration' (i, p. 45); of Dryden's *Troilus and Cressida* he wrote: 'The play as a play is better, I believe, than Shakespeare's, which is hardly a play at all' (i, p. 50); he held that Crowne acted in good taste in making an adaptation of only the first three acts of *Henry 6, Part 2* since 'I have always felt that in themselves they constitute an excellent play, and regretted that Shakespeare had, after the downfall of this noble pair, added the trifling episodes of the Jack Cade Rebellion and York's revolt against his sovereign' (i, p. 64). Similarly Hazelton Spencer found the Prospero–Miranda exposition scene in *The Tempest* 'a tedious affair', well below Shakespeare's best (p. 195), believed that structurally Dryden's *Troilus* was superior to Shakespeare's (pp. 231–2), that structurally Crowne's *Henry 6* was better than Shakespeare's (p. 308), and expressed indifference about D'Urfey's *Injured Princess* since '*Cymbeline* is not among those plays about which one feels outraged by the adapter's clumsy hand. Much of it is botchwork, and its plethora of ungainly expositions, as well as its unconscionably protracted

denouement, ill accords with those matchless songs and lyric passages with which it is so plentifully sprinkled' (p. 318). It was never more clear that to evaluate Shakespeare's critics exposes one's own status as a Shakespeare critic.

20 See M. W. Black and M. A. Shaaber, *Shakespeare's Seventeenth Century Editors, 1632–85* (New York, 1937).

21 Ben Jonson, *Discoveries 1641, Conversations with William Drummond of Hawthornden 1619*, ed. G. B. Harrison (1923) pp. 3–4.

22 See G. E. Bentley, *Shakespeare and Jonson, Their Reputations in the Seventeenth Century Compared* (2 vols, Cambridge, 1945), with some details of computation corrected by D. L. Frost, 'Shakespeare in the seventeenth century', *Shakespeare Quarterly* xvi (1965) pp. 81–9.

23 Quoted from *Critical Essays of the Seventeenth Century* ed. J. E. Spingarn (London, 1908, 1957) iii, p. 48.

24 Cited in Thorn-Drury, *op. cit.* p. 38.

25 *Aubrey's Brief Lives*, ed. O. L. Dick (Penguin Books, 1962) p. 335. In the next sentence Aubrey attacked Jonson's 'small Latine and less Greek': 'he understood Latine pretty well: for he had been in his younger yeares a schoolmaster in the countrey'. He noted that he had this information 'from Mr. Beeston' and had this claim (whether true or not) been available in the eighteenth century (it was first published in 1813) it might well have influenced the status of Shakespeare's reputation.

26 D. N. Smith, *Eighteenth Century Essays on Shakespeare* (Glasgow, 1903) pp. xiii f, 305; *Shakespeare in the Eighteenth Century* (Oxford, 1928) p. 7.

27 H. Spencer, *op. cit.* p. 4.

Note on the Text

The texts in this collection are taken from the first printed edition, unless otherwise stated. The date under which a piece is filed is that of the first edition, with two exceptions; plays, for which the first performance is used (for such information I have relied on *The London Stage* for the period 1660 to 1800); and those works for which the author gives a date of composition substantially earlier than its first printing. The place of publication is London, unless otherwise indicated.

Spelling and punctuation are those of the original editions except where they seemed likely to create ambiguities for the modern reader. Spelling has, however, been standardised for writers' names (Jonson not Johnson, Rymer not Rhimer), for play titles, and for Shakespearian characters.

Small omissions in the text are indicated by three dots: [. . .]; larger ones by three asterisks.

Footnotes intended by the original authors are distinguished with an asterisk, dagger and so on; those added by the editor are numbered. Editorial notes within the text are placed within square brackets.

Act, scene and line-numbers have been supplied in all quotations from Shakespeare, in the form 2.1.85 (Act 2, scene 1, line 85). The text used for this purpose was the *Tudor Shakespeare* ed. P. Alexander (Collins, 1951).

Classical quotations have been identified, and translations added, usually those in the Loeb library.

1. Ben Jonson on Shakespeare

1623, c. 1630

Ben Jonson (1573?–1637) was a life-long friend and rival of Shakespeare. His tribute in the First Folio was dismissed by Dryden as 'An Insolent, Sparing, and Invidious Panegyrick' (Preface to Juvenal's *Satires*, 1693, iii), and that judgment has been echoed many times. But Jonson's only reservation is on the grounds of Shakespeare's knowledge of classical languages and, properly understood, means that Shakespeare equalled the achievement of the Greek and Roman dramatists without having the learning to be indebted to them; he excelled by Nature, not Art. For the rest, Jonson's praise is both perceptive and generous.

In his *Timber: or Discoveries; made upon men and matter: as they have flow'd out of his daily Readings*. . . . (a notebook kept between 1626 and 1637, and published for the first time in 1640) he similarly keeps a balance between criticism and celebration.

(a) *To the memory of my beloved, The Author Mr. William Shakespeare: And what he hath left us*, in *Mr. William Shakespeares Comedies, Histories, & Tragedies* (1623):

> To draw no envy (*Shakespeare*) on thy name,
>   Am I thus ample to thy Booke, and Fame:
> While I confesse thy writings to be such,
>   As neither *Man*, nor *Muse*, can praise too much.
> 'Tis true, and all mens suffrage. But these wayes
>   Were not the paths I meant unto thy praise:
> For seeliest Ignorance on these may light,
>   Which, when it sounds at best, but eccho's right;
> Or blinde Affection, which doth ne're advance
>   The truth, but gropes, and urgeth all by chance;
>   Or crafty Malice, might pretend this praise,
>   And thinke to ruine, where it seem'd to raise.

These are, as some infamous Baud, or Whore,
  Should praise a Matron. What could hurt her more?
But thou art proofe against them, and indeed
  Above th' ill fortune of them, or the need.
I, therefore will begin. Soule of the Age!
  The applause! delight! the wonder of our Stage!
My *Shakespeare*, rise; I will not lodge thee by
  Chaucer, or *Spenser*, or bid *Beaumont* lye
A little further, to make thee a roome:
  Thou art a Moniment, without a tombe,
And art alive still, while thy Booke doth live,
  And we have wits to read, and praise to give.
That I not mixe thee so, my braine excuses;
  I meane with great, but disproportion'd *Muses*:
For, if I thought my judgement were of yeeres,
  I should commit thee surely with thy peeres,
And tell, how farre thou didstst our *Lyly* out-shine,
  Or sporting *Kyd*, or *Marlowe*'s mighty line.
And though thou hadst small *Latine*, and lesse *Greeke*,
  From thence to honour thee, I would not seeke
For names; but call forth thund'ring *Æschylus*,
  Euripides, and *Sophocles* to us,
Paccuvius, *Accius*, him of *Cordova* dead,
  To life againe, to heare thy Buskin tread,
And shake a Stage: Or, when thy Sockes were on,
  Leave thee alone, for the comparison
Of all, that insolent *Greece*, or haughtie *Rome*
  sent forth, or since did from their ashes come.
Triumph, my *Britaine*, thou hast one to showe,
  To whom all Scenes of *Europe* homage owe.
He was not of an age, but for all time!
  And all the *Muses* still were in their prime,
When like *Apollo* he came forth to warme
  Our eares, or like a *Mercury* to charme!
Nature her selfe was proud of his designes,
  And joy'd to weare the dressing of his lines!
Which were so richly spun, and woven so fit,
  As, since, she will vouchsafe no other Wit.
The merry *Greeke*, tart *Aristophanes*,
  Neat *Terence*, witty *Plautus*, now not please;

But antiquated, and deserted lye
 As they were not of Natures family.
Yet must I not give Nature all: Thy Art,
 My gentle *Shakespeare*, must enjoy a part.
For though the *Poets* matter, Nature be,
 His Art doth give the fashion. And, that he,
Who casts to write a living line, must sweat,
 (such as thine are) and strike the second heat
Upon the *Muses* anvile: turne the same,
 (And himselfe with it) that he thinkes to frame;
Or for the lawrell, he may gaine a scorne,
 For a good *Poet*'s made, as well as borne.
And such wert thou. Looke how the fathers face
 Lives in his issue, even so, the race
Of *Shakespeare's* minde, and manners brightly shines
 In his well torned, and true filed lines:
In each of which, he seemes to shake a Lance,
 As brandish't at the eyes of Ignorance.
Sweet Swan of *Avon*! what a sight it were
 To see thee in our waters yet appeare,
And make those flights upon the bankes of *Thames*,
 That so did take *Eliza*, and our *James*!
But stay, I see thee in the *Hemisphere*
 Advanc'd, and made a Constellation there!
Shine forth, thou Starre of *Poets*, and with rage,
 Or influence, chide, or cheere the drooping Stage;
Which, since thy flight from hence, hath mourn'd like night,
 And despaires day, but for thy Volumes light.

(b) 'De Shakespeare nostrati', from *Timber*, first printed in Jonson's *Works* (1640), ii, pp. 97–8.

For 'the players'' tribute see Introduction, p. 1. The lines in *Julius Caesar* which Jonson objected to read in the Folio text:

> Know, *Caesar* doth not wrong, nor without cause
> Will he be satisfied. (3.1.47–8)

It seems likely that Shakespeare had altered them in response to Jonson's criticism.

De Shakespeare nostrati.

I remember, the Players have often mentioned it as an honour to *Shakespeare*, that in his writing, (whatsoever he penn'd) hee never blotted out line. My answer hath beene, would he had blotted a thousand. Which they thought a malevolent speech. I had not told posterity this, but for their ignorance, who choose that circumstance to commend their friend by, wherein he most faulted. And to justifie mine owne candor, (for I lov'd the man, and doe honour his memory (on this side Idolatry) as much as any.) Hee was (indeed) honest, and of an open, and free nature: had an excellent *Phantsie*; brave notions, and gentle expressions: wherein hee flow'd with that facility, that sometime it was necessary he should be stop'd: *Sufflaminandus erat*;[1] as *Augustus* said of *Haterius*. His wit was in his owne power; would the rule of it had beene so too. Many times hee fell into those things, could not escape laughter: As when hee said in the person of *Cæsar*, one speaking to him; *Cæsar thou dost me wrong*. Hee replyed: *Cæsar did never wrong, but with just cause*: and such like; which were ridiculous. But hee redeemed his vices, with his vertues. There was ever more in him to be praysed, than to be pardoned.

[1] M. Seneca, *Controversiae* 4. *Pref.* 7: 'He needed brakes.'

2. Leonard Digges, commendatory verses

1640

Upon Master William Shakespeare, the Deceased Authour, and his Poems, prefixed to Shakespeare's *Poems* (1640).

Leonard Digges (1588–1635) was a poet and translator who probably knew Shakespeare personally. He contributed a poem to his memory in the First Folio.

Poets are borne not made; when I would prove
This truth, the glad rememberance I must love
Of never dying *Shakespeare*, who alone,
Is argument enough to make that one.
First, that he was a Poet none would doubt,
That heard th' applause of what he sees set out
Imprinted; where thou hast (I will not say)
Reader his Workes (for to contrive a Play:
To him twas none) the patterne of all wit,
Art without Art unparaleld as yet.
Next Nature onely helpt him, for looke thorow
This whole Booke, thou shalt find he doth not borrow,
One phrase from Greekes, nor Latines imitate,
Nor once from vulgar Languages Translate,
Nor Plagiari-like from others gleane,
Nor begges he from each witty friend a Scene
To peece his Acts with; all that he doth write,
Is pure his owne, plot, language exquisite.
But oh! what praise more powerfull can we give
The dead, than that by him the Kings men live,
His Players, which should they but have shar'd the Fate,
All else expir'd within the short Termes date;
How could the Globe have prospered, since through want
Of change, the Plaies and Poems had growne scant.

But happy Verse thou shalt be sung and heard,
When hungry quills shall be such honour bard.
Then vanish upstart Writers to each Stage,
You needy Poetasters of this Age,
Where *Shakespeare* liv'd or spake, Vermine forbeare,
Least with your froth you spot them, come not neere;
But if you needs must write, if poverty
So pinch, that otherwise you starve and die,
On Gods name may the Bull or Cockpit have
Your lame blancke Verse, to keepe you from the grave:
Or let new Fortunes younger brethren see,
What they can picke from your leane industry.
I doe not wonder when you offer at
Blacke-Friers, that you suffer: tis the fate
Of richer veines, prime judgements that have far'd
The worse, with this deceased man compar'd.
So have I seene, when Cesar would appeare,
And on the Stage at halfe-sword parley were,
Brutus and *Cassius*: oh how the Audience,
Were ravish'd, with what wonder they went thence,
When some new day they would not brooke a line,
Of tedious (though well laboured) *Catiline*;
Sejanus too was irkesome, they priz'de more
Honest *Iago*, or the jealous Moore.
And though the Fox and subtill Alchimist,
Long intermitted could not quite be mist,
Though these have sham'd all the Ancients, and might raise,
Their Authours merit with a crowne of Bayes.
Yet these sometimes, even at a friend's desire
Acted, have scarce defrai'd the Seacoale fire
And doore-keepers: when let but *Falstaff* come,
Hal, Poins, the rest you scarce shall have a roome
All is so pester'd: let but *Beatrice*
And *Benedick* be seene, loe in a trice
The Cockpit Galleries, Boxes, all are full
To heare *Malvolio* that crosse garter'd Gull.
Briefe, there is nothing in his wit fraught Booke,
Whose sound we would not heare, on whose worth looke
Like old coynd gold, whose lines in every page,
Shall passe true currant to succeeding age.

But why doe I dead *Shakespeare's* praise recite,
Some second *Shakespeare* must of *Shakespeare* write;
For me tis needlesse, since an host of men,
Will pay to clap his praise, to free my Pen.

3. Abraham Wright on *Othello* and *Hamlet*

c. 1655

From Abraham Wright's commonplace book, British Museum Add. MS. 22608.

Abraham Wright (1611–90), Vicar of Okeham, included in his notebook a list of contemporary plays for the benefit of his son James (1643–1713), who indeed became a theatrical historian (*Historia Histrionica: an Historical Account of the English Stage*, 1699). The full text of Wright's notes is given by A. C. Kirsch in 'A Caroline commentary on the drama', *Modern Philology* lxvi (1968), pp. 256–61.

Othello, by Shakespeare.

A very good play both for lines and plot, but especially the plot. Iago for a rogue, and Othello for a jealous husband 2 parts well pend. Act: 3 the scene beetwixt Iago and Othello, and the 1 sce: of the 4 Act between the same shew admirably the villanous humour of Iago when hee persuades Othello to his jalousy.

Hamlet, a Tragedie by Shakespeare.

But an indifferent play, the lines but meane: and in nothing like *Othello*. Hamlet is an indifferent good part for a madman, and the scene in the beeginning of the 5ᵗ Act beetweene Hamlet and the grave-maker a good scene but since betterd in the *Jealous Lovers*.[1]

[1] By Thomas Randolph, 1632.

4. Samuel Pepys on Shakespeare in the theatre

1660-9

Diary ed. H. B. Wheatley, 8 vols (1913); text checked against the edition in progress by R. C. Latham and W. Matthews (1970 onwards).

Pepys's comments are one of the few records we possess by Restoration playgoers. But they are not necessarily typical: as the contexts will show Pepys often went to the theatre with a troubled conscience, which may be reflected in his comments on specific plays.

11 October 1660
Here, in the Park, we met with Mr. Salisbury, who took Mr. Creed and me to the Cockpitt to see *The Moore of Venice*, which was well done. Burtt acted the Moore; by the same token, a very pretty lady that sat by me, called out, to see Desdemona smothered. (I, 24)

1 March 1662
. . . . thence to the Opera, and there saw *Romeo and Juliet*, the first time it was ever acted; but it is a play of itself the worst that ever I heard in my life. . . . (II, 185)

29 September 1662
. . . . and then to the King's Theatre, where we saw *Midsummer Night's Dream*, which I had never seen before, nor shall ever again, for it is the most insipid ridiculous play that ever I saw in my life. I saw, I confess, some good dancing and some handsome women, which was all my pleasure. (II, 326)

6 January 1663
. . . . after dinner to the Duke's house, and there saw *Twelfth Night* acted well, though it be but a silly play, and not related at all to the name or day. (III, 6)

5 November 1664

. . . . and so with my wife to the Duke's house to a play, *Macbeth*
[D'Avenant's operatic version], a pretty good play, but admirably
acted. (IV, 264)

20 August 1666

Up, and to Deptford by water, reading *Othello, Moore of Venice*, which
I ever heretofore esteemed a mighty good play, but having so lately
read *The Adventures of Five Houres*,[1] it seems a mean thing. (V, 382–3)

28 December 1666

From hence to the Duke's house, and there saw *Macbeth* most excellently acted, and a most excellent play for variety. (VI, 110)

7 January 1667

. . . . thence to the Duke's house, and saw *Macbeth*, which, though I saw
it lately, yet appears a most excellent play in all respects, but especially
in divertissement, though it be a deep tragedy; which is a strange
perfection in a tragedy, it being most proper here, and suitable. (VI, 118)

19 April 1667

Here we saw *Macbeth*, which, though I have seen it often, yet is it one
of the best plays for a stage, and variety of dancing and musique,
that ever I saw. (VI, 261)

15 August 1667

And so went to the King's, and there saw *The Merry Wives of Windsor*:
which did not please me at all, in no part of it. . . . (VII, 64)

2 November 1667

. . . . to the King's playhouse, and there saw *Henry the Fourth*: and contrary to expectation, was pleased in nothing more than in Cartwright's
speaking of Falstaff's speech about 'What is Honour?' (VII, 172)

7 November 1667

. . . . resolved with Sir W. Pen to go see *The Tempest*, an old play of
Shakespeare's, acted, I hear, the first day. . . . the most innocent play
that ever I saw; and a curious piece of musique in an echo[2] of half
sentences, the echo repeating the former half, while the man goes on to
the latter; which is mighty pretty. The play [has] no great wit, but yet
good, above ordinary plays. (VII, 176–7)

---

[1] A play by Sir Samuel Tuke commissioned by Charles II.
[2] Ferdinand's song from D'Avenant and Dryden's adaptation: below, p. 102.

3 February 1668

. . . . and thence after dinner to the Duke of York's house, to the play, *The Tempest*, which we have often seen, but yet I was pleased again, and shall be again to see it, it is so full of variety, and particularly this day I took pleasure to learn the tune of the seaman's dance, which I have much desired to be perfect in, and have made myself so. (VII, 282)

20 January 1669

. . . . and thence to the Duke of York's house, and saw *Twelfth Night*, as it is now revived; but, I think, one of the weakest plays that ever I saw on the stage. (VIII, 193)

5. Sir William D'Avenant, from his adaptation of *Measure for Measure* with *Much Ado*

1662

From *The Law Against Lovers*, in D'Avenant's *Works* (1673), ii, pp. 272–329.

Sir William D'Avenant (1606–68) is the major figure linking Caroline and Restoration drama. He wrote plays and masques for the court of Charles I, became Poet Laureate in 1638, and was a theatre manager at the closing of the theatres in 1642. A pioneer in the presentation of operas in the 1650s, after the Restoration he became one of the two patentees. His conflation of *Much Ado* with *Measure for Measure* was performed on 15 February 1662. Benedick becomes Angelo's brother; Beatrice, 'a great Heiress' and Angelo's ward, joins Benedick in helping Isabella and the lovers; Mariana is omitted, as are all the comic characters from *Measure for Measure*; Lucio becomes a gentleman.

---

*   *   *

[Act III, Scene iii. Turin.]

*   *   *

Isab. What says my Brother?
Claud. Death is a fearful thing.
Isab. And living shame more hateful.
Sure you have study'd what it is to dye.
   Claud. Oh Sister, 'tis to go we know not whither.
We lye in silent darkness, and we rot;
Where long our motion is not stopt; for though
In Graves none walk upright (proudly to face
The Stars) yet there we move again, when our

33

Corruption makes those worms in whom we crawl.
Perhaps the Spirit (which is future life)
Dwells *Salamander*-like, unharm'd in fire:
Or else with wand'ring winds is blown about
The world. But if condemn'd like those
Whom our incertain thought imagines howling;
Then the most loath'd and the most weary life
Which Age, or Ache, want, or imprisonment
Can lay on Nature, is a Paradise
To what we fear of death.

   Isab. Alas, alas!

   Claud. Sweet Sister! I would live,
Were not the ransom of my life much more
Than all your honour and your virtue too
(By which you are maintain'd) can ever pay,
Without undoing both.

   Isab. Prepare yourself, your line of life is short.

   Claud. I am prepar'd: but Sister, if
Your Brother you did ever love; or if
Our Mothers pity may your pattern be,
Let *Juliet* in your tender bosom dwell;
Who has no blemish, if such Laws
As innocent antiquity allow'd,
Were now of force, or if Religion here
In *Turin*, did not more subsist
By publick form, than private use.

   Isab. You want Authority to tax the Law.
Let your submission your last virtue be.

   Claud. Will you be good to *Juliet*?

   Isab. I will invite her to my breast, and to
A cloyster'd shade, where we with mutual grief
Will mourn, in sad remembrance of our loss.

   Claud. Your promise is now register'd in Heaven.
Bear her this fatal pledge of our first Vows.   [*Gives her a Ring.*
Farewel. To cloyst'rall kindness both
Retire, where you may ever live above
The rage of pow'r, and injuries of love.   [*Exit, and the Duke*

   Duke. Vouchsafe a word, young Sister, but one word.   [*steps in.*

   Isab. What is your will?

   Duke. I would some satisfaction crave of that,

In which you likewise may have benefit.

    Isab. My sorrows, Father, hasten me away.
I must beseech you to be brief.

    Duke. The hand which made you fair, has made you good.
Th' assault which *Angelo* has to
Your virtue given, chance to my knowledge brings.
I have o'reheard you, and with much astonishment
I gaze on th' Image you have made of *Angelo.*

    Isab. How is the noble Duke deceiv'd in such
A Substitute! whose wickedness I will
Proclaim to all the world.

    Duke. Your accusation he will soon avoid,
By saying he but tryal of
Your virtue made; therefore I wish you would
Conceal his horrid purpose till fit time
Shall serve you at the Duke's return:
Do you conceive my counsel good?

    Isab. Father I am oblig'd to follow it.

    Duke. Where lodge you, virtuous Maid?

    Isab. The Sisterhood of Saint *Clare* will soon inform you.
I lodge in the Apartment for probation.

    Duke. There I'll attend you Daughter. Grace preserve you.

                                  [*Exeunt several ways.*

                  [Act III, Scene iv.]

Enter Benedick *and* Beatrice *at several doors, and* Viola *with her.*

    Beat. O Sir! you are a very princely Lover!
You cannot woo but by Ambassadors;
And may chance to marry by Proxy.

    Ben. Your wit flows so fast
That I'll not stem the tyde; I'll cast Anchor,
And consult in your Cabin how t'avoid
Danger. The Rocks are very near us.

    Beat. How now? afraid of the Deputy's Ghost
E're he be dead? my Sister shall lead you
Through the dark.

    Ben. There is the pardon
Sign'd for *Juliet* and for *Claudio* too.

    Beat. I thank you, *Benedick.* Give it me.

                     35

Ben. You are as nimble as a Squirrel, but
The Nuts are not so soon crackt.

Beat. Unless I have it I'll take back my thanks.

Ben. If it be possible to fix Quick-silver
Stay but a little.

*   *   *

[Act IV, Scene i.]

*   *   *

Enter Viola *dancing a Saraband awhile with Castanietos.*

*   *   *

[Act IV, Scene vi.]

Enter Angelo, *Servant.*

Ang. Attend her in, and then wait you at distance.   [*Ex. Serv.*
O Love! how much thy borrow'd shapes disguise,
Even to themselves, the valiant and the wise?

Enter Isabella.

Ang. Had you not fear'd th'approach of *Claudio's* fate
(Which shews you are to him compassionate,
Though not to me) I had not seen you here.
He may your pity thank, and I your fear.

Isab. My Lord, I hardly could myself forgive
For suing still to have my Brother live,
But that a higher hope directs my aim;
Which, saving his frail life, would yours reclaim.

Ang. How desp'rate all your hopeful visits prove!
You bring me counsel still instead of love.
And would in storms of passion make me wise.
Bid Pilots preach to winds when tempests rise.

Isab. But yet as tempests are by showers allay'd,
So may your anger by my tears be sway'd.

Ang. You must by yielding teach me to relent.
Make haste! the Mourners tears are almost spent,
Courtiers to Tyrant-Death who basely wait,

36

To do that Tyrant honour whom they hate.
Inviting formal Fools to see his Feast
To which your Brother is th'unwilling Guest.
And the absolving Priest must say the Grace:
Night's progress done, *Claudio* begins his Race.
    Isab. And with the mornings wings your cruel doom
He shall convey where you must trembling come,
Before that Judge, whose pow'r you use so ill,
As if, like Law, 'twere subject to your will.
The cruel there shall wish they had been just,
And that their seeming love had not been lust.
    Ang. These useless sayings were from Cloysters brought:
You cannot teach so soon as you were taught.
You must example to my mercy give;
First save my life, and then let *Claudio* live.
    Isab. Have you no words but what are only good,
Because their ill is quickly understood?
Dispose of *Claudio*'s life! whilst cruel you
Seem dead, by being deaf to all that sue.
Till by long custom of forgiving none
Y' are so averse to all forgiveness grown.
That in your own behalf you shall deny,
To hear of absolution when you dye.
    Ang. How *Isabel*! from calms of bashfulness
(Even such as suppliant Saints to Heaven express,
When patience makes herself a Sacrifice)
Can you to storms of execration rise?   [*Isabel is going out.*
Leave me not full of evil wonder, stay!
    Isab. Can it be good to hear what you would say?
                       [*He steps in and reaches a Cabinet.*
    Ang. In this behold Nature's Reserves of light,
When the lost day yields to advancing night.
When that black Goddess fine in Frosts appears,
Then starry Jewels bright as these she wears.
The wealth of many Parents who did spare
In plenteous peace, and get by prosperous War.
    Isab. Of that which evil life may get, you make
        A wonder in a monstrous boast;
      Which death from you as certainly will take,
        As 'tis already by your Parents lost.

37

Ang. Be in this world, like other mortals, wise;
And take this treasure as your Beauty's prize.
Wealth draws a Curtain o're the face of shame;
Restores lost beauty, and recovers fame.

    Isab. Catch Fools in Nets without a Covert laid;
Can I, who see the treason, be betray'd?   *[Going out.*

    Ang. Stay *Isabel!* stay but a moments space!
You know me not by knowing but my face,
My heart does differ from my looks and tongue.
To know you much, I have deceiv'd you long.

    Isab. Have you more shapes, or would you new devise?

    Ang. I'll now at once cast off my whole disguise.
Keep still your virtue, which is dignify'd
And has new value got by being try'd.
Claudio shall live longer than I can do,
Who was his Judge, but am condemn'd by you.
The Marshal of the Guards keeps secretly
His pardon seal'd; nor meant I he should dye.

    Isab. By shifting your disguise, you seem much more
In borrow'd darkness than you were before.

    Ang. Forgive me who, till now, thought I should find
Too many of your beauteous Sex too kind.
I strove, as jealous Lovers curious grow,
Vainly to learn, what I was loth to know.
And of your virtue I was doubtful grown,
As men judge womens frailties by their own.
But since you fully have endur'd the test,
And are not only good, but prove the best
Of all your Sex, submissively I woo
To be your Lover, and your Husband too.

    Isab. Can I when free, be by your words subdu'd,
Whose actions have my Brother's life pursu'd?

    Ang. I never meant to take your Brother's life;
But if in tryal how to chuse a wife,
I have too diffident, too curious been,
I'll pardon ask for folly, as for sin;
I lov'd you e're your pretious beauties were
In your probation shaded at Saint *Clare*:
And when with sacred Sisterhood confin'd,
A double enterprise perplext my mind;

By *Claudio*'s danger to provoke you forth
From that blest shade, and then to try your worth.

   Isab. She that can credit give to things so strange,
And can comply with such a sudden change,
Has mighty faith, and kindness too so strong,
That the extream cannot continue long.
I am so pleas'd with *Claudio*'s liberty,
That the example shall preserve me free.

   Ang. Was I when bad so quickly understood;
And cannot be believ'd when I am good?

   Isab. In favour of my Sex and not of you,
I wish your love so violent and true,
That those who shall hereafter curious be,
To seek that frailty, which they would not see,
May by your punishment become afraid,
To use those Nets which you ignobly laid.

   Ang. Ah *Isabel*! you blam'd my cruelty!
Will you, when I shew mercy, cruel be?

   Isab. You might have met a weaker breast than mine,
Which at approach to parley would incline:
How little honour then you had obtain'd,
If, where but little was, you that had stain'd?
Had you been great of mind, you would have strove
T' have hid, or helpt the weaknesses of love;
And not have us'd temptations to the frail,
Or pow'r, where 'twas dishonour to prevail.
You will (if now your love dissembled be)
Deceive your self, in not deceiving me.
If it be true, you shall not be believ'd,
Lest you should think me apt to be deceiv'd.   [*Exit.*

   Ang. Break heart! farewel the cruel and the just!
Fools seek belief, where they have bred distrust:
Because she doubts my virtue I must dye;
Who did with vitious arts her virtue try.   [*Exit.*

[Act V, Scene i.]

Enter Duke and Isabel.

   Duke. You told me, Daughter, that the Marshal has
Your Brother's pardon seal'd, and I shall watch

All means to keep him safe, lest *Angelo*
Should turn his clemency into revenge.
Do not th' assurance of his freedom buy
With hazard of a Virgins liberty.
   Isab. I shall with patience follow your instruction.
   Duke. Night's shady Curtains are already drawn;
And you shall hear strange news before the dawn.   [*Exit Duke.*

Enter Francisca.

   Franc. Is the good Father gone?
   Isab. Yes, Sister, and has left my breast in peace.   [*A Bell rings.*
   Franc. This Bell does nightly warn us e're we sleep,
T' appease offended Heaven. Let us go pray,
That the worlds crimes may vanish with the day.   [*Exeunt.*

Enter Benedick, Eschalus, Beatrice, Viola, Lucio, *singing a Chorus within.*

   Esch. Your Brother, Sir, has an unquiet mind:
'Tis late, and he would take his rest.
   Viol. We'll sing him asleep.
   Ben. Shall he who should
Live lean with care of the whole Common-wealth,
Grow fat with sleep like a *Groenland*-Bear?
   Esch. Rulers are but mortal; and should have rest.
   Ben. A States-man should take a nap in his Chair,
And only dream of sleep.
   Beat. These great tame Lions of the Law
(Who make Offenders of the weak)
Should still seem watchful, and like wild Lions
Sleep with their eyes open.
   Esch. Is night a season for singing?
   Viol. We'll sing like Nightingales, and they sing at night.
   Esch. Take heed; for the Grand-Watch does walk the Round.
   Beat. Signior, when did you hear of Nightingales
Taken by the Watch?
   Luc. Madam, we'll sing. The Governour
May come (if he please) and sigh to the Chorus.
   Esch. I'll bear no part, Sir, in your Song,
Nor in your punishment.   [*Exit* Eschalus.

The SONG.

Luc.   Our Ruler has got the vertigo of State;
       The world turns round in his politick pate.
  He stears in a Sea, where his Course cannot last;
  And bears too much sail for the strength of his Mast.
Cho.   Let him plot all he can,
       Like a politick man,
  Yet Love though a Child may fit him.
       The small Archer though blind,
       Such an Arrow will find,
  As with an old trick shall hit him.

2.

Beat.   Sure *Angelo* knows Loves party is strong;
      Love melts, like soft wax, the hearts of the young.
  And none are so old but they think on the taste,
  And weep with remembrance of kindnesses past.
Cho.   Let him plot all he can, &c.

3.

Ben.   Love in the wisest is held a mad fit;
     And madness in Fools is reckon'd for Wit.
  The Wise value Love, just as Fools Wisdom prize;
  Which when they cann't gain, they seem to dispise.
Cho.   Let him plot all he can, &c.

4.

Viol.   Cold Cowards all perils of anger shun;
     To dangers of Love they leap when they run.
  The valiant in frolicks did follow the Boy,
  When he led them a Dance from *Greece* to old *Troy*.
Cho.   Let him plot all he can, &c.

*   *   *

6. Margaret Cavendish on Shakespeare's wit

1662

Letter 113, from *CCXI Sociable Letters, written by the Thrice Noble, Illustrious, and Excellent Princess, The Lady Marchioness of Newcastle* (1664), pp. 224–8.

Margaret Cavendish, Duchess of Newcastle (1624?–75), was a prolific poet, dramatist, and essay-writer. Although she invokes the neoclassic concept of decorum to defend Shakespeare she writes with unpedantic enthusiasm and knowledge.

MADAM,

I Wonder how that Person you mention in your Letter, could either have the Conscience, or Confidence to Dispraise *Shakespeare*'s Playes, as to say they were made up onely with Clowns, Fools, Watchmen, and the like; But to Answer that Person, though *Shakespeare*'s Wit will Answer for himself, I say, that it seems by his Judging, or Censuring, he Understands not Playes, or Wit; for to Express Properly, Rightly, Usually, and Naturally, a Clown's, or Fool's Humour, Expressions, Phrases, Garbs, Manners, Actions, Words, and Course of Life, is as Witty, Wise, Judicious, Ingenious, and Observing, as to Write and Express the Expressions, Phrases, Garbs, Manners, Actions, Words, and Course of Life, of Kings and Princes; and to Express Naturally, to the Life, a Mean Country Wench, as a Great Lady, a Courtesan, as a Chast Woman, a Mad man, as a Man in his right Reason and Senses, a Drunkard, as a Sober man, a Knave, as an Honest man, and so a Clown, as a Well-bred man, and a Fool, as a Wise man; nay, it Expresses and Declares a Greater Wit, to Express, and Deliver to Posterity, the Extravagancies of Madness, the Subtilty of Knaves, the Ignorance of Clowns, and the Simplicity of Naturals, or the Craft of Feigned Fools, than to Express Regularities, Plain Honesty, Courtly Garbs, or Sensible Discourses, for 'tis harder to Express Nonsense than

42

Sense, and Ordinary Conversations, than that which is Unusual; and
'tis Harder, and Requires more Wit to Express a Jester, than a Grave
Statesman; yet *Shakespeare* did not want Wit, to Express to the Life
all Sorts of Persons, of what Quality, Profession, Degree, Breeding, or
Birth soever; nor did he want Wit to Express the Divers, and Different
Humours, or Natures, or Several Passions in Mankind; and so Well
he hath Express'd in his Playes all Sorts of Persons, as one would think
he had been Transformed into every one of those Persons he hath
Described; and as sometimes one would think he was Really himself
the Clown or Jester he Feigns, so one would think, he was also the
King, and Privy Counsellor; also as one would think he were Really
the Coward he Feigns, so one would think he were the most Valiant,
and Experienced Souldier; Who would not think he had been such a
man as his Sir *John Falstaff*? and who would not think he had been
Harry the Fifth? & certainly *Julius Cæsar*, *Augustus Cæsar*, and *Antonius*,
did never Really Act their parts Better, if so Well, as he hath Described
them, and I believe that *Antonius* and *Brutus* did not Speak Better to the
People, than he hath Feign'd them; nay, one would think that he had
been Metamorphosed from a Man to a Woman, for who could
Describe *Cleopatra* Better than he hath done, and many other Females
of his own Creating, as *Nan Page*, Mrs. *Page*, Mrs. *Ford*, the Doctors
Maid, *Beatrice*, Mrs. *Quickly*, *Doll Tearsheet*, and others, too many to
Relate? and in his Tragick Vein, he Presents Passions so Naturally, and
Misfortunes so Probably, as he Peirces the Souls of his Readers with
such a True Sense and Feeling thereof, that it Forces Tears through their
Eyes, and almost Perswades them, they are Really Actors, or at least
Present at those Tragedies. Who would not Swear he had been a
Noble Lover, that could Woo so well? and there is not any person he
hath Described in his Book, but his Readers might think they were
Well acquainted with them; indeed *Shakespeare* had a Clear Judgment,
a Quick Wit, a Spreading Fancy, a Subtil Observation, a Deep Ap-
prehension, and a most Eloquent Elocution; truly, he was a Natural
Orator, as well as a Natural Poet, and he was not an Orator to Speak
Well only on some Subjects, as Lawyers, who can make Eloquent
Orations at the Bar, and Plead Subtilly and Wittily in Law-Cases, or
Divines, that can Preach Eloquent Sermons, or Dispute Subtilly and
Wittily in Theology, but take them from that, and put them to other
Subjects, and they will be to seek; but *Shakespeare*'s Wit and Eloquence
was General, for, and upon all Subjects, he rather wanted Subjects for
his Wit and Eloquence to Work on, for which he was Forced to take

some of his Plots out of History, where he only took the Bare Designs, the Wit and Language being all his Own; and so much he had above others, that those, who Writ after him, were Forced to Borrow of him, or rather to Steal from him; I could mention Divers Places, that others of our Famous Poets have Borrow'd, or Stoln, but lest I should Discover the Persons, I will not Mention the Places, or Parts, but leave it to those that Read his Playes, and others, to find them out. I should not have needed to Write this to you, for his Works would have Declared the same Truth: But I believe, those that Dispraised his Playes, Dispraised them more out of Envy, than Simplicity or Ignorance, for those that could Read his Playes, could not be so Foolish to Condemn them, only the Excellency of them caused an Envy to them. By this we may perceive, Envy doth not Leave a man in the Grave, it Follows him after Death, unless a man be Buried in Oblivion, but if he Leave any thing to be Remembred, Envy and Malice will be still throwing Aspersion upon it, or striving to Pull it down by Detraction. But leaving *Shakespeare*'s Works to their own Defence, and his Detractors to their Envy, and you to your better Imployments, than Reading my Letter, I rest,

    Madam,

Your faithful Friend
and humble Servant.

7. Richard Flecknoe, from
A Short Discourse of the English Stage

1664

Added to *Love's Kingdom* (1664), an alteration of his play *Love's Dominion* (1654).

Richard Flecknoe (*c.* 1620–78) was a poet and dramatist, who had the misfortune to be satirised by Dryden. His remarks here anticipate many of Dryden's critical discussions.

*   *   *

In this time were Poets and Actors in their greatest flourish, *Jonson*, *Shakespeare*, with *Beaumont* and *Fletcher* their Poets, and *Field* and *Burbidge* their Actors.

For Playes, *Shakespeare* was one of the first who inverted the Dramatick Stile, from dull History to quick Comedy, upon whom *Jonson* refin'd; as *Beaumont* and *Fletcher* first writ in the Heroick way, upon whom *Suckling* and others endeavoured to refine agen; one saying wittily of his *Aglaura*, that 'twas full of fine flowers, but they seem'd rather stuck, than growing there; as another, of *Shakespeare*'s writings, that 'twas a fine Garden, but it wanted weeding.

There are few of our English Playes (excepting onely some few of *Jonson*'s) without some faults or other; and if the French have fewer than our English, 'tis because they confine themselves to narrower limits, and consequently have less liberty to erre.

The chief faults of ours, are our huddling too much matter together, and making them too long and intricate; we imagining we never have intrigue enough, till we lose our selves and Auditors, who shu'd be led in a Maze, but not a Mist; and through turning and winding wayes, but so still as they may finde their way at last.

A good Play shu'd be like a good stuff, closely and evenly wrought, without any breakes, thrums, or loose ends in 'um, or like a good Picture well painted and designed; the Plot or Contrivement, the Design, the Writing, the Colors, and Counterplot, the Shaddowings, with other Embellishments: or finally, it shu'd be like a well contriv'd Garden, cast into its Walks and Counterwalks, betwixt an Alley and a Wilderness, neither too plain nor too confus'd. Of all Arts, that of the Dramatick Poet is the most difficult and most subject to censure; for in all others, they write onely of some particular subject, as the Mathematician of Mathematicks, or Philosopher of Philosophy; but in that, the Poet must write of every thing, and every one undertakes to judge of it.

A Dramatick Poet is to the Stage as a Pilot to the Ship, and to the Actors, as an Architect to the Builders, or Master to his Schollars: he is to be a good moral Philosopher, but yet more learned in Men than Books. He is to be a wise, as well as a witty Man, and a good man, as well as a good Poet; and I'de allow him to be so far a good fellow too, to take a chearful cup to whet his wits, so he take not so much to dull 'um, and whet 'um quite away.

To compare our English Dramatick Poets together (without taxing them) *Shakespeare* excelled in a natural Vein, *Fletcher* in Wit, and *Jonson* in Gravity and ponderousness of Style; whose onely fault was he was too elaborate; and had he mixt less erudition with his Playes, they had been more pleasant and delightful than they are. Comparing him with *Shakespeare*, you shall see the difference betwixt Nature and Art; and with *Fletcher*, the difference betwixt Wit and Judgement: Wit being an exuberant thing, like *Nilus*, never more commendable than when it overflowes; but Judgement, a stayed and reposed thing, always containing it self within its bounds and limits. (Sig G_5^r–G_6^r).

*   *   *

8. Sir William D'Avenant, from his adaptation of *Macbeth*

1664

From *Macbeth a Tragedy. With all the Alterations, Amendments, Additions, and New Songs* (1674).

D'Avenant's version of *Macbeth* may have been performed for the first time on 5 November 1664. It was a considerable success, as Downes records (No. 46 in vol. 2).

D'Avenant added 'spectacle'; and he produced a symmetrical ethical structure by developing Lady Macduff as a paragon of virtue, an exact anti-type to Lady Macbeth. In addition to much small-scale alteration of Shakespeare's language (especially his metaphors), D'Avenant omits the porter's scene and gives Macbeth a dying speech.

[Act I, Scene i.] An Open place.

Thunder and Lightning.

Enter three Witches.

1. *Witch.* When shall we three meet again,
In Thunder, Lightning, and in Rain?
2. When the Hurly-burly's done,
When the Battle's lost and won.
3. And that will be e're set of Sun.
1. Where's the place?
2. Upon the Heath.
3. There we resolve to meet *Macbeth.*   [*A shriek like an Owl.*
1. I come Gray *Malkin.*
All. Paddock calls!
To us fair weather's foul, and foul is fair!
Come hover through the foggy, filthy Air.   [*Ex. flying.*

[Act I, Scene ii.] A camp near Forres.

Enter King, Malcolm, Donalbine *and* Lenox, *with Attendants meeting* Seyton *wounded.*

King. What aged man is that? if we may guess
His message by his looks, he can relate the
Issue of the Battle!
   Malc. This is the valiant *Seyton;*
Who like a good and hardy Souldier fought
To save my liberty. Hail, Worthy Friend,
Inform the King in what condition you
Did leave the Battle?
   Seyton. It was doubtful;
As two spent swimmers, who together cling
And choak their Art: the merciless *Mackdonald*
(Worthy to be a Rebel, to which end
The multiplying Villanies of Nature
Swarm'd thick upon him) from the Western Isles
With Kernes and Gallow-glasses was supply'd.
Whom Fortune with her smiles oblig'd a while;
But brave *Macbeth* (who well deserves that name)
Did with his frowns put all her smiles to flight:
And Cut his passage to the Rebels person:
Then having Conquer'd him with single force,
He fix'd his head upon our Battlements.
   King. O valiant Cousin! Worthy Gentleman!
   Seyton. But then this Day-break of our Victory
Serv'd but to light us into other Dangers
That, sprung from whence our hopes did seem to rise,
Produc'd our hazard: for no sooner had
The justice of your Cause, Sir, (arm'd with valour,)
Compell'd these nimble Kernes to trust their Heels;
But the *Norweyan* Lord, (having expected
This opportunity) with new supplies
Began a fresh assault.
   King. Dismaid not this our Generals, *Macbeth*
And *Banquo?*
   Seyton. Yes, as sparrows Eagles, or as hares do Lions;
As flames are heighten'd by access of fuel,

So did their valours gather strength, by having
Fresh Foes on whom to exercise their Swords:
Whose thunder still did drown the dying groans
Of those they slew, which else had been so great,
Th' had frighted all the rest into Retreat.
My spirits faint: I would relate the wounds
Which their Swords made; but my own silence me.
   King. So well thy wounds become thee as thy words:
Th' are full of Honour both: Go get him Surgeons——
                                 [Ex. Cap. and Attendants.

Enter Macduff.

But, who comes there?
   Malc. Noble *Macduff*!
   Lenox. What haste looks through his eyes!
   Donal. So should he look who comes to speak things strange.
   Macd. Long live the King!
   King. Whence com'st thou, worthy *Thane*?
   Macd. From *Fife*, Great King; where the *Norwean* Banners
Darkned the Air; and fann'd our people cold:
Norwey himself with infinite supplies,
(Assisted by that most disloyal *Thane*
Of *Cawdor*) long maintain'd a dismal Conflict,
Till brave *Macbeth* oppos'd his bloody rage,
And check'd his haughty spirits, after which
His Army fled: Thus shallow streams may flow
Forward with violence a while; but when
They are oppos'd, as fast run back agen.
In brief, the Victory was ours.
   King. Great Happiness!
   Malcol. And now the *Norway* King craves Composition.
We would not grant the burial of his men,
Until at *Colems-Inch* he had disburs'd
Great heaps of Treasure to our Generals use.
   King. No more that *Thane of Cawdor* shall deceive
Our confidence: pronounce his present Death;
And with his former Title greet *Macbeth*.
He has deserv'd it.
   Macd. Sir! I'le see it done.
   King. What he hath lost, Noble *Macbeth* has won.   *[Exeunt.*

[Act I, Scene iii.] A blasted heath.

Thunder and Lightning.

Enter three Witches flying.

*   *   *

Macb. *Glamis* and *Thane* of *Cawdor*!
The greatest is behind; my noble Partner!
Do you not hope your Children shall be Kings?
When those who gave to me the *Thane* of *Cawdor*
Promis'd no less to them.
   Banq. If all be true,
You have a Title to a Crown, as well
As to the *Thane* of *Cawdor*. It seems strange;
But many times to win us to our harm,
The Instruments of darkness tell us truths,
And tempt us with low trifles, that they may
Betray us in the things of high concern.
   Macb. Th'have told me truth as to the name of *Cawdor*,   [*Aside.*
That may be Prologue to the name of King.
Less Titles shou'd the greater still fore-run,
The morning Star doth usher in the Sun.
This strange Prediction in as strange a manner
Deliver'd neither can be good nor ill;
If ill, 'twou'd give no earnest of success,
Beginning in a truth: I'm *Thane* of *Cawdor*;
If good, Why am I then perplext with doubt?
My future bliss causes my present fears,
Fortune, methinks, which rains down Honour on me,
Seems to rain bloud too: *Duncan* does appear
Clouded by my increasing Glories: but
These are but dreams.
   Banq. Look how my Partner's rap'd!
   Macb. If Chance will have me King; Chance may bestow
A Crown without my stir.
   Banq. His Honours are surprizes, and resemble
New Garments, which but seldom fit men well,
Unless by help of use.

Macb. Come, what come may;
Patience and time run through the roughest day.
  Banq. Worthy *Macbeth*! we wait upon your leisure.
  Macb. I was reflecting upon past transactions;
Worthy *Macduff*; your pains are registred
Where every day I turn the leaf to read them.
Let's hasten to the King: we'll think upon
These accidents at more convenient time.
When w'have maturely weigh'd them, we'll impart
Our mutual judgments to each others breasts.
  Banq. Let it be so.
  Macb. Till then, enough. Come Friends.   [*Exeunt.*

*   *   *

[Act I, Scene v.] Inverness. Macbeth's Castle.

Enter Lady Macbeth, *and Lady* Macduff, *Lady* Macbeth *having a Letter in her hand.*

  La. Macb. Madam, I have observ'd since you came hither,
You have been still disconsolate. Pray tell me,
Are you in perfect health?
  La. Macd. Alas! how can I?
My Lord, when Honour call'd him to the War,
Took with him half of my divided soul,
Which lodging in his bosom, lik'd so well
The place, that 'tis not yet return'd.
  La. Macb. Methinks
That should not disorder you: for, no doubt
The brave *Macduff* left half his soul behind him,
To make up the defect of yours.
  La. Macd. Alas!
The part transplanted from his breast to mine,
(As 'twere by sympathy) still bore a share
In all the hazards which the other half
Incurr'd, and fill'd my bosom up with fears.
  La. Macb. Those fears, methinks, should cease now he is safe.
  La. Macd. Ah, Madam, dangers which have long prevail'd
Upon the fancy; even when they are dead
Live in the memory a-while.
  La. Macb. Although his safety has not power enough to put

51

Your doubts to flight, yet the bright glories which
He gain'd in Battel might dispel those Clouds.

La. Macd. The world mistakes the glories gain'd in war,
Thinking their Lustre true: alas, they are
But Comets, Vapours! by some men exhal'd
From others bloud, and kindl'd in the Region
Of popular applause, in which they live
A-while; then vanish: and the very breath
Which first inflam'd them, blows them out agen.

La. Macb. I willingly would read this Letter; but   [*Aside.*
Her presence hinders me; I must divert her.
If you are ill, repose may do you good;
Y'had best retire; and try if you can sleep.

L. Macd. My doubtful thoughts too long have kept me waking,
Madam! I'll take your Counsel.   [*Ex. La. Macd.*

La. Macb. Now I have leisure, peruse this Letter.
His last brought some imperfect news of things
Which in the shape of women greeted him
In a strange manner. This perhaps may give
More full intelligence.   [*She reads.*

Reads. *They met me in the day of success; and I have been told they have
more in them than mortal Knowledge. When I desired to question them
further; they made themselves air. Whilest I entertain'd myself with the wonder
of it, came Missives from the King, who call'd me* Thane of Cawdor: *by
which Title, these weyward Sisters had saluted me before, and referr'd me to
the comming on of time; with, Hail King that shall be. This have I imparted
to thee, (my dearest Partner of Greatness) that thou might'st not lose thy
rights of rejoycing, by being ignorant of what is promis'd. Lay it to thy heart,
and farewel.*

Glamis thou art, and *Cawdor,* and shalt be
What thou art promis'd: yet I fear thy Nature
Has too much of the milk of humane kindness
To take the nearest way: thou wouldst be great:
Thou do'st not want ambition: but the ill
Which should attend it: what thou highly covet'st
Thou covet'st holily! alas, thou art
Loath to play false; and yet would'st wrongly win!
Oh how irregular are thy desires!
Thou willingly, Great *Glamis,* would'st enjoy

The end without the means! Oh haste thee thither,
That I may pour my spirits in thy ear:
And chastise with the valour of my tongue
Thy too effeminate desires of that
Which supernatural assistance seems
To Crown thee with.

Enter Servant.

What may be your news?
    Macb. Ser. The King comes hither to night.
    La. Macb. Th'art mad to say it:
Is not thy Master with him? Were this true,
He would give notice for the preparation.
    Macb. Ser. So please you, it is true: our *Thane* is coming;
One of my fellows had the speed of him;
Who almost dead for breath, had scarcely more
Than would make up his Message.
    La. Macb. See him well look'd to: he brings welcome news.
There wou'd be musick in a Raven's voice,
Which should but croke the entrance of the King
Under my Battlements. Come all you spirits
That wait on mortal thoughts: unsex me here:
Empty my Nature of humanity,
And fill it up with cruelty: make thick
My bloud, and stop all passage to remorse;
That no relapses into mercy may
Shake my design, nor make it fall before
'Tis ripen'd to effect: you murthering spirits,
(Where ere in fightless substances you wait
On Natures mischief) com, and fill my breasts
With Gall instead of Milk: make haste dark night,
And hide me in a smoak as black as hell;
That my keen steel see not the wound it makes:
Nor Heav'n peep through the Curtains of the dark,
To cry, hold! hold!

Enter Macbeth.

Great *Glamis*! worthy *Cawdor*!
Greater than both, by the all-Hail hereafter;
Thy Letters have transported me beyond

My present posture; I already feel
The future in the instant.
  Macb. Dearest Love,
Duncan comes here to night.
    La. Macb. When goes he hence?
    Macb. To morrow as he purposes.
    La. Macb. O never!
Never may any Sun that morrow see.
Your face, my *Thane*, is as a book, where men
May read strange matters to beguile the time.
Be chearful, Sir; bear welcome in your eye,
Your hand, your tongue: Look like the innocent flower,
But be the Serpent under't: He that's coming
Must be provided for: And you shall put
This nights great bus'ness into my dispatch;
Which shall to our future nights and days
Give soveraign Command: we will with-draw,
And talk on't further: Let your looks be clear,
Your change of Count'nance does betoken fear.   [*Exeunt.*

[Act I, Scene vi.] Before Macbeth's Castle.

Enter King, Malcolme, Donalbine, Banquo, Lenox, Macduff, *Attendants.*

  King. This Castle has a very pleasant seat;
The air does sweetly recommend itself
To our delighted senses.
  Banq. The Guest of Summer,
The Temple-haunting *Martin* by his choice
Of this place for his Mansion, seems to tell us,
That here Heavens breath smells pleasantly. No window,
Buttrice, nor place of vantage; but this Bird
Has made his pendant bed and cradle where
He breeds and haunts. I have observ'd the Air,
'Tis delicate.

Enter Lady Macbeth.

  King. See, see our honoured Hostess,
By loving us, some persons cause our trouble;
Which still we thank as love: herein I teach

You how you should bid us welcome for your pains,
And thank you for your trouble.
   La. Macb. All our services
In every point twice done, would prove but poor
And single gratitude, if weigh'd with these
Obliging honours which
Your Majesty confers upon our house;
For dignities of old and later date
(Being too poor to pay) we must be still
Your humble debtors.
   Macd. Madam, we are all joyntly, to night, your trouble;
But I am your trespasser upon another score.
My Wife, I understand, has in my absence
Retir'd to you.
   La. Macb. I must thank her: for whilst she came to me
Seeking a Cure for her own solitude,
She brought a remedy to mine: her fears
For you, have somewhat indispos'd her, Sir,
She's now with-drawn, to try if she can sleep:
When she shall wake, I doubt not but your presence
Will perfectly restore her health.
   King. Where's the *Thane* of *Cawdor*?
We cours'd him at the heels, and had a purpose
To be his purveyor: but he rides well,
And his great love (sharp as his spur) has brought him
Hither before us. Fair and Noble Lady,
We are your Guests to night.
   La. Macb. Your servants
Should make their Audit at your pleasure, Sir,
And still return it as their debt.
   King. Give me your hand.
Conduct me to *Macbeth*: we love him highly,
And shall continue our affection to him.   [*Exeunt.*

[Act I, Scene vii.]

Enter Macbeth.

   Macb. If it were well when done, then it were well
It were done quickly; if his Death might be
Without the Death of nature in myself

And killing my own rest, it wou'd suffice;
But deeds of this complexion still return
To plague the doer, and destroy his peace:
Yet let me think; he's here in double trust.
First, as I am his Kinsman, and his Subject,
Strong both against the Deed: then as his Host,
Who should against this murderer shut the door,
Not bear the sword myself. Besides, this *Duncan*
Has born his faculties so meek, and been
So clear in his great Office that his Virtues,
Like Angels, plead against so black a deed;
Vaulting Ambition! thou o're-leap'st thyself
To fall upon another: now, what news?

* * *

[Act II, Scene i.]

* * *

Macb. Go bid your Mistress, when she is undrest,
To strike the Closet-bell and I'le go to bed.
Is this a dagger which I see before me?
The hilt draws towards my hand; come, let me grasp thee:
I have thee not, and yet I see thee still;
Art thou not, fatal Vision, sensible
To feeling as to sight? or, art thou but
A dagger of the mind, a false creation
Proceeding from the brain, opprest with heat?
My eyes are made the fools of th'other senses,
Or else worth all the rest: I see thee still,
And on thy blade are stains of reeking blood.
It is the bloody business that thus
Informs my eye-sight; now, to half the world
Nature seems dead, and wicked dreams infect
The health of sleep; now witchcraft celebrates
Pale *Heccate*'s Offerings; now murder is
Alarm'd by his nights Centinel: the wolf,
Whose howling seems the watch-word to the dead:
But whilst I talk, he lives: hark, I am summon'd;
O *Duncan*, hear it not, for 'tis a bell
That rings my Coronation, and thy Knell.   [*Exit.*

[Act II, Scene ii.]

*   *   *

Macb. Methoughts I heard a noise cry, sleep no more:
Macbeth has murder'd sleep, the innocent sleep;
Sleep, that locks up the senses from their care;
The death of each days life; tir'd labours bath;
Balm of hurt minds; great natures second course;
Chief nourisher in life's feast.
    La. Macb. What do you mean?
    Macb. Still it cry'd, sleep no more, to all the house.
Glamis hath murder'd sleep, and therefore *Cawdor*
Shall sleep no more; *Macbeth* shall sleep no more.
    La. Macb. Why do you dream thus? go get some water
And cleanse this filthy witness from your hands.
Why did you bring the daggers from the place?
They must be there, go carry them, and stain
The sleepy Grooms with blood.
    Macb. I'le go no more;
I am afraid to think what I have done.
What then with looking on it, shall I do?
    La. Macb. Give me the daggers, the sleeping and the dead
Are but as pictures; 'tis the eye of childhood
That fears a painted Devil: with his blood
I'le stain the faces of the Grooms; by that
It will appear their guilt.   [*Ex. La. Macbeth.*
                                          [*Knock within.*

    Macb. What knocking's that?
How is't with me, when every noise affrights me?
What hands are here! can the Sea afford
Water enough to wash away the stains?
No, they would sooner add a tincture to
The Sea, and turn the green into a red.

Enter Lady Macbeth.

    La. Macbeth. My hands are of your colour; but I scorn
To wear an heart so white. Heark,   [*Knock.*
I hear a knocking at the Gate: to your Chamber;
A little water clears us of this deed.

Your fear has left you unmann'd; heark, more knocking.
Get on your Gown, lest occasions call us,
And shews us to be watchers; be not lost
So poorly in your thoughts.   [*Exit.*

    Macb. Disguis'd in blood, I scarce can find my way.
Wake *Duncan* with this knocking, wou'd thou could'st.   [*Exit.*

[Act II, Scene iii.]

Enter Lenox *and* Macbeth's *servant.*

    Lenox. You sleep soundly, that so much knocking
Could not wake you.
    Serv. Labour by day causes rest by night.

Enter Macduff.

    Len. See the noble *Macduff.*
Good morrow my Lord, have you observ'd
How great a mist does now possess the air;
It makes me doubt whether't be day or night.
    Macd. Rising this morning early, I went to look out of my
Window, and I cou'd scarce see farther than my breath:
The darkness of the night brought but few objects
To our eyes, but too many to our ears.
Strange claps and creekings of the doors were heard;
The *Screech-Owl* with his screams, seem'd to foretel
Some deed more black than night.

           ★   ★   ★

[Act II, Scene v.]

SCENE; *An Heath.*

Enter Lady Macduff, *Maid, and Servant.*

    La. Macd. Art sure this is the place my Lord appointed
Us to meet him?
    Serv. This is the entrance o'th' Heath; and here
He order'd me to attend him with the Chariot.
    La. Macd. How fondly did my Lord conceive that we
Should shun the place of danger by our flight
From *Everness?* The darkness of the day

Makes the Heath seem the gloomy walks of death.
We are in danger still: they who dare here
Trust Providence, may trust it any where.

    Maid. But this place, Madam, is more free from terror:
Last night methoughts I heard a dismal noise
Of shrieks and groanings in the air.

    La. Macd. 'Tis true, this is a place of greater silence;
Not so much troubled with the groans of those
That die; nor with the out-cries of the living.

    Maid. Yes, I have heard stories, how some men
Have in such lonely places been affrighted
With dreadful shapes and noises.   [*Macduff hollows.*

    La. Macd. But hark, my Lord sure hollows;
'Tis he; answer him quickly.

    Serv. Illo, ho, ho, ho.

Enter Macduff.

    La. Macd. Now I begin to see him: are you afoot,
My Lord?

    Macd. Knowing the way to be both short and easie,
And that the Chariot did attend me here,
I have adventur'd. Where are our Children?

    La. Macd. They are securely sleeping in the Chariot.

First Song by Witches.

    1 Witch. Speak, Sister, speak; is the deed done?

    2 Witch. Long ago, long ago:
Above twelve glasses since have run.

    3 Witch. Ill deeds are seldom slow;
Nor single: following crimes on former wait.
The worst of creatures fastest propagate.
Many more murders must this one ensue,
As if in death were propagation too.

    2 Witch. He will.

    1 Witch. He shall.

    3 Witch. He must spill much more bloud;
And become worse, to make his Title good.

    1 Witch. Now let's dance.

    2 Witch. Agreed.

    3 Witch. Agreed.

4 Witch. Agreed.

Chorus. We shou'd rejoyce when good Kings bleed.
      When Cattel die, about we go,
      What then, when Monarchs perish, should we do?

Macd. What can this be?

La. Macd. This is most strange: but why seem you affraid?
Can you be capable of fears, who have
So often caus'd it in your Enemies?

Macd. It was an hellish Song; I cannot dread
Ought that is mortal, but this is something more.

Second Song.

Let's have a dance upon the Heath;
We gain more life by *Duncan*'s death.
Sometimes like brinded Cats we shew,
Having no musick but our mew.
Sometimes we dance in some old Mill,
Upon the Hopper, Stones, and Wheel.
To some old Saw, or Bardish Rhime,
Where still the Mill-clack does keep time.
Sometimes about an hollow tree,
A round, a round, a round dance we.
Thither the chirping Cricket comes,
And Beetle, singing drowsie hums.
Sometimes we dance o're Fens and Furs,
To howls of Wolves, and barks of Curs.
And when with none of those we meet,
We dance to th' Ecchoes of our feet.
At the night-Raven's dismal voice,
Whilst others tremble, we rejoyce;
And nimbly, nimbly dance we still
To th' Ecchoes from an hollow Hill.

Macd. I am glad you are not affraid.

La. Macd. I would not willingly to fear submit:
None can fear ill, but those that merit it.

Macd. Am I made bold by her? How strong a guard   [*Aside.*
Is innocence! If any one would be
Reputed valiant, let him learn of you;
Vertue both courage is, and safety too.   [*A dance of Witches.*

Enter three Witches.

Macd. These seem foul spirits; I'll speak to 'em.
If you can any thing by more than nature know;
You may in these prodigious times fore-tell
Some ill we may avoid.
 1 Witch. Saving thy bloud will cause it to be shed;
 2 Witch. He'll bleed by thee, by whom thou first hast bled.
 3 Witch. Thy Wife shall shunning danger, dangers find,
And fatal be, to whom she most is kind   [*Ex. Witches.*
 La. Macd. Why are you alter'd, Sir? Be not so thoughtful:
The Messengers of Darkness never spake
To men, but to deceive them.
 Macd. Their words seem to fore-tell some dire Predictions.
 La. Macd. He that believes ill news from such as these,
Deserves to find it true. Their words are like
Their shape; nothing but Fiction.
Let's hasten to our journey.
 Macd. I'll take your counsel; for to permit
Such thoughts upon our memories to dwell,
Will make our minds the Registers of Hell.   [*Exeunt omnes.*

    ★ ★ ★

   [Act III, Scene ii.] Fife. Macduff's Castle.

Enter Macduff, *and Lady* Macduff.

 Macd. It must be so. Great *Duncan's* bloody death
Can have no other Author but *Macbeth.*
His Dagger now is to a Scepter grown;
From *Duncan's* Grave he has deriv'd his Throne.
 La. Macd. Ambition urg'd him to that bloody deed:
May you be never by Ambition led:
Forbid it Heav'n, that in revenge you shou'd
Follow a Copy that is writ in blood.
 Macd. From *Duncan's* Grave, methinks I hear a groan
That calls aloud for justice.
 La. Macd. If the Throne
Was by *Macbeth* ill gain'd, Heavens may,
Without your Sword, sufficient vengeance pay.

Usurpers lives have but a short extent,
Nothing lives long in a strange Element.

   Macd. My Countreys dangers call for my defence
Against the bloody Tyrants violence.

   La. Macd. I am afraid you have some other end,
Than meerly *Scotland*'s freedom to defend.
You'd raise yourself, whilst you wou'd him dethrone;
And shake his Greatness to confirm your own.
That purpose will appear, when rightly scann'd,
But usurpation at the second hand.
Good Sir, recal your thoughts.

   Macd. What if I shou'd
Assume the Scepter for my Countreys good?
Is that an usurpation? can it be
Ambition to procure the liberty
Of this sad Realm; which does by Treason bleed?
That which provokes, will justifie the deed.

   La. Macd. If the Design should prosper, the Event
May make us safe, but not you Innocent.
For whilst to set our fellow Subjects free
From present Death, or future Slavery,
You wear a Crown (not by your Title due)
Defence in them is an Offence in you.
That deed's unlawful, though it cost no Blood,
In which you'l be at best unjustly Good.
You, by your Pity, which for us you plead,
Weave but Ambition of a finer thread.

   Macd. Ambition does the height of power affect,
My aim is not to Govern, but Protect:
And he is not ambitious that declares,
He nothing seeks of Scepters but their cares.

   La. Macd. Can you so patiently your self molest,
And lose your own to give your Countrey rest!
In *Plagues* what sound Physician wou'd endure
To be infected for another's Cure?

   Macd. If by my troubles I cou'd yours release,
My Love wou'd turn those torments to my ease:
I shou'd at once be sick, and healthy too,
Though Sickly in my self, yet Well in you.

   La. Macd. But then reflect upon the Danger, Sir,

Which you by your aspiring wou'd incur.
From Fortunes Pinacle, you will too late
Look down, when you are giddy with your height:
Whilst you with *Fortune* play to win a Crown,
The Peoples Stakes are greater than your own.
   Macd. In hopes to have the common Ills redrest,
Who wou'd not venture single interest?

Enter Servant.

   Ser. My Lord, a Gentleman, just now arriv'd
From Court, has brought a Message from the King:
   Macd. One sent from him, can no good Tidings bring!
   La. Macd. What wou'd the Tyrant have?
   Macd. Go, I will hear
The News, though it a dismal Accent bear;
Those who expect and do not fear their Doom,
May hear a Message though from Hell it come.   [*Exeunt.*

[Act III, Scene iii.] Forres. The Palace.

         ★   ★   ★

   Macb. Alas, we have but scorch'd the Snake, not kill'd it,
She'l close and be her self, whilst our poor malice
Remains in danger of her former Sting.
But let the frame of all things be disjoynt
E're we will eat our bread in fear; and sleep
In the affliction of those horrid Dreams
That shake us mightily! Better be with him
Whom we to gain the Crown, have sent to peace;
Than on the torture of the mind to lie
In restless Agony. *Duncan* is dead;
He, after life's short feaver, now sleeps; Well,
Treason has done its worst; nor Steel, nor Poyson,
Nor Foreign force, nor yet Domestick Malice
Can touch him further.
   La. Macb. Come on, smooth your rough brow.
Be free and merry with your guests to night.
   Macb. I shall, and so I pray be you, but still,
Remember to apply your self to *Banquo*:

Present him kindness with your Eye and Tongue.
In how unsafe a posture are our honours
That we must have recourse to flattery,
And make our Faces Vizors to our hearts.

La. Macb. You must leave this.

Macb. How full of Scorpions is my mind! Dear Wife
Thou know'st that *Banquo* and his *Fleance* lives.

La. Macb. But they are not Immortal, there's comfort yet in that.

Macb. Be merry then, for ere the *Bat* has flown
His Cloyster'd flight; ere to black *Heccate*'s Summons,
The sharp brow'd Beetle with his drowsie hums,
Has rung nights second Peal:
There shall be done a deed of dreadful Note.

La. Macb. What is't?

Macb. Be innocent of knowing it, my Dear,
Till thou applaud the deed. Come dismal Night
Close up the Eye of the quick-sighted Day
With thy invisible and bloody hand.
The Crow makes wing to the thick shady Grove,
Good things of day grow dark and overcast,
Whilst Nights black Agents to their Preys make hast.
Thou wonder'st at my Language, wonder still,
Things ill begun, strengthen themselves by ill.   [*Exeunt.*

[Act III, Scene iv.] Forres. Outside the Palace.

Enter three Murtherers.

1 Mur. The time is almost come,
The *West* yet glimmers with some streaks of day,
Now the benighted Traveller spurs on,
To gain the timely Inn.

2 Mur. Hark, I hear Horses, and saw some body alight
At the Park gate.

3 Mur. Then 'tis he; the rest
That are expected are i'th' Court already.

1 Mur. His horses go about almost a Mile,
And men from hence to th' *Pallace* make it their usual walk. [*Exeunt.*

Enter Banquo *and* Fleance.

Banq. It will be rain to night.

Flean. We must make haste:

Banq. Our haste concerns us more than being wet.
The King expects me at his feast to night,
To which he did invite me with a kindness,
Greater than he was wont to express.   *[Exeunt.*

Re-enter Murtherers with drawn Swords.

1 Mur. Banquo, thou little think'st what bloody feast
Is now preparing for thee.

2 Mur. Nor to what shades the darkness of this night,
Shall lead thy wandring spirit.   *[Exeunt after* Banquo.
                    [Clashing of Swords is heard from within.
Re-enter Fleance *pursu'd by one of the Murtherers.*

Flean. Murther, help, help, my Father's kill'd.   *[Exe. running.*

★   ★   ★

[Act III, Scene vi.] Fife. Macduff's Castle.

Enter Macduff *and Lady* Macduff.

La. Macd. Are you resolved then to be gone?

Macd. I am:
I know my Answer cannot but inflame
The Tyrants fury to pronounce my death,
My life will soon be blasted by his breath.

La. Macd. But why so far as *England* must you fly?

Macd. The farthest part of *Scotland* is too nigh.

La. Macd. Can You leave me, your Daughter and young Son,
To perish by that Tempest which you shun?
When Birds of stronger Wing are fled away,
The Ravenous *Kite* do's on the weaker prey.

Macd. He will not injure you, he cannot be
Possest with such unmanly cruelty:
You will your safety to your weakness owe
As Grass escapes the Syth by being low.
Together we shall be too slow to fly:
Single, we may out-ride the Enemy.
I'll from the *English* King such Succours crave,
As shall revenge the Dead, and Living save.
My greatest misery is to remove,
With all the wings of haste from what I love.

65

La. Macd. If to be gone seems misery to you,
Good Sir, let us be miserable too.
 Macd. Your Sex which here is your security,
Will by the toyls of flight your Danger be.   [*Enter Messenger.*
What fatal News do's bring thee out of breath?
 Mess. Sir, *Banquo's* kill'd.
 Macd. Then I am warn'd of Death.
Farewell; our safety, Us, a while must sever:
 La. Macd. Fly, fly, or we may bid farewel for ever.
 Macd. Flying from Death, I am to life unkind,
For leaving you, I leave my Life behind.   [*Exit.*
 La. Macd. Oh my dear Lord, I find now thou art gone,
I am more valiant when unsafe alone.
My heart feels man-hood, it does Death despise,
Yet I am still a Woman in my eyes.
And of my Tears thy absence is the cause,
So falls the Dew when the bright Sun withdraws.   [*Exeunt.*

[Act III, Scene viii.] The Heath.

Thunder. **Enter three Witches meeting** Hecate.

 1 Witch. How? *Hecat,* you look angerly.
 Hecate. Have I not reason *Beldams?*
Why did you all Traffick with *Macbeth*
'Bout Riddles and affairs of Death,
And call'd not me? All you have done
Hath been but for a Weyward Son:
Make some amends now: get you gon,
And at the pit of *Achæron*
Meet me i'th' morning: Thither he
Will come to know his Destiny.
Dire business will be wrought ere Noon,
For on a corner of the Moon,
A drop my Spectacles have found,
I'll catch it ere it come to ground.
And that distill'd shall yet ere night,
Raise from the Center such a Spright:
As by the strength of his Illusion,
Shall draw *Macbeth* to his Confusion.

[*Musick and Song.*
Heccate, Heccate, Heccate! O come away:

Hark, I am call'd, my little Spirit see,
Sits in a foggy Cloud, and stays for me.

[*Machine descends.*

[*Sing within.*
Come away *Heccate, Heccate!* Oh come away:

Hec. I come, I come, with all the speed I may,
With all the speed I may.
Where's *Stadling*?
    2. Here.
    Hec. Where's *Puckle*?
    3. Here, and *Hopper* too, and *Helway* too.
    1. We want but you, we want but you:
Come away, make up the Count.
    Hec. I will but Noint, and then I mount,
I will but, &c.
    1. Here comes down one to fetch his due, a Kiss,
A Cull, a sip of bloud.
And why thou stay'st so long, I muse,
Since th' Air's so sweet and good.
    2. Oh art thou come! What News?
All goes fair for our delight,
Either come, or else refuse,
Now I'm furnish'd for the flight,
Now I go, and now I fly,
Malking my sweet Spirit and I.
    3. Oh what a dainty pleasure's this!
To sail i'th' Air
While the *Moon* shines fair;
To Sing, to Toy, to Dance and Kiss;
Over Woods, high Rocks and Mountains;
Over Hills, and misty Fountains;
Over Steeples, Towers, and Turrets:
We fly by night 'mongst troops of Spirits.
No Ring of Bells to our Ears sounds,
No Howls of Wolves, nor Yelps of Hounds;

67

No, nor the noise of Waters breach,
Nor Cannons Throats our Height can reach.
   1. Come let's make haste, she'll soon be back again.
   2. But whilst she moves through the foggy Air,
Let's to the Cave and our dire Charms prepare.

★   ★   ★

[Act IV, Scene iv.] Dunsinane. Macbeth's Castle.

Enter Macbeth *and* Seaton.

   Macb. Seaton, go bid the Army March.
   Seat. The posture of Affairs requires your Presence.
   Macb. But the Indisposition of my Wife
Detains me here.
   Seat. Th' Enemy is upon our borders, *Scotland's* in danger.
   Macb. So is my Wife, and I am doubly so.
I am sick in her, and my Kingdom too.
Seaton.
   Seat. Sir.
   Macb. The spur of my Ambition prompts me to go
And make my Kingdom safe, but Love which softens me
To pity her in her distress, curbs my Resolves.
   Seat. He's strangely disorder'd.   [*Aside.*
   Macb. Yet why should Love since confin'd, desire
To controul Ambition, for whose spreading hopes
The world's too narrow? It shall not; great Fires
Put out the less; *Seaton* go bid my Grooms
Make ready; I'le not delay my going.
   Seat. I go.
   Macb. Stay *Seaton*, stay, Compassion calls me back.
   Seat. He looks and moves disorderly.   [*Aside.*
   Macb. I'll not go yet.   [*Enter a Servant, who*
   Seat. Well Sir.   *whispers* Macbeth.
   Macb. Is the Queen asleep?
   Seat. What makes 'em whisper and his countenance change? [*Aside.*
Perhaps some new design has had ill success.
   Macb. Seaton, go see what posture our affairs are in.
   Seat. I shall, and give you notice Sir.   [*Exit* Seat.

Enter Lady Macbeth.

68

Macb. How does my gentle Love?

La. Macb. Duncan is dead.

Macb. No words of that.

La. Macb. And yet to me he lives.
His fatal Ghost is now my shadow, and pursues me
Where e're I go.

Macb. It cannot be my Dear,
Your Fears have mis-inform'd your eyes.

La. Macb. See there; Believe your own.
Why do you follow me? I did not do it.

Macb. Methinks there's nothing.

La. Macb. If you have Valour force him hence.
Hold, hold, he's gone. Now you look strangely.

Macb. 'Tis the strange error of your eyes.

La. Macb. But the strange error of my eyes
Proceeds from the strange action of your Hands.
Distraction does by fits possess my head,
Because a Crown unjustly covers it.
I stand so high that I am giddy grown.
A Mist does cover me, as Clouds the tops
Of Hills. Let us get down apace.

Macb. If by your high ascent you giddy grow,
'Tis when you cast your eyes on things below.

La. Macb. You may in peace resign the ill gain'd Crown.
Why should you labour still to be unjust?
There has been too much blood already spilt.
Make not the Subjects Victims to your guilt.

Macb. Can you think that a Crime, which you did once
Provoke me to commit? Had not your breath
Blown my Ambition up into a Flame
Duncan had yet been living.

La. Macb. You were a man,
And by the Charter of your Sex you shou'd
Have govern'd me, there was more crime in you
When you obey'd my Councels, than I contracted
By my giving it. Resign your Kingdom now,
And with your Crown put off your guilt.

Macb. Resign the Crown, and with it both our Lives.
I must have better Counsellors.

La. Macb. What, your Witches?

Curse on your Messengers of Hell. Their breath
Infected first my Breast: See me no more.
As King your Crown sits heavy on your Head,
But heavier on my heart: I have had too much
Of Kings already. See, the Ghost again.   *[Ghost appears.*
    Macb. Now she relapses.
    La. Macb. Speak to him if thou canst.
Thou look'st on me, and shew'st thy wounded breast.
Shew it the Murderer.
    Macb. Within there, Ho.   *[Enter Women.*
    La. Macb. Am I ta'ne Prisoner? then the Battle's lost.   *[Exit.*
                    [Lady Macbeth *led out by Women.*
    Macb. She does from *Duncan*'s death to sickness grieve,
And shall from *Malcom*'s death her health receive.
When by a Viper bitten, nothing's good
To cure the Venom but a Viper's blood.   *[Exit*

★   ★   ★

[Act V, Scene i.]

Enter Seaton, *and a Lady.*

    Lady. I have seen her rise from her bed, throw
Her Night-Gown on her, unlock her Closet,
Take forth Paper, fold it, write upon't, read it,
Afterwards Seal it, and again return to Bed,
Yet all this while in a most fast sleep.
    Seat. 'Tis strange she should receive the Benefit
Of sleep, and do the Effects of waking.
In this disorder what at any time have
You heard her say?
    Lady. That Sir, which I will not report of her.
    Seat. You may to me; and 'tis most meet you shou'd.
    Lady. Neither to You, nor any one living;
Having no witness to confirm my Speech.

Enter Lady Macbeth.

See here she comes: observe her, and stand close.
    Seat. You see her eyes are open.
    Lady. Ay, But her Sense is shut.

70

Seat. What is't she does now? Look how she rubs her hands.

Lady. It is an accustom'd action with her to seem
Thus washing her hands: I have known
Her continue in this a quarter of an hour.

La. Macb. Yet out, out, here's a spot.

Seat. Heark, she speaks.

La. Macb. Out, out, out I say. One, two: Nay then
'Tis time to do't: Fie my Lord, fy, a Souldier,
And affraid? What need we fear? Who knows it?
There's none dares call our Power to account.
Yet who would have thought the old Man had
So much Bloud in him?

Seat. Do you mark that?

La. Macb. Macduff had once a Wife; where is she now?
Will these hands ne're be clean? Fie my Lord,
You spoil all with this starting: Yet here's
A smell of bloud; not all the perfumes of *Arabia*
Will sweeten this little Hand. Oh, oh, oh.　　　　　　　*[Exit.*

★　　★　　★

[Act V, Scene iii.] Dunsinane. Before Macbeth's castle.

Enter Macbeth, Seaton *and Attendants.*

Macb. Bring me no more Reports: Let 'em fly all.
Till *Byrnam* Wood remove to *Dunsinane*
I cannot fear. What's the Boy *Malcolm*? What
Are all the *English*? Are they not of Women
Born? And t'all such I am invincible;
Then fly false *Thanes,*
By your Revolt you have inflam'd my Rage,
And now have borrowed *English* bloud to quench it.

Enter a Messenger.

Now Friend, what means thy change of Countenance?

Mess. There are Ten Thousand, Sir.

Macb. What, Ghosts?

Mess. No, Armed men.

Macb. But such as shall be Ghosts ere it be Night,
Art thou turn'd Coward too, since I made thee Captain?

71

Go Blush away thy Paleness, I am sure
Thy Hands are of another Colour; thou hast Hands
Of Bloud, but Looks of Milk.

    Mess. The *English* Force so please you——
    Macb. Take thy Face hence.

He has Infected me with Fear;
I am sure to die by none of Woman born.
And yet the *English* Drums beat an Alarm,
As fatal to my Life as are the Crokes
Of *Ravens,* when they flutter about the Windows
Of departing men.
My hopes are great, and yet methinks I fear;
My Subjects cry out Curses on my Name,
Which like a North-wind seems to blast my Hopes.

    Seat. That Wind is a contagious Vapour exhal'd from Bloud. [*Aside.*

Enter Second Messenger.

What news more?

    2 Mess. All's confirm'd, my Leige, that was Reported.
    Macb. And my Resolves in spite of Fate shall be as firmly.
Send out more Horse; and Scout the Country round.
How do's my Wife?

    Seat. Not so sick, my Lord, as she is troubled
With disturbing Fancies, that keep her from her rest.

    Macb. And I, methinks, am sick of her Disease:
Seaton send out; Captain, the *Thanes* flie from thee:
Wou'd she were well, I'de quickly win the Field.
Stay *Seaton* Stay, I'll bear you company,
The *English* cannot long maintain the Fight;
They come not here to Kill, but to be Slain;
Send out our Scouts.

    Seat. Sir, I am gone.
Not to obey your Orders, but the Call of Justice.   [*Aside.*
I'll to the *English* Train whose Hopes are built
Upon their Cause, and not on Witches Prophesies.   [*Exit.*

    Macb. Poor *Thanes,* you vainly hope for Victory:
You'l find *Macbeth* Invincible; or if
He can be o'recome, it must be then
By *Birnam Oaks,* and not by English-men.   [*Exit.*

✷   ✷   ✷

[Act V, Scene viii.] Another part of the field.

Enter Macbeth.

Macb. Why should I play the *Roman* Fool and Fall,
On my own Sword, while I have living Foes
To Conquer? My Wounds shew better upon them.

Enter Macduff.

Macd. Turn, Hell-Hound, Turn.
Macb. Of all Men else, I have avoided Thee;
But get thee back, my Soul is too much clog'd
With Blood of thine already.
Macd. I'le have no Words, thy Villanies are worse
Than ever yet were Punisht with a Curse.
Macb. Thou mayst as well attempt to Wound the Air,
As me; my Destiny's reserv'd for some Immortal Power,
And I must fall by Miracle; I cannot Bleed.
Macd. Have thy black Deeds then turn'd thee to a Devil.
Macb. Thou wouldst but share the Fate of *Lenox.*
Macd. Is *Lenox* slain? and by a Hand that would Damn all it kills,
But that their Cause preserves 'em.
Macb. I have a Prophecy secures my Life.
Macd. I have another which tells me I shall have his Blood,
Who first shed mine.
Macb. None of Woman born can spill my Blood.
Macd. Then let the Devils tell thee, *Macduff*
Was from his Mothers Womb untimely Ript.
Macb. Curst be that tongue that tells me so,
And double Damn'd be they who with a double sence
Make Promises to our Ears and Break at last
That Promise to our sight: I will not Fight with thee.
Macd. Then yield thy self a Prisoner to be led about
The World, and Gaz'd on as a Monster, a Monster
More Deform'd then ever Ambition Fram'd,
Or Tyranny could shape.
Macb. I scorn to Yield. I will in spite of Enchantment
Fight with thee, though *Birnam* Wood be come
To *Dunsinane*:
And thou art of no Woman Born. I'le try,   ⎰*They Fight, Macbeth*
If by a Man it be thy Fate to Die.   ⎱*falls. They shout within.*

73

Macd. This for my Royal Master *Duncan*,
This for my dearest Friend my Wife,
This for those Pledges of our Loves, my Children.
Hark I hear a Noise, sure there are more   [*Shout within.*
Reserves to Conquer.
I'le as a Trophy bear away his Sword,
To witness my Revenge.   [*Exit Macduff.*
    Macb. Farewel vain World, and what's most vain in it, Ambition.
                                   [*Dies.*

[Act V, Scene ix.]

Enter *Malcolm, Seymour, Donalbain, Fleance, Seaton,* and *Souldiers.*

    Malc. I wish *Macduff* were safe Arriv'd, I am
In doubt for him; for *Lenox* I'me in grief.
    Seym. Consider *Lenox,* Sir, is nobly Slain:
They who in Noble Causes fall, deserve
Our Pity, not our Sorrow. Look where the Tyrant is.
    Seat. The Witches, Sir, with all the Power of Hell,
Could not preserve him from the Hand of Heaven.

Enter *Macduff* with *Macbeths* Sword.

    Macd. Long Live *Malcolm,* King of *Scotland,* so you are;
And though I should not Boast, that one
Whom Guilt might easily weigh down, fell
By my Hand; yet here I present you with
The Tyrants Sword, to shew that Heaven appointed
Me to take Revenge for you, and all
That Suffered by his Power.
    Malc. Macduff, we have more Ancient Records
Than this of your successful Courage.
    Macd. Now *Scotland,* thou shalt see bright Day again,
That Cloud's remov'd that did Eclipse thy Sun,
And Rain down Blood upon thee. As your Arms
Did all contribute to this Victory;
So let your Voices all concur to give
One joyful Acclamation.
Long live Malcom, King of Scotland.   [*All shout.*
    Malc. We shall not make a large Expence of time
Before we Reckon with your several Loves,

And make us even with you. *Thanes* and Kinsman,
Henceforth be Earls, the first that ever *Scotland*
Saw Honour'd with that Title: And may they still Flourish
On your Families, though like the Laurels
You have Won to Day they Spring from a Field of Blood.
Drag his body hence, and let it Hang upon
A Pinnacle in *Dunsinane*, to shew
To future Ages what to those is due,
Who others Right, by Lawless Power pursue.
   Macd. So may kind Fortune Crown your Raign with Peace,
As it has Crown'd your Armies with Success;
And may the Peoples Prayers still wait on you,
As all their Curses did *Macbeth* pursue:
His Vice shall make your Virtue shine more Bright,
As a Fair Day succeeds a Stormy Night.

9. Sir William D'Avenant and John Dryden, from their adaptation of *The Tempest*

1667

From *The Tempest, or the Enchanted Island. A Comedy* (1670).

In the last of his major adaptations (performed 11 November 1667), D'Avenant was joined by Dryden (1631–1700), who in the preface gives a full account of their collaboration. Dryden's rapture was shared by contemporary audiences, for this became one of the most successful versions, holding the stage until the late eighteenth century. As in *Macbeth* the principle of structural balance is carried to its logical conclusion in the invention of new characters; and as with Lucio, another 'low' character is elevated to a more proper social status—Stephano is transformed from a butler to a ship's captain.

[Preface]

The writing of Prefaces to Plays was probably invented by some very ambitious Poet, who never thought he had done enough: Perhaps by some Ape of the French Eloquence, which uses to make a business of a Letter of gallantry, an examen of a Farce; and in short, a great pomp and ostentation of words on every trifle. This is certainly the talent of that Nation, and ought not to be invaded by any other. They do that out of gayety which would be an imposition upon us.

We may satisfie our selves with surmounting them in the Scene, and safely leave them those trappings of writing, and flourishes of the Pen, with which they adorn the borders of their Plays, and which are indeed no more than good Landskips to a very indifferent Picture. I must proceed no farther in this argument, lest I run my self beyond my excuse for writing this. Give me leave therefore to tell you, Reader, that I do it not to set a value on any thing I have written in this Play, but out of gratitude to the memory of Sir *William Davenant*, who did me the honour to joyn me with him in the alteration of it.

It was originally *Shakespeare*'s: a Poet for whom he had particularly a high veneration, and whom he first taught me to admire. The Play it self had formerly been acted with success in the *Black-Fryers*: and our excellent *Fletcher* had so great a value for it, that he thought fit to make use of the same Design, not much varied, a second time. Those who have seen his *Sea-Voyage*, may easily discern that it was a Copy of *Shakespeare*'s *Tempest*: the Storm, the desart Island, and the Woman who had never seen a Man, are all sufficient testimonies of it. But *Fletcher* was not the only Poet who made use of *Shakespeare*'s Plot: Sir *John Suckling*, a profess'd admirer of our Author, has follow'd his footsteps in his *Goblins*; his *Regmella* being an open imitation of *Shakespeare*'s *Miranda*; and his Spirits, though counterfeit, yet are copied from *Ariel*. But Sir *William Davenant*, as he was a man of quick and piercing imagination, soon found that somewhat might be added to the Design of Shakespeare, of which neither *Fletcher* nor *Suckling* had ever thought: and therefore to put the last hand to it, he design'd the Counterpart to *Shakespeare*'s Plot, namely that of a Man who had never seen a Woman; that by this means those two Characters of Innocence and Love might the more illustrate and commend each other. This excellent contrivance he was pleas'd to communicate to me, and to desire my assistance in it. I confess that from the very first moment it so pleas'd me, that I never writ any thing with more delight. I must likewise do him that justice to acknowledge, that my writing received daily his amendments, and that is the reason why it is not so faulty as the rest which I have done without the help or correction of so judicious a friend. The Comical parts of the Saylors were also his invention, and for the most part his writing, as you will easily discover by the style. In the time I writ with him I had the opportunity to observe somewhat more neerly of him than I had formerly done, when I had only a bare acquaintance with him: I found him then of so quick a fancy, that nothing was propos'd to him, on which he could not suddenly produce a thought extreamly pleasant and surprizing: and those first thoughts of his, contrary to the old Latine Proverb, were not alwaies the least happy. And as his fancy was quick, so likewise were the products of it remote and new. He borrowed not of any other; and his imaginations were such as could not easily enter into any other man. His corrections were sober and judicious: and he corrected his own writings much more severely than those of another man, bestowing twice the time and labour in polishing which he us'd in invention. It had perhaps been easie enough for me to have arrogated more to my self than was my due in the writing of this Play, and to have pass'd by his name with silence in the publication of it, with the same ingratitude which others have us'd to him, whose Writings he hath not only corrected, as he has done this, but has had a greater inspection over them, and sometimes added whole Scenes together, which may as easily be distinguish'd from the rest, as true Gold from counterfeit by the weight. But besides the unworthiness of the action which deterred me from it (there being nothing so base as to rob the dead of his reputation) I am satisfi'd I could never have receiv'd so much honour in being thought the Author of any Poem how excellent soever, as I shall from the joining my imperfections with the merit and name of *Shakespeare* and Sir *William Davenant.*

Decemb. 1.
    1669.

JOHN DRYDEN.

[Prologue]

As when a Tree's cut down the secret root
Lives under ground, and thence new Branches shoot
So, from old *Shakespeare*'s honour'd dust, this day
Springs up and buds a new reviving Play.
Shakespeare, who (taught by none) did first impart
To *Fletcher* Wit, to labouring *Jonson* Art.
He Monarch-like gave those his subjects law,
And is that Nature which they paint and draw.
Fletcher reach'd that which on his heights did grow,
Whilst *Jonson* crept and gather'd all below.
This did his Love, and this his Mirth digest:
One imitates him most, the other best.
If they have since out-writ all other men,
'Tis with the drops which fell from *Shakespeare*'s Pen.
The Storm which vanish'd on the Neighb'ring shore,
Was taught by *Shakespeare*'s Tempest first to roar.
That innocence and beauty which did smile
In *Fletcher*, grew on this *Enchanted Isle.*

But *Shakespeare*'s Magick could not copy'd be,
Within that Circle none durst walk but he.
I must confess 'twas bold, nor would you now,
That liberty to vulgar Wits allow,
Which works by Magick supernatural things:
But *Shakespeare*'s pow'r is sacred as a King's.
Those Legends from old Priest-hood were receiv'd,
And he then writ, as people then believ'd.
But, if for *Shakespeare* we your grace implore,
We for our Theatre shall want it more:
Who by our dearth of Youths are forc'd t'employ
One of our Women to present a Boy.
And that's a transformation you will say
Exceeding all the Magick in the Play.
Let none expect in the last Act to find,
Her sex transform'd from man to Woman-kind.
What e're she was before the Play began,
All you shall see of her is perfect man.
Or if your fancy will be farther led,
To find her Woman, it must be abed.

Dramatis Personæ

Alonzo Duke of *Savoy*, and Usurper of the Dukedom of *Mantua*.
Ferdinand his Son.
Prospero right Duke of *Millain*.
Antonio his Brother, Usurper of the Dukedom.
Gonzalo a Noble man of *Savoy*.
Hippolito, one that never saw Woman, right Heir of the Dukedom of
    Mantua.
Stephano Master of the Ship.
Mustacho his Mate.
Trincalo Boatswain.
Ventoso a Mariner.
Several Mariners.
A Cabbin-Boy.
Miranda and⎫
Dorinda ⎬ (Daughters to *Prospero*) that never saw man.
Ariel an aiery Spirit, attendant on *Prospero*.

79

[*Milcha* an airy Spirit, female.]
Caliban ⎫
⎬ Two Monsters of the Isle.
Sycorax his Sister ⎭

[Act I, Scene i.] The Ship.

Enter Mustacho *and* Ventoso.

Vent. What a Sea comes in!
Must. A hoaming Sea! we shall have foul weather.

Enter Trincalo.

Trinc. The Scud comes against the Wind, 'twill blow hard.

Enter Stephano.

Steph. Bosen!
Trinc. Here, Master, what cheer?
Steph. Ill weather! let's off to Sea.
Must. Let's have Sea-room enough, and then let it blow the Devils
head off.

Steph. Boy!

Enter Cabin-boy.
Boy. Yaw, yaw, here Master.
Steph. Give the Pilot a dram of the Bottle.   [*Exeunt* Stephano
                                                            and Boy.

Enter Mariners and pass over the Stage.

Trinc. Heigh, my hearts, chearly, chearly, my hearts, yare, yare.

Enter Alonzo, Antonio, Gonzalo.

Alon. Good Bosen have a care; where's the Master?
Play the men.
Trinc. Pray keep below.
Anto. Where's the Master, Bosen?
Trinc. Do you not hear him? you mar our labour: keep your Cabins,
you help the storm.
Gonz. Nay, good friend be patient.
Trinc. Aye, when the Sea is hence; what care these roarers for the
name of Duke? to Cabin; silence; trouble us not.
Gonz. Good friend, remember whom thou hast aboard.
Trinc. None that I love more than my self. You are a Counsellour,

if you can advise these Elements to silence, use your wisdom: if you cannot, make your self ready in the Cabin for the ill hour. Cheerly good hearts! out of our way, Sirs.   [*Exeunt* Trincalo *and Mariners.*

Gonz. I have great comfort from this Fellow; methinks his complexion is perfect Gallows; stand fast, good fate, to his hanging; make the Rope of his destiny our Cable, for our own does little advantage us; if he be not born to be hang'd we shall be drown'd.   [*Exit.*

Enter Trincalo *and* Stephano.

Trinc. Up aloft Lads. Come, reef both Top-sails.
Steph. Let's weigh, Let's weigh, and off to Sea.   [*Ex.* Stephano.

Enter two Mariners and pass over the Stage.

Trinc. Hands down! man your main-Capstorm.

Enter Mustacho *and* Ventoso *at the other door.*

Must. Up aloft! and man your jeere-Capstorm.
Vent. My Lads, my hearts of Gold, get in your Capstorm-Bar: Hoa up, hoa up, &c.   [*Exeunt* Mustacho *and* Ventoso.

Enter Stephano.

Steph. Hold on well! hold on well! nip well there,
Quarter-Master, get's more Nippers.   [*Exit* Stephano.

Enter two Mariners and pass over again.

Trinc. Turn out, turn out all hands to Capstorm!
You dogs, is this a time to sleep?
Heave together Lads.   [Trincalo *whistles.*
     [*Exeunt* Mustacho *and* Ventoso.
Must. within. Our Viol's broke.
Vent. within. 'Tis but our Viol-block has given way. Come heave Lads! we are fix'd again. Heave together Bullyes.

Enter Stephano.

Steph. Cut off the Hamocks! cut off the Hamocks, come my Lads: Come *Bullys*, chear up! heave lustily.
The Anchor's a peek.
Trinc. Is the Anchor a peek?
Steph. Is a weigh! Is a weigh!
Trinc. Up aloft my Lads upon the Fore-Castle!
Cut the Anchor, cut him.

All within. Haul Catt, Haul Catt, &c. Haul Catt, haul: haul, Catt, haul. Below.

Steph. Aft, Aft! and loose the Misen!

Trinc. Get the Misen-tack aboard. Haul Aft Misen-sheat!

Enter Mustacho.

Must. Loose the main Top-sail!

Steph. Furle him again, there's too much Wind.

Trinc. Loose Fore-sail! Haul Aft both sheats! trim her right afore the Wind. Aft! Aft! Lads, and hale up the Misen here.

Must. A Mackrel-Gale, Master.

Steph. within. Port hard, port! the Wind grows scant, bring the Tack aboard. Port is. Star-board, star-board, a little steady; now steady, keep her thus, no neerer you cannot come.

Enter Ventoso.

Vent. Some hands down: the Guns are loose.   [*Ex.* Must.

Trinc. Try the Pump, try the Pump!   [*Exit* Ventoso.

Enter Mustacho *at the other door.*

Must. O Master! six foot Water in Hold.

Steph. Clap the Helm hard aboard! Flat, flat, flat in the Fore-sheat there.

Trinc. Over-haul your fore-boling.

Steph. Brace in the Lar-board.   [*Exit.*

Trinc. A curse upon this howling,   [*A great cry within.* They are louder than the weather.

Enter Antonio *and* Gonzalo.

Yet again, what do you here! shall we give o're, and drown? ha' you a mind to sink?

Gonz. A Pox o' your throat, you bawling, blasphemous, uncharitable dog.

Trinc. Work you then.

Anto. Hang, Cur, hang, you whorson insolent noise-maker, we are less afraid to be drown'd than thou art.

Trinc. Brace off the Fore-yard.   [*Exit.*

Gonz. I'le warrant him for drowning, though the Ship were no stronger than a Nut-shell, and as leaky as an unstanch'd Wench.

Enter Alonzo *and* Ferdinand.

Ferd. For my self I care not, but your loss
Brings a thousand Deaths to me.

Alonzo. O name not me, I am grown old, my Son;
I now am tedious to the world, and that,
By use, is so to me; but, *Ferdinand*,
I grieve my subjects loss in thee: Alas!
I suffer justly for my crimes, but why
Thou shouldest — O Heaven!   *[A cry within.*
Heark, farewel my Son! a long farewel!

Ferd. Some lucky Plank, when we are lost by shipwrack,
Waft hither, and submit it self beneath you.
Your blessing, and I dye contented.   *[Embrace and Exeunt.*

Enter Trincalo, Mustacho, *and* Ventoso.

Trinc. What, must our mouths be cold then?

Vent. All's lost. To prayers, to prayers.

Gonz. The Duke and Prince are gone within to prayers.
Let's assist them.

Must. Nay, we may e'en pray too; our case is now alike.

Ant. We are meerly cheated of our lives by Drunkards.
This wide chopt Rascal: would thou might'st lye drowning
The long washing of ten Tides.
             [Exeunt Trincalo, Mustacho, *and* Ventoso.

Gonz. He'll be hang'd yet, though every drop of water swears
against it; now would I give ten thousand Furlongs of Sea for one
Acre of barren ground, Long-heath, Broom-furs, or any thing. The
wills above be done, but I would fain dye a dry death.   *[A confused*
                                             noise within.

Ant. Mercy upon us! we split, we split.

Gonz. Let's all sink with the Duke, and the young Prince.   *[Exeunt.*

Enter Stephano, Trincalo.

Trinc. The Ship is sinking.   *[A new cry within.*
Steph. Run her ashore!

Trinc. Luffe! luffe! or we are all lost! there's a Rock upon the Star-
board Bow.

Steph. She strikes, she strikes! All shift for themselves.   *[Exeunt.*

[Act I, Scene ii.] The Island.

Enter Prospero *and* Miranda.

    Prosp. Miranda! where's your Sister?
    Miran. I left her looking from the pointed Rock,
At the walks end, on the huge beat of Waters.
    Prosp. It is a dreadful object.
    Mir. If by your Art, my dearest Father, you have
Put them in this roar, allay 'em quickly.
Had I been any God of power, I would
Have sunk the Sea into the Earth, before
It should the Vessel so have swallowed.
    Prosp. Collect your self, and tell your piteous heart,
There's no harm done.
    Mir. O woe the day!
    Prosp. There is no harm:
I have done nothing but in care of thee,
My Daughter, and thy pretty Sister:
You both are ignorant of what you are,
Not knowing whence I am, nor that I'm more
Than *Prospero*, Master of a narrow Cell,
And thy unhappy Father.

*   *   *

    Prosp. Hag-seed hence!
Fetch us in fewel, and be quick
To answer other business: shrugst thou (malice)?
If thou neglectest or dost unwillingly what I command,
I'le wrack thee with old Cramps, fill all thy bones with
Aches, make thee roar, that Beasts shall tremble
At thy Din.
    Calib. No prethee!
I must obey. His Art is of such power,   [*Aside.*
It would controul my Dam's God, *Setebos,*
And make a Vassal of him.
    Prosp. So Slave, hence.   [*Exeunt* Prospero *and* Caliban *severally.*

Enter Dorinda.

    Dor. Oh Sister! what have I beheld?

Mir. What is it moves you so?

Dor. From yonder Rock,
As I my Eyes cast down upon the Seas,
The whistling winds blew rudely on my face,
And the waves roar'd; at first I thought the War
Had bin between themselves, but strait I spy'd
A huge great Creature.

Mir. O you mean the Ship.

Dor. Is't not a Creature then? it seem'd alive.

Mir. But what of it?

Dor. This floating Ram did bear his Horns above;
All ty'd with Ribbands, ruffling in the wind,
Sometimes he nodded down his head a while,
And then the Waves did heave him to the Moon;
He clamb'ring to the top of all the Billows,
And then again he curtsy'd down so low,
I could not see him: till, at last, all side long
With a great crack his belly burst in pieces.

Mir. There all had perisht
Had not my Father's magick Art reliev'd them.
But, Sister, I have stranger news to tell you;
In this great Creature there were other Creatures,
And shortly we may chance to see that thing,
Which you have heard my Father call, a Man.

Dor. But what is that? for yet he never told me.

Mir. I know no more than you: but I have heard
My Father say we Women were made for him.

Dor. What, that he should eat us, Sister?

Mir. No sure, you see my Father is a man, and yet
He does us good. I would he were not old.

Dor. Methinks indeed it would be finer, if we two
Had two young Fathers.

Mir. No Sister, no, if they were young, my Father
Said that we must call them Brothers.

Dor. But pray how does it come that we two are
Not Brothers then, and have not Beards like him?

Mir. Now I confess you pose me.

Dor. How did he come to be our Father too?

Mir. I think he found us when we both were little,
And grew within the ground.

Dor. Why could he not find more of us? pray sister
Let you and I look up and down one day,
To find some little ones for us to play with.

Mir. Agreed; but now we must go in. This is the hour
Wherein my Father's Charm will work,
Which seizes all who are in open Air:
Th'effect of his great Art I long to see,
Which will perform as much as Magick can.

Dor. And I, methinks, more long to see a Man.   [*Exeunt.*

[Act II, Scene i.]

Enter Alonzo, Antonio, Gonzalo, *Attendants.*

Gonz. Beseech your Grace be merry; you have cause,
So have we all, of joy for our strange scape:
Then wisely, good Sir, weigh
Our sorrow with our comfort.

Alonz. Prithee peace!
You cram these words into my Ears against
My stomack. How can I rejoyce,
When my dear Son, perhaps this very moment,
Is made a meal to some strange Fish?

Ant. Sir, he may live,
I saw him beat the billows under him,
And ride upon their backs; he trod the Water,
Whose enmity he flung aside, and breasted
The most swoln surge that met him; his bold head
'Bove the contentious waves he kept, and oar'd
Himself with his strong arms to shore. I do not doubt
He came alive to land.

Alonz. No, no, he's gone;
And you and I, *Antonio*, were those who caus'd his death.

Ant. How could we help it?

Alonz. Then, then, we should have helpt it,
When thou betrayedst thy Brother *Prospero*,
And *Mantua*'s Infant Sovereign, to my power:
And when I, too ambitious, took by force
Anothers right; then lost we *Ferdinand*,
Then forfeited our Navy to this Tempest.

Ant. Indeed we first broke truce with Heav'n;

You to the waves an Infant Prince expos'd,
And on the waves have lost an only Son;
I did usurp my Brother's fertile lands, and now
Am cast upon this desert Isle.

   Gonz. These, Sir, 'tis true, were crimes of a black Dye,
But both of you have made amends to Heav'n,
By your late Voyage into *Portugal*,
Where, in defence of Christianity,
Your valour has repuls'd the *Moors* of *Spain*.

   Alonz. O name it not, *Gonzalo*,
No act but penitence can expiate guilt.
Must we teach Heaven what price to set on Murthers?
What rate on lawless power, and wild ambition?
Or dare we traffick with the Powers above,
And sell by weight a good deed for a bad?   [*Musick within.*

   Gonz. Musick! and in the air! sure we are shipwrackt
On the Dominions of some merry Devil.

   Ant. This Isle's inchanted ground, for I have heard
Swift voices flying by my Ear, and groans
Of lamenting Ghosts.

   Alonz. I pull'd a Tree, and Blood pursu'd my hand;
O Heaven! deliver me from this dire place,
And all the after actions of my life
Shall mark my penitence and my bounty.
Heark! the sounds approach us.

     A Dialogue within sung in parts.

   1. Devil. Where does proud Ambition dwell?
   2. In the lowest Rooms of Hell.
   1. Of the damn'd who leads the Host?
   2. He who did oppress the most.
   1. Who such Troops of damned brings?
   2. Most are led by fighting Kings.
     Kings who did Crowns unjustly get,
     Here on burning Thrones are set.
   Chor. Kings who did Crowns, &c.

   Ant. Do you hear, Sir, how they lay our Crimes before us?
   Gonz. Do evil Spirits imitate the good,
In shewing men their sins?

Alonz. But in a different way,
Those warn from doing, these upbraid 'em done.

1. Devil. Who are the Pillars of Ambitions Court?
2. Grim Deaths and Scarlet Murthers it support.
1. What lyes beneath her feet?
2.   Her footsteps tread,
   On Orphans tender breasts, and Brothers dead.
1. Can Heaven permit such Crimes should be
   Rewarded with felicity?
2. Oh no! uneasily their Crowns they wear,
   And their own guilt amidst their Guards they fear.
   Cares when they wake their minds unquiet keep,
   And we in visions lord it o're their sleep.
Cho. Oh no! uneasily their Crowns, &c.

Alonz. See where they come in horrid shapes!

*Enter the two that sung, in the shape of Devils, placing themselves at two
   corners of the Stage.*
Ant. Sure Hell is open'd to devour us quick.

1. Devil. Say Brother, shall we bear these mortals hence?
2. First let us shew the shapes of their offence.
1. We'll muster then their crimes on either side:
   Appear! appear! their first begotten, Pride.

Enter Pride.

Pride. Lo! I am here, who led their hearts astray,
   And to Ambition did their minds betray.

Enter Fraud.

Fraud. And guileful Fraud does next appear,
   Their wandring steps who led,
   When they from virtue fled,
   And in my crooked paths their course did steer.

Enter Rapine.

Rap. From Fraud to Force they soon arrive,
   Where Rapine did their actions drive.

Enter Murther.

Murd. There long they cannot stay,
   Down the deep precipice they run,
   And to secure what they have done,
   To murder bend their way.
                 [*After which they fall into a round encompassing the*
                                  Duke, &c. Singing.

    Around, around, we pace
    About this cursed place,
    Whilst thus we compass in
    These mortals and their sin.   [*Dance.*
                                [*All the spirits vanish.*

Ant. Heav'n has heard me! they are vanish'd.
Alonz. But they have left me all unman'd;
I feel my sinews slacken'd with the fright,
And a cold sweat trills down o're all my limbs,
As if I were dissolving into Water.
O *Prospero*! my crimes 'gainst thee sit heavy on my heart.
   Ant. And mine, 'gainst him and young *Hippolito.*
   Gonz. Heav'n have mercy on the penitent!
   Alonz. Lead from this cursed ground;
The Seas, in all their rage, are not so dreadful.
This is the Region of despair and death.
   Gonz. Shall we not seek some food?
   Alonz. Beware all fruit but what the birds have peck'd,
The shadows of the Trees are poisonous too;
A secret venom slides from every branch.
My conscience doth distract me, O my Son!
Why do I speak of eating or repose,
Before I know thy fortune?   [*Exeunt.*

            ★   ★   ★

[Act II, Scene iv.]

Enter Prospero *alone.*

   Prosp. 'Tis not yet fit to let my Daughters know I kept
The infant Duke of *Mantua* so near them in this Isle,
Whose Father dying bequeath'd him to my care,
Till my false Brother (when he design'd t'usurp
My Dukedom from me) expos'd him to that fate

He meant for me. By calculation of his birth
I saw death threat'ning him, if, till some time were
Past, he should behold the face of any Woman:
And now the danger's nigh: *Hippolito!*

Enter Hippolito.

   Hip. Sir, I attend your pleasure.
   Prosp. How I have lov'd thee from thy infancy,
Heav'n knows, and thou thy self canst bear me witness,
Therefore accuse not me for thy restraint.
   Hip. Since I knew life, you've kept me in a Rock,
And you this day have hurry'd me from thence,
Only to change my Prison, not to free me.
I murmur not, but I may wonder at it.
   Prosp. O gentle Youth, Fate waits for thee abroad,
A black Star threatens thee, and death unseen
Stands ready to devour thee.
   Hip. You taught me not to fear him in any of his shapes:
Let me meet death rather than be a Prisoner.
   Prosp. 'Tis pity he should seize thy tender youth.
   Hip. Sir, I have often heard you say, no creature liv'd
Within this Isle, but those which Man was Lord of,
Why then should I fear?
   Prosp. But here are creatures which I nam'd not to thee,
Who share man's soveraignty by Nature's Laws,
And oft depose him from it.
   Hip. What are those Creatures, Sir?
   Prosp. Those dangerous enemies of men call'd women.
   Hip. Women! I never heard of them before.
But have I Enemies within this Isle, and do you
Keep me from them? do you think that I want
Courage to encounter 'em?
   Prosp. No courage can resist 'em.
   Hip. How then have you, Sir,
Liv'd so long unharm'd among them?
   Prosp. O they despise old age, and spare it for that reason:
It is below their conquest, their fury falls
Alone upon the young.
   Hip. Why then the fury of the young should fall on them again.
Pray turn me loose upon 'em: but, good Sir,

What are women like?

Prosp. Imagine something between young men and Angels:
Fatally beauteous, and have killing Eyes,
Their voices charm beyond the Nightingales,
They are all enchantment, those who once behold 'em,
Are made their slaves for ever.

Hip. Then I will wink and fight with 'em.

Prosp. 'Tis but in vain, for when your eyes are shut,
They through the lids will shine, and pierce your soul;
Absent, they will be present to you.
They'l haunt you in your very sleep.

Hip. Then I'le revenge it on 'em when I wake.

Prosp. You are without all possibility of revenge,
They are so beautiful that you can ne're attempt,
Nor wish to hurt them.

Hip. Are they so beautiful?

Prosp. Calm sleep is not so soft, nor Winter Suns,
Nor Summer Shades so pleasant.

Hip. Can they be fairer than the Plumes of Swans?
Or more delightful than the Peacocks Feathers?
Or than the gloss upon the necks of Doves?
Or have more various beauty than the Rain-bow?
These I have seen, and without danger wondred at.

Prosp. All these are far below 'em. Nature made
Nothing but Woman dangerous and fair:
Therefore if you should chance to see 'em,
Avoid 'em streight, I charge you.

Hip. Well, since you say they are so dangerous,
I'le so far shun 'em as I may with safety of the
Umblemish'd honour which you taught me.
But let 'em not provoke me, for I'm sure I shall
Not then forbear them.

Prosp. Go in and read the Book I gave you last.
To morrow I may bring you better news.

Hip. I shall obey you, Sir.   [*Exit* Hippolito.

Prosp. So, so; I hope this lesson has secur'd him,
For I have been constrain'd to change his Lodging
From yonder Rock where first I bred him up,
And here have brought him home to my own Cell,
Because the Shipwrack happen'd near his Mansion.

I hope he will not stir beyond his limits,
For hitherto he hath been all obedience.
The Planets seem to smile on my designs,
And yet there is one sullen cloud behind,
I would it were disperst.

Enter Miranda *and* Dorinda.

How, my daughters! I thought I had instructed   [*Aside.*
Them enough: Children! retire;
Why do you walk this way?

Mir. It is within our bounds, Sir.

Prosp. But both take heed, that path is very dangerous.
Remember what I told you.

Dor. Is the man that way, Sir?

Prosp. All that you can imagine is ill there,
The curled Lyon, and the rugged Bear
Are not so dreadful as that man.

Mir. Oh me, why stay we here then?

Dor. I'le keep far enough from his Den, I warrant him.

Mir. But you have told me, Sir, you are a man;
And yet you are not dreadful.

Prosp. I child! but I am a tame man; old men are tame
By Nature, but all the danger lies in a wild
Young man.

Dor. Do they run wild about the Woods?

Prosp. No, they are wild within Doors, in Chambers,
And in Closets.

Dor. But Father, I would stroak 'em and make 'em gentle,
Then sure they would not hurt me.

Prosp. You must not trust them, Child: no woman can come
Neer 'em but she feels a pain full nine Months:
Well I must in; for new affairs require my
Presence: be you, *Miranda*, your Sister's Guardian.

[*Exit* Prospero.

Dor. Come, Sister, shall we walk the other way?
The man will catch us else, we have but two legs,
And he perhaps has four.

Mir. Well, Sister, though he have; yet look about you
And we shall spy him ere he comes too near us.

Dor. Come back, that way is towards his Den.

Mir. Let me alone; I'le venture first, for sure he can
Devour but one of us at once.

Dor. How dare you venture?

Mir. We'll find him sitting like a Hare in's Form,
And he shall not see us.

Dor. Aye, but you know my Father charg'd us both.

Mir. But who shall tell him on't? we'll keep each
Others Counsel.

Dor. I dare not for the world.

Mir. But how shall we hereafter shun him, if we do not
Know him first?

Dor. Nay I confess I would
Fain see him too. I find it in my Nature,
Because my Father has forbidden me.

Mir. Aye, there's it, Sister, if he had said nothing
I had been quiet. Go softly, and if you see him first,
Be quick and becken me away.

Dor. Well, if he does catch me, I'le humble my self to him,
And ask him pardon, as I do my Father,
When I have done a fault.

Mir. And if I can but scape with life, I had rather be
In pain nine Months, as my Father threatn'd,
Than lose my longing.   [*Exeunt.*

[Act II, Scene v.]

The Scene changes, and discovers Hippolito *in a Cave walking, his face
from the Audience.*

Hip. Prospero has often said that Nature makes
Nothing in vain: why then are women made?
Are they to suck the poyson of the Earth,
As gaudy colour'd Serpents are? I'le ask that
Question, when next I see him here.

Enter Miranda *and* Dorinda *peeping.*

Dor. O Sister, there it is, it walks about like one of us.

Mir. Aye, just so, and has legs as we have too.

Hip. It strangely puzzles me: yet 'tis most likely
Women are somewhat between men and spirits.

Dor. Heark! it talks, sure this is not it my Father meant,

93

For this is just like one of us: methinks I am not half
So much afraid on't as I was; see, now it turns this way.
  Mir. Heaven! what a goodly thing it is!
  Dor. I'le go nearer it.
  Mir. O no, 'tis dangerous, Sister! I'le go to it.
I would not for the world that you should venture.
My Father charg'd me to secure you from it.
  Dor. I warrant you this is a tame man, dear Sister,
He'll not hurt me, I see it by his looks.
  Mir. Indeed he will! but go back, and he shall
Eat me first: Fye, are you not asham'd
To be so much inquisitive?
  Dor. You chide me for't, and wou'd give your self.
  Mir. Come back, or I will tell my Father.
Observe how he begins to stare already.
I'le meet the danger first, and then call you.
  Dor. Nay, Sister, you shall never vanquish me in kindness.
I'le venture you, no more than you will me.
  Prosp. within. Miranda, Child, where are you?
  Mir. Do you not hear my Father call? go in.
  Dor. 'Twas you he nam'd, not me; I will but say my Prayers,
And follow you immediately.
  Mir. Well, Sister, you'l repent it.   [*Exit* Miranda.
  Dor. Though I dye for't, I must have th'other peep.
  Hip. seeing her. What thing is that? sure 'tis some Infant of
The Sun, dress'd in his Fathers gayest Beams,
And comes to play with Birds: my sight is dazl'd,
And yet I find I'm loth to shut my Eyes.
I must go nearer it—but stay a while;
May it not be that beauteous murderer, Woman,
Which I was charg'd to shun? Speak, what art thou?
Thou shining Vision!
  Dor. Alas I know not; but I'm told I am a Woman;
Do not hurt me, pray, fair thing.
  Hip. I'd sooner tear my eyes out, than consent
To do you any harm; though I was told
A Woman was my Enemy.
  Dor. I never knew what 'twas to be an Enemy,
Nor can I e're prove so to that which looks
Like you: for though I have been charg'd by him

(Whom yet I never disobey'd) to shun
Your presence, yet I'd rather dye than lose it;
Therefore I hope you will not have the heart
To hurt me: though I fear you are a man,
That dangerous thing of which I have been warn'd;
Pray tell me what you are?

    Hip. I must confess, I was inform'd I am a man,
But if I fright you, I shall wish I were some other Creature.
I was bid to fear you too.

    Dor. Ay me! Heav'n grant we be not poyson to each other!
Alas, can we not meet but we must die?

    Hip. I hope not so! for when two poysonous Creatures,
Both of the same kind, meet, yet neither dies.
I've seen two Serpents harmless to each other,
Though they have twin'd into a mutual Knot:
If we have any venome in us, sure, we cannot be more
Poysonous, when we meet, than Serpents are.
You have a hand like mine, may I not gently touch it?

                                          [Takes her hand.

    Dor. I've touch'd my Father's and my Sister's hands
And felt no pain; but now, alas! there's something,
When I touch yours, which makes me sigh: just so
I've seen two Turtles mourning when they met;
Yet mine's a pleasing grief; and so methought was theirs;
For still they mourn'd, and still they seem'd to murmur too,
And yet they often met.

    Hip. Oh Heavens! I have the same sense too: your hand
Methinks goes through me; I feel at my heart,
And find it pleases, though it pains me.

    Prosp. within. Dorinda!

    Dor. My Father calls agen, ah, I must leave you.

    Hip. Alas, I'm subject to the same command.

    Dor. This is my first offence against my Father,
Which he, by severing us, too cruelly does punish.

    Hip. And this is my first trespass too: but he hath more
Offended truth than we have him:
He said our meeting would destructive be,
But I no death but in our parting see.

                                         [Exeunt several ways.

[Act III, Scene i.]

Enter Prospero *and* Miranda.

Prosp. Excuse it not, *Miranda*, for to you
(The elder, and, I thought the more discreet)
I gave the conduct of your Sister's actions.

Mir. Sir, when you call'd me thence, I did not fail
To mind her of her duty to depart.

Prosp. How can I think you did remember hers,
When you forgot your own? Did you not see
The man whom I commanded you to shun?

Mir. I must confess I saw him at a distance.

Prosp. Did not his Eyes infect and poyson you?
What alteration found you in your self?

Mir. I only wondred at a sight so new.

Prosp. But have you no desire once more to see him.
Come, tell me truly what you think of him.

Mir. As of the gayest thing I ever saw,
So fine that it appear'd more fit to be
Belov'd than fear'd, and seem'd so near my kind,
That I did think I might have call'd it Sister.

Prosp. You do not love it?

Mir. How is it likely that I should,
Except the thing had first lov'd me?

Prosp. Cherish those thoughts: you have a gen'rous soul;
And since I see your mind not apt to take
The light impressions of a sudden love,
I will unfold a secret to your knowledge.
That Creature which you saw, is of a kind
Which nature made a prop and guide to yours.

Mir. Why did you then propose him as an object
Of terrour to my mind? you never us'd
To teach me any thing but God-like truths,
And what you said I did believe as sacred.

Prosp. I fear'd the pleasing form of this young man
Might unawares possess your tender breast,
Which for a nobler Guest I had design'd;
For shortly my *Miranda*, you shall see
Another of his kind, the full blown-flower,
Of which this youth was but the op'ning-bud.

Go in, and send your sister to me.
  Mir. Heav'n still preserve you, Sir.   [*Ex.* Miranda.
  Prosp. And make thee fortunate.
Dorinda now must be examin'd too
Concerning this late interview. I'm sure
Unartful truth lies open in her mind,
As Crystal streams their sandy bottom show.
I must take care her love grow not too fast,
For innocence is Love's most fertile soil,
Wherein he soon shoots up and widely spreads.
Nor is that danger which attends *Hippolito* yet overpast.

Enter Dorinda.

  Prosp. O, come hither! You have seen a man to day,
Against my strict command.
  Dor.   Who I?
Indeed I saw him but a little, Sir.
  Prosp. Come, come, be clear. Your Sister told me all.
  Dor. Did she? truly she would have seen him more
Than I, but that I would not let her.
  Prosp.   Why so?
  Dor. Because, methought, he would have hurt me less
Than he would her. But if I knew you'd not
Be angry with him, I could tell you, Sir,
That he was much to blame.
  Prosp.   Hah! was he to blame?
Tell me, with that sincerity I taught you,
How you became so bold to see the man?
  Dor. I hope you will forgive me, Sir, because
I did not see him much till he saw me.
Sir, he would needs come in my way, and star'd,
And star'd upon my face; and so I thought
I would be reveng'd of him, and therefore I gaz'd
On him as long; but if I e're come neer
A man again——
  Prosp.   I told you he was dangerous;
But you would not be warn'd.
  Dor.   Pray be not angry, Sir,
If I tell you, you are mistaken in him;
For he did me no great hurt.

Prosp. But he may do you more harm hereafter.

Dor. No, Sir, I'm as well as e're I was in all my life,
But that I cannot eat nor drink for thought of him.
That dangerous man runs ever in my mind.

Prosp. The way to cure you, is no more to see him.

Dor. Nay pray, Sir, say not so, I promis'd him
To see him once agen; and you know, Sir,
You charg'd me I should never break my promise.

Prosp. Wou'd you see him who did you so much mischief?

Dor. I warrant you I did him as much harm
As he did me, for when I left him, Sir,
He sigh'd so as it griev'd my heart to hear him.

Prosp. Those sighs were poysonous, they infected you:
You say they griev'd you to the heart.

Dor. 'Tis true; but yet his looks and words were gentle.

Prosp. These are the Day-dreams of a maid in love,
But still I fear the worst.

Dor. O fear not him, Sir,
I know he will not hurt you for my sake;
I'le undertake to tye him to a hair,
And lead him hither as my Pris'ner to you.

Prosp. Take heed, *Dorinda*, you may be deceiv'd;
This Creature is of such a Salvage race,
That no mild usage can reclaim his wildness;
But, like a Lyon's whelp bred up by hand,
When least you look for't, Nature will present
The Image of his Fathers bloody Paws,
Wherewith he purvey'd for his couching Queen;
And he will leap into his native fury.

Dor. He cannot change from what I left him, Sir.

Prosp. You speak of him with too much passion; tell me
(And on your duty tell me true, *Dorinda*)
What past betwixt you and that horrid creature?

Dor. How, horrid, Sir? if any else but you
Should call it so, indeed I should be angry.

Prosp. Go to! you are a foolish Girl; but answer
To what I ask; what thought you when you saw it?

Dor. At first it star'd upon me and seem'd wild,
And then I trembled, yet it look'd so lovely,
That when I would have fled away, my feet

Seem'd fasten'd to the ground. Then it drew near,
And with amazement askt to touch my hand;
Which, as a ransom for my life, I gave:
But when he had it, with a furious gripe
He put it to his mouth so eagerly,
I was afraid he would have swallow'd it.
   Prosp. Well, what was his behaviour afterwards?
   Dor. He on a sudden grew so tame and gentle,
That he became more kind to me than you are;
Then, Sir, I grew I know not how, and touching
His hand agen, my heart did beat so strong
As I lackt breath to answer what he ask'd.
   Prosp. You have been too fond, and I should chide you for it.
   Dor. Then send me to that creature to be punisht.
   Prosp. Poor Child! thy passion like a lazy Ague
Has seiz'd thy blood; instead of striving thou humour'st
And feed'st thy languishing disease. Thou fight'st
The Battels of thy Enemy, and 'tis one part of what
I threaten'd thee, not to perceive thy danger.
   Dor. Danger, Sir?
If he would hurt me, yet he knows not how:
He hath no Claws, nor Teeth, nor Horns to hurt me,
But looks about him like a Callow-bird
Just straggl'd from the Nest: pray trust me, Sir,
To go to him agen.
   Prosp. Since you will venture,
I charge you bear yourself reserv'dly to him,
Let him not dare to touch your naked hand,
But keep at distance from him.
   Dor. This is hard.
   Prosp. It is the way to make him love you more;
He will despise you if you grow too kind.
   Dor. I'le struggle with my heart to follow this,
But if I lose him by it, will you promise
To bring him back agen?
   Prosp. Fear not, *Dorinda*;
But use him ill and he'l be yours for ever.
   Dor. I hope you have not couzen'd me agen.   [*Exit* Dorinda.
   Prosp. Now my designs are gathering to a head.
My spirits are obedient to my charms.

What, *Ariel*! my servant *Ariel*, where art thou?

Enter Ariel.

   Ariel. What wou'd my potent Master? here I am.
   Prosp. Thou and thy meaner fellows your last service
Did worthily perform, and I must use you
In such another work: how goes the day?
   Ariel. On the fourth, my Lord, and on the sixth you said
Our work should cease.
   Prosp.   And so it shall;
And thou shalt have the open air at freedom.
   Ariel. Thanks my great Lord.
   Prosp. But tell me first, my spirit,
How fares the Duke, my Brother, and their followers?
   Ariel. Confin'd together, as you gave me order,
In the Lime-Grove which weather-fends your Cell;
Within that Circuit up and down they wander,
But cannot stir one step beyond their compass.
   Prosp. How do they bear their sorrows?
   Ariel. The two Dukes appear like men distracted, their
Attendants brim-full of sorrow mourning over 'em;
But chiefly, he you term'd the good *Gonzalo*:
His tears run down his Beard, like Winter-drops
From Eaves of Reeds. Your Vision did so work 'em,
That if you now beheld 'em, your affections
Would become tender.
   Prosp. Dost thou think so, Spirit?
   Ariel. Mine would, Sir, were I humane.
   Prosp. And mine shall:
Hast thou, who art but air, a touch, a feeling of their
Afflictions, and shall not I (a man like them, one
Who as sharply relish passions as they) be kindlier
Mov'd than thou art? though they have pierc'd
Me to the quick with injuries, yet with my nobler
Reason 'gainst my fury I will take part;
The rarer action is in virtue than in vengeance.
Go, my *Ariel*, refresh with needful food their
Famish'd bodies. With shows and cheerful
Musick comfort 'em.

Ariel. Presently, Master.

Prosp. With a twinckle, *Ariel.*

Ariel. Before you can say come and go,
And breath twice, and cry so; so,
Each spirit tripping on his toe,
Shall bring 'em meat with mop and moe,
Do you love me, Master, aye, or no?

Prosp. Dearly, my dainty *Ariel,* but stay, spirit;
What is become of my Slave *Caliban,*
And *Sycorax* his Sister?

Ariel. Potent Sir!
They have cast off your service, and revolted
To the wrack'd Mariners, who have already
Parcell'd your Island into Governments.

Prosp. No matter, I have now no need of 'em;
But, spirit, now I stay thee on the Wing;
Haste to perform what I have given in charge:
But see they keep within the bounds I set 'em.

Ariel. I'le keep 'em in with Walls of Adamant,
Invisible as air to mortal Eyes,
But yet unpassable.

Prosp. Make hast then.   [*Exeunt severally.*

*   *   *

[Act III, Scene iv.]

Enter Ferdinand, *and* Ariel (*invisible*).

Ferd. How far will this invisible Musician conduct
My steps? he hovers still about me, whether
For good or ill I cannot tell, nor care I much;
For I have been so long a slave to chance, that
I'm as weary of her flatteries as her frowns.
But here I am——

Ariel.   Here I am.

Ferd. Hah! art thou so? the Spirit's turn'd an Eccho:
This might seem pleasant, could the burthen of my
Griefs accord with any thing but sighs,

And my last words, like those of dying men,
Need no reply. Fain I would go to shades, where
Few would wish to follow me.
    Ariel.   Follow me.
    Ferd. This evil Spirit grows importunate,
But I'le not take his counsel.
    Ariel.   Take his counsel.
    Ferd. It may be the Devil's counsel. I'le never take it.
    Ariel.   Take it.
    Ferd. I will discourse no more with thee,
Nor follow one step further.
    Ariel.   One step further.
    Ferd. This must have more importance than an Eccho.
Some Spirit tempts to a precipice.
I'le try if it will answer when I sing
My sorrows to the murmurs of this Brook.
        He Sings.
                 Go thy way.
    Ariel.   Go thy way.
    Ferd.   Why should'st thou stay?
    Ariel.   Why should'st thou stay?
    Ferd. Where the Winds whistle, and where the streams creep,
         Under yond Willow-tree, fain would I sleep.
                 Then let me alone,
                   For 'tis time to be gone.
    Ariel.   For 'tis time to be gone.
    Ferd. What cares or pleasures can be in this Isle?
             Within this desart place
             There lives no humane race;
         Fate cannot frown here, nor kind fortune smile.
    Ariel. Kind Fortune smiles, and she
         Has yet in store for thee
         Some strange felicity.
         Follow me, follow me,
         And thou shalt see.

    Ferd. I'le take thy word for once;
Lead on Musician.   [*Exeunt and return.*

[Act III, Scene v.]

Scene changes, and discovers Prospero *and* Miranda.

  Prosp. Advance the fringed Curtains of thine Eyes,
And say what thou seest yonder.
  Mir.   Is it a Spirit?
Lord! how it looks about! Sir, I confess
It carries a brave form. But 'tis a Spirit.
  Prosp. No Girl, it eats and sleeps, and has such senses
As we have. This young Gallant, whom thou see'st,
Was in the wrack; were he not somewhat stain'd
With grief (beauty's worst Cancker) thou might'st call him
A goodly person; he has lost his company,
And strays about to find 'em.
  Mir.   I might call him
A thing divine, for nothing natural
I ever saw so noble.
  Prosp.   It goes on   [*Aside.*
As my Soul prompts it: Spirit, fine Spirit,
I'le free thee within two days for this.
  Ferd.   She's sure the Mistress,
On whom these airs attend. Fair Excellence,
If, as your form declares, you are divine,
Be pleas'd to instruct me how you will
Be worship'd; so bright a beauty cannot sure
Belong to humane kind.
  Mir.   I am, like you,
A mortal, if such you are.
  Ferd.   My language too!
O Heavens! I am the best of them who speak
This speech, when I'm in my own Country.
  Prosp.   How, the best?
What wert thou if the Duke of *Savoy* heard thee?
  Ferd. As I am now, who wonders to hear thee speak
Of *Savoy*: he does hear me, and that he does I weep.
My self am *Savoy*, whose fatal Eyes (e're since
At ebbe) beheld the Duke my Father wrackt.
  Mir. Alack! for pity.
  Prosp. At the first sight they have chang'd Eyes; dear *Ariel*, [*Aside.*
I'le set thee free for this.—Young Sir, a word.

With hazard of yourself you do me wrong.

    Mir. Why speaks my Father so ungently?
This is the third man that e're I saw, the first whom
E're I sigh'd for. Sweet Heaven move my Father
To be inclin'd my way.

    Ferd. O! if a Virgin! and your affection not gone forth,
I'le make you Mistress of *Savoy*.

    Prosp. Soft, Sir! one word more.
They are in each others powers, but this swift   [*Aside.*
Bus'ness I must uneasie make, lest too light
Winning make the prize light.—One word more:
Thou usurp'st the name not due to thee, and hast
Put thy self upon this Island as a spy to get the
Government from me, the Lord of it.

    Ferd. No, as I'm a man.

    Mir. There's nothing ill can dwell in such a Temple:
If th' Evil Spirit hath so fair a house,
Good things will strive to dwell with it.

    Prosp. No more. Speak not you for him, he's a Traytor.
Come! thou art my Pris'ner and shalt be in bonds.
Sea-water shalt thou drink, thy food shall be
The fresh-Brook-Mussels, wither'd Roots, and Husks,
Wherein the Acorn cradl'd; follow.

    Ferd. No, I will resist such entertainment
Till my Enemy has more power.

                [*He draws, and is charm'd from moving.*

    Mir. O dear Father! make not too rash a tryal
Of him, for he's gentle and not fearful.

    Prosp. My child my Tutor! put thy Sword up, Traytor,
Who mak'st a show, but dar'st not strike: thy
Conscience is possest with guilt. Come from
Thy Ward, for I can here disarm thee with
This Wand, and make thy Weapon drop.

    Mir. 'Beseech you, Father.

    Prosp. Hence: hang not on my Garment.

    Mir. Sir, have pity, I'le be his Surety.

    Prosp. Silence! one word more shall make me chide thee,
If not hate thee: what, an advocate for an impostor?
Sure thou think'st there are no more such shapes as his?
To the most of men this is a *Caliban*,

And they to him are Angels.

Mir. My affections are then most humble,
I have no ambition to see a goodlier man.

Prosp. Come on, obey:
Thy Nerves are in their infancy agen,
And have no vigour in them.

Ferd.   So they are:
My Spirits, as in a Dream, are all bound up:
My Father's loss, the weakness which I feel,
The wrack of all my friends, and this man's threats,
To whom I am subdu'd, would seem light to me,
Might I but once a day through my Prison
Behold this maid: all corners else 'o'th' Earth
Let liberty make use of: I have space
Enough in such a prison.

Prosp.   It works: come on: [*Aside.*
Thou hast done well, fine *Ariel*: follow me.   [*Whispers* Ariel.
Heark what thou shalt more do for me.

Mir. Be of comfort!
My Father's of a better nature, Sir,
Than he appears by speech: this is unwonted
Which now came from him.

Prosp. Thou shalt be as free as Mountain Winds:
But then exactly do all points of my command.

Ariel. To a Syllable.   [*Exit* Ariel.

Prosp. to Mir. Go in that way, speak not a word for him:
I'le separate you.   [*Exit* Miranda.

Ferd. As soon thou may'st divide the waters
When thou strik'st 'em, which pursue thy bootless blow,
And meet when 'tis past.

Prosp. Go practise your Philosophy within,
And if you are the same you speak yourself,
Bear your afflictions like a Prince.—That Door
Shews you your Lodging.

Ferd. 'Tis in vain to strive, I must obey.   [*Exit.* Ferd.

Prosp. This goes as I would wish it.
Now for my second care, *Hippolito*:
I shall not need to chide him for his fault,
His passion is become his punishment.
Come forth, *Hippolito*.   [*Enter* Hippolito.

Hip. entring. 'Tis *Prospero's* voice.

Prosp. Hippolito! I know you now expect
I should severely chide you: you have seen a woman,
In contempt of my commands.

Hip. But, Sir, you see I am come off unharm'd;
I told you, that you need not doubt my courage.

Prosp. You think you have receiv'd no hurt.

Hip. No, none Sir.
Try me agen, when e're you please I'm ready:
I think I cannot fear an Army of 'em.

Prosp. How much in vain it is to bridle Nature!   [*Aside.*
Well! what was the success of your encounter?

Hip. Sir, we had none, we yielded both at first,
For I took her to mercy, and she me.

Prosp. But are you not much chang'd from what you were?

Hip. Methinks I wish and wish! for what I know not,
But still I wish—yet if I had that woman,
She, I believe, could tell me what I wish for.

Prosp. What wou'd you do to make that Woman yours?

Hip. I'd quit the rest o'th' world that I might live
Alone with her; she never should be from me.
We two would sit and look till our eyes ak'd.

Prosp. You'd soon be weary of her.

Hip. O, Sir, never.

Prosp. But you'l grow old and wrinckl'd, as you see me now,
And then you will not care for her.

Hip. You may do what you please, but, Sir,
We two can never possibly grow old.

Prosp. You must, *Hippolito.*

Hip. Whether we will or no, Sir, who shall make us?

Prosp. Nature, which made me so.

Hip. But you have told me her works are various;
She made you old, but she has made us young.

Prosp. Time will convince you.
Mean while be sure you tread in honour's paths
That you may merit her; and that you may not want
Fit occasions to employ your virtue, in this next
Cave there is a stranger lodg'd, one of your kind,
Young, of a noble presence, and as he says himself,
Of Princely birth. He is my Pris'ner and in deep

Affliction: visit, and comfort him; it will become you.

   Hip. It is my duty, Sir.   [*Exit* Hippolito.

   Prosp. True, he has seen a woman, yet he lives;
Perhaps I took the moment of his birth amiss;
Perhaps my Art itself is false.
On what strange grounds we build our hopes and fears.
Mans life is all a mist, and in the dark
Our fortunes meet us.
If Fate be not, then what can we foresee,
Or how can we avoid it, if it be?
If by free-will in our own paths we move,
How are we bounded by Decrees above?
Whether we drive, or whether we are driven,
If ill 'tis ours, if good the act of Heaven.   [*Exit* Prospero.

[Act III, Scene vi.] *Scene, a Cave*

Enter Hippolito *and* Ferdinand.

   Ferd. Your pity, noble youth, doth much oblige me,
Indeed 'twas sad to lose a Father so.

   Hip. Aye, and an only Father too, for sure you said
You had but one.

   Ferd. But one Father! he's wondrous simple!   [*Aside.*

   Hip. Are such misfortunes frequent in your world,
Where many men live?

   Ferd.   Such we are born to.
But gentle youth, as you have question'd me,
So give me leave to ask you, what you are?

   Hip. Do not you know?

   Ferd.   How should I?

   Hip. I well hop'd I was a man, but by your ignorance
Of what I am, I fear it is not so:
Well, *Prospero!* this is now the second time   [*Aside.*
You have deceiv'd me.

   Ferd. Sir, there is no doubt you are a man:
But I would know of whence?

   Hip. Why, of this world, I never was in yours.

   Ferd. Have you a Father?

   Hip.   I was told I had one,
And that he was a man, yet I have bin
So much deceived, I dare not tell't you for

A truth; but I have still been kept a Prisoner
For fear of women.

 Ferd. They indeed are dangerous, for since I came
I have beheld one here, whose beauty pierc'd my heart.

 Hip. How did she pierce? you seem not hurt.

 Ferd. Alas! the wound was made by her bright eyes,
And festers by her absence.
But to speak plainer to you, Sir, I love her.

 Hip. Now I suspect that love's the very thing,
That I feel too! pray tell me truly, Sir,
Are you not grown unquiet since you saw her?

 Ferd. I take no rest.

 Hip.   Just, just my disease.
Do you not wish you do not know for what?

 Ferd. O no! I know too well for what I wish.

 Hip. There, I confess, I differ from you, Sir:
But you desire she may be always with you?

 Ferd. I can have no felicity without her.

 Hip. Just my condition! alas, gentle Sir,
I'le pity you, and you shall pity me.

 Ferd. I love so much, that if I have her not,
I find I cannot live.

 Hip.   How! do you love her?
And would you have her too? that must not be:
For none but I must have her.

 Ferd. But perhaps, we do not love the same:
All beauties are not pleasing alike to all.

 Hip. Why are there more fair Women, Sir,
Besides that one I love?

 Ferd. That's a strange question. There are many more
Besides that beauty which you love.

 Hip. I will have all of that kind, if there be a hundred of 'em.

 Ferd. But noble youth, you know not what you say.

 Hip. Sir, they are things I love, I cannot be
Without 'em: O, how I rejoyce! more women!

 Ferd. Sir, if you love you must be ty'd to one.

 Hip. Ty'd! how ty'd to her?

 Ferd. To love none but her.

 Hip. But, Sir, I find it is against my Nature.
I must love where I like, and I believe I may like all,

All that are fair: come! bring me to this Woman,
For I must have her.
    Ferd.   His simplicity   *[Aside.*
Is such that I can scarce be angry with him.
Perhaps, sweet youth, when you behold her,
You will find you do not love her.
    Hip. I find already I love, because she is another Woman.
    Ferd. You cannot love two women, both at once.
    Hip. Sure 'tis my duty to love all who do resemble
Her whom I've already seen. I'le have as many as I can,
That are so good, and Angel-like, as she I love.
And will have yours.
    Ferd.   Pretty youth, you cannot.
    Hip. I can do any thing for that I love.
    Ferd. I may, perhaps, by force restrain you from it.
    Hip. Why, do so if you can. But either promise me
To love no Woman, or you must try your force.
    Ferd. I cannot help it, I must love.
    Hip. Well, you may love, for *Prospero* taught me
Friendship too: you shall love me and other men
If you can find 'em, but all the Angel-women
Shall be mine.
    Ferd. I must break off this conference, or he will   *[Aside.*
Urge me else beyond what I can bear.
Sweet youth! some other time we will speak
Further concerning both our loves; at present
I am indispos'd with weariness and grief,
And would, if you are pleas'd, retire a while.
    Hip. Some other time be it; but, Sir, remember
That I both seek and much intreat your friendship,
For next to Women, I find I can love you.
    Ferd. I thank you, Sir, I will consider of it.   *[Exit* Ferdinand.
    Hip. This Stranger does insult and comes into my
World to take those heavenly beauties from me,
Which I believe I am inspir'd to love,
And yet he said he did desire but one.
He would be poor in love, but I'le be rich:
I now perceive that *Prospero* was cunning;
For when he frighted me from woman-kind,
Those precious things he for himself design'd.   *[Exit.*

[Act IV, Scene i.]

Enter Prospero, *and* Miranda.

Prosp. Your suit has pity in't, and has prevail'd.
Within this Cave he lies, and you may see him:
But yet take heed; let Prudence be your Guide;
You must not stay, your visit must be short.   [*She's going.*
One thing I had forgot; insinuate into his mind
A kindness to that youth, whom first you saw;
I would have friendship grow betwixt 'em.
   Mir. You shall be obey'd in all things.
   Prosp. Be earnest to unite their very souls.
   Mir. I shall endeavour it.
   Prosp. This may secure *Hippolito* from that
Dark danger which my art forebodes;
For friendship does provide a double strength
T'oppose th'assaults of fortune.   [*Exit* Prospero.

Enter Ferdinand.

   Ferd. To be a Pris'ner where I dearly love,
Is but a double tye; a Link of fortune
Joyn'd to the chain of love; but not to see her,
And yet to be so near her, there's the hardship.
I feel myself as on a Rack, stretch'd out,
And nigh the ground, on which I might have ease,
Yet cannot reach it.
   Mir.   Sir! my Lord? where are you?
   Ferd. Is it your voice, my Love? or do I dream?
   Mir. Speak softly, it is I.
   Ferd.   O heavenly Creature!
Ten times more gentle, than your Father's cruel,
How on a sudden all my griefs are vanish'd!
   Mir. I come to help you to support your griefs.
   Ferd. While I stand gazing thus, and thus have leave
To touch your hand, I do not envy freedom.
   Mir. Heark! heark! is't not my Father's voice I hear?
I fear he calls me back again too soon.
   Ferd. Leave fear to guilty minds: 'tis scarce a virtue
When it is paid to Heaven.

Mir. But there 'tis mix'd with love, and so is mine;
Yet I may fear, for I am guilty when
I disobey my Fathers will in loving you too much.

Ferd. But you please Heav'n in disobeying him,
Heav'n bids you succour Captives in distress.

Mir. How do you bear your Prison?

Ferd. 'Tis my Palace while you are here, and love
And silence wait upon our wishes; do but think
We chuse it, and 'tis what we would chuse.

Mir. I'm sure what I would.
But how can I be certain that you love me?
Look to't; for I will dye when you are false.
I've heard my Father tell of Maids, who dy'd,
And haunted their false Lovers with their Ghosts.

Ferd. Your Ghost must take another form to fright me,
This shape will be too pleasing: do I love you?
O Heav'n! O Earth! bear witness to this sound,
If I prove false—

Mir. Oh hold, you shall not swear;
For Heav'n will hate you if you prove forsworn.

Ferd. Did I not love, I could no more endure
This undeserved captivity, than I
Could wish to gain my freedom with the loss of you.

Mir. I am a fool to weep at what I'm glad of:
But I have a suit to you, and that, Sir, shall
Be now the only tryal of your love.

Ferd. Y'ave said enough, never to be deny'd,
Were it my life; for you have far o'rebid
The price of all that humane life is worth.

Mir. Sir, 'tis to love one for my sake, who for
His own deserves all the respect which you
Can ever pay him.

Ferd. You mean your Father: do not think his usage
Can make me hate him; when he gave you being,
He then did that which cancell'd all these wrongs.

Mir. I meant not him, for that was a request
Which if you love I should not need to urge.

Ferd. Is there another whom I ought to love?
And love him for your sake?

Mir. Yes, such a one, who for his sweetness and

His goodly shape, (if I, who am unskill'd
In forms, may judge) I think can scarce be equall'd:
'Tis a youth, a Stranger too as you are.

Ferd. Of such a graceful feature, and must I
For your sake love?

Mir. Yes, Sir, do you scruple to grant the first
Request I ever made? he's wholly unacquainted
With the world, and wants your conversation.
You should have compassion on so meer a stranger.

Ferd. Those need compassion whom you discommend,
Not whom you praise.

Mir. I only ask this easie tryal of you.

Ferd. Perhaps it might have easier bin
If you had never ask'd it.

Mir. I cannot understand you; and methinks am loth
To be more knowing.

Ferd. He has his freedom, and may get access, when my
Confinement makes me want that blessing.
I his compassion need, and not he mine.

Mir. If that be all you doubt, trust me for him.
He has a melting heart, and soft to all the Seals
Of kindness; I will undertake for his compassion.

Ferd. O Heavens! would I were sure I did not need it.

Mir. Come, you must love him for my sake: you shall.

Ferd. Must I for yours, and cannot for my own?
Either you do not love, or think that I do not:
But when you bid me love him, I must hate him.

Mir. Have I so far offended you already,
That he offends you only for my sake?
Yet sure you would not hate him, if you saw
Him as I have done, so full of youth and beauty.

Ferd. O poyson to my hopes!
When he did visit me, and I did mention this   [*Aside.*
Beauteous Creature to him, he did then tell me
He would have her.

Mir. Alas, what mean you?

Ferd. It is too plain: like most of her frail Sex,   [*Aside.*
She's false, but has not learnt the art to hide it;
Nature has done her part, she loves variety:
Why did I think that any Woman could

112

Be innocent, because she's young?
No, no, their Nurses teach them change,
When with two Nipples they divide their liking.

   Mir. I fear I have offended you, and yet
I meant no harm: but if you please to hear me—   [*A noise within.*
Heark! Sir! now I am sure my Father comes, I know
His steps; dear Love retire a while, I fear
I've stay'd too long.

   Ferd. Too long indeed, and yet not long enough: oh jealousie!
Oh Love! how you distract me!   [*Exit* Ferdinand.

   Mir. He appears displeas'd with that young man, I know
Not why: but, till I find from whence his hate proceeds,
I must conceal it from my Fathers knowledge,
For he will think that guiltless I have caus'd it;
And suffer me no more to see my Love.

Enter Prospero.

   Prosp. Now I have been indulgent to your wish,
You have seen the Prisoner?

   Mir. Yes.

   Prosp. And he spake to you?

   Mir. He spoke; but he receiv'd short answers from me.

   Prosp. How like you his converse?

   Mir. At second sight
A man does not appear so rare a Creature.

   Prosp. aside. I find she loves him much because she hides it.
Love teaches cunning even to innocence,
And where he gets possession, his first work is to
Dig deep within a heart, and there lie hid,
And like a Miser in the dark to feast alone.
But tell me, dear *Miranda,* how does he suffer
His imprisonment?

   Mir. I think he seems displeas'd.

   Prosp. O then 'tis plain his temper is not noble,
For the brave with equal minds bear good
And evil fortune.

   Mir. O, Sir, but he's pleas'd again so soon
That 'tis not worth your noting.

   Prosp. To be soon displeas'd and pleas'd so suddenly again,
Does shew him of a various froward Nature.

Mir. The truth is, Sir, he was not vex'd at all, but only
Seem'd to be so.

Prosp. If he be not and yet seems angry, he is a dissembler,
Which shews the worst of Natures.

Mir. Truly, Sir, the man has faults enough; but in
My conscience that's none of 'em. He can be no
Dissembler.

Prosp. aside.   How she excuses him, and yet desires
That I should judge her heart indifferent to him!
Well, since his faults are many, I am glad you love him not.

Mir. 'Tis like, Sir, they are many,
But I know none he has, yet let me often see him
And I shall find 'em all in time.

Prosp. I'le think on't.
Go in, this is your hour of Orizons.

Mir. aside. Forgive me, truth, for thus disguising thee;
If I can make him think I do not love
The stranger much, he'll let me see him oftner.   [*Exit* Miranda.

Prosp. Stay! stay—I had forgot to ask her what she has said
Of young *Hippolito*: Oh! here he comes! and with him
My *Dorinda*. I'le not be seen, let
Their loves grow in secret.   [*Exit* Prospero.

Enter Hippolito *and* Dorinda.

Hip. But why are you so sad?

Dor. But why are you so joyful?

Hip. I have within me all, all the various Musick of
The Woods. Since last I saw you I have heard brave news!
I'le tell you, and make you joyful for me.

Dor. Sir, when I saw you first, I through my eyes drew
Something in, I know not what it is;
But still it entertains me with such thoughts
As makes me doubtful whether joy becomes me.

Hip. Pray believe me;
As I'm a man, I'le tell you blessed news.
I have heard there are more Women in the World,
As fair as you are too.

Dor. Is this your news? you see it moves not me.

Hip. And I'le have 'em all.

Dor. What will become of me then?

Hip. I'le have you too.
But are not you acquainted with these Women?
   Dor. I never saw but one.
   Hip. Is there but one here?
This is a base poor world, I'le go to th' other;
I've heard men have abundance of 'em there.
But pray where is that one Woman?
   Dor. Who, my Sister?
   Hip. Is she your Sister? I'm glad o'that: you shall
Help me to her, and I'le love you for't.   [*Offers to take her hand.*
   Dor. Away! I will not have you touch my hand.
My Father's counsel which enjoyn'd reservedness,   [*Aside.*
Was not in vain I see.
   Hip. What makes you shun me?
   Dor. You need not care, you'l have my Sisters hand.
   Hip. Why must not he who touches hers touch yours?
   Dor. You mean to love her too.
   Hip. Do not you love her?
Then why should not I do so?
   Dor. She is my Sister, and therefore I must love her:
But you cannot love both of us.
   Hip. I warrant you I can:
Oh that you had more Sisters!
   Dor. You may love her, but then I'le not love you.
   Hip. O but you must;
One is enough for you, but not for me.
   Dor. My Sister told me she had seen another;
A man like you, and she lik'd only him;
Therefore if one must be enough for her,
He is that one, and then you cannot have her.
   Hip. If she like him, she may like both of us.
   Dor. But how if I should change and like that man?
Would you be willing to permit that change?
   Hip. No, for you lik'd me first.
   Dor. So you did me.
   Hip. But I would never have you see that man;
I cannot bear it.
   Dor. I'le see neither of you.
   Hip. Yes, me you may, for we are now acquainted;
But he's the man of whom your Father warn'd you:

O! he's a terrible, huge, monstrous creature,
I am but a Woman to him.

Dor. I will see him,
Except you'l promise not to see my Sister.

Hip. Yes, for your sake I needs must see your Sister.

Dor. But she's a terrible, huge Creature too; if I were not
Her Sister she would eat me; therefore take heed.

Hip. I heard that she was fair, and like you.

Dor. No, indeed, she's like my Father, with a great Beard,
'Twould fright you to look on her,
Therefore that man and she may go together,
They are fit for no body but one another.

Hip. looking in. Yonder he comes with glaring eyes, fly! fly!
Before he sees you.

Dor.   Must we part so soon?

Hip. Y'are a lost Woman if you see him.

Dor. I would not willingly be lost, for fear you
Should not find me. I'le avoid him.   [*Exit* Dorinda.

Hip. She fain would have deceived me, but I know her
Sister must be fair, for she's a Woman;
All of a Kind that I have seen are like to one
Another: all the Creatures of the Rivers and
The Woods are so.

Enter Ferdinand.

Ferd. O! well encounter'd, you are the happy man!
Y' have got the hearts of both the beauteous Women.

Hip. How! Sir? pray, are you sure on't?

Ferd. One of 'em charg'd me to love you for her sake.

Hip. Then I must have her.

Ferd. No, not till I am dead.

Hip. How dead? what's that? but whatsoe're it be
I long to have her.

Ferd. Time and my grief may make me dye.

Hip. But for a friend you should make haste; I ne're ask'd
Any thing of you before.

Ferd. I see your ignorance;
And therefore will instruct you in my meaning.
The Woman, whom I love, saw you and lov'd you.
Now, Sir, if you love her you'l cause my death.

Hip. Be sure I'le do't then.

Ferd. But I am your friend;
And I request you that you would not love her.

Hip. When friends request unreasonable things,
Sure th'are to be deny'd: you say she's fair,
And I must love all who are fair; for, to tell
You a secret, Sir, which I have lately found
Within myself, they all are made for me.

Ferd. That's but a fond conceit: you are made for one,
And one for you.

Hip. You cannot tell me, Sir,
I know I'm made for twenty hundred Women.
(I mean if there so many be i'th' World)
So that if once I see her I shall love her.

Ferd. Then do not see her.

Hip. Yes, Sir, I must see her.
For I wou'd fain have my heart beat again,
Just as it did when I first saw her Sister.

Ferd. I find I must not let you see her then.

Hip. How will you hinder me?

Ferd. By force of Arms.

Hip. By force of Arms?
My Arms perhaps may be as strong as yours.

Ferd. He's still so ignorant that I pity him, and fain   [*Aside.*
Would avoid force. — Pray, do not see her, she was
Mine first; you have no right to her.

Hip. I have not yet consider'd what is right, but, Sir,
I know my inclinations are to love all Women:
And I have been taught that to dissemble what I
Think is base. In honour then of truth, I must
Declare that I do love, and I will see your Woman.

Ferd. Wou'd you be willing I should see and love your
Woman, and endeavour to seduce her from that
Affection which she vow'd to you?

Hip. I wou'd not you should do it, but if she should
Love you best, I cannot hinder her.
But, Sir, for fear she shou'd, I will provide against
The worst, and try to get your Woman.

Ferd. But I pretend no claim at all to yours;
Besides you are more beautiful than I,

117

And fitter to allure unpractis'd hearts.
Therefore I once more beg you will not see her.

   Hip. I'm glad you let me know I have such beauty.
If that will get me Women, they shall have it
As far as e're 'twill go: I'le never want 'em.

   Ferd. Then since you have refused this act of friendship,
Provide your self a Sword; for we must fight.

   Hip. A Sword, what's that?

   Ferd. Why such a thing as this.

   Hip. What should I do with it?

   Ferd. You must stand thus, and push against me,
While I push at you, till one of us fall dead.

   Hip. This is brave sport,
But we have no Swords growing in our World.

   Ferd. What shall we do then to decide our quarrel?

   Hip. We'll take the Sword by turns, and fight with it.

   Ferd. Strange ignorance! you must defend your life,
And so must I: but since you have no Sword
Take this; for in a corner of my Cave   [*Gives him his sword.*
I found a rusty one, perhaps 'twas his who keeps
Me Pris'ner here: that I will fit:
When next we meet prepare yourself to fight.

   Hip. Make haste then, this shall ne're be yours agen.
I mean to fight with all the men I meet, and
When they are dead, their Women shall be mine.

   Ferd. I see you are unskilful; I desire not to take
Your life, but if you please we'll fight on
These conditions: he who first draws bloud,
Or who can take the others Weapon from him,
Shall be acknowledg'd as the Conquerour,
And both the Women shall be his.

   Hip. Agreed,
And ev'ry day I'le fight for two more with you.

   Ferd. But win these first.

   Hip. I'le warrant you I'le push you.   [*Exeunt severally.*

       ★   ★   ★

[Act IV, Scene iii.]

Enter Ferdinand, Hippolito, (*with their swords drawn.*)

Ferd. Come, Sir, our Cave affords no choice of place,
But the ground's firm and even: are you ready?
  Hip. As ready as yourself, Sir.
  Ferd. You remember on what conditions we must fight?
Who first receives a Wound is to submit.
  Hip. Come, come, this loses time, now for the women, Sir.
                    [*They fight a little,* Ferdinand *hurts him.*
  Ferd. Sir, you are wounded.
  Hip. No.
  Ferd. Believe your blood.
  Hip. I feel no hurt, no matter for my blood.
  Ferd. Remember our Conditions.
  Hip. I'le not leave, till my Sword hits you too.
                    [Hip. *presses on,* Ferd. *retires and wards.*
  Ferd. I'm loth to kill you, you are unskilful, Sir.
  Hip. You beat aside my Sword, but let it come as near
As yours, and you shall see my skill.
  Ferd. You faint for loss of blood, I see you stagger,
Pray, Sir, retire.
  Hip. No! I will ne're go back—
Methinks the Cave turns round, I cannot find—
  Ferd. Your eyes begin to dazle.
  Hip. Why do you swim so, and dance about me?
Stand but still till I have made one thrust.
                    [Hippolito *thrusts and falls.*
  Ferd. O help, help, help!
Unhappy man! what have I done?
  Hip. I'm going to a cold sleep, but when I wake
I'le fight agen. Pray stay for me.   [*Swounds.*
  Ferd. He's gone! he's gone! O stay sweet lovely Youth!
Help, help!

Enter Prospero.

  Prosp. What dismal noise is that?
  Ferd. O see, Sir, see!
What mischief my unhappy hand has wrought.
  Prosp. Alas! how much in vain doth feeble Art endeavour

To resist the will of Heaven!   [*Rubs* Hippolito.
He's gone for ever; O thou cruel Son of an
Inhumane Father! all my designs are ruin'd
And unravell'd by this blow.
No pleasure now is left me but Revenge.
   Ferd. Sir, if you knew my innocence—
   Prosp. Peace, peace,
Can thy excuses give me back his life?
What, *Ariel*! sluggish spirit, where art thou?

Enter Ariel.

   Ariel. Here, at thy beck, my Lord.
   Prosp.   Aye, now thou com'st,
When Fate is past and not to be recall'd.
Look there, and glut the malice of thy Nature,
For as thou art thy self, thou canst not be
But glad to see young Virtue nipt i'th' Blossom.
   Ariel. My Lord, the Being high above can witness
I am not glad: we Airy Spirits are not of temper
So malicious as the Earthy,
But of a Nature more approaching good,
For which we meet in swarms, and often combat
Betwixt the Confines of the Air and Earth.
   Prosp. Why did'st thou not prevent, at least foretell
This fatal action then?
   Ariel. Pardon, great Sir,
I meant to do it, but I was forbidden
By the ill Genius of *Hippolito*,
Who came and threatn'd me if I disclos'd it,
To bind me in the bottom of the Sea,
Far from the lightsome Regions of the Air,
(My native fields) above a hundred years.
   Prosp. I'le chain thee in the North for thy neglect,
Within the burning Bowels of Mount *Hecla*,
I'le sindge thy airy wings with sulph'rous flames,
And choak thy tender nostrils with blew smoak,
At ev'ry Hick-up of the belching Mountain
Thou shalt be lifted up to taste fresh Air,
And then fall down agen.
   Ariel. Pardon, dread Lord.

Prosp. No more of pardon than just Heav'n intends thee
Shalt thou e're find from me: hence! flye with speed,
Unbind the Charms which hold this Murtherer's
Father, and bring him with my Brother streight
Before me.
    Ariel. Mercy, my potent Lord, and I'le outfly thy thought.
                                                    [*Exit* Ariel.

    Ferd. O Heavens! what words are those I heard
Yet cannot see who spoke 'em? Sure the Woman
Whom I lov'd was like this, some aiery Vision.
    Prosp. No, Murd'rer, she's, like thee, of mortal mould,
But much too pure to mix with thy black Crimes;
Yet she had faults and must be punish'd for 'em.
Miranda and *Dorinda*! where are ye?
The will of Heaven's accomplish'd: I have
Now no more to fear, and nothing left to hope,
Now you may enter.

Enter Miranda *and* Dorinda.

    Mir. My Love! is it permitted me to see you once again?
    Prosp. You come to look your last; I will
For ever take him from your Eyes.
But, on my blessing, speak not, nor approach him.
    Dor. Pray, Father, is not this my Sisters man?
He has a noble form; but yet he's not so excellent
As my *Hippolito.*
    Prosp. Alas poor Girl, thou hast no man: look yonder;
There's all of him that's left.
    Dor. Why, was there ever any more of him?
He lies asleep, Sir, shall I waken him?
                        [*She kneels by* Hippolito, *and jogs him.*
    Ferd. Alas! he's never to be wak'd agen.
    Dor. My Love, my Love! will you not speak to me?
I fear you have displeas'd him, Sir, and now
He will not answer me. He's dumb and cold too,
But I'le run streight, and make a fire to warm him.
                                            [*Exit* Dorinda *running.*
Enter Alonzo, Gonzalo, Antonio; Ariel (*invisible.*)

    Alonz. Never were Beasts so hunted into toyls,
As we have been pursu'd by dreadful shapes.

But is not that my Son? O *Ferdinand*!
If thou art not a Ghost, let me embrace thee.

Ferd. My Father! O sinister happiness! Is it
Decreed I should recover you alive, just in that
Fatal hour when this brave Youth is lost in Death,
And by my hand?

Ant. Heaven! what new wonder's this?

Gonz. This Isle is full of nothing else.

Alonz. I thought to dye, and in the walks above,
Wand'ring by Star-light, to have sought thee out;
But now I should have gone to Heaven in vain,
Whilst thou art here behind.

Ferd. You must indeed in vain have gone thither
To look for me. Those who are stain'd with such black
Crimes as mine, come seldom there.

Prosp. And those who are, like him, all foul with guilt,
More seldom upward go. You stare upon me as
You ne'er had seen me; have fifteen years
So lost me to your knowledge, that you retain
No memory of *Prospero*?

Gonz. The good old Duke of *Millain*!

Prosp. I wonder less, that thou *Antonio* know'st me not,
Because thou did'st long since forget I was thy Brother,
Else I never had bin here.

Ant. Shame choaks my words.

Alonz. And wonder mine.

Prosp. For you, usurping Prince,   [*To* Alonzo.
Know, by my Art, you shipwrackt on this Isle,
Where, after I a while had punish'd you, my vengeance
Wou'd have ended; I design'd to match that Son
Of yours with this my Daughter.

Alonz. Pursue it still, I am most willing to't.

Prosp. So am not I. No marriages can prosper
Which are with Murd'rers made. Look on that Corps:
This, whilst he liv'd, was young *Hippolito*, that
Infant Duke of *Mantua*, Sir, whom you expos'd
With me; and here I bred him up till that blood-thirsty
Man, that *Ferdinand*——
But why do I exclaim on him, when Justice calls
To unsheath her Sword against his guilt?

Alonz. What do you mean?

Prosp. To execute Heav'ns Laws.
Here I am plac'd by Heav'n, here I am Prince,
Though you have dispossess'd me of my *Millain.*
Blood calls for blood; your *Ferdinand* shall dye,
And I in bitterness have sent for you
To have the sudden joy of seeing him alive,
And then the greater grief to see him dye.

Alonz. And think'st thou I or these will tamely stand
To view the execution?   [*Lays hand upon his Sword.*

Ferd. Hold, dear Father! I cannot suffer you
T' attempt against his life who gave her being
Whom I love.

Prosp. Nay then, appear my Guards!

[*He stamps, and many Spirits appear.*
—I thought no more   [*Aside.*
To use their aids (I'm curs'd because I us'd it),
But they are now the Ministers of Heaven,
Whilst I revenge this murder.

Alonz. Have I for this found thee my Son, so soon agen
To lose thee? *Antonio, Gonzalo,* speak for pity:
He may hear you.

Ant. I dare not draw that blood upon myself, by
Interceding for him.

Gonz. You drew this judgment down when you usurp'd
That Dukedom which was this dead Prince's right.

Alonz. Is this a time t'upbraid me with my sins, when
Grief lies heavy on me? y'are no more my friends,
But crueller than he, whose sentence has
Doom'd my Son to death.

Ant. You did unworthily t'upbraid him.

Gonz. And you do worse t'endure his crimes.

Ant. *Gonzalo,* we'll meet no more as friends.

Gonz. Agreed, *Antonio*: and we agree in discord.

Ferd. to Mir. Adieu my fairest Mistress.

Mir. Now I can hold no longer; I must speak.
Though I am loth to disobey you, Sir,
Be not so cruel to the man I love,
Or be so kind to let me suffer with him.

Ferd. Recall that Pray'r, or I shall wish to live,

Though death be all the mends that I can make.

   Prosp. This night I will allow you, *Ferdinand*, to fit
You for your Death; that Cave's your Prison.

   Alonz. Ah, *Prospero*! hear me speak. You are a Father,
Look on my age, and look upon his youth.

   Prosp. No more! all you can say is urg'd in vain,
I have no room for pity left within me.
Do you refuse! help, *Ariel*, with your fellows
To drive 'em in; *Alonzo* and his Son bestow in
Yonder Cave, and here *Gonzalo* shall with
Antonio lodge.   [*Spirits drive 'em in, as they are appointed.*

Enter Dorinda.

   Dor. Sir, I have made a fire, shall he be warm'd?

   Prosp. He's dead, and vital warmth will ne'er return.

   Dor. Dead, Sir, what's that?

   Prosp. His soul has left his body.

   Dor. When will it come agen?

   Prosp. O never, never!
He must be laid in Earth, and there consume.

   Dor. He shall not lye in earth, you do not know
How well he loves me: indeed he'l come agen;
He told me he would go a little while,
But promis'd me he would not tarry long.

   Prosp. He's murder'd by the man who lov'd your Sister.
Now both of you may see what 'tis to break
A Father's precept; you would needs see men, and by
That sight are made for ever wretched.
Hippolito is dead, and *Ferdinand* must dye
For murdering him.

   Mir. Have you no pity?

   Prosp. Your disobedience has so much incens'd me, that
I this night can leave no blessing with you.
Help to convey the body to my Couch,
Then leave me to mourn over it alone.
           [*They bear off the body of* Hippolito.

Enter Miranda, *and* Dorinda *again*; Ariel *behind 'em.*

   Ariel. I've bin so chid for my neglect by *Prospero*,   [*Aside.*
That I must now watch all and be unseen.

Mir. Sister, I say agen, 'twas long of you
That all this mischief happen'd.

Dor. Blame not me for your own fault, your
Curiosity brought me to see the man.

Mir. You safely might have seen him and retir'd, but
You wou'd needs go near him and converse. You may
Remember my Father call'd me thence, and I call'd you.

Dor. That was your envy, Sister, not your love;
You call'd me thence, because you could not be
Alone with him your self; but I am sure my
Man had never gone to Heaven so soon, but
That yours made him go.   [*Crying.*

Mir. Sister, I could not wish that either of 'em shou'd
Go to Heaven without us, but it was his fortune,
And you must be satisfi'd.

Dor. I'le not be satisfi'd: My Father says he'l make
Your man as cold as mine is now, and when he
Is made cold, my Father will not let you strive
To make him warm agen.

Mir. In spight of you mine never shall be cold.

Dor. I'm sure 'twas he that made me miserable,
And I will be reveng'd. Perhaps you think 'tis
Nothing to lose a man.

Mir. Yes, but there is some difference betwixt
My *Ferdinand*, and your *Hippolito*.

Dor. Aye, there's your judgment. Your's is the oldest
Man I ever saw except it were my Father.

Mir. Sister, no more. It is not comely in a Daughter,
When she says her Father's old.

Dor. But why do I stay here, whilst my cold Love
Perhaps may want me?
I'le pray my Father to make yours cold too.

Mir. Sister, I'le never sleep with you agen.

Dor. I'le never more meet in a Bed with you,
But lodge on the bare ground and watch my Love.

Mir. And at the entrance of that Cave I'le lye,
And eccho to each blast of wind a sigh.

        [*Exeunt severally, looking discontentedly on one another.*

Ariel. Harsh discord reigns throughout this fatal Isle,
At which good Angels mourn, ill Spirits smile;

Old *Prospero*, by his Daughters rob'd of rest,
Has in displeasure left 'em both unblest.
Unkindly they abjure each others bed,
To save the living, and revenge the dead.
Alonzo and his Son are Pris'ners made,
And good *Gonzalo* does their crimes upbraid.
Antonio and *Gonzalo* disagree,
And wou'd, though in one Cave, at distance be.
The Seamen all that cursed Wine have spent,
Which still renew'd their thirst of Government;
And, wanting subjects for the food of Pow'r,
Each wou'd to rule alone the rest devour.
The Monsters *Sycorax* and *Caliban*
More monstrous grow by passions learn'd from man.
Even I, not fram'd of warring Elements,
Partake and suffer in these discontents.
Why shou'd a mortal by Enchantments hold
In chains a spirit of ætherial mould?
Accursed Magick we our selves have taught,
And our own pow'r has our subjection wrought!   [*Exit.*

[Act V, Scene i.]

Enter Prospero *and* Miranda.

   Prosp. You beg in vain; I cannot pardon him,
He has offended Heaven.
   Mir. Then let Heaven punish him.
   Prosp. It will by me.
   Mir. Grant him at least some respite for my sake.
   Prosp. I by deferring Justice should incense the Deity
Against my self and you.
   Mir. Yet I have heard you say, The Powers above are slow
In punishing: and shou'd not you resemble them?
   Prosp. The Powers above may pardon or reprieve,
As Sovereign Princes may dispense with Laws,
Which we, as Officers, must execute. Our Acts of grace
To Criminals are Treason to Heavens prerogative.
   Mir. Do you condemn him for shedding blood?
   Prosp. Why do you ask that question? you know I do.
   Mir. Then you must be condemn'd for shedding his,

And he who condemns you, must dye for shedding
Yours, and that's the way at last to leave none living.
 Prosp. The Argument is weak, but I want time
To let you see your errours; retire and if you love him
Pray for him.   *[He's going.*
 Mir. O stay, Sir, I have yet more Arguments.
 Prosp. But none of any weight.
 Mir. Have you not said you are his Judge?
 Prosp. 'Tis true, I am; what then?
 Mir. And can you be his Executioner?
If that be so, then all men may declare their
Enemies in fault; and Pow'r without the Sword
Of Justice, will presume to punish what e're
It calls a crime.
 Prosp. I cannot force *Gonzalo* or my Brother, much
Less the Father, to destroy the Son; it must
Be then the Monster *Caliban*, and he's not here.
But *Ariel* strait shall fetch him.

Enter Ariel.

 Ariel. My potent Lord, before thou call'st, I come,
To serve thy will.
 Prosp. Then Spirit fetch me here my salvage Slave.
 Ariel. My Lord, it does not need.
 Prosp. Art thou then prone to mischief, wilt thou be
Thy self the Executioner?
 Ariel. Think better of thy aiery Minister, who
For thy sake, unbid, this night has flown
O're almost all the habitable World.
 Prosp. But to what purpose was all thy diligence?
 Ariel. When I was chidden by my mighty Lord
For my neglect of young *Hippolito*,
I went to view his body, and soon found
His soul was but retir'd, not sally'd out,
And frighted lay at skulk in th'inmost corner
Of his scarce-beating heart.
 Prosp. Is he not dead?
 Ariel.   Hear me my Lord!
I prun'd my wings, and, fitted for a journey,
From the next Isles of our *Hesperides*,

127

I gather'd Moly first, thence shot my self
To *Palestine*, and watch'd the trickling Balm,
Which caught, I glided to the British Isles,
And there the purple Panacea found.
  Prosp. All this to night?
  Ariel. All this, my Lord, I did,
Nor was *Hippolito*'s good Angel wanting, who
Climbing up the circle of the Moon,
While I below got Simples for the Cure, went to
Each Planet which o're-rul'd those Herbs,
And drew it's virtue to increase their pow'r:
Long ere this hour had I been back again,
But that a Storm took me returning back
And flag'd my tender Wings.
  Prosp. Thou shalt have rest, my spirit;
But hast thou search'd the wound?
  Ariel. My Lord I have, and 'twas in time I did it; for
The soul stood almost at life's door, all bare
And naked, shivering like Boys upon a Rivers
Bank, and loth to tempt the cold air. But I took
Her and stop'd her in, and pour'd into his mouth
The healing juice of vulnerary Herbs.
  Prosp. Thou art my faithful servant.
  Ariel. His only danger was his loss of blood, but now
He's wak'd, my Lord, and just this hour
He must be dress'd again, as I have done it.
Anoint the Sword which pierc'd him with this
Weapon-Salve, and wrap it close from air till
I have time to visit him again.
  Prosp. It shall be done. Be it your task, *Miranda*,
Because your Sister is not present here,
While I go visit your dear *Ferdinand*,
From whom I will a while conceal this news,
That it may be more welcome.
  Mir. I obey you, and with a double duty, Sir: for now
You twice have given me life.
  Prosp. My *Ariel*, follow me.   [*Exeunt severally.*

[Act V, Scene ii.]

[Hippolito *discovered on a Couch*, Dorinda *by him*.

Dor. How do you find your self?

Hip. I'm somewhat cold, can you not draw me nearer
To the Sun? I am too weak to walk.

Dor. My Love, I'le try.

She draws the chair nearer the Audience.

I thought you never would have walk'd agen,
They told me you were gone away to Heaven;
Have you bin there?

Hip. I know not where I was.

Dor. I will not leave you till you promise me
You will not dye agen.

Hip. Indeed I will not.

Dor. You must not go to Heav'n unless we go together,
For I've heard my Father say that we must strive
To be each others Guide, the way to it will else
Be difficult, especially to those who are so young.
But I much wonder what it is to dye.

Hip. Sure 'tis to dream, a kind of breathless sleep
When once the Soul's gone out.

Dor. What is the Soul?

Hip. A small blew thing that runs about within us.

Dor. Then I have seen it in a frosty morning run
Smoaking from my mouth.

Hip. But if my Soul had gone, it should have walk'd
Upon a Cloud just over you, and peep'd,
And thence I would have call'd you.

Dor. But I should not have heard you, 'tis so far.

Hip. Why then I would have rain'd and snow'd upon you,
And thrown down Hail-stones gently till I hit you,
And made you look at least. But dear *Dorinda*
What is become of him who fought with me?

Dor. O, I can tell you joyful news of him,
My Father means to make him dye to day,
For what he did to you.

Hip. That must not be, my dear *Dorinda*; go and beg your
Father he may not dye, it was my fault he hurt me,

I urg'd him to it first.

   Dor. But if he live, he'll never leave killing you.

   Hip. O no! I just remember when I fell asleep
I heard him calling me a great way off
And crying over me as you wou'd do.
Besides, we have no cause of quarrel now.

   Dor. Pray how began your difference first?

   Hip. I fought with him for all the Women in the World.

   Dor. That hurt you had was justly sent from Heaven,
For wishing to have any more but me.

   Hip. Indeed I think it was, but I repent it.
The fault was only in my blood, for now
'Tis gone, I find I do not love so many.

   Dor. In confidence of this, I'le beg my Father,
That he may live. I'm glad the naughty blood
That made you love so many, is gone out.

   Hip. My Dear, go quickly, lest you come too late.   [*Exit* Dor.

Enter Miranda *at the other door, with* Hippolito's *sword wrapt up.*

   Hip. Who's this who looks so fair and beautiful, as
Nothing but *Dorinda* can surpass her? O!
I believe it is that Angel Woman,
Whom she calls Sister.

   Mir. Sir, I am sent hither to dress your wound,
How do you find your strength?

   Hip. Fair Creature, I am faint with loss of blood.

   Mir. I'm sorry for't.

   Hip. Indeed and so am I, for if I had that blood, I then
Should find a great delight in loving you.

   Mir. But, Sir, I am anothers, and your love is given
Already to my Sister.

   Hip. Yet I find that if you please I can love still a little.

   Mir. I cannot be unconstant, nor shou'd you.

   Hip. O my wound pains me.

   Mir. I am come to ease you.   [*She unwraps the Sword.*

   Hip. Alas! I feel the cold air come to me,
My wound shoots worse than ever.   [*She wipes and anoints the Sword.*

   Mir. Does it still grieve you?

   Hip. Now methinks there's something laid just upon it.

   Mir. Do you find no ease?

Hip. Yes, yes, upon the sudden all the pain
Is leaving me. Sweet Heaven how I am eas'd!

Enter Ferdinand *and* Dorinda *to them.*

 Ferd. to Dor. Madam, I must confess my life is yours,
I owe it to your generosity.
 Dor. I am o'rejoy'd my Father lets you live, and proud
Of my good fortune, that he gave your life to me.
 Mir. How? gave his life to her!
 Hip. Alas! I think she said so, and he said he ow'd it
To her generosity.
 Ferd. But is not that your Sister with *Hippolito*?
 Dor. So kind already?
 Ferd. I came to welcome life, and I have met
The cruellest of deaths.
 Hip. My dear *Dorinda* with another man?
 Dor. Sister, what bus'ness have you here?
 Mir. You see I dress *Hippolito*.
 Dor. Y'are very charitable to a Stranger.
 Mir. You are not much behind in charity,
To beg a pardon for a man,
Whom you scarce ever saw before.
 Dor. Henceforward let your Surgery alone,
For I had rather he should dye,
Than you should cure his wound.
 Mir. And I wish *Ferdinand* had dy'd before
He ow'd his life to your entreaty.
 Ferd. to Hip. Sir, I'm glad you are so well recover'd.
You keep your humour still to have all Women?
 Hip. Not all, Sir; you except one of the number,
Your new Love there, *Dorinda*.
 Mir. Ah *Ferdinand*! can you become inconstant?
If I must lose you, I had rather death should take
You from me than you take your self.
 Ferd. And if I might have chose, I would have wish'd
That death from *Prospero*, and not this from you.
 Dor. Aye, now I find why I was sent away,
That you might have my Sisters company.
 Hip. *Dorinda*, kill me not with your unkindness,
This is too much, first to be false yourself,

And then accuse me too.

Ferd. We all accuse each other, and each one denys their guilt,
I should be glad it were a mutual errour.
And therefore first to clear myself from fault,
Madam, I beg your pardon, while I say I only love
Your Sister.   [*To* Dorinda.

Mir. O blest word!
I'm sure I love no man but *Ferdinand.*

Dor. Nor I, Heav'n knows, but my *Hippolito.*

Hip. I never knew I lov'd so much, before I fear'd
Dorinda's constancy; but now I am convinc'd that
I lov'd none but her, because none else can
Recompence her loss.

Ferd. 'Twas happy then you had this little tryal.
But how we all so much mistook, I know not.

Mir. I have only this to say in my defence: my Father sent
Me hither, to attend the wounded Stranger.

Dor. And *Hippolito* sent me to beg the life of *Ferdinand.*

Ferd. From such small errours, left at first unheeded,
Have often sprung sad accidents in love:
But see, our Fathers and our friends are come
To mix their joys with ours.

Enter Prospero, Alonzo, Antonio, Gonzalo.

Alon. to Prosp. Let it no more be thought of. Your purpose,
Though it was severe, was just. In losing *Ferdinand*
I should have mourn'd, but could not have complain'd.

Prosp. Sir, I am glad kind Heaven decreed it otherwise.

Dor. O wonder!
How many goodly Creatures are there here!
How beauteous mankind is!

Hip. O brave new World that has such people in't!

Alon. to Ferd. Now all the blessings of a glad Father
Compass thee about,
And make thee happy in thy beauteous choice.

Gonz. I've inward wept, or should have spoke ere this.
Look down sweet Heav'n, and on this Couple drop
A blessed Crown, for it is you chalk'd out
The way which brought us hither.

Ant. Though penitence forc'd by necessity can scarce

Seem real, yet dearest Brother I have hope
My blood may plead for pardon with you. I resign
Dominion, which 'tis true I could not keep,
But Heaven knows too I would not.

 Prosp. All past crimes I bury in the joy of this
Blessed day.

 Alonz. And that I may not be behind in justice, to this
Young Prince I render back his Dukedom,
And as the Duke of *Mantua* thus salute him.

 Hip. What is it that you render back? Methinks
You give me nothing.

 Prosp. You are to be Lord of a great People,
And o're Towns and Cities.

 Hip. And shall these people be all Men and Women?

 Gonz. Yes, and shall call you Lord.

 Hip. Why then I'le live no longer in a Prison, but
Have a whole Cave to my self hereafter.

 Prosp. And that your happiness may be compleat,
I give you my *Dorinda* for your Wife. She shall
Be yours for ever, when the Priest has made you one.

 Hip. How can he make us one, shall I grow to her?

 Prosp. By saying holy words you shall be joyn'd
In marriage to each other.

 Dor. I warrant you those holy words are charms.
My Father means to conjure us together.

 Prosp. to his daughter. My *Ariel* told me, when last night you
  quarrel'd,
You said you would for ever part your beds;
But what you threaten'd in your anger, Heaven
Has turn'd to Prophecy:
For you, *Miranda*, must with *Ferdinand*,
And you, *Dorinda*, with *Hippolito*
Lye in one Bed hereafter.

 Alonz. And Heaven make those Beds still fruitful in
Producing Children to bless their Parents
Youth, and Gransires age.

 Mir. to Dor. If Children come by lying in a Bed,
I wonder you and I had none between us.

 Dor. Sister it was our fault, we meant like fools
To look 'em in the fields, and they it seems

Are only found in Beds.

Hip. I am o'rejoy'd that I shall have *Dorinda* in a Bed,
We'll lye all night and day together there,
And never rise again.

Ferd. aside to him. Hippolito! you yet are ignorant of your great
Happiness, but there is somewhat which for
Your own and fair *Dorinda*'s sake I must instruct
You in.

Hip. Pray teach me quickly how Men and Women in your
World make love, I shall soon learn
I warrant you.

Enter Ariel *driving in* Steph. Trinc. Must. Vent. Calib. Syc.

Prosp. Why that's my dainty *Ariel*, I shall miss thee,
But yet thou shalt have freedom.

Gonz. O look, Sir, look the Master and the Saylors—
The Bosen too—my Prophecy is out, that if
A Gallows were on land, that man could n'ere
Be drown'd.

Alonz. to Trinc. Now Blasphemy, what not one Oath ashore?
Hast thou no mouth by land? why star'st thou so?

Trinc. What, more Dukes yet? I must resign my Dukedom.
But 'tis no matter, I was almost starv'd in't.

Must. Here's nothing but wild Sallads without Oyl or Vinegar.

Steph. The Duke and Prince alive! would I had now
Our gallant Ship agen, and were her Master,
I'd willingly give all my Island for her.

Vent. And I my Vice-Roy-ship.

Trinc. I shall need no hangman, for I shall e'en hang
My self, now my friend Butt has shed his
Last drop of life. Poor Butt is quite departed.

Ant. They talk like mad men.

Prosp. No matter, time will bring 'em to themselves,
And now their Wine is gone they will not quarrel.
Your Ship is safe and tight, and bravely rigg'd,
As when you first set Sail.

Alonz. This news is wonderful.

Ariel. Was it well done, my Lord?

Prosp. Rarely, my diligence.

Gonz. But pray, Sir, what are those mishapen Creatures?

Prosp. Their Mother was a Witch, and one so strong
She would controul the Moon, make Flows
And Ebbs, and deal in her command without
Her power.

Syc. O *Setebos*! these be brave Sprights indeed.

Prosp. to Calib. Go Sirrah to my Cell, and as you hope
For pardon, trim it up.

Calib. Most carefully. I will be wise hereafter.
What a dull fool was I to take those Drunkards
For Gods, when such as these were in the world!

Prosp. Sir, I invite your Highness and your Train
To my poor Cave this night; a part of which
I will imploy in telling you my story.

Alonz. No doubt it must be strangely taking, Sir.

Prosp. When the morn draws I'le bring you to your Ship,
And promise you calm Seas and happy Gales.
My *Ariel*, that's thy charge: then to the Elements
Be free, and fare thee well.

Ariel. I'le do it Master.

> *Sings.* Where the Bee sucks there suck I,
> In a Cowslips Bell, I lye,
> There I couch when Owls do cry,
> On the Swallows wing I flye
> After Summer merrily.
> Merrily, merrily shall I live now
> Under the Blossom that hangs on the Bough.

Syc. I'le to Sea with thee, and keep thee warm in thy Cabin.

Trinc. No my dainty Dy-dapper, you have a tender constitution,
and will be sick a Ship-board. You are partly Fish and may swim after
me. I wish you a good Voyage.

Prosp. Now to this Royal Company, my servant,
Be visible, And entertain them with a Dance
Before they part.

Ariel. I have a gentle Spirit for my Love,
Who twice seven years hath waited for my Freedom,
It shall appear and foot it featly with me.
Milcha, my Love, thy *Ariel* calls thee.

Enter Milcha.

Milcha. Here!

[*They dance a Saraband.*

Prosp. Henceforth this Isle to the afflicted be
A place of Refuge as it was to me;
The Promises of blooming Spring live here,
And all the Blessings of the rip'ning year;
On my retreat let Heaven and Nature smile,
And ever flourish the *Enchanted Isle.*   [*Exeunt.*

10. John Dryden, from *An Essay of Dramatick Poesie*

1668

From *Of Dramatick Poesie, An Essay* (1668). In the Dedication
Dryden recorded that he had begun writing this work in the
country, after the theatres were closed by the plague in May/
June 1665: however, a number of references show that he was
still writing, or revising, it in the summer of 1667. Although
dated 1668 it was probably published late in 1667.

This dialogue is one of Dryden's major attempts to work out
his own position in the competing claims of Ancients against
Moderns, French against English dramatists, Art and Rules
against Nature and Genius. The characters in the dialogue are
traditionally identified as follows: Neander: Dryden himself;
Eugenius: Charles Sackville, Lord Buckhurst; Crites: Sir Robert
Howard; Lisideius: Sir Charles Sedley.

*   *   *

['Neander' prefers the English drama to the more 'correct' models of
the French]

'Now what I beseech you is more easie than to write a regular French

Play, or more difficult than to write an irregular English one, like those of *Fletcher*, or of *Shakespeare*?

If they content themselves as *Corneille* did, with some flat design, which, like an ill Riddle, is found out ere it be half propos'd; such Plots we can make every way regular as easily as they: but when e're they endeavour to rise up to any quick turns and counterturns of Plot, as some of them have attempted, since *Corneille*'s Playes have been less in vogue, you see they write as irregularly as we, though they cover it more speciously. Hence the reason is perspicuous, why no French Playes, when translated, have, or ever can succeed upon the English Stage. For, if you consider the Plots, our own are fuller of variety, if the writing ours are more quick and fuller of spirit: and therefore 'tis a strange mistake in those who decry the way of writing Playes in verse, as if the English therein imitated the French. We have borrow'd nothing from them; our Plots are weav'd in English Loomes: we endeavour therein to follow the variety and greatness of characters which are deriv'd to us from *Shakespeare* and *Fletcher*: the copiousness and well-knitting of the intrigues we have from *Jonson*, and for the verse it self we have English precedents of elder date than any of *Corneille*'s Playes. . . . I can show in Shakespeare, many Scenes of rhyme together, and the like in *Ben Jonson*'s Tragedies. . . .

But to return from whence I have digress'd, I dare boldly affirm these two things of the English *Drama*: First, That we have many Playes of ours as regular as any of theirs; and which, besides, have more variety of Plot and Characters: And secondly, that in most of the irregular Playes of *Shakespeare* or *Fletcher* (for *Ben. Jonson*'s are for the most part regular) there is a more masculine fancy and greater spirit in all the writing, than there is in any of the French. I could produce even in *Shakespeare*'s and *Fletcher*'s Works, some Playes which are almost exactly form'd; as the *Merry Wives of Windsor*, and the *Scornful Lady*: but because (generally speaking) *Shakespeare*, who writ first, did not perfectly observe the Laws of Comedy, and *Fletcher*, who came nearer to perfection, yet through carelessness made many faults; I will take the pattern of a perfect Play from *Ben. Jonson*, who was a careful and learned observer of the Dramatique Laws, and from all his Comedies I shall select *The Silent Woman*; of which I will make a short Examen, according to those Rules which the French observe.'

As *Neander* was beginning to examine the *Silent Woman*, *Eugenius*, looking earnestly upon him; 'I beseech you *Neander*,' said he, 'gratifie the company and me in particular so far, as before you speak of the

Play, to give us a Character of the Authour; and tell us franckly your opinion, whether you do not think all Writers, both French and English, ought to give place to him?'

'I fear,' replied *Neander*, 'That in obeying your commands I shall draw a little envy upon my self. Besides, in performing them, it will be first necessary to speak somewhat of *Shakespeare* and *Fletcher*, his Rivalls in Poesie; and one of them, in my opinion, at least his equal, perhaps his superiour.

To begin then with *Shakespeare*; he was the man who of all Modern, and perhaps Ancient Poets, had the largest and most comprehensive soul. All the Images of Nature were still present to him, and he drew them not laboriously, but luckily: when he describes any thing, you more than see it, you feel it too. Those who accuse him to have wanted learning, give him the greater commendation: he was naturally learn'd; he needed not the spectacles of Books to read Nature; he look'd inwards, and found her there. I cannot say he is every where alike; were he so, I should do him injury to compare him with the greatest of Mankind. He is many times flat, insipid; his Comick wit degenerating into clenches, his serious swelling into Bombast. But he is always great, when some great occasion is presented to him: no man can say he ever had a fit subject for his wit, and did not then raise himself as high above the rest of Poets,

> *Quantum lenta solent, inter viberna cupressi.*[1]

The consideration of this made Mr. *Hales* of *Eaton* say, That there was no subject of which any Poet ever writ, but he would produce it much better treated of in *Shakespeare*; and however others are now generally prefer'd before him, yet the Age wherein he liv'd, which had contemporaries with him, *Fletcher* and *Jonson*, never equall'd them to him in their esteem: And in the last Kings Court, when *Ben*'s reputation was at highest, Sir *John Suckling*, and with him the greater part of the Courtiers, set our *Shakespeare* far above him.

Beaumont and *Fletcher* of whom I am next to speak, had with the advantage of *Shakespeare*'s wit, which was their precedent, great natural gifts, improv'd by study. *Beaumont* especially being so accurate a judge of Playes, that *Ben. Jonson* while he liv'd, submitted all his Writings to his Censure, and 'tis thought, us'd his judgement in correcting, if not contriving all his Plots. What value he had for him,

[1] Virgil, *Eclogue* 1.25: '[But this city has reared her head as high among all other cities] as cypresses oft do among the bending osiers.'

appears by the Verses he writ to him; and therefore I need speak no farther of it. The first Play which brought *Fletcher* and him in esteem was their *Philaster*: for before that, they had written two or three very unsuccessfully: as the like is reported of *Ben. Jonson*, before he writ *Every Man in his Humour*. Their Plots were generally more regular than *Shakespeare*'s, especially those which were made before *Beaumont*'s death; and they understood and imitated the conversation of Gentlemen much better; whose wilde debaucheries, and quickness of wit in reparties, no Poet can ever paint as they have done. This Humour of which *Ben. Jonson* deriv'd from particular persons, they made it not their business to describe: they represented all the passions very lively, but above all, Love. I am apt to believe the English Language in them arriv'd to its highest perfection; what words have since been taken in, are rather superfluous than necessary. Their Playes are now the most pleasant and frequent entertainments of the Stage; two of theirs being acted through the year for one of *Shakespeare*'s or *Jonson*'s: the reason is, because there is a certain gayety in their Comedies, and Pathos in their more serious Playes, which suits generally with all mens humours. *Shakespeare*'s language is likewise a little obsolete, and *Ben. Jonson*'s wit comes short of theirs. . . . (45–9)

If I would compare [*Ben Jonson*] with *Shakespeare*, I must acknowledge him the more correct Poet, but *Shakespeare* the greater wit. *Shakespeare* was the *Homer*, or Father of our Dramatick Poets; *Jonson* was the *Virgil*, the pattern of elaborate writing; I admire him, but I love *Shakespeare*. To conclude of him, as he has given us the most correct Playes, so in the precepts which he has laid down in his *Discoveries*, we have as many and profitable Rules for perfecting the Stage as any wherewith the French can furnish us.' (50)

✱   ✱   ✱

['Neander' discusses Morose, the 'humour' character of Jonson's *Epicoene*]

'. . . I am assur'd from diverse persons, that *Ben. Jonson* was actually acquainted with such a man, one altogether as ridiculous as he is here represented. Others say it is not enough to find one man of such an humour; it must be common to more, and the more common the more natural. To prove this, they instance in the best of Comical Characters, *Falstaff*: There are many men resembling him; Old, Fat, Merry, Cowardly, Drunken, Amorous, Vain, and Lying: But to convince these people, I need but tell them, that humour is the ridiculous extravagance of conversation, wherein one man differs from all others. If then it be common, or communicated to many, how differs it from other mens? or what indeed causes it to be ridiculous so much as the singularity of it? As for *Falstaff*, he is not properly one humour, but a Miscellany of Humours or Images, drawn from so many several men; that wherein he is singular is his wit, or those things he sayes, *praeter expectatum*, unexpected by the Audience; his quick evasions when you imagine him surpriz'd, which as they are extreamly diverting of themselves, so receive a great addition from his person; for the very sight of such an unwieldy old debauch'd fellow is a Comedy alone.' (51–2)

★   ★   ★

['Crites' attacks the use of rhyme in drama, but 'Neander' defends the practice]

'And this, Sir, calls to my remembrance the beginning of your discourse, where you told us we should never find the Audience favourable to this kind of writing, till we could produce as good Playes in Rhyme, as *Ben. Jonson*, *Fletcher*, and *Shakespeare*, had writ out of it. But it is to raise envy to the living, to compare them with the dead. They are honour'd, and almost ador'd by us, as they deserve; neither do I know any so presumptuous of themselves as to contend with them. Yet give me leave to say thus much, without injury to their Ashes, that not onely we shall never equal them, but they could never equal themselves, were they to rise and write again. We acknowledge them our Fathers in wit, but they have ruin'd their Estates themselves before they came to their childrens hands. There is scarce an Humour, a Character, or any kind of Plot, which they have not blown upon: all comes sullied or wasted to us: and were they to entertain this Age, they could not make so plenteous treatments out of such decay'd Fortunes. This therefore will be a good Argument to us either not to write at all, or to attempt some other way.' (64–5)

★   ★   ★

11. John Dryden?, prologue to *Julius Caesar*

1672

From *Covent-Garden Drollery* (1672).

This prologue is accepted as authentic by James Kinsley in his edition of Dryden's *Poems*, 1958 (pp. 142, 1854), but not by the editors of the California *Dryden* (1956—). However, Dryden's attack, in the same year, on the coarseness of some characters in Jonsonian comedy (see No. 12) is the most striking of several echoes in this poem of Dryden's authenticated opinions: I believe the ascription to be more likely than not.

In Country Beauties as we often see,
Something that takes in their simplicity.
Yet while they charm, they know not they are fair,
And take without the spreading of the snare.
Such Artless beauty lies in *Shakespeare*'s wit,
'Twas well in spight of him whate're he writ.
His Excellencies came and were not sought,
His words like casual Atoms made a thought:
Drew up themselves in Rank and File, and writ,
He wondring how the Devil it was such wit.
Thus like the drunken Tinker, in his Play,
He grew a Prince, and never knew which way.
He did not know what trope or Figure meant,
But to perswade is to be eloquent;
So in this Cæsar which today you see,
Tully ne'r spoke as he makes *Antony*.
Those then that tax his Learning are to blame,
He knew the thing, but did not know the Name:
Great *Jonson* did that Ignorance adore,
And though he envi'd much, admir'd him more.

The faultless *Jonson* equally writ well,
Shakespeare made faults; but then did more excel.
One close at Guard like some old Fencer lay,
T'other more open, but he shew'd more play.
In Imitation *Jonson's* wit was shown,
Heaven made his men; but *Shakespeare* made his own.
Wise *Jonson's* talent in observing lay,
But others follies still made up his play.
He drew the life in each elaborate line,
But *Shakespeare* like a Master did design.
Jonson with skill dissected humane kind,
And show'd their faults that they their faults might find:
But then as all Anatomists must do,
He to the meanest of mankind did go,
And took from Gibbets such as he would show.
Both are so great that he must boldly dare,
Who both of 'em does judge and both compare.
If amongst Poets one more bold there be,
The man that dare attempt in either way, is he.

12. John Dryden on the Jacobean dramatists

1672

(a) Epilogue to the Second Part of *The Conquest of Granada by the Spaniards*, 1672.

They, who have best succeeded on the Stage,
Have still conform'd their Genius to their Age.
Thus *Jonson* did Mechanique humour show,
When men were dull, and conversation low.
Then, Comedy was faultless, but 'twas coarse:
Cobb's Tankard was a jest, and *Otter's* horse.
And as their Comedy, their love was mean;
Except by chance, in some one labour'd Scene;

Which must atone for an ill-written Play.
They rose; but at their height could seldome stay.
Fame then was cheap, and the first commer sped;
And they have kept it since, by being dead.
But were they now to write, when Critiques weigh
Each Line, and ev'ry word, throughout a Play,
None of 'em, no not *Jonson* in his height,
Could pass, without allowing grains for weight.
Think it not envy that these truths are told,
Our Poet's not malicious, though he's bold.
'Tis not to brand 'em that their faults are shown,
But, by their errours, to excuse his own.
If Love and Honour now are higher rais'd,
'Tis not the Poet, but the Age is prais'd.
Wit's now arriv'd to a more high degree;
Our native Language more refin'd and free.
Our Ladies and our men now speak more wit
In conversation, than those Poets writ.
Then, one of these is, consequently, true;
That what this Poet writes comes short of you,
And imitates you ill (which most he fears),
Or else his writing is not worse than theirs.
Yet, though you judge (as sure the Critiques will),
That some before him writ with greater skill,
In this one praise he has their fame surpast,
To please an Age more Gallant than the last.

(*b*) From *A Defence of the Epilogue, Or, An Essay on the Dramatique Poetry of the Last Age* (1672).

This apologia finds Dryden enduring the pressure of the past less charitably than in *An Essay of Dramatick Poesie.*

★   ★   ★

The truth is, I have so farr ingag'd my self in a bold *Epilogue* to this Play, wherein I have somewhat tax'd the former writing, that it was necessary for me either not to print it, or to show that I could defend it. Yet, I would so maintain my opinion of the present Age, as not to be wanting in my veneration for the past: I would ascribe to dead Authors their just praises, in those things wherein they have excell'd us: and in those wherein we contend with them for the preheminence, I would acknowledge our advantages to the Age, and claim no victory from our wit. This being what I have propos'd to my self, I hope I shall not be thought arrogant when I inquire into their Errors. For, we live in an Age, so Sceptical, that as it determines little, so it takes nothing from Antiquity on trust, and I profess to have no other ambition in this Essay, than that Poetry may not go backward, when all other Arts and Sciences are advancing. ...

[Dryden cites in his defence Horace's argument that]

...Antiquity alone is no plea for the excellency of a Poem: but, that one Age learning from another, the last (if we can suppose an equallity of wit in the writers,) has the advantage of knowing more, and better than the former. And this I think is the state of the question in dispute. It is therefore my part to make it clear, that the Language, Wit, and Conversation of our Age are improv'd and refin'd above the last: and then it will not be difficult, to inferr, that our Playes have receiv'd some part of those advantages.

In the first place, therefore, it will be necessary to state, in general, what this refinement is of which we treat: and that I think will not be defin'd amiss: *An improvement of our Wit, Language, and Conversation, or, an alteration in them for the better.*

To begin with *Language.* That an Alteration is lately made in ours or since the Writers of the last Age (in which I comprehend *Shakespeare, Fletcher* and *Jonson*) is manifest. Any man who reads those excellent Poets, and compares their language with what is now written, will see it almost in every line. But, that this is an *Improvement* of the Language, or an alteration for the better, will not so easily be granted. For many are of a contrary opinion, that the English tongue was then in the height of its perfection; that, from *Jonson's* time to ours, it has been in a continual declination; like that of the *Romans* from the Age of *Virgil* to *Statius,* and so downward to *Claudian:* of which, not onely *Petronius,* but *Quintilian* himself so much complains, under the person of *Secundus,* in his famous Dialogue *de causis corruptæ eloquentiæ.*

But, to shew that our Language is improv'd; and that those people have not a just value for the Age in which they live, let us consider in what the refinement of a language principally consists: that is, *either in rejecting such old words or phrases which are ill sounding, or improper, or in admitting new, which are more proper, more sounding and more signifi-cant.*

The Reader will easily take notice, that when I speak of rejecting improper words and phrases I mention not such as are Antiquated by custome onely: and, as I may say, without any fault of theirs: for in this case the refinement can be but accidental: that is when the words and phrases which are rejected happen to be improper. Neither would I be understood (when I speak of impropriety in Language) either wholly to accuse the last Age, or to excuse the present; and least of all my self. For all writers have their imperfections and failings, but I may safely conclude in the general, that our improprieties are less frequent, and less gross than theirs. One Testimony of this is un-deniable, that we are the first who have observ'd them; and, certainly, to observe errours is a great step to the correcting of them. But, malice and partiality set apart, let any man who understands English, read diligently the works of *Shakespeare* and *Fletcher*; and I dare undertake that he will find in every page either some *Solecism* of Speech, or some notorious flaw in Sence: and yet these men are reverenc'd when we are not forgiven. That their wit is great and many times their expressions noble, envy it self cannot deny.

> —————*Neque ego illi detrahere ausim*
> *Haerentem capiti, cum multa laude coronam:*[1]

but the times were ignorant in which they liv'd. Poetry was then, if not in its infancy among us, at least not arriv'd to its vigor and maturity: witness the lameness of their Plots: many of which, especially those which they writ first, (for even that Age refin'd itself in some measure,) were made up of some ridiculous, incoherent story, which, in one Play many times took up the business of an Age. I suppose I need not name *Pericles Prince* of *Tyre*, nor the Historical Plays of *Shakespeare*. Besides many of the rest as the *Winter's Tale, Love's Labour's Lost, Measure for Measure*, which were either grounded on impossibilities, or at least, so meanly written, that the Comedy neither caus'd your mirth, nor the serious part your concernment. If I would expatiate on this Subject, I could easily demonstrate that our admir'd *Fletcher*, who writ after him, neither understood correct Plotting, nor that which they call *the Decorum of the Stage*. I would not search in his worst

---

[1] Horace, *Satire* 1.10.48f.: 'Nor would I dare to wrest from him the crown that clings to his brow with so much glory.'

Playes for examples: he who will consider his *Philaster*, his *Humorous Lieutenant*, his *Faithful Shepheardess*; and many others which I could name, will find them much below the applause which is now given them. He will see *Philaster* wounding his Mistriss, and afterwards his Boy, to save himself: Not to mention the Clown who enters immediately, and not only has the advantage of the Combat against the Heroe, but diverts you from your serious concernment, with his ridiculous and absurd Raillery. In his *Humorous Lieutenant* you find his *Demetrius* and *Leoncius* staying in the midst of a routed Army to hear the cold mirth of the *Lieutenant*: and *Demetrius* afterwards appearing with a Pistol in his hand, in the next Age to *Alexander* the Great. And for his *Shepheard*, he falls twice into the former indecency of wounding Women. But these absurdities, which those Poets committed, may more properly be call'd the Ages fault than theirs, for, besides the want of Education and Learning, (which was their particular unhappiness) they wanted the benefit of converse; but of that, I shall speak hereafter, in a place more proper for it. Their Audiences knew no better: and therefore were satisfy'd with what they brought. Those who call theirs the *Golden Age of Poetry*, have only this reason for it, that they were then content with Acorns, before they knew the use of Bread: or that Ἅλις δρυός [1] was become a Proverb. They had many who admir'd them, and few who blam'd them; and, certainly, a severe Critique is the greatest help to a good Wit. He does the Office of a Friend, while he designs that of an Enemy: and his malice keeps a Poet within those bounds, which the Luxuriancy of his Fancy would tempt him to overleap.

But it is not their Plots which I meant, principally to tax: I was speaking of their Sence and Language, and I dare almost challenge any man to show me a page together, which is correct in both. As for *Ben. Jonson*, I am loath to name him, because he is a most Judicious Writer; yet he very often falls into these errors. And I once more beg the Readers pardon for accusing him or them. Onely let him consider that I live in an age where my least faults are severely censur'd: and that I have no way left to extenuate my failings but my showing as great in those whom we admire.

Cædimus inque vicem præbemus cura sagittis. [2]

---

[1] Enough of acorns.

[2] Persius, *Satire* 4.42: 'We keep smiting by turns and by turns presenting our own legs to the arrow.'

I cast my eyes but by chance on *Catiline*; and in the three or four first pages, found enough to conclude that *Jonson* writ not correctly.

> ——————————Let the long hid seeds
> Of treason, in thee, now shoot forth in deeds
> Ranker than horrour.

In reading some bombast speeches of *Macbeth*, which are not to be understood, he us'd to say that it was horrour, and I am much afraid that this is so. (160-5)

★   ★   ★

[Dryden then lists more faults of language]

But I am willing to close the Book, partly out of veneration to the Author, partly out of weariness to pursue an argument which is so fruitful in so small a compass. And what correctness, after this, can be expected from *Shakespeare* or from *Fletcher*, who wanted that Learning and Care which *Jonson* had? I will therefore spare my own trouble of inquiring into their faults: who had they liv'd now, had doubtless written more correctly. I suppose it will be enough for me to affirm (as I think I safely may) that these and the like errors which I tax'd in the most correct of the last Age, are such, into which we doe not ordinarily fall. I think few of our present Writers would have left behind them such a line as this,

> *Contain your Spirit in more stricter bounds.*

But that gross way of two Comparatives was then, ordinary: and therefore more pardonable in *Jonson*.

As for the other part of refining, which consists in receiving new Words and Phrases, I shall not insist much on it. 'Tis obvious that we have admitted many: some of which we wanted, and, therefore our Language is the richer for them: as it would be by importation of Bullion: others are rather Ornamental than Necessary; yet by their admission, the Language is become more courtly: and our thoughts are better drest. These are to be found scatter'd in the Writers of our Age: and it is not my business to collect them. They who have lately written with most care, have, I believe, taken the Rule of *Horace* for their guide; that is, not to be too hasty in receiving of Words: but rather to stay till Custome has made them familiar to us,

Quem penes arbitrium est & jus & norma loquendi.[1]

For I cannot approve of their way of refining, who corrupt our *English* Idiom by mixing it too much with *French*: that is a Sophistication of Language, not an improvement of it: a turning *English* into *French*, rather than a refining of *English* by *French*. We meet daily with those Fopps, who value themselves on their Travelling, and pretend they cannot express their meaning in *English*, because they would put off to us some *French* Phrase of the last Edition: without considering that, for ought they know, we have a better of our own; but these are not the men who are to refine us: their Talent is to prescribe Fashions, not Words: at best they are onely serviceable to a Writer, so as *Ennius* was to *Virgil*. He may *Aurum ex stercore colligere*[2] for 'tis hard if, amongst many insignificant Phrases, there happen not something worth preserving: though they themselves, like *Indians*, know not the value of their own Commodity.

There is yet another way of improving Language, which Poets especially have practic'd in all Ages: that is by applying receiv'd words to a new Signification, and this I believe, is meant by *Horace*, in that Precept which is so variously constru'd by Expositors:

> *Dixeris Egregie, notum si callida verbum*
> *Reddiderit iunctura novum.*[3]

And, in this way, he himself had a particular happiness: using all the Tropes, and particularly Metaphors, with that grace which is observable in his Odes: where the Beauty of Expression is often greater than that of thought, as in that one example, amongst an infinite number of others: *Et vultus nimium lubricus aspici.*[4]

And therefore though he innovated little, he may justly be call'd a great Refiner of the *Roman* Tongue. This choice of words, and height'ning of their natural signification, was observ'd in him by the Writers of the following Ages: for *Petronius* says of him *& Horatii curiosa fælicitas.*[5] By this graffing, as I may call it, on old words, has our Tongue been Beautified by the three fore-mention'd Poets,

---

[1] Horace, *A.P.* 72: 'In whose hands [Usage] lies the judgement, the right and the rule of speech.'

[2] 'Find gold in a dung-heap.'

[3] *A.P.* 47f.: 'You will express yourself most happily, if a skilful setting makes a familiar word new.'

[4] Horace, *Odes* 1.19.8: 'I am enamoured of . . . her face seductive to behold.'

[5] *Satyricon* 118: 'The studied felicity of Horace.'

Shakespeare, Fletcher and *Jonson*: whose Excellencies I can never enough admire, and in this, they have been follow'd especially by Sir *John Suckling* and Mr. *Waller*, who refin'd upon them. Neither have they who now succeed them, been wanting in their endeavours to adorn our Mother Tongue: but it is not so lawful for me to praise my living Contemporaries, as to admire my dead Predecessors.

I should now speak of the Refinement of Wit: but I have been so large on the former Subject that I am forc'd to contract my self in this. I will therefore onely observe to you, that the wit of the last Age, was yet more incorrect than their language. *Shakespeare*, who many times has written better than any Poet, in any Language, is yet so far from writing Wit always, or expressing that Wit according to the Dignity of the Subject, that he writes in many places, below—the dullest Writer of ours, or of any precedent Age. Never did any Author precipitate himself from such heights of thought to so low expressions, as he often does. He is the very *Janus* of Poets; he wears, almost every where two faces: and you have scarce begun to admire the one, ere you despise the other. Neither is the Luxuriance of *Fletcher*, (which his friends have tax'd in him,) a less fault than the carelessness of *Shakespeare*. He does not well always, and, when he does, he is a true *Englishman*; he knows not when to give over. If he wakes in one Scene he commonly slumbers in another: And if he pleases you in the first three Acts, he is frequently so tir'd with his labor, that he goes heavily in the fourth, and sinks under his burden in the fifth.

For *Ben. Jonson*, the most judicious of Poets, he always writ properly, and as the Character requir'd: and I will not contest farther with my Friends who call that Wit. It being very certain, that even folly it self, well represented, is Wit in a larger signification: and that there is Fancy, as well as Judgement in it; though not so much or noble: because all Poetry being imitation, that of Folly is a lower exercise of Fancy, though perhaps as difficult as the other: for 'tis a kind of looking downward in the Poet; and representing that part of Mankind which is below him.

In these low Characters of Vice and Folly, lay the excellency of that inimitable Writer: who, when at any time, he aim'd at Wit, in the stricter sence, that is, Sharpness of Conceit, was forc'd either to borrow from the Ancients, as, to my knowledge he did very much from *Plautus*: or, when he trusted himself alone, often fell into meanness of expression. Nay, he was not free from the lowest and most groveling king of Wit, which we call clenches; of which, *Every Man in his*

Humour, is infinitely full; and, which is worse, the wittiest persons in the *Drama* speak them. His other Comedies are not exempted from them. . . .

This was then the mode of wit, the vice of the Age and not *Ben. Jonson*'s, for you see, a little before him, that admirable wit, Sir *Philip Sidney*, perpetually playing with his words. In his time, I believe, it ascended first into the Pulpit: where (if you will give me leave to clench too) it yet finds the benefit of its Clergy, for they are commonly the first corrupters of Eloquence, and the last reform'd from vicious Oratory: as a famous *Italian* has observ'd before me, in his Treatise of the Corruption of the *Italian Tongue*; which he principally ascribes to Priests and preaching Friars.

But, to conclude with what brevity I can; I will only add this in the defence of our present Writers, that if they reach not some excellencies of *Ben. Jonson*; (which no Age, I am confident, ever shall) yet, at least, they are above that meanness of thought which I have tax'd, and which is frequent in him.

That the wit of this Age is much more Courtly, may easily be prov'd by viewing the Characters of Gentlemen which were written in the last. First, for *Jonson*, *True-Wit* in the *Silent Woman*, was his Master-piece, and *True-wit* was a Scholar-like kind of man, a Gentleman with an allay of Pedantry: a man who seems mortifi'd to the world, by much reading. The best of his discourse, is drawn, not from the knowledge of the Town, but Books, and, in short, he would be a fine Gentleman, in an University. *Shakespeare* show'd the best of his skill in his *Mercutio*, and he said himself, that he was forc'd to kill him in the third Act, to prevent being kill'd by him. But, for my part, I cannot find he was so dangerous a person: I see nothing in him but what was so exceeding harmless, that he might have liv'd to the end of the Play, and dy'd in his bed, without offence to any man.

Fletcher's *Don John* is our onely Bug-bear: and yet, I may affirm, without suspition of flattery, that he now speaks better, and that his Character is maintain'd with much more vigour in the fourth and fifth Acts than it was by *Fletcher* in the three former. I have always acknow-ledg'd the wit of our Predecessors, with all the veneration which becomes me, but, I am sure, their wit was not that of Gentlemen, there was ever somewhat that was ill-bred and Clownish in it: and which confest the conversation of the Authors.

And this leads me to the last and greatest advantage of our writing, which proceeds from conversation. In the Age, wherein those Poets liv'd, there was less of gallantry than in ours; neither did they keep the best company of theirs. Their fortune has been much like that of *Epicurus*, in the retirement of his Gardens: to live almost unknown, and to be celebrated after their decease. I cannot find that any of them were conversant in Courts, except *Ben. Jonson*: and his *genius* lay not so much that way, as to make an improvement by it. Greatness was not, then, so easy of access, nor conversation so free as now it is. I cannot, therefore, conceive it any insolence to affirm, that, by the knowledge, and pattern of their wit, who writ before us, and by the advantage of our own conversation, the discourse and Raillery of our *Comedies* excell what has been written by them, and this will be deny'd by none, but some few old fellows who value themselves on their acquaintance with the *Black-Friars*: who, because they saw their Playes, would pretend a right to judge ours. The memory of these grave Gentlemen is their only Plea for being Wits. They can tell a story of *Ben. Jonson*, and perhaps have had fancy enough to give a supper in *Apollo* that they might be call'd his Sons: and because they were drawn in to be laught at in those times, they think themselves now sufficiently intitled to laugh at ours. Learning I never saw in any of them, and wit no more than they could remember. In short, they were unlucky to have been bred in an unpolish'd Age, and more unlucky to live to a refin'd one. They have lasted beyond their own, and are cast behind ours: and not contented to have known little at the age of twenty, they boast of their ignorance at threescore.

Now, if any ask me, whence it is that our conversation is so much refin'd? I must freely, and without flattery, ascribe it to the Court: and, in it, particularly to the King; whose example gives a law to it. His own mis-fortunes and the Nations, afforded him an opportunity, which is rarely allow'd to Sovereign Princes, I mean of travelling, and being conversant in the most polish'd Courts of *Europe*; and, thereby, of cultivating a Spirit, which was form'd by Nature, to receive the impressions of a gallant and generous education. At his return, he found a Nation lost as much in Barbarism as in Rebellion, and as the excellency of his Nature forgave the one, so the excellency of his manners reform'd the other. The desire of imitating so great a pattern, first waken'd the dull and heavy spirits of the *English*, from their natural reserv'dness: loosen'd them, from their stiff forms of conversation; and made them easy and plyant to each other in discourse. Thus, insensibly, our way of living became more free: and the fire of the English wit, which was before stifled under a constrain'd melancholy way of breeding, began first to display its force: by mixing the solidity of our Nation, with the air and gayety of our neighbours. This being granted to be true, it would be a wonder, if the Poets, whose work is imitation, should be the onely persons in three Kingdoms, who should not receive advantage by it: or, if they should not more easily imitate the wit and conversation of the present age, than of the past.

Let us therefore admire the beauties and the heights of *Shakespeare*, without falling after him into a carelesness and (as I may call it) a Lethargy of thought, for whole Scenes together. Let us imitate, as we are able, the quickness and easiness of *Fletcher*, without proposing him as a pattern to us, either in the redundancy of his matter, or the incorrectness of his language. Let us admire his wit and sharpness of conceit; but, let us at the same time acknowledge that it was seldome so fix'd, and made proper to his characters, as that the same things might not be spoken by any person in the Play. Let us applaud his Scenes of Love; but, let us confess that he understood not either greatness or perfect honour in the parts of any of his women. In fine, let us allow, that he had so much fancy, as when he pleas'd he could write wit: but that he wanted so much Judgment as seldome to have written humour; or describ'd a pleasant folly. Let us ascribe to *Jonson* the height and accuracy of Judgment, in the ordering of his Plots, his choice of characters, and maintaining what he had chosen, to the end; but let us not think him a perfect pattern of imitation, except it be in humour: for Love, which is the foundation of all *Comedies* in other Languages, is scarcely mention'd in any of his Playes, and for humour it self, the Poets of this Age will be more wary than to imitate the meanness of his persons. Gentlemen will now be entertain'd with the follies of each other: and though they allow *Cob* and *Tib* to speak properly, yet they are not much pleas'd with their Tankard or with their Raggs. And, surely, their conversation can be no jest to them on the *Theatre*, when they would avoid it in the street.

To conclude all, let us render to our Predecessors what is their due, without confineing our selves to a servile imitation of all they writ: and, without assuming to our selves the Title of better Poets, let us ascribe to the gallantry and civility of our age the advantage which we have above them; and to our knowledge of the customs and manners of it, the happiness we have to please beyond them. (167–75)

13. Thomas Shadwell?, from the operatic version of *The Tempest* adaptation

1674

From *The Tempest, or the Enchanted Island* (1674).

The ascription of this adaptation to Shadwell (1642?–92) is not certain, despite the authority of John Downes (No. 46 in volume 2). The actor Betterton is another candidate, while some scholars have suggested that it was a collaborative effort. This 'operatic' version (performed on about 30 April 1674) took the Dryden–D'Avenant adaptation and added music and spectacle. The stage directions give some idea of the impressionistic effects sought after: their contemporary success is witnessed by Downes.

[Act I, Scene i.]

The Front of the Stage is open'd, and the Band of 24 Violins, with the Harpsicals and Theorbo's which accompany the Voices, are plac'd between the Pit and the Stage. While the Overture is playing, the Curtain rises, and discovers a new Frontispiece, joyn'd to the great Pylasters, on each side of the Stage. This Frontispiece is a noble Arch, supported by large wreathed Columns of the Corinthian Order; the wreathings of the Columns are beautifi'd with Roses wound round them, and several Cupids flying about them. On the Cornice, just over the Capitals, sits on either side a Figure, with a Trumpet in one hand, and a Palm in the other, representing Fame. A little farther on the same Cornice, on each side of a Compass-pediment, lie a Lion and a Unicorn, the Supporters of the Royal Arms of England. In the middle of the Arch are several Angels, holding the Kings Arms, as if they were placing them in the midst of that Compass-pediment. Behind this is the Scene, which represents a thick Cloudy Sky, a very Rocky Coast, and a Tempestuous Sea in perpetual Agitation. This Tempest (suppos'd to be rais'd by Magick) has many dreadful Objects in it, as several Spirits in horrid shapes flying down amongst the Sailers, then rising and crossing in the Air. And when the Ship is sinking, the whole House is darken'd, and a shower of Fire falls upon 'em. This is accompanied with Lightning, and several Claps of Thunder, to the end of the Storm.

★   ★   ★

[Act I, Scene ii.]

In the midst of the Shower of Fire the Scene changes. The Cloudy Sky, Rocks, and Sea vanish; and when the Lights return, discover that Beautiful part of the Island, which was the habitation of Prospero. *'Tis compos'd of three Walks of Cypress-trees; each Side-walk leads to a Cave, in one of which* Prospero *keeps his Daughters, in the other* Hippolito: *The Middle-Walk is of a great depth, and leads to an open part of the Island.*

★   ★   ★

Ariel. I thank thee, Master.

Prosp. If thou more murmurest, I will rend an Oak,
And peg thee in his knotty entrails, till thou
Hast houl'd away twelve Winters more.

Ariel. Pardon, Master,
I will be correspondent to command, and be
A gentle spirit.

Prosp. Do so, and after two days I'l discharge thee.

Ariel. Thanks, my great Master. But I have yet one request.

Prosp. What's that, my spirit?

Ariel. I know that this days business is important,
Requiring too much toyl for one alone.
I have a gentle spirit for my Love,
Who twice seven years has waited for my freedom:
Let it appear, it will assist me much,
And we with mutual joy shall entertain
Each other. This I beseech you grant me.

Prosp. You shall have your desire.

Ariel. That's my noble Master. *Milcha!*

[Milcha flies down to his assistance.

Milc. I am here, my Love.

Ariel. Thou art free! welcome, my dear! what shall we do?

154

Say, say, what shall we do?
 Prosp.   Be subject to
No sight but mine, invisible to every Eye-ball else.
Hence with diligence, anon thou shalt know more.
        [They both fly up and cross in the air.

    ★ ★ ★

[Act II, Scene i.]

*The Scene changes to the wilder part of the Island; 'tis compos'd of divers
sorts of Trees, and barren places, with a prospect of the Sea at a great
distance.*

    ★ ★ ★

[Act II, Scene iii.] *A wild Island.*

 Alon. O name it not, *Gonzalo;*
No act but penitence can expiate guilt!
Must we teach Heav'n what price to set on Murder?
What rate on lawless Power and wild Ambition?
Or dare we traffick with the Powers above,
And sell by weight a good deed for a bad?
        [A flourish of Musick.
 Gonz. Musick! and in the air! sure we are Shipwrack'd
On the Dominions of some merry Devil!
 Anto. This Isle's Inchanted ground; for I have heard
Swift voices flying by my ear, and groans
Of lamenting ghosts.
 Alon. I pull'd a Tree, and bloud pursu'd my hand.
Heav'n deliver me from this dire place,
And all the after-actions of my life
Shall mark my penitence and my bounty. *[Musick agen lowder.*
Hark, the sounds approach us!

   The Stage opens in several places.

 Anto. Lo the Earth opens to devour us quick.
These dreadful horrors, and the guilty sense
Of my foul Treason, have unmann'd me quite.
 Alon. We on the brink of swift destruction stand;

       155

No means of our escape is left.

[*Another flourish of Voyces under the Stage.*

Anto. Ah! what amazing sounds are these we hear!

Gonz. What horrid Masque will the dire Fiends present?

Sung under the Stage.

1. Dev. Where does the black Fiend Ambition reside,
With the mischievous Devil of Pride?

2. Dev. In the lowest and darkest Caverns of Hell
Both Pride and Ambition does dwell.

1. Dev. Who are the chief Leaders of the damned Host?

3. Dev. Proud Monarchs, who tyrannize most.

1. Dev. Damned Princes there
The worst of torments bear;

3. Dev. Who in Earth all others in pleasures excel,
Must feel the worst torments of Hell.

[*They rise singing this Chorus.*

Anto. Oh Heav'ns! what horrid Vision's this?
How they upbraid us with our crimes!

Alon. What fearful vengeance is in store for us!

1. Dev. Tyrants by whom their Subjects bleed,
Should in pains all others exceed;

2. Dev. And barb'rous Monarchs who their Neighbours invade,
And their Crowns unjustly get;
And such who their Brothers to death have betrai'd,
In Hell upon burning Thrones shall be set.

3. Dev.⎫ ——In Hell, in Hell with flames they shall reign,
Chor. ⎭ And for ever, for ever shall suffer the pain.

Anto. Oh my Soul; for ever, for ever shall suffer the pain.

Alon. Has Heav'n in all its infinite stock of mercy
No overflowings for us? poor, miserable, guilty men!

Gonz. Nothing but horrors do encompass us!
For ever, for ever must we suffer!

Alon. For ever we shall perish! O dismal words, for ever!

1. Dev. Who are the Pillars of the Tyrants Court?

2. Dev. Rapine and Murder his Crown must support!

3. Dev. ——His cruelty does tread
On Orphans tender breasts, and Brothers dead!

2. Dev. Can Heav'n permit such crimes should be
       Attended with felicity?
1. Dev. No Tyrants their Scepters uneasily bear,
      In the midst of their Guards they their Consciences fear.
2. Dev. ⎱ Care their minds when they wake unquiet will keep,
Chor. ⎰ And we with dire visions disturb all their sleep.

Anto. Oh horrid sight! how they stare upon us!
The Fiends will hurry us to the dark Mansion.
Sweet Heav'n, have mercy on us!

[The devils stage the masque of Pride, Fraud, Rapine and Murder,
substantially as above, pp. 88 f.]

            ★   ★   ★

Alonz. Beware all fruit, but what the Birds have peck'd.
The shadows of the Trees are poisonous too:
A secret venom slides from every branch!
My Conscience does distract me! O my Son!
Why do I speak of eating or repose,
Before I know thy fortune?

                    [As they are going out, a Devil rises just before them,
                              at which they start, and are frighted.

Alonz. O Heavens! yet more Apparitions!

Devil sings. Arise, arise! ye subterranean winds,
        More to disturb their guilty minds.
      And all ye filthy damps and vapours rise,
        Which use t' infect the Earth, and trouble all the Skies;
      Rise you, from whom devouring plagues have birth:
      You that i' th' vast and hollow womb of Earth,
      Engender Earthquakes, make whole Countreys shake,
      And stately Cities into Desarts turn;
And you who feed the flames by which Earths entrals burn.
      Ye raging winds, whose rapid force can make
      All but the fix'd and solid Centre shake:
      Come drive these Wretches to that part o' th' Isle,
        Where Nature never yet did smile:

Cause Fogs and Storms, Whirlwinds and Earthquakes there:
There let 'em houl and languish in despair.
Rise and obey the pow'rful Prince o' th' Air.

[*Two Winds rise, Ten more enter and dance: At the end of the
Dance, Three winds sink, the rest drive* Alon. Anto. Gonz. *off.
Act Ends.*

    ★   ★   ★

[Act III, Scene iii.]

    ★   ★   ★

[*Dance of fantastick Spirits; after the Dance, a Table furnish'd with Meat
and Fruit is brought in by two Spirits. . . . Two Spirits descend, and flie
away with the Table.*

    ★   ★   ★

[Act IV, Scene ii.]

    ★   ★   ★

[*A Table rises, and four Spirits with Wine and Meat enter, placing it, as
they dance, on the Table: The Dance ended, the Bottles vanish, and the
Table sinks agen.*

    ★   ★   ★

[Act V, Scene ii.]

    ★   ★   ★

Prosp. Sir, I invite your Highness and your Train
To my poor Cave this night; a part of which
I will employ, in telling you my story.
    Alonz. No doubt it must be strangely taking, Sir.
    Prosp. When the morn draws, I'l bring you to your Ship,
And promise you calm Seas, and happy Gales.
My *Ariel*, that's thy charge: then to the Elements
Be free, and fare thee well.
    Ariel. I'll do it, Master.
    Prosp. Now to make amends

For the rough treatment you have found to day,
I'll entertain you with my Magick Art:
I'll, by my power, transform this place, and call
Up those that shall make good my promise to you.

> [*Scene changes to the Rocks, with the Arch of Rocks,*
> *and calm Sea. Musick playing on the Rocks.*

Prosp. Neptune, and your fair *Amphitrite*, rise;
Oceanus, with your *Tethys* too, appear;
All ye Sea-Gods, and Goddesses, appear!
Come, all ye *Trytons*; all ye *Nereides*, come,
And teach your sawcy Element to obey:
For you have Princes now to entertain,
And unsoil'd Beauties, with fresh youthful Lovers.

> [Neptune, Amphitrite, Oceanus *and* Tethys *appear in a*
> *Chariot drawn with Sea-horses; on each side of the Chariot,*
> *Sea-gods and Goddesses, Tritons and Nereides.*

Alonz. This is prodigious.
Anto. Ah! what amazing Objects do we see!
Gonz. This Art doth much exceed all humane skill.

SONG.

Amph.   My Lord: Great *Neptune*, for my sake,
  On these bright Beauties pity take:
   And to the rest allow
    Your mercy too.
 Let this inraged Element be still,
  Let *Æolus* obey my will:
 Let him his boystrous Prisoners safely keep
  In their dark Caverns, and no more
 Let 'em disturb the bosome of the Deep,
  Till these arrive upon their wish'd-for shore.
Neptune. So much my *Amphitrite*'s love I prize,
  That no commands of hers I can despise.
  Tethys no furrows now shall wear,
  Oceanus no wrinkles on his brow,
  Let your serenest looks appear!
   Be calm and gentle now.

Nep. &⎫ Be calm, ye great Parents of the Flouds and the Springs,
Amph. ⎭ While each *Nereide* and *Triton* Plays, Revels, and Sings.
Oceanus.   Confine the roaring Winds, and we
              Will soon obey you cheerfully
Chorus of ⎫ Tie up the Winds, and we'll obey,   ⎡*Here the Dancers*
Tritons   ⎬ Upon the Flouds we'll sing and play,   ⎨*mingle with the*
and Ner. ⎭ And celebrate a *Halcyon* day.   ⎣*Singers.*
                                                       [*Dance.*

Nept.   Great Nephew *Æolus* make no noise,
              Muzle your roaring Boys.   [*Æolus appears.*
Amph.   Let 'em not bluster to disturb our ears,
              Or strike these Noble Passengers with fears.
Nept.   Afford 'em onely such an easie Gale,
              As pleasantly may swell each Sail.
Amph.   While fell Sea-monsters cause intestine jars,
              This Empire you invade with foreign Wars.
Nept.   But you shall now be still,
              And shall obey my *Amphitrites* will.
Æolus ⎫ You I'll obey, who at one stroke can make,
descends.⎭ With your dread Trident, the whole Earth to quake.
              Come down, my Blusterers, swell no more,
                Your stormy rage give o'r.   ⎧*Winds from the four*
                Let all black Tempests cease—   ⎨*corners appear.*
              And let the troubled Ocean rest:
              Let all the Sea enjoy as calm a peace,
              As where the *Halcyon* builds her quiet Nest.
                To your Prisons below,
                Down, down you must go:
              You in the Earths Entrals your Revels may keep;
              But no more till I call shall you trouble the Deep.
                                                   [*Winds fly down.*
              Now they are gone, all stormy Wars shall cease:
              Then let your Trumpeters proclaim a Peace.
Amph.   *Tritons*, my Sons, your Trumpets sound,
              And let the noise from Neighbouring Shores rebound.
                                        ⎡Sound a Calm.
                                        ⎢Sound a Calm.
                              Chorus.⎨Sound a Calm.
                                        ⎢   a Calm.
                                        ⎣Sound a Calm.

[Here the Trytons, *at every repeat of* Sound a Calm,
*changing their Figure and Postures, seem to sound their
wreathed* Trumpets *made of Shells.*
*A Short Symphony of Musick, like Trumpets, to which
four* Trytons *Dance.*

Nept.   See, see, the Heavens smile, all your troubles are past,
           Your joys by black Clouds shall no more be o'rcast.
Amph. On this barren Isle ye shall lose all your fears
           Leave behind all your sorrows, and banish your cares.
Both.   { And your Loves and your Lives shall in safety enjoy;
         { No influence of Stars shall your quiet destroy.
Chorus { And your Loves, &c.
of all. { No influence, &c.
               [Here the Dancers mingle with the Singers.
Oceanus. We'll safely convey you to your own happy Shore,
           And yours and your Countrey's soft peace we'll restore.
Tethys. To treat you blest Lovers, as you sail on the Deep,
           The *Trytons* and *Sea-Nymphs* their Revels shall keep.
Both.   { On the swift Dolphins backs they shall sing and shall play
         { They shall guard you by night, and delight you by day.
Chorus { On the swift, &c.
of all. { And shall guard, &c.
               [Here the Dancers mingle with the Singers.
                  [A Dance of twelve Tritons.*

Miran. What charming things are these?
Dor. What heavenly power is this?
Prosp. Now, my *Ariel*, be visible
And let the rest of your Aerial Train
Appear, and entertain 'em with a Song;
And then farewell my long lov'd *Ariel*.

*[Scene changes to the Rising Sun, and a number of Aerial Spirits in the
Air.* Ariel *flying from the Sun, advances towards the Pit.*

Alon. Heav'n! what are these we see?
Prosp. They are Spirits, with which the Air abounds
In swarms, but that they are not subject
To poor feeble mortal Eyes:
Anto. O wondrous skill!
Gonz. O power Divine!

Ariel *and the rest sing the following Song.*

Ariel.   Where the Bee sucks, there suck I,
In a Cowslips Bed I lie;
There I couch when Owls do cry.
On the Swallows wings I fly
After Summer merrily.
Merrily, merrily shall I live now,
Under the Blossom that hangs on the Bow.

[*Song ended,* Ariel *speaks, hovering in the Air.*
Ariel. My Noble Master!
May theirs and your blest Joys never impair.
And for the freedom I enjoy in Air,
I will be still your *Ariel,* and wait
On Aiery accidents that work for Fate.
What ever shall your happiness concern,
From your still faithful *Ariel* you shall learn.
Prosp. Thou hast been always diligent and kind!
Farewell, my long lov'd *Ariel,* thou shalt find,
I will preserve thee ever in my mind.
Henceforth this Isle to the afflicted be
A place of Refuge, as it was to me:
The promises of blooming Spring live here,
And all the blessings of the ripening Year.
On my retreat, let Heav'n and Nature smile,
And ever flourish the *Enchanted Isle.*

[*Exeunt.*

14. John Dryden, from *All For Love*

From *All For Love: Or, The World well lost. A Tragedy* . . .
Written in Imitation of Shakespeare's Stile (1678).

Dryden's version of the Antony and Cleopatra story was performed on about 12 December 1667. It is not a proper adaptation,
but contains many echoes and some deliberate imitations. Dryden
observes the unities of place and time (the action opens after the
battle of Actium and is limited to the lovers' last day); the number
of characters is severely reduced (Octavius is omitted); Ventidius
takes over much of the function of Enobarbus as a representative
of Roman duty, and to complete the conventional opposition
between love and honour, Alexas (Cleopatra's eunuch) stands for
the claims of love.

Preface.

The death of *Antony* and *Cleopatra*, is a Subject which has been treated
by the greatest Wits of our Nation, after *Shakespeare*; and by all so
variously, that their example has given me the confidence to try my self
in this Bowe of *Ulysses* amongst the Crowd of Sutors; and, withal,
to take my own measures, in aiming at the Mark. I doubt not but the
same Motive has prevailed with all of us in this attempt; I mean the
excellency of the Moral: for the chief persons represented, were
famous patterns of unlawful love; and their end accordingly was
unfortunate. All reasonable men have long since concluded, That the
Heroe of the Poem, ought not to be a character of perfect Virtue, for,
then, he could not, without injustice, be made unhappy; nor yet
altogether wicked, because he could not then be pitied: I have therefore
steer'd the middle course; and have drawn the character of *Antony*
as favourably as *Plutarch*, *Appian*, and *Dion Cassius* wou'd give me
leave: the like I have observ'd in *Cleopatra*. That which is wanting to
work up the pity to a greater heighth, was not afforded me by the

story: for the crimes of love which they both committed, were not occasion'd by any necessity, or fatal ignorance, but were wholly voluntary; since our passions are, or ought to be, within our power.

The Fabrick of the Play is regular enough, as to the inferior parts of it; and the Unities of Time, Place and Action, more exactly observ'd, than, perhaps, the English Theater requires. Particularly, the Action is so much one, that it is the only of the kind without Episode, or Underplot; every Scene in the Tragedy conducing to the main design, and every Act concluding with a turn of it. The greatest errour in the contrivance seems to be in the person of *Octavia*: For, though I might use the priviledge of a Poet, to introduce her into *Alexandria*, yet I had not enough consider'd, that the compassion she mov'd to her self and children, was destructive to that which I reserv'd for *Antony* and *Cleopatra*; whose mutual love being founded upon vice, must lessen the favour of the Audience to them, when Virtue and Innocence were oppress'd by it. And, though I justified *Antony* in some measure, by making *Octavia*'s departure, to proceed wholly from herself; yet the force of the first Machine still remain'd; and the dividing of pity, like the cutting of a River into many Channels, abated the strength of the natural stream.

∗   ∗   ∗

It remains that I acquaint the Reader, that I have endeavoured in this Play to follow the practise of the Ancients, who, as Mr. *Rymer* has judiciously observ'd, are and ought to be our Masters. . . .

Yet, though their Models are regular, they are too little for English Tragedy; which requires to be built in a larger compass. I could give an instance in the *Oedipus Tyrannus*, which was the Masterpiece of *Sophocles*; but I reserve it for a more fit occasion, which I hope to have hereafter. In my Stile I have profess'd to imitate the Divine *Shakespeare*; which that I might perform more freely, I have dis-incumber'd my self from Rhyme. Not that I condemn my former way, but that this is more proper to my present purpose. I hope I need not to explain my self, that I have not Copy'd my Author servilely: Words and Phrases must of necessity receive a change in succeeding Ages: but 'tis almost a Miracle that much of his Language remains so pure; and that he who began Dramatique Poetry amongst us, untaught by any, and, as *Ben Jonson* tells us, without Learning, should by the force of his own Genius perform so much, that in a manner he has left no praise for any who come after him. The occasion is fair, and the subject would be pleasant to handle the difference of Stiles betwixt him and *Fletcher*, and wherein, and how far they are both to be imitated. But since I must not be over-confident of my own performance after him, it will be prudence in me to be silent. Yet I hope I may affirm, and without vanity, that by imitating him, I have excell'd my self throughout the Play; and particularly, that I prefer the Scene betwixt *Antony* and *Ventidius* in the first Act, to any thing which I have written in this kind.

*　　*　　*

[Prologue]

*　　*　　*

[Our poet] fights this day unarmed,—without his rhyme;—
And brings a tale which often has been told;
As sad as *Dido*'s; and almost as old.
His hero, whom you wits his bully call,
Bates of his mettle, and scarce rants at all:
He's somewhat lewd; but a well-meaning mind;
Weeps much; fights little; but is wond'rous kind.

*　　*　　*

Dramatis Personae

Mark Antony.
Ventidius, his General.
Dolabella, his Friend.
Alexas, the Queen's Eunuch.
Serapion, Priest of Isis.
Myris, another Priest.
Servants to Antony.

Cleopatra, Queen of Egypt.
Octavia, Antony's Wife.
Charmion,⎫
Iras,　　⎬Cleopatra's Maids.
Antony's two little daughters.

SCENE: Alexandria

[Act I, Scene i.] The Temple of Isis.

*   *   *

Alex. . . . Her own Birth-day
Our Queen neglected, like a vulgar Fate,
That pass'd obscurely by.
   Ven. Would it had slept,
Divided far from his; till some remote
And future Age had call'd it out, to ruin
Some other Prince, not him.
   Alex. Your Emperor,
Tho grown unkind, would be more gentle, than
T'upbraid my Queen, for loving him too well.
   Ven. Does the mute Sacrifice upbraid the Priest?
He knows him not his Executioner.
O, she has deck'd his ruin with her love,
Led him in golden bands to gaudy slaughter,
And made perdition pleasing: She has left him
The blank of what he was;
I tell thee, Eunuch, she has quite unman'd him:
Can any Roman see, and know him now,
Thus alter'd from the Lord of half Mankind,
Unbent, unsinew'd, made a Womans Toy,
Shrunk from the vast extent of all his honors,
And crampt within a corner of the World?
O, *Antony*!
Thou bravest Soldier, and thou best of Friends!
Bounteous as Nature; next to Nature's God!
Could'st thou but make new Worlds, so wouldst thou give 'em,
As bounty were thy being. Rough in Battel,
As the first *Romans*, when they went to War;
Yet, after Victory, more pitiful,
Than all their Praying Virgins left at home!
   Alex. Would you could add to those more shining Virtues,
His truth to her who loves him.
   Ven. Would I could not!
But, Wherefore waste I precious hours with thee?

Thou art her darling mischief, her chief Engin,
Antony's other Fate. Go, tell thy Queen,
Ventidius is arriv'd, to end her Charms.
Let your *Ægyptian* Timbrels play alone;
Nor mix Effeminate Sounds with *Roman* Trumpets.
You dare not fight for *Antony*; go Pray,
And keep your Cowards-Holyday in Temples.　　　[*Exeunt* Alex.
　　　　　　　　　　　　　　　　　　　　　　　Serap.
Enter a Gentleman of M. Antony.

2. Gent. The Emperor approaches, and commands,
On pain of Death, that none presume to stay.
1. Gent. I dare not disobey him.　　　[*Going out with the other.*
Vent. Well, I dare.
But, I'll observe him first unseen, and find
Which way his humour drives: the rest I'll venture.　　　[*Withdraws.*

Enter Antony, *walking with a disturb'd Motion, before he speaks.*

Antony. They tell me, 'tis my Birth-day, and I'll keep it
With double pomp of sadness.
'Tis what the day deserves, which gave me breath.
Why was I rais'd the Meteor of the World,
Hung in the Skies, and blazing as I travel'd,
Till all my fires were spent; and then cast downward
To be trod out by *Cæsar*?
Ven. aside. On my Soul,
'Tis mournful, wondrous mournful!
Ant. Count thy gains.
Now, *Antony*, Wouldst thou be born for this?
Glutton of Fortune, thy devouring youth
Has starv'd thy wanting Age.
Ven. How sorrow shakes him!　　　　　　　　　　　[*Aside.*
So, now the Tempest tears him up by th' Roots,
And on the ground extends the noble ruin.
Ant. having thrown himself down. Lye there, thou shadow of an
　　　　　　　　　　　　　　　　　Emperor;
The place thou pressest on thy Mother Earth
Is all thy Empire now: now it contains thee;
Some few dayes hence, and then twill be too large,
When thou'rt contracted in thy narrow Urn,

Shrunk to a few cold Ashes; then *Octavia*,
(For *Cleopatra* will not live to see it)
Octavia then will have thee all her own,
And bear thee in her Widow'd hand to *Cæsar*;
Cæsar will weep, the Crocodile will weep,
To see his Rival of the Universe
Lye still and peaceful there. I'll think no more on't.
Give me some Musick; look that it be sad:
I'll sooth my Melancholy, till I swell,
And burst myself with sighing.——   [*Soft Musick.*
'Tis somewhat to my humor. Stay, I fancy
I'm now turn'd wild, a Commoner of Nature;
Of all forsaken, and forsaking all;
Live in a shady Forrest's *Sylvan* Scene,
Stretch'd at my length beneath some blasted Oke;
I lean my head upon the Mossy Bark,
And look just of a piece, as I grew from it:
My uncomb'd Locks, matted like *Misleto*,
Hang o're my hoary Face; a murm'ring Brook
Runs at my foot.

    Ven.   Methinks I fancy   [*Aside.*
Myself there too.

    Ant.   The Herd come jumping by me,
And fearless, quench their thirst, while I look on,
And take me for their fellow-Citizen.
More of this Image, more; it lulls my thoughts.

                    [*Soft Musick again.*

    Ven. I must disturb him; I can hold no longer.   [*Stands before him.*
    Ant. starting up. Art thou *Ventidius*?
    Ven. Are you *Antony*?
I'm liker what I was, than you to him
I left you last.
    Ant. I'm angry.
    Vent. So am I.
    Ant. I would be private: leave me.
    Ven. Sir, I love you,
And therefore will not leave you.
    Ant. Will not leave me?
Where have you learnt that Answer? Who am I?
    Ven. My Emperor; the Man I love next Heaven:

If I said more, I think 'twere scarce a Sin;
Y'are all that's good, and god-like.
 Ant. All that's wretched.
You will not leave me then?
 Ven. 'Twas too presuming
To say I would not; but I dare not leave you:
And, 'tis unkind in you to chide me hence
So soon, when I so far have come to see you.
 Ant. Now thou hast seen me, art thou satisfy'd?
For, if a Friend, thou hast beheld enough;
And, if a Foe, too much.
 Ven. weeping. Look, Emperor, this is no common Deaw,
I have not wept this Forty year; but now
My Mother comes afresh into my eyes;
I cannot help her softness.
 Ant. By Heav'n, he weeps; poor good old Man, he weeps!
The big round drops course one another down
The furrows of his cheeks. Stop 'em, *Ventidius*,
Or I shall blush to death: they set my shame,
That caus'd 'em, full before me.
 Ven. I'll do my best.
 Ant. Sure there's contagion in the tears of Friends:
See, I have caught it too. Believe me, 'tis not
For my own griefs, but thine.———Nay, Father!
 Ven. Emperor?
 Ant. Emperor! Why, that's the stile of Victory.
The Conqu'ring Soldier, red with unfelt wounds,
Salutes his General so: but never more
Shall that sound reach my ears.
 Ven. I warrant you.
 Ant. Actium, Actium! Oh—
 Ven. It sits too near you.
 Ant. Here, here it lies; a lump of Lead by day,
And, in my short distracted nightly slumbers,
The Hag that rides my Dreams———
 Ven. Out with it; give it vent.
 Ant. Urge not my shame.
I lost a Battel.
 Ven. So has *Julius* done.
 Ant. Thou favour'st me, and speak'st not half thou think'st;

For *Julius* fought it out, and lost it fairly:
But *Antony*———
   Ven. Nay, stop not!
   Ant. Antony,
(Well, thou wilt have it) like a coward, fled,
Fled while his Soldiers fought; fled first, *Ventidius.*
Thou long'st to curse me, and I give thee leave.
I know thou cam'st prepar'd to rail.
   Ven. I did.
   Ant. I'll help thee.—I have been a Man, *Ventidius,—*
   Ven. Yes, and a brave one; but———
   Ant. I know thy meaning.
But, I have lost my Reason, have disgrac'd
The name of Soldier, with inglorious ease.
In the full Vintage of my flowing honors,
Sate still, and saw it prest by other hands.
Fortune came smiling to my youth, and woo'd it,
And purple greatness met my ripen'd years.
When first I came to Empire, I was born
On Tides of People, crouding to my Triumphs:
The wish of Nations; and the willing World
Receiv'd me as its pledge of future peace;
I was so great, so happy, so belov'd,
Fate could not ruine me; till I took pains
And work'd against my Fortune, chid her from me,
And turn'd her loose; yet still she came again.
My careless dayes, and my luxurious nights,
At length have weary'd her, and now she's gone,
Gone, gone, divorc'd for ever. Help me, Soldier,
To curse this Mad-man, this industrious Fool,
Who labour'd to be wretched: pr'ythee curse me.
   Ven. No.
   Ant. Why?
   Ven. You are too sensible already
Of what y'have done, too conscious of your failings,
And like a Scorpion, whipt by others first
To fury, sting your self in mad revenge.
I would bring Balm, and pour it in your wounds,
Cure your distemper'd mind, and heal your fortunes.
   Ant. I know thou would'st,

Ven. I will.

Ant. Ha, ha, ha, ha!

Ven. You laugh.

Ant. I do, to see officious love
Give Cordials to the dead.

Ven. You would be lost then?

Ant. I am.

Ven. I say, you are not. Try your fortune.

Ant. I have, to th'utmost. Dost thou think me desperate?
Without just cause? No, when I found all lost
Beyond repair, I hid me from the World,
And learnt to scorn it here; which now I do
So heartily, I think it is not worth
The cost of keeping.

Ven. Cæsar thinks not so:
He'l thank you for the gift he could not take.
You would be kill'd, like *Tully*, would you? do,
Hold out your Throat to *Cæsar*, and dye tamely!

Ant. No, I can kill my self; and so resolve.

Ven. I can dy with you too, when time shall serve;
But Fortune calls upon us now to live,
To fight, to Conquer.

Ant. Sure thou Dream'st, *Ventidius.*

Ven. No; 'tis you Dream; you sleep away your hours
In desperate sloth, miscall'd *Phylosophy.*
Up, up, for Honor's sake; twelve Legions wait you,
And long to call you Chief: by painful journeys,
I led 'em, patient, both of heat and hunger,
Down from the *Parthian* Marches, to the *Nile.*
'Twill do you good to see their Sun-burnt faces,
Their skar'd cheeks, and chopt hands; there's virtue in 'em,
They'l sell those mangled limbs at dearer rates
Than yon trim Bands can buy.

Ant. Where left you them?

Ven. I said, in lower *Syria.*

Ant. Bring 'em hither;
There may be life in these.

Ven. They will not come.

Ant. Why did'st thou mock my hopes with promis'd aids
To double my despair? They'r mutinous.

Ven. Most firm and loyal.

Ant. Yet they will not march
To succor me. Oh trifler!

Ven. They petition
You would make hast to head 'em.

Ant. I'm besieg'd.

Ven. There's but one way shut up: How came I hither?

Ant. I will not stir.

Ven. They would perhaps desire
A better reason.

Ant. I have never us'd
My Soldiers to demand a reason of
My actions. Why did they refuse to March?

Ven. They said they would not fight for *Cleopatra*.

Ant. What was't they said?

Ven. They said, they would not fight for *Cleopatra*.
Why should they fight indeed, to make her Conquer,
And make you more a Slave? to gain you Kingdoms,
Which, for a kiss, at your next midnight Feast,
You'l sell to her? then she new names her Jewels,
And calls this Diamond such or such a Tax,
Each Pendant in her ear shall be a Province.

Ant. Ventidius, I allow your Tongue free licence
On all my other faults; but, on your life,
No word of *Cleopatra*: She deserves
More Worlds than I can lose.

Ven. Behold, you Pow'rs,
To whom you have intrusted Humankind;
See *Europe*, *Africk*, *Asia* put in ballance,
And all weigh'd down by one light worthless Woman!
I think the gods are *Antony's*, and give
Like Prodigals, this neather World away,
To none but wastful hands.

Ant. You grow presumptuous.

Ven. I take the priviledge of plain love to speak.

Ant. Plain love! plain arrogance, plain insolence:
Thy Men are Cowards; thou, an envious Traitor,
Who, under seeming honesty, hast vented
The burden of thy rank o'reflowing Gall.
O that thou wert my equal; great in Arms

As the first *Cæsar* was, that I might kill thee
Without a Stain to Honor!
   Ven. You may kill me;
You have done more already, call'd me Traitor.
   Ant. Art thou not one?
   Ven. For showing you your self,
Which none else durst have done; but had I been
That name, which I disdain to speak again,
I needed not have sought your abject fortunes,
Come to partake your fate, to dye with you.
What hindred me t' have led my Conqu'ring Eagles
To fill *Octavius*'s Bands? I could have been
A Traitor then, a glorious happy Traitor,
And not have been so call'd.
   Ant. Forgive me, Soldier:
I've been too passionate.
   Ven. You thought me false;
Thought my old age betray'd you: kill me, Sir,
Pray kill me; yet you need not, your unkindness
Has left your Sword no work.
   Ant. I did not think so;
I said it in my rage: pr'ythee forgive me:
Why did'st thou tempt my anger, by discovery
Of what I would not hear?
   Ven. No Prince but you,
Could merit that sincerity I us'd,
Nor durst another Man have ventur'd it;
But you, ere Love misled your wandring eyes,
Were sure the chief and best of Human Race,
Fram'd in the very pride and boast of Nature,
So perfect, that the gods who form'd you wonder'd
At their own skill, and cryd, A lucky hit
Has mended our design. Their envy hindred,
Else you had been immortal, and a pattern,
When Heav'n would work for ostentation sake,
To copy out again.
   Ant. But *Cleopatra*————
Go on; for I can bear it now.
   Ven. No more.
   Ant. Thou dar'st not trust my Passion; but thou may'st:

Thou only lov'st; the rest have flatter'd me.

Ven. Heav'n's blessing on your heart, for that kind word.
May I believe you love me? speak again.

Ant. Indeed I do. Speak this, and this, and this.   [*Hugging him.*
Thy praises were unjust; but, I'll deserve 'em,
And yet mend all. Do with me what thou wilt;
Lead me to victory, thou know'st the way!

Ven. And, Will you leave this——

Ant. Pr'ythee do not curse her,
And I will leave her; though, Heav'n knows, I love
Beyond Life, Conquest, Empire; all, but Honor:
But I will leave her.

Ven. That's my Royal Master.
And, Shall we fight?

Ant. I warrant thee, old Soldier,
Thou shalt behold me once again in Iron,
And at the head of our old Troops, that beat
The *Parthians*, cry alloud, Come follow me.

Ven. O now I hear my Emperor! in that word
Octavius fell. Gods, let me see that day,
And, if I have ten years behind, take all;
I'll thank you for th' exchange.

Ant. Oh *Cleopatra*!

Ven. Again?

Ant. I've done: in that last sigh, she went.
Cæsar shall know what 'tis to force a Lover,
From all he holds most dear.

Ven. Methinks you breathe
Another Soul: Your looks are more Divine;
You speak a Heroe, and you move a God.

Ant. O, thou hast fir'd me; my Soul's up in Arms,
And Mans each part about me: once again,
That noble eagerness of fight has seiz'd me;
That eagerness, with which I darted upward
To *Cassius*'s Camp: In vain the steepy Hill,
Oppos'd my way; in vain a War of Speares
Sung round my head; and planted all my shield:
I won the Trenches, while my formost Men
Lag'd on the Plain below.

Ven. Ye Gods, ye Gods,

For such another hour!
   Ant. Come on, My Soldier!
Our hearts and armes are still the same: I long
Once more to meet our foes; that Thou and I,
Like Time and Death, marching before our Troops,
May taste fate to 'em; Mowe 'em out a passage,
And, entring where the foremost Squadrons yield,
Begin the noble Harvest of the Field.   [*Exeunt.*

★   ★   ★

[Act III, Scene i.] The Palace.

★   ★   ★

   Ant. . . . Canst thou remember
When, swell'd with hatred, thou beheld'st her first
As accessary to thy Brothers death?
   Dolla. Spare my remembrance; 'twas a guilty day,
And still the blush hangs here.
   Ant. To clear her self,
For sending him no aid, she came from *Egypt.*
Her Gally down the Silver *Cydnos* row'd,
The Tackling Silk, the Streamers wav'd with Gold,
The gentle Winds were lodg'd in Purple sails:
Her Nymphs, like *Nereids,* round her Couch, were plac'd;
Where she, another Sea-born *Venus,* lay.
   Dolla. No more: I would not hear it.
   Ant. O, you must!
She lay, and leant her cheek upon her hand,
And cast a look so languishingly sweet,
As if, secure of all beholders hearts,
Neglecting she could take 'em. Boys, like *Cupids,*
Stood fanning, with their painted wings, the winds
That plaid about her face: but if she smil'd,
A darting glory seem'd to blaze abroad:
That mens desiring eyes were never weary'd;
But hung upon the object. To soft Flutes
The Silver Oars kept time; and while they plaid,
The hearing gave new pleasure to the sight;

175

And both to thought. 'Twas Heav'n, or somewhat more;
For she so charm'd all hearts, that gazing crowds
Stood panting on the shore, and wanted breath
To give their welcome voice.
Then, *Dollabella*, where was then thy Soul?
Was not thy fury quite disarm'd with wonder?
Didst thou not shrink behind me from those eyes,
And whisper in my ear, Oh tell her not
That I accus'd her of my Brothers death?
    Dolla. And should my weakness be a plea for yours?
Mine was an age when love might be excus'd,
When kindly warmth, and when my springing youth
Made it a debt to Nature. Yours——
    Ven. Speak boldly.
Yours, he would say, in your declining age,
When no more heat was left but what you forced,
When all the sap was needful for the trunk,
When it went down, then you constrained the course,
And robbed from nature, to supply desire;
In you (I would not use so harsh a word)
'Tis but plain dotage.

*   *   *

[Act V, Scene i.] The Palace.

*   *   *

    Ant. 'Tis too plain;
Else wou'd she have appear'd, to clear her self.
    Alex. Too fatally she has; she could not bear
To be accus'd by you; but shut her self
Within her Monument: look'd down, and sigh'd;
While, from her unchang'd face, the silent tears
Dropt, as they had not leave, but stole their parting.
Some undistinguish'd words she inly murmur'd;
At last, she rais'd her eyes; and, with such looks
As dying *Lucrece* cast,——
    Ant. My heart forebodes.——
    Ven. All for the best: go on.

Alex. She snatch'd her Ponyard,
And, ere we cou'd prevent the fatal blow,
Plung'd it within her breast: then turn'd to me,
Go, bear my Lord (said she) my last Farewel;
And ask him if he yet suspect my Faith.
More she was saying, but death rush'd betwixt.
She half pronounc'd your Name with her last breath,
And bury'd half within her.
   Ven. Heav'n be prais'd!
   Ant. Then art thou innocent, my poor dear Love?
And art thou dead?
O those two words! their sound shou'd be divided:
Hadst thou been false, and dy'd; or hadst thou liv'd,
And hadst been true—— But Innocence and Death!
This shows not well above. Then what am I,
The Murderer of this Truth, this Innocence!
Thoughts cannot form themselves in words so horrid
As can express my guilt!
   Ven. Is't come to this? The Gods have been too gracious:
And thus you thank 'em for't.
   Ant. to Alex. Why stay'st thou here?
Is it for thee to spy upon my Soul,
And see its inward mourning? Get thee hence;
Thou art not worthy to behold, what now
Becomes a *Roman* Emperor to perform.
   Alex. aside. He loves her still:
His grief betrays it. Good! The joy to find
She's yet alive, compleats the reconcilement.
I've sav'd my self, and her. But, Oh! the *Romans*!
Fate comes too fast upon my Wit,
Hunts me too hard, and meets me at each double.   [*Exit.*
   Ven. Wou'd she had dy'd a little sooner, tho,
Before *Octavia* went; you might have treated:
Now 'twill look tame, and wou'd not be receiv'd.
Come, rouze your self, and lets die warm together.
   Ant. I will not fight: there's no more work for War.
The bus'ness of my angry hours is done.
   Ven. Cæsar is at your Gates.
   Ant. Why, let him enter;
He's welcom now.

Ven. What Lethargy has crept into your Soul?

Ant. 'Tis but a scorn of life, and just desire
To free my self from bondage.

Ven. Do it bravely.

Ant. I will; but not by fighting. O, *Ventidius*!
What shou'd I fight for now? My Queen is dead.
I was but great for her; my Pow'r, my Empire,
Were but my Merchandise to buy her love;
And conquer'd Kings, my Factors. Now she's dead,
Let *Cæsar* take the World,———
An Empty Circle, since the Jewel's gone
Which made it worth my strife: my being's nauseous;
For all the bribes of life are gone away.

Ven. Wou'd you be taken?

Ant. Yes, I wou'd be taken;
But, as a *Roman* ought, dead, my *Ventidius*:
For I'll convey my Soul from *Cæsar*'s reach,
And lay down life my self. 'Tis time the World
Shou'd have a Lord, and know whom to obey.
We two have kept its homage in suspence,
And bent the Globe on whose each side we trod,
Till it was dinted inwards: Let him walk
Alone upon 't; I'm weary of my part.
My Torch is out; and the World stands before me
Like a black Desart, at th' approach of night:
I'll lay me down, and stray no farther on.

Ven. I cou'd be griev'd,
But that I'll not out-live you. Choose your death;
For, I have seen him in such various shapes,
I care not which I take: I'm only troubled
The life I bear, is worn to such a rag,
'Tis scarce worth giving. I cou'd wish indeed
We threw it from us with a better grace;
That, like two Lyons taken in the Toils,
We might at least thrust out our paws, and wound
The Hunters that inclose us.

Ant. I have thought on't.
Ventidius, you must live.

Ven. I must not, Sir.

Ant. Wilt thou not live, to speak some good of me?

To stand by my fair Fame, and guard th' approaches
From the ill Tongues of Men?
    Ven. Who shall guard mine,
For living after you?
    Ant. Say, I command it.
    Ven. If we die well, our deaths will speak themselves,
And need no living witness.
    Ant. Thou hast lov'd me,
And fain I wou'd reward thee: I must die;
Kill me, and take the merit of my death
To make thee Friends with *Cæsar.*
    Ven. Thank your kindness.
You said I lov'd you; and, in recompence,
You bid me turn a Traitor: did I think
You wou'd have us'd me thus? that I shou'd die
With a hard thought of you?
    Ant. Forgive me, *Roman.*
Since I have heard of *Cleopatra*'s death,
My reason bears no rule upon my tongue,
But lets my thoughts break all at random out:
I've thought better; do not deny me twice.
    Ven. By Heav'n, I will not.
Let it not be t'out-live you.
    Ant. Kill me first,
And then die thou: for 'tis but just thou serve
Thy Friend, before thy self.
    Ven. Give me your hand.
We soon shall meet again. Now, Farewel, Emperor!   [*Embrace.*
Methinks that word's too cold to be my last:
Since Death sweeps all distinctions, Farewel, Friend.
That's all.———
I will not make a bus'ness of a trifle:
And yet I cannot look on you, and kill you;
Pray turn your face.
    Ant. I do: strike home be sure.
    Ven. Home, as my Sword will reach.   [*Kills himself.*
    Ant. O, thou mistak'st;
That wound was none of thine: give it me back:
Thou robb'st me of my death.
    Ven. I do indeed;

179

But, think 'tis the first time I e'er deceiv'd you;
If that may plead my pardon. And you, Gods,
Forgive me, if you will; for I die perjur'd,
Rather than kill my Friend.   [*Dies.*

   Ant. Farewel! Ever my Leader, ev'n in death!
My Queen and thou have got the start of me,
And I'm the lag of Honour.——Gone so soon?
Is death no more? He us'd him carelessly,
With a familiar kindness: ere he knock'd,
Ran to the door, and took him in his arms,
As who shou'd say, Y'are welcome at all hours,
A Friend need give no warning. Books had spoil'd him;
For all the Learn'd are Cowards by profession.
'Tis not worth
My farther thought; for death, for ought I know,
Is but to think no more. Here's to be satisfi'd.

[*Falls on his Sword.*

I've mist my heart. O unperforming hand!
Thou never cou'dst have err'd in a worse time.
My Fortune jades me to the last; and death,
Like a great Man, takes state, and makes me wait
For my admittance.——   [*Trampling within.*
Some perhaps from *Cæsar*:
If he shou'd find me living, and suspect
That I plaid booty with my life! I'll mend
My work, ere they can reach me.   [*Rises upon his knees.*

Enter Cleopatra, Charmion, Iras.

   Cleop. Where is my Lord? where is he?
   Char. There he lies,
And dead *Ventidius* by him.
   Cleop. My fears were Prophets; I am come too late.
O that accurs'd *Alexas*!   [*Runs to him.*
   Ant. Art thou living?
Or am I dead before I knew? and thou
The first kind Ghost that meets me?
   Cleop. Help me seat him.
Send quickly, send for help.   [*They place him in a Chair.*
   Ant. I am answer'd.

We live both. Sit thee down, my *Cleopatra*:
I'll make the most I can of life, to stay
A moment more with thee.
   Cleop. How is it with you?
   Ant. 'Tis as with a man
Removing in a hurry; all pack'd up,
But one dear Jewel that his haste forgot;
And he, for that, returns upon the spur:
So I come back, for thee.
   Cleop. Too long, you Heav'ns, you have been cruel to me;
Now show your mended Faith, and give me back
His fleeting life.
   Ant. It will not be, my Love.
I keep my Soul by force.
Say but thou art not false.
   Cleop. 'Tis now too late
To say I'm true: I'll prove it, and die with you.
Unknown to me, *Alexas* feign'd my death:
Which, when I knew, I hasted, to prevent
This fatal consequence. My Fleet betray'd
Both you and me.
   Ant. And *Dollabella*?———
   Cleop. Scarce esteem'd before he lov'd; but hated now.
   Ant. Enough: my life's not long enough for more.
Thou sayst thou wilt come after: I believe thee;
For I can now believe whate'er thou sayst,
That we may part more kindly.
   Cleop. I will come:
Doubt not, my life, I'll come, and quickly too:
Cæsar shall triumph o'er no part of thee.
   Ant. But grieve not, while thou stay'st
My last disastrous times:
Think we have had a clear and glorious day;
And Heav'n did kindly to delay the storm
Just till our close of ev'ning. Ten years love,
And not a moment lost, but all improv'd
To th' utmost joys: What Ages have we liv'd!
And now to die each others; and, so dying,
While hand in hand we walk in Groves below,
Whole Troops of Lovers Ghosts shall flock about us,

And all the Train be ours.

    Cleop. Your words are like the Notes of dying Swans,
Too sweet to last. Were there so many hours
For your unkindness, and not one for love?

    Ant. No, not a minute.——This one kiss——more worth
Than all I leave to *Cæsar*.   [*Dies.*

    Cleop. O, tell me so again,
And take ten thousand kisses, for that word.
My Lord, my Lord: speak, if you yet have being;
Sigh to me, if you cannot speak; or cast
One look: Do any thing that shows you live.

    Iras. He's gone too far, to hear you;
And this you see, a lump of sensless Clay,
The leavings of a Soul.

    Char. Remember, Madam,
He charg'd you not to grieve.

    Cleop. And I'll obey him.
I have not lov'd a *Roman* not to know
What should become his Wife; his Wife, my *Charmion*!
For 'tis to that high Title I aspire,
And now I'll not die less. Let dull *Octavia*
Survive, to mourn him dead: my Nobler Fate
Shall knit our Spousals with a tie too strong
For *Roman* Laws to break.

    Iras. Will you then die?

    Cleop. Why shou'dst thou make that question?

    Iras. Cæsar is merciful.

    Cleop. Let him be so
To those that want his mercy: my poor Lord
Made no such Cov'nant with him, to spare me
When he was dead. Yield me to *Cæsar*'s pride?
What, to be led in triumph through the Streets,
A spectacle to base *Plebeian* eyes;
While some dejected Friend of *Antony*'s,
Close in a corner, shakes his head, and mutters
A secret curse on her who ruin'd him?
I'll none of that.

    Char. Whatever you resolve,
I'll follow ev'n to death.

    Iras. I only fear'd

For you; but more shou'd fear to live without you.

   Cleop. Why, now 'tis as it shou'd be. Quick, my Friends,
Dispatch; ere this, the Town's in *Cæsar*'s hands:
My Lord looks down concern'd, and fears my stay,
Lest I shou'd be surpriz'd;
Keep him not waiting for his love too long.
You, *Charmion*, bring my Crown and richest Jewels,
With 'em, the Wreath of Victory I made
(Vain Augury!) for him who now lies dead;
You, *Iras*, bring the cure of all our ills.

   Iras. The Aspicks, Madam?

   Cleop. Must I bid you twice?

                         [*Exeunt* Char. *and* Iras.

'Tis sweet to die, when they wou'd force life on me,
To rush into the dark aboad of death,
And seize him first; if he be like my Love,
He is not frightful sure.
We're now alone, in secresie and silence;
And is not this like Lovers? I may kiss
These pale, cold lips; *Octavia* does not see me;
And, Oh! 'tis better far to have him thus,
Than see him in her arms.——O welcome, welcome.

Enter Charmion, Iras.

   Char. What must be done?

   Cleop. Short Ceremony, Friends;
But yet it must be decent. First, this Laurel
Shall crown my Hero's Head: he fell not basely,
Nor left his Shield behind him.—Only thou
Cou'dst triumph o'er thy self; and thou alone
Wert worthy so to triumph.

   Char. To what end
These Ensigns of your Pomp and Royalty?

   Cleop. Dull, that thou art! why, 'tis to meet my Love;
As when I saw him first, on *Cydnos* bank,
All sparkling, like a Goddess; so adorn'd,
I'll find him once again: my second Spousals
Shall match my first in Glory. Haste, haste, both,
And dress the Bride of *Antony*.

Char. 'Tis done.

Cleop. Now seat me by my Lord. I claim this place;
For I must conquer *Cæsar* too, like him,
And win my share o'th' World. Hail, you dear Relicks
Of my Immortal Love!
O let no Impious hand remove you hence;
But rest for ever here: let *Egypt* give
His death that peace, which it deny'd his life.
Reach me the Casket.

 Iras. Underneath the fruit the Aspick lies.

 Cleop. putting aside the leaves. Welcom, thou kind Deceiver!
Thou best of Thieves; who, with an easie key,
Dost open life, and, unperceiv'd by us,
Ev'n steal us from our selves: discharging so
Death's dreadful office, better than himself,
Touching our limbs so gently into slumber,
That Death stands by, deceiv'd by his own Image,
And thinks himself but Sleep.

 Serap. within. The Queen, where is she?
The Town is yielded, *Cæsar*'s at the Gates.

 Cleop. He comes too late t' invade the Rights of Death.
Haste, bare my Arm, and rouze the Serpent's fury.

       [Holds out her Arm, and draws it back.

Coward Flesh——
Wou'dst thou conspire with *Cæsar*, to betray me,
As thou wert none of mine? I'll force thee to't,
And not be sent by him,
But bring my self my Soul to *Antony*.

       [Turns aside, and then shows her Arm bloody.

Take hence; the work is done.

 Serap. within. Break ope the door,
And guard the Traitor well.

 Char. The next is ours.

 Iras. Now, *Charmion*, to be worthy
Of our great Queen and Mistress.   *[They apply the Aspicks.*

 Cleop. Already, Death, I feel thee in my Veins;
I go with such a will to find my Lord,
That we shall quickly meet.

A heavy numness creeps through every limb,
And now 'tis at my head: my eye-lids fall,
And my dear Love is vanish'd in a mist.
Where shall I find him, where? O turn me to him,
And lay me on his breast.——*Cæsar*, thy worst;
Now part us, if thou canst.

> [*Dies*. Iras *sinks down at her feet, and dies;* Charmion *stands
> behind her Chair, as dressing her head.*

Enter Serapion, *two Priests,* Alexas *bound, Egyptians.*

2. Priests. Behold, *Serapion*, what havock Death has made!
    Serap. 'Twas what I fear'd.
Charmion, is this well done?
    Char. Yes, 'tis well done, and like a Queen, the last
Of her great Race: I follow her.   [*Sinks down; Dies.*
    Alexas. 'Tis true,
She has done well: much better thus to die,
Than live to make a Holy-day in *Rome*.
    Serap. See, see how the Lovers sit in State together,
As they were giving Laws to half Mankind.
Th' impression of a smile left in her face,
Shows she dy'd pleas'd with him for whom she liv'd,
And went to charm him in another World.
Cæsar's just entring; grief has now no leisure.
Secure that Villain, as our pledge of safety
To grace th'Imperial Triumph. Sleep, blest Pair,
Secure from humane chance, long Ages out,
While all the Storms of Fate fly o'er your Tomb;
    And Fame, to late Posterity, shall tell,
    No Lovers liv'd so great, or dy'd so well.

15. Thomas Rymer, from *The Tragedies of the Last Age*

1677

From *The Tragedies of the Last Age Consider'd and Examin'd by the Practice of the Ancients, and by the Common Sense of all Ages* (1677).

Thomas Rymer (1641–1713) was an antiquary and archaeologist (he became Historiographer Royal in 1693) who is best remembered for his *Foedera*, a great collection of treaties between English rulers and foreign powers. His ambitions as a dramatist were thwarted by the failure of his rhymed heroic tragedy *Edgar*. Before turning to his real occupation he delivered himself of his grievances against English drama.

---

*   *   *

I would not examin the *proportions*, the *unities* and *outward* regularities, the *mechanical part* of Tragedies: there is no talking of Beauties when there wants Essentials; 'tis not necessary for a man to have a nose on his face, nor to have two legs: he may be a *true* man, though aukward and unsightly, as the *Monster* in the *Tempest*.

Nor have I much troubl'd their phrase and expression. I have not vex'd their language with the *doubts*, the *remarks* and eternal triflings of the *French Grammaticasters*: much less have I cast about for Jests, and gone a quibble-catching.

I have chiefly consider'd the *Fable* or *Plot*, which all conclude to be the *Soul* of a *Tragedy*; which, with the *Ancients*, is always found to be a *reasonable Soul*; but *with us*, for the most part, a *brutish*, and often worse than *brutish*. (3–4)

*   *   *

These objectors urge, that there is also another great *accident*, which is, that *Athens* and *London* have not the same *Meridian*.

186

Certain it is, that *Nature* is the same, and *Man* is the same; he *loves, grieves, hates, envies,* has the same *affections* and *passions* in both places, and the same *springs* that give them *motion.* What mov'd *pity* there, will *here* also produce the same effect.

This must be confest, unless they will, in effect, say that we have not that *delicate tast* of things; we are not so *refin'd,* nor so *vertuous;* that *Athens* was more *civiliz'd* by their *Philosophers,* than we with both our *Philosophers* and *twelve Apostles.*

But were it to be suppos'd that *Nature* with us is a *corrupt* and deprav'd *Nature,* that we are *Barbarians,* and *humanity* dwells not amongst us; shall our *Poet* therefore pamper this *corrupt* nature, and indulge our barbarity? Shall he not rather *purge* away the corruption, and reform our *manners?* (6–7)

★   ★   ★

[Rymer then surveys the history of tragedy]

After much new-modelling, many changes and alterations, *Æschylus* came with a *second* Actor on the Stage, and lessen'd the business of the *Chorus* proportionably. But *Sophocles* adding a *third* Actor, and *painted* Scenes, gave (in *Aristotle*'s opinion,) the utmost *perfection* to Tragedy.

And now it was that (the *men* of *sense* grown weary with discoursing of *Atoms* and *empty Space,* and the *humour* of *Mechanical* Philosophy near spent) *Socrates* set up for *Morality,* and all the buz in *Athens* was now about vertue and good life.

Comrades with him, and Confederates in his worthy design, were our *Sophocles* and *Euripides*: But these took a different method.

He instructed in a pleasant facetious manner, by witty *questions, allusions* and *parables.*

These were for teaching by *examples,* in a graver way, yet extremely *pleasant* and *delightful.* And, finding in History, the same *end* happen to the *righteous* and to the *unjust, vertue* often opprest, and *wickedness* on the Throne: they saw these particular *yesterday-truths* were imperfect and unproper to illustrate the *universal* and *eternal truths* by them intended. Finding also that this *unequal* distribution of rewards and punishments did perplex the *wisest,* and by the *Atheist* was made a scandal to the *Divine Providence,* They concluded, that a *Poet* must of necessity see *justice* exactly administred, if he intended to please. For, said they, if the World can scarce be satisfie'd with God Almighty, whose holy will and purposes are not to be *comprehended*; a *Poet* (in these matters) shall never be pardon'd, who (they are sure) is not *incomprehensible*; whose *ways* and *walks* may, without *impiety*, be penetrated and examin'd. They knew indeed, that many things naturally unpleasant to the World in *themselves*, yet gave *delight* when well *imitated*. These they consider'd as the picture of some *deform'd* old Woman, that might cause *laughter*, or some light, superficial, and *comical* pleasure; but never to be endur'd on serious occasions, where the attention of the mind, and where the heart was engaged. . . . (13–15)

They found that *History*, grosly taken, was neither proper to *instruct*, nor apt to *please*; and therefore they would not trust History for their examples, but refin'd upon the History; and thence contriv'd something more *philosophical*, and more *accurate* than *History*. But whether our *English* Authors of Tragedy lay their foundation so deep, whether they had any *design* in their *designs*, and whether it was to *prudence* or to *chance* that they sacrific'd, is the business of this present enquiry. (15–16)

* * *

[Rymer then analyses three tragedies by Fletcher, beginning with *Rollo, Duke of Normandy*. He criticises the characterisation of Aubrey, rightful heir to the throne, who becomes King after the fatal dispute between the brothers Rollo and Otto]

Aubrey should in all his words and actions appear great, promising, and Kingly, to deserve that care which Heaven manifests so wonderfully in his Restoration.

And because this, of the two Brothers killing each other, is an action *morally* unnatural; therefore, by way of *preparation*, the *Tragedy* would have begun with Heaven and Earth in disorder, *nature* troubl'd, unheard-of *prodigies*; something (if I may so say) *physically* unnatural, and against the ordinary course of nature. Perhaps the first *Scene* would have shew'd the Usurper's *Ghost* from Hell, full of horror for his crime, cursing his Sons, and sending some infernal *fury* amongst them.

And, by the way, he might relate all things fit to be known, which past out of the *Drama*.

The nicety in writing upon this *Fable*, would have chiefly been in the *characters* of the two Brothers. These are the persons kill'd, and, of all things, a Poet must be tender of a mans life, and never *sacrifice* it to his *Maggot* and *Capriccio*. Therefore, as (I said) the Brothers were not to be *wicked*, so likewise they ought not to be absolutely innocent. For if they had refused to succeed their Father, and when they might have sat on the Throne, have humbled themselves at *Aubrey*'s feet; then no *Poetical Justice* could have touch'd them: guilty they were to be, in enjoying their Father's crime; but not of committing any new. And this guilt of theirs was also either to be palliated, or else to be past over in silence, lest, laid too open, the compassion of the Audience might be abated. Neither would it suffice that these Brothers kill each other by some chance; but it should appear, that agitated by their Father's crime, like *Machines*, they unavoidably clash against each other; whilst their proper *inclination* in vain strives against the *violence*.

If the *English Theatre* requires more *intrigue*, an Author may multiply the *Incidents*, may add *Episods*, and *thicken* the *Plot*, as he sees occasion; provided that all the *lines* tend to the same *center*; more of a main *Plot*, *Virgil* requir'd not for his *Epic* Poem. (22–4)

* * *

In former times *Poetry* was another thing than *History*, or than the *Law* of the Land. *Poetry* discover'd crimes, the *Law* could never find out; and punish'd those the *Law* had acquitted. The *Areopagus* clear'd *Orestes*, but with what *Furies* did the *Poets* haunt and torment him? and what a wretch made they of *Oedipus*, when the *Casuist* excus'd his *invincible* ignorance?

The *Poets* consider'd, that naturally men were affected with *pitty*, when they saw others suffer more than their fault deserv'd; and *vice*, they thought, could never be painted too ugly and frightful; therefore, whether they would move *pitty*, or make *vice* detested, it concern'd them to be somewhat of the severest in the punishments they inflicted. Now, because their hands were tied, that they could not punish beyond such a degree; they were oblig'd to have a strict eye on their Malefactor, that he transgrest not too far, that he committed not *two* crimes, when but responsible for *one*: nor, indeed, be so far guilty, as by the Law to deserve death. For though *historical Justice* might rest there; yet *poetical Justice* could not be so content. It would require that the satisfaction be compleat and full, ere the *Malefactor* goes off the *Stage*, and nothing left to God Almighty, and another World. Nor will it suffer that the Spectators trust the *Poet* for a *Hell* behind the *Scenes*; the fire must roar in the conscience of the *Criminal*, the *fiends* and *furies* be conjur'd up to their faces, with a world of *machines* and horrid spectacles; and yet the *Criminal* could never move *pitty*. Therefore amongst the *Ancients* we find no Malefactors of this kind; a wilful Murderer is with them as strange and unknown, as a *Paricide* to the old *Romans*. Yet need we not fancy that they were squeamish, or unacquainted with any of these great *lumping* crimes in that age; when we remember their *Oedipus*, *Orestes*, or *Medea*. But they took care to wash the Viper, to cleanse away the venom, and with such art to prepare the morsel: they made it all Junket to the tast, and all Physick in the operation.

They so qualifi'd, so allaid, and cover'd the *crime* with circumstances, that little could appear on the *Stage*, but either the causes and provocations before it, or the remorse and penitence, the despairs and horrors of conscience which follow'd, to make the *Criminal* every way a fit object for *pitty*. Nor can we imagin their Stage so rarely endur'd any bloodshed, and that the sight was displeasing, because the Spectators were some sort of effeminate, unfighting fellows, when we remember the Battels of *Marathon* and *Salamis*; and with what small number these very Spectators had routed *Xerxes* and the greatest Armies in the World. For now it was that the *arms* of the *Athenians* (as well as their *arts*) shin'd in their greatest glory.

The truth is, the *Poets* were to move pitty; and this pitty was to be mov'd for the living, who remain'd; and not for the dead. And they found in nature, that men could not so easily pardon a crime committed before their faces; and consequently could not be so easily dispos'd to bestow that pitty on the *Criminal* which the Poets labour'd for. The Poets, I say, found that the sight of the fact made so strong an impression, as no art of theirs could afterwards fully conquer. (25-8)

* * *

Tragedy requires not what is only Natural, but what is great in Nature, and such thoughts as quality and Court-education might inspire. She might indeed be surpriz'd, and at the first let the meer Natural woman [Edith] escape a little, but one or two so harsh and barbarous repulses should have rouz'd that Tragical spirit so vilely prostituted, and made her reflect on the other bloody scenes, so lately acted before her eyes, and caus'd her to despair before she had troubl'd us with her endless impertinencies.

Nor indeed comes short of her for tongue and wind, the old *Dutchess* [Sophia], when in all reason one might expect that so violent grief and passions would choak them; they run chattering, as if the concern were no more than a *gossiping*: theirs are not of the old cut, *Curæ leves loquuntur ingentes stupent. . . .*[1] (43–4)

Says *Sophia*,

> *Divide me first, and tear me limb by limb,*
> *And let them find as many several graves,*
> *As there are Vilages in* Normandy. . . .

After the three first words she flies from the only thought that was proper, high enough, and proportionable to her passion: she is for being split in as many pieces as there are *Villages* in *Normandy*; which expression scatters the thought, breaks the resemblance and carries all remote from the occasion, and must in effect move but very indifferently. From thence she plunges into such impertinent and inconsistent wild *jargon* as is obvious to any man. That of the Diamond is a good thought in it self; but in this place comes very cold from her mouth, 'tis no more than if she had said, *Divide the Dukedom, divide me first, nay divide a Diamond,* &c. Naturally in a great passion none have leisure to ramble for comparisons, much less to compute the value of Diamonds whole or broken. (50–4)

★　　★　　★

[Rymer then discusses *A King and No King*, and the correct presentation of Kings in tragedy]

Kings of *Tragedy* are all Kings by the Poet's *Election*, and if such as these must be elected, certainly no *Polish* Diet would ever suffer Poet to have a voice in choosing a King for them. Nor will it serve that *Arbaces* is not truly a King, for he is actually such, and intended for a true and rightful King before the Poet has done with him; what wants in Birth the Poet should make up in his Merit: every one is to consent and wish him King, because the Poet designs him for one; 'tis (besides) observ'd that Usurpers generally take care to deserve by their conduct what is deny'd them by right.

We are to presume the greatest vertues, where we find the highest of rewards; and though it is not necessary that all *Heroes* should be Kings, yet undoubtedly all crown'd heads by *Poetical right* are *Heroes*. This Character is a flower, a prerogative, so certain, so inseparably annex'd to the *Crown*, as by no Poet, no *Parliament* of Poets, ever to be invaded.

[1] Seneca, *Hippolytus* 607: 'Light troubles speak; the weighty are struck dumb.'

Arbaces indeed is of a different mould, he no sooner comes on the Stage, but lays about him with his tongue at so nauseous a rate, Captain *Bessus* is all Modesty to him; to mend the matter his friend, shaking an empty skull, says *'Tis pity that valour should be thus drunk.* Had he been content to brag only amongst his own Vassals, the fault might be more sufferable, but the King of *Armenia* is his prisoner, he must bear the load of all; he must be swagger'd at, insulted over, and trampl'd on without any provocation. We have a *Scene* of his sufferings in each *Act* of the Play: *Bajazet* in the *Cage* was never so carried about, or felt half the barbarous indignities which are thrown on this unfortunate Prince by our monster of a King.

If the Poet would teach that victory makes a man insolent; he must at the same time make victory blush, and fly to the other side; as a just punishment for him that had abused her favours. (60–2)

★　　★　　★

[Arbaces threateningly draws his sword on the Queen-mother; Rymer contrasts the scene in the *Aeneid* (II. 575–95) where Aeneas thinks momentarily of revenging the fall of Troy on Helen, but refrains]

We need not make a controversy whether *Virgil* or his *Criticks* be in the right: But if *Virgil* will not in a man allow the *thought* of striking a Woman in any circumstances, unless he condemns himself for that *thought*; And if his *Criticks* will not permit a *thought* of that kind with any *qualifications* whatsoever; then we may well conclude, that *Poetry* to be very *gross*, where the *men* both think, and speak, and act their *cruelties* against *Women*, without any shame or restraint.

But *Arbaces*, though mad, and flash'd upon by never so great a *hurrican* of provocations, was not to be allow'd to think of striking; because the Womans *quality* was above his, and made her sacred. Neither in this point is there a difference betwixt an *Epick* Poem and a *Tragedy*; when the conclusion of both is *prosperous*. . . . (73–4)

I know with the Ancients, *Orestes* kill'd his Mother, *Hercules* his Wife and Children, *Agamemnon* his Daughter. But the first was an act of *Justice*; the second of *Frenzy*; the last of *Religion*. But these were all Tragedies unhappy in the *catastrophe*, And the business so well prepar'd that every one might see, that these Worthies had rather have laid violent hands on themselves, had not their *will* and choice been over-rul'd. Every step they made, appear'd so contrary to their inclinations, as all the while shew'd them unhappy, and render'd them the most *deserving* of pitty in the World.

Another *Canker* in the heart of this *Tragedy*, is the incestuous love (for such it appears) between *Arbaces* and *Panthea*, I mean, the *conduct* of it. When any *design* on the *Stage* is in agitation, the Poet must take care that he engage the affections, take along the heart, and secure the good will of the Audience. If the *design* be wicked, as here the making approaches towards an *incestuous* enjoyment, the *Audience* will *naturally* loath and detest it, rather than favour or accompany it with their good wishes. 'Tis the sad effects and consequences of an ill *design* which the *Audience* love to have represented: 'tis then that the *penitence, remorse* and *despairs* move us: 'tis then that we grieve with the sorrowful, and weep with those that weep.

Therefore, were the Ancients to make an *incestuous* love their subject they would *take* it in the *fall*, as it rowls down headlong to desperation and misery. (74–6)

*   *   *

[Finally Rymer discusses *The Maid's Tragedy*]

From these considerations we might gather that the Poet's intent was to show the dismal consequences of *fornication*. And if so, then the Title of the Tragedy should have related to the King.

Whil'st thus we are uncertain what ought to be the *title*, we may suspect that the *Action* of the Tragedy is *double*; where there seem two centers, neither can be right; and the lines leading towards them must all be false and confus'd; the *preparation* I mean, and conduct must be all at random, since not directed to any one certain end.

But what ever the Poet design'd; nothing in *History* was ever so *unnatural*, nothing in *Nature* was ever so *improbable* as we find the whole conduct of this Tragedy, so far are we from any thing accurate, and Philosophical as Poetry requires. . . . (106–7)

A King of History might marry his Concubine to another man for a Maid; might hinder that man from the enjoyment. But would not then turn them into the bed-chamber to be all night together; nor would come in the morning to interrogate and question him, and torture the soul of him, as we find in this Tragedy, nor would impose it on a husband thus affronted, whom he calls *honest* and *valiant*, to be the pimp to his bride. To have taken *Amintors* head off had been clemency in comparison of these outrages without any cause or colour. (107–8)

✳   ✳   ✳

Now Nature knows nothing in the *manners* which so properly and particularly distinguishes woman as doth her modesty. Consonant therefore to our principles and Poetical, is what some writers of Natural History have reported; that women when drowned swim with their faces downwards, though men on the contrary.

Tragedy cannot represent a woman without modesty as natural and essential to her.

If a woman has got any accidental historical impudence, if, documented in the School of *Nanna* or *Heloisa*, she is furnish'd with some stock of acquired impudence, she is no longer to stalk in Tragedy on her high shoes; but must rub off and pack down with the Carriers into the *Province* of Comedy, there to be kickt about and expos'd to laughter. (113–14)

✳   ✳   ✳

If it be said that the King was accessary to the falshood, I question whether in Poetry a King can be an accessary to a crime. If the King commanded *Amintor*, *Amintor* should have begg'd the King's pardon, should have suffer'd all the racks and tortures a Tyrant could inflict; and from *Perillus*'s Bull should have still bellowed out that eternal truth, that his *Promise was to be kept*, that he is true to *Aspatia*, that he dies for his Mistress; then would his memory have been precious and sweet to after-ages, and the Midsummer-Maydens would have *offer'd* their Garlands all at his grave. . . .

But if the Poet intended to make an example of this King, and that the King right or wrong must be kill'd, *Amintor* only felt the highest provocations, and he alone should have been drawn out for the wicked instrument; for *Melantius* had no reason to be angry at any but at his Sister *Evadne*, nor could she have any pretence to exercise her hands, unless it were against her self.

If I mistake not, in Poetry no woman is to kill a man, except her quality gives her the advantage above him; nor is a Servant to kill the Master, nor a Private Man, much less a Subject to kill a King, nor on the contrary.

Poetical decency will not suffer death to be dealt to each other by such persons, whom the Laws of Duel allow not to enter the lists together. . . . (115–17)

*   *   *

In *Epick Poetry* enemies are kill'd; and *Mezentius* must be a wicked Tyrant, the better to set off *Æneas*'s piety. In Tragedy, all the clashing is amongst friends, no *panegyrick* is design'd, nor ought intended but pitty and terror: and consequently no shadow of sense can be pretended for bringing any wicked persons on the Stage. (120)

*   *   *

And certainly, of all the characters, this of *Amintor* is the most unreasonable. No reason appears why he was contracted to *Aspatia*, and less why he forsook her for *Evadne*; and least of all for his dissembling, and bearing so patiently the greatest of provocations that could possibly be given. Certainly no spectacle can be more displeasing, than to see a man ty'd to a post, and another buffetting him with an immoderate tongue. . . .

Poetry will allow no provocation or injury, where it allows no revenge. And what pleasure can there be in seeing a King threaten and hector without cause; when none may be suffer'd to make a return? Poetry will not permit an affront, where there can be no reparation. But well was it for us all, that *Amintor* was by the Poet his *maker* endu'd with a restraining grace, and had his hands ty'd.

The King should first have kill'd his own Mother to have made him mad enough, and fitted him for such a monstrous provocation. And *Amintor* too should have been guilty of some enormous crime (as he is indeed), that drew this curse upon him, and prepar'd him to receive so horrid an out-rage. Both should have been ripe for punishment, which this occasion pulls down upon them, by making them kill each other. Then *Poetical Justice* might have had its course, though no way could pitty be due to either of them. (125–6)

*   *   *

Some would blame me for insisting and examining only what is apt to *please*, without a word of what might profit.

1. I believe the end of all Poetry is to *please*.

2. Some sorts of Poetry please without profiting.

3. I am confident whoever writes a Tragedy cannot please but must also profit; 'tis the Physick of the mind that he makes palatable.

And besides the *purging* of the *passions* something must stick by observing that constant order, that harmony and beauty of Providence, that necessary relation and chain whereby the causes and the effects, the vertues and rewards, the vices and their punishments are proportion'd and link'd together; how deep and dark soever are laid the Springs, and however intricate and involv'd are their operations.

But these enquiries I leave to men of more flegm and consideration.

Othello comes next to hand, but laying my Papers together without more scribling, I find a volumn, and a greater burthen then I dare well obtrude upon you. (140-1)

16. John Dryden, *Heads of an Answer to Rymer*

c. 1677

From the Preface to Tonson's edition of Beaumont and Fletcher (1711), I. xii-xxvi.

In his preface Tonson records that Rymer sent a copy of his *Tragedies of the Last Age* to Dryden, 'who on the Blank Leaves, before the Beginning, and after the End of the Book, made several Remarks, as if he design'd an Answer to Mr. *Rymer*'s Reflections. . . .' (p. xii)

He who undertakes to Answer this Excellent Critick of Mr. *Rymer*, in behalf of our *English* Poets against the *Greek*, ought to do it in this manner.

Either by yielding to him the greatest part of what he contends for, which consists in this, that the μυθος (*i. e.*) the Design and Conduct of it is more conducing in the *Greeks*, to those Ends of Tragedy which *Aristotle* and he propose, namely, to cause Terror and Pity; yet the granting this does not set the *Greeks* above the *English* Poets.

But the Answerer ought to prove two things; First, That the Fable is not the greatest Master-Piece of a Tragedy, tho' it be the Foundation of it.

Secondly, That other Ends, as suitable to the Nature of Tragedy, may be found in the *English*, which were not in the *Greek*.

Aristotle places the Fable first; not *quoad dignitatem, sed quoad fundamentum*; for a Fable never so Movingly contriv'd, to those Ends of his, Pity and Terror, will operate nothing on our Affections, except the Characters, Manners, Thoughts and Words are suitable.

So that it remains for Mr. *Rymer* to prove, That in all those, or the greatest part of them, we are inferior to *Sophocles* and *Euripides*: And this he has offer'd at in some measure, but, I think, a little partially to the Ancients.

To make a true Judgment in this Competiton, between the *Greek* Poets and the *English* in Tragedy, Consider,

I. How *Aristotle* has defin'd a Tragedy.

II. What he assigns the End of it to be.

III. What he thinks the Beauties of it.

IV. The Means to attain the End propos'd. Compare the *Greek* and *English* Tragick Poets justly and without Partiality, according to those Rules.

Then, Secondly, consider, whether *Aristotle* has made a just Definition of Tragedy, of its Parts, of its Ends, of its Beauties; and whether he having not seen any others but those of *Sophocles, Euripides,* &c. had or truly could determine what all the Excellencies of Tragedy are, and wherein they consist.

Next show in what ancient Tragedy was deficient; for Example, in the narrowness of its Plots, and fewness of Persons, and try whether that be not a Fault in the *Greek* Poets; and whether their Excellency was so great, when the Variety was visibly so little; or whether what they did was not very easie to do.

Then make a Judgment on what the *English* have added to their Beauties: as for Example, not only more Plot, but also new Passions; as namely, that of Love, scarce touch'd on by the Ancients, except in this one Example of *Phædra*, cited by Mr. *Rymer*, and in that how short they were of *Fletcher*.

Prove also that Love, being an Heroique Passion, is fit for Tragedy, which cannot be deny'd; because of the Example alledged of *Phædra*: And how far *Shakespeare* has outdone them in Friendship, &c.

To return to the beginning of this Enquiry, consider if Pity and Terror be enough for Tragedy to move, and I believe upon a true definition of Tragedy, it will be found that its Work extends farther, and that it is to reform Manners by delightful Representation of Human Life in great Persons, by way of Dialogue. If this be true, then not only Pity and Terror are to be mov'd as the only Means to bring us to Virtue, but generally Love to Virtue, and Hatred to Vice, by shewing the Rewards of one, and Punishments of the other; at least by rendring Virtue always amiable, though it be shown unfortunate; and Vice detestable, tho' it be shown Triumphant.

If then the Encouragement of Virtue, and Discouragement of Vice, be the proper End of Poetry in Tragedy: Pity and Terror, tho' good Means, are not the only: For all the Passions in their turns are to be set in a Ferment; as Joy, Anger, Love, Fear, are to be used as the Poets common Places; and a general Concernment for the principal Actors is to be rais'd, by making them appear such in their Characters, their Words and Actions, as will Interest the Audience in their Fortunes.

And if after all, in a large Sense, Pity comprehends this Concernment for the Good, and Terror includes Detestation for the Bad; then let us consider whether the *English* have not answer'd this End of Tragedy, as well as the Ancients, or perhaps better.

And here Mr. *Rymer*'s Objections against these Plays are to be impartially weigh'd; that we may see whether they are of weight enough to turn the Ballance against our Country-men.

'Tis evident those Plays which he arraigns have mov'd both those Passions in a high Degree upon the Stage.

To give the Glory of this away from the Poet, and to place it upon the Actors, seems unjust.

One Reason is, because whatever Actors they have found, the Event has been the same, that is, the same Passions have been always mov'd: which shows, that there is something of Force and Merit in the Plays themselves, conducing to the Design of Raising those two Passions: And suppose them ever to have been excellently acted, yet Action only adds Grace, Vigour, and more Life upon the Stage, but cannot give it wholly where it is not first. But Secondly, I dare appeal to those who have never seen them acted, if they have not found those two Passions mov'd within them; and if the general Voice will carry it, Mr. *Rymer*'s Prejudice will take off his single Testimony.

This being matter of Fact, is reasonably to be Established by this Appeal: As if one Man say 'tis Night, when the rest of the World conclude it to be Day, there needs no further Argument against him that it is so.

If he urge, that the general Taste is deprav'd; his Arguments to prove this can at best but evince, that our Poets took not the best way to raise those Passions; but Experience proves against him, that those Means which they have us'd, have been successful, and have produc'd them.

And one Reason of that Success is, in my Opinion, this, that *Shakespeare* and *Fletcher* have written to the Genius of the Age and Nation in which they liv'd: For tho' Nature, as he objects, is the same in all Places, and Reason too the same; yet the Climate, the Age, the Dispositions of the People to whom a Poet writes, may be so different, that what pleas'd the *Greeks*, would not satisfie an *English* Audience.

And if they proceeded upon a Foundation of truer Reason to please the *Athenians*, than *Shakespeare* and *Fletcher* to please the *English*, it only shows that the *Athenians* were a more judicious People: But the Poet's business is certainly to please the Audience.

Whether our *English* Audience have been pleas'd hitherto with Acorns, as he calls it, or with Bread, is the next Question; that is, whether the Means which *Shakespeare* and *Fletcher* have us'd in their Plays to raise those Passions before-named, be better applied to the ends by the *Greek* Poets than by them; and perhaps we shall not grant him this wholly. Let it be yielded that a Writer is not to run down with the Stream, or to please the People by their own usual Methods, but rather to reform their Judgments: It still remains to prove that our Theater needs this total Reformation.

The Faults which he has found in their Designs, are rather wittily aggravated in many places, than reasonably urg'd; and as much may be return'd on the *Greeks*, by one who were as witty as himself.

Secondly, They destroy not, if they are granted, the Foundation of the Fabrick, only take away from the Beauty of the Symmetry. For Example: The faults in the Character of the *King and no King*, are not, as he makes them, such as render him detestable; but only Imperfections which accompany human Nature, and for the most part excus'd by the Violence of his Love; so that they destroy not our Pity or Concernment for him. This Answer may be applied to most of his Objections of that kind.

And *Rollo* committing many Murders, when he is answerable but for one, is too severely arraign'd by him; for it adds to our Horror and Detestation of the Criminal: And Poetique Justice is not neglected neither, for we stab him in our Minds for every Offence which he commits; and the point which the Poet is to gain upon the Audience, is not so much in the Death of an Offender, as the raising an Horror of his Crimes.

That the Criminal should neither be wholly Guilty, nor wholly Innocent, but so participating of both, as to move both Pity and Terror, is certainly a good Rule; but not perpetually to be observed, for that were to make all Tragedies too much alike; which Objection he foresaw, but has not fully answered.

To conclude therefore, if the Plays of the Ancients are more correctly Plotted, ours are more beautifully written; and if we can raise Passions as high on worse Foundations, it shows our Genius in Tragedy is greater, for in all other parts of it the *English* have manifestly excell'd them.

For the Fable it self, 'tis in the *English* more adorn'd with Episodes, and larger than in the *Greek* Poets, consequently more diverting; for, if the Action be but one, and that plain, without any Counterturn of Design or Episode (*i.e.*) Under-plot, how can it be so pleasing as the *English*, which have both Under-plot, and a turn'd Design, which keeps the Audience in Expectation of the Catastrophe? whereas in the *Greek* Poets we see through the whole Design at first.

For the Characters, they are neither so many nor so various in *Sophocles* and *Euripides*, as in *Shakespeare* and *Fletcher*; only they are more adapted to those ends of Tragedy which *Aristotle* commends to us; Pity and Terror.

The Manners flow from the Characters, and consequently must partake of their Advantages and Disadvantages.

The Thoughts and Words, which are the fourth and fifth Beauties of Tragedy, are certainly more Noble and more Poetical in the *English* than in the *Greek*, which must be proved by comparing them somewhat more Equitably than Mr. *Rymer* has done.

After all, we need not yield that the *English* way is less conducing to move Pity and Terror; because they often shew Virtue oppress'd, and Vice punish'd; where they do not both or either, they are not to be defended.

That we may the less wonder why Pity and Terror are not now the only Springs on which our Tragedies move, and that *Shakespeare* may be more excus'd, *Rapin* confesses that the *French* Tragedies now all run upon the *Tendre*, and gives the Reason, because Love is the Passion which most Predominates in our Souls; and that therefore the Passions represented become insipid, unless they are conformable to the Thoughts of the Audience; but it is to be concluded, that this Passion works not now among the *French* so strongly, as the other two did amongst the Ancients: Amongst us, who have a stronger Genius for Writing, the Operations from the Writing are much stronger; for the raising of *Shakespeare*'s Passions are more from the Excellency of the Words and Thoughts, than the Justness of the Occasion; and if he has been able to pick single Occasions, he has never founded the whole reasonably; yet by the Genius of Poetry, in Writing he has succeeded.

The Parts of a Poem, Tragique or Heroique, are,

I. The Fable it self.

II. The Order or Manner of its Contrivance, in relation of the parts to the whole.

III. The Manners, or Decency of the Characters in Speaking or Acting what is proper for them, and proper to be shewn by the Poet.

IV. The Thoughts which express the Manners.

V. The Words which express those Thoughts.

In the last of these *Homer* excels *Virgil*, *Virgil* all other ancients Poets, and *Shakespeare* all Modern Poets.

For the second of these, the Order; the meaning is, that a Fable ought to have a beginning, middle, and an end, all just and natural, so that that part which is the middle, could not naturally be the beginning or end, and so of the rest; all are depending one on another, like the links of a curious Chain.

If Terror and Pity are only to be rais'd; certainly this Author follows *Aristotle*'s Rules, and *Sophocles*' and *Euripides*' Example; but Joy may be rais'd too, and that doubly, either by seeing a wicked Man Punish'd, or a good Man at last Fortunate; or perhaps Indignation, to see Wickedness prosperous, and Goodness depress'd: both these may be profitable to the end of Tragedy, Reformation of Manners; but the last improperly, only as it begets Pity in the Audience; tho' *Aristotle*, I confess, places Tragedies of this kind in the second Form.

And, if we should grant that the *Greeks* perform'd this better; perhaps it may admit of Dispute whether Pity and Terror are either the Prime, or at least the Only Ends of Tragedy.

'Tis not enough that *Aristotle* has said so, for *Aristotle* drew his Models of Tragedy from *Sophocles* and *Euripides*; and if he had seen ours, might have chang'd his Mind.

And chiefly we have to say (what I hinted on Pity and Terror in the last Paragraph save one) that the Punishment of Vice, and Reward of Virtue, are the most Adequate ends of Tragedy, because most conducing to good Example of Life; now Pity is not so easily rais'd for a Criminal (as the Ancient Tragedy always Represents its chief Person such) as it is for an Innocent Man: and the Suffering of Innocence and Punishment of the Offender, is of the Nature of *English* Tragedy; contrary in the *Greek*, Innocence is unhappy often, and the Offender escapes.

Then we are not touch'd with the Sufferings of any sort of Men so much as of Lovers; and this was almost unknown to the Antients; so that they neither administred Poetical Justice (of which Mr. *Rymer* boasts) so well as we, neither knew they the best common Place of Pity, which is Love.

He therefore unjustly blames us for not building upon what the Antients left us, for it seems, upon consideration of the Premises, that we have wholly finished what they begun.

My Judgment on this Piece is this; that it is extreamly Learned; but that the Author of it is better Read in the *Greek* than in the *English* Poets; that all Writers ought to Study this Critick as the best Account I have ever seen of the Ancients; that the Model of Tragedy he has here given, is Excellent, and extream Correct; but that it is not the only Model of all Tragedy; because it is too much circumscrib'd in Plot, Characters, &c. and lastly, that we may be taught here justly to Admire and Imitate the Antients, without giving them the Preference, with this Author, in Prejudice to our own Country.

Want of Method, in this Excellent Treatise, makes the Thoughts of the Author sometimes obscure.

His Meaning, that Pity and Terror are to be mov'd, is that they are to be mov'd as the Means conducing to the Ends of Tragedy, which are Pleasure and Instruction.

And these two Ends may be thus distinguish'd. The chief End of the Poet is to please; for his immediate Reputation depends on it.

The great End of the Poem is to Instruct, which is perform'd by making Pleasure the Vehicle of that Instruction: For Poetry is an Art, and all Arts are made to Profit (*Rapin*).

The Pity which the Poet is to Labour for, is for the Criminal, not for those, or him, whom he has murder'd, or who have been the Occasion of the Tragedy: The Terror is likewise in the Punishment of the same Criminal, who if he be represented too great an Offender, will not be pitied; if altogether Innocent, his Punishment will be unjust.

Another Obscurity is where he says, *Sophocles* perfected Tragedy, by introducing the third Actor; that is, he meant three kinds of Action, one Company singing or speaking, another Playing on the Musick, a third Dancing.

Rapin attributes more to the *Dictio*, that is, to the Words and Discourses of a Tragedy, than *Aristotle* has done, who places them in the last Rank of Beauties; perhaps only last in Order, because they are the last Product of the Design: of the Disposition or Connexion of its Parts, of the Characters, of the Manners of those Characters, and of the Thoughts proceeding from those Manners.

Rapin's Words are Remarkable:

' 'Tis not the admirable Intrigue, the surprizing Events, and extraordinary Incidents that make the Beauty of a Tragedy, 'tis the Discourses, when they are Natural and Passionate.'

So are *Shakespeare*'s.

17. Thomas Shadwell, from his adaptation of *Timon of Athens*

1678

From *The History of Timon of Athens, the Man-Hater . . . Made into a Play* (1678).

Shadwell's adaptation was performed (probably) in January 1678. The major change is the addition of a love plot, for Timon is betrothed to Melissa and is loved by his mistress Evandra: when he loses his fortune it is the mistress who proves loyal. The steward Flavius becomes Demetrius, and is changed from a loyal to a faithless servant. Shadwell links the Alcibiades and Timon plots by making Melissa waver between the two, depending on their current success. At least his additions take a similar ethical direction to Shakespeare's plot. The masque (with music by Purcell) contributed to the great success of this version in the eighteenth century.

Dedication to George, Duke of Buckingham.

I am now to present your Grace with this History of *Timon*, which you were pleased to tell me you liked, and it is the more worthy of you, since it has the inimitable hand of *Shakespeare* in it, which never made more Masterly strokes than in this. Yet I can truly say, I have made it into a Play. . . .

[Act I, Scene i.]

Enter Demetrius.

Dem. How strange it is to see my Riotous Lord
With careless Luxury betray himself!
To Feast and Revel all his hours away;
Without account how fast his Treasure ebbs,
How slowly flows, and when I warn'd him of
His following dangers, with his rigorous frowns

He nipt my growing honesty i'th' Bud,
And kill'd it quite; and well for me he did so.
It was a barren Stock would yield no Fruit:
But now like Evil Councellours I comply,
And lull him in his soft Lethargick life.
And like such cursed Politicians can
Share in the head-long ruine, and will rise by't:
What vast rewards to nauseous Flatterers,
To Pimps, and Women, what Estates he gives!
And shall I have no share? Be gon, all Honesty,
Thou foolish, slender, thredbare, starving thing, be gon!

Enter Poet.

Here's a fellow-horseleech: How now Poet, how goes the world?
Poet. Why, it wears as it grows: but is Lord *Timon* visible?
Dem. Hee'll come out suddenly, what have you to present him?
Poet. A little Off-spring of my fruitful Muse: She's in travail daily
for his honour.
Dem. For your own profit, you gross flatterer.   [*Aside.*
By his damn'd Panegyricks he has written
Himself up to my Lords Table,
Which he seldom fails; nay, into his Chariot,
Where he in publick does not blush to own
The sordid Scribler.
Poet. The last thing I presented my Noble Lord was Epigram: But
this is in Heroick style.
Dem. What d'ye mean by style? that of good sence is all alike; that
is to say, with apt and easie words, not one too little or too much:
And this I think good style.
Poet. O Sir, you are wide o'th' matter! apt and easie!
Heroicks must be lofty and high sounding;
No easie language in Heroick Verse;
'Tis most unfit: for should I name a Lion,
I must not in Heroicks call him so!
Dem. What then?
Poet. I'de as soon call him an Ass. No thus——
The fierce *Numidian* Monarch of the Beasts.
Dem. That's lofty, is it?
Poet. O yes! but a Lion would sound so baldly, not to be
Endur'd, and a Bull too—but

The mighty Warriour of the horned Race:
Ah—how that sounds!

   Dem. Then I perceive sound's the great matter in this way.
   Poet. Ever while you live.
   Dem. How would you sound a Fox as you call it?
   Poet. A Fox is but a scurvey Beast for Heroick Verse.
   Dem. Hum—is it so? how will a Raven do in Heroick?
   Poet. Oh very well, Sir.

That black and dreadful fate-denouncing fowl.

   Dem. An excellent sound—But let me see your Piece.
   Poet. I'le read it—'Tis a good morrow to the Lord *Timon.*
   Dem. Do you make good morrow sound loftily?
   Poet. Oh very loftily!——

> The fringed Vallance of your eyes advance,
> Shake off your Canopy'd and downie trance:
> *Phœbus* already quaffs the morning dew,
> Each does his daily lease of life renew.

Now you shall hear description, 'tis the very life of Poetry.

> He darts his beams on the Larks mossie-house,
> And from his quiet tenement does rouze
> The little charming and harmonious Fowl,
> Which sings its lump of Body to a Soul:
> Swiftly it clambers up in the steep air
> With warbling throat, and makes each noat a stair.

There's rapture for you! hah!——

   Dem. Very fine.

> *Poet.*   This the sollicitous Lover straight alarms,
> Who too long slumber'd in his *Cœlia's* arms:
> And now the swelling Spunges of the night
> With aking heads stagger from their delight:
> Slovenly Taylors to their needles hast:
> Already now the moving shops are plac'd
> By those who crop the treasures of the fields,
> And all those Gems the ripening Summer yields.

Who d'ye think are now? Why—Nothing but Herb-women: there
are fine lofty expressions for Herb-women! ha!——

> Already now, &c.

Dem. But what's all this to my Lord?

Poet. No, that's true, 'tis description though.

Dem. Yes, in twenty lines to describe to him that 'tis about
The fourth hour in the morning——I'le in and let
Him know in three words 'tis the seventh.

                                              [*Exit* Demetrius.

★   ★   ★

Phæax. Let the Villain be soundly punish'd for his
Licentious tongue.

Tim. No, the man is honest, 'tis his humour: 'Tis odd,
And methinks pleasant. You must dine with me
Apemantus.

Apem. I devour no Lords.

Tim. No, if you did, the Ladies wou'd be angry.

Apem. Yet they with all their modest simperings,
And varnish'd looks can swallow Lords, and get
Great bellies by't, yet keep their virtuous
Vizors on, till a poor little Bastard steals into
The world, and tells a tale.

Enter Nicius.

Tim. My Noble Lord, welcome! most welcom to my arms!
You are the Fountain from which all my happiness
Did spring! your matchless Daughter, fair *Mellissa.*

Nic. You honour us too much my Lord.

Tim. I cannot, she is the joy of *Athens*! the chief delight
Of Nature, the only life I live by: Oh, that her vows
Were once expir'd; it is methinks an Age till that blest day
When we shall joyn our hands and hearts together.

Nic. 'Tis but a week, my Lord.

Tim. 'Tis a thousand years.

Apem. Thou miserable Lord, hast thou to compleat
All thy calamities, that plague of Love,
That most unmanly madness of the mind,
That specious cheat, as false as friendship is?
Did'st thou but see how like a sniveling thing
Thou look'st and talk'st, thou would'st abhor or laugh at
Thy own admir'd Image.

Tim. Peace: I will hear no railing on this subject.

Apem. *Oh vile corrupted time, that men should be*
Deaf to good Counsel, not to Flatterie.

Tim. Come my dear friends, let us now visit our gardens,
And refresh our selves with some cool Wines and Fruit:
I am transported with your Visits!
There is not now a Prince whom I can envy,
Unless it be in that he can more bestow
Upon the men he loves.

Ælius. My Noble Lord, who would not wed your friendship,
Though without a Dowrie?

Isodor. Most worthy *Timon*! who has a life
You may not call your own?

Phæax.   We are all your slaves.

Poet. The joy of all Mankind.

Jewel.   Great spirit of Nobleness.

Tim. We must not part this day my Friends.

Apem. So, so, crouching slaves, aches contract and make your supple
Joynts to wither; that there should be so little
Love among these Knaves, yet all this courtesie!
They hate and scorn each other, yet they kiss
As if they were of different Sexes: Villains, Villains.

[*Exeunt Omnes.*

[Act I, Scene ii.]

Enter Evandra. *Re-enter* Timon.

Tim. Hail to the fair *Evandra*! methinks your looks are chang'd,
And clouded with some grief that misbecomes 'em.

Evan. My Lord, my ears this morning were saluted with
The most unhappy news, the dismal'st story
The only one cou'd have afflicted me;
My dream foretold it, and I wak'd affrighted,
With a cold sweat o're all my limbs.

Tim. What was it Madam?

Evan. You speak not with the kindness you were wont;
I have been us'd to tenderer words than these:
It is too true, and I am miserable!

Tim. What is't disturbs you so? too well I guess.   [*Aside.*

Evan. I hear I am to lose your Love, which was

The only earthly blessing I enjoy'd,
And that on which my life depended.

 Tim. No, I must ever love my Excellent *Evandra*!

 Evan. Melissa will not suffer it: Oh cruel *Timon*,
Thou well may'st blush at thy ingratitude!
Had I so much towards thee, I ne're shou'd show
My face without confusion: Such a guilt,
As if I had destroy'd thy Race, and ruin'd
All thy Estate, and made thee infamous!
Thy Love to me I cou'd prefer before
All cold respects of Kindred, Wealth and Fame.

 Tim. You have been kind so far above return,
That 'tis beyond expression.

 Evan. Call to mind
Whose Race I sprung from, that of great *Alcides*,
Though not my Fortune, my Beauty and my Youth
And my unspotted Fame yielded to none.
You on your knees a thousand times have sworn,
That they exceeded all, and yet all these,
The only treasures a poor Maid possest,
I sacrific'd to you, and rather chose
To throw my self away, than you shou'd be
Uneasie in your wishes; since which happy
And yet unhappy time, you have been to me,
My Life, my Joy, my Earth, my Heaven, my All,
I never had one single wish beyond you;
Nay, every action, every thought of mine,
How far soe're their large circumference
Stretcht out, yet center'd all in you: You were
My End, the only thing could fill my mind.

 Tim. She strikes me to the heart! I would I had   [*Aside.*
Not seen her.

 Evan. Ah *Timon*, I have lov'd you so, that had
My eyes offended you, I with these fingers
Had pluckt 'em by the roots, and cast them from me:
Or had my heart contain'd one thought that was
Not yours, I with this hand would rip it open:
Shew me a Wife in *Athens* can say this;
And yet I am not one, but you are now to marry.

 Tim. That I have lov'd you, you and Heav'n can witness

By many long repeated acts of Love,
And Bounty I have shew'd you——
   Evan. Bounty! ah *Timon!*
I am not yet so mean, but I contemn
Your transitory dirt, and all rewards,
But that of Love. Your person was the bound
Of all my thoughts and wishes, in return
You *have* lov'd me! Oh miserable sound!
I would you never had, or always would.
   Tim. Man is not master of his appetites,
Heav'n swayes our mind to Love.
   Evan. But Hell to falsehood:
How many thousand times y' have vow'd and sworn
Eternal Love; Heav'n has not yet absolv'd
You of your Oaths to me; nor can I ever,
My Love's as much too much as yours too little.
   Tim. If you love me, you'l love my happiness,
Melissa; Beauty and her Love to me
Has so inflam'd me, I can have none without her.
   Evan. If I had lov'd another, when you first,
My dear, false *Timon* swore to me, would you
Have wisht I might have found my happiness
Within anothers armes? No, no, it is
To love a contradiction.
   Tim. 'Tis a truth I cannot answer.
   Evan. Besides, *Melissa*'s beauty
Is not believ'd to exceed my little stock,
Even modesty may praise it self when 'tis
Aspers'd: But her Love is mercenary,
Most mercenary, base, 'tis Marriage Love:
She gives her person, but in vile exchange
She does demand your liberty: But I
Could generously give without mean bargaining:
I trusted to your honour, and lost mine,
Lost all my Friends and Kindred: but little thought
I should have lost my Love, and cast it on
A barren and ungrateful soil that would return no fruit.
   Tim. This does perplex me, I must break it off.   [*Aside.*
   Evan. The first storm of your Love did shake me so,
It threw down all my leaves, my hopeful blossoms,

Pull'd down my branches; but this latter tempest of your hate
Strikes at my root, and I must wither now,
Like a desertless, sapless tree: must fall——
   Tim. You are secure against all injuries
While I have breath——
   Evan. And yet you do the greatest.
   Timon. You shall be so much partner of my fortune
As will secure you full respect from all,
And may support your quality in what pomp
You can desire.
   Evan. I am not of so coarse a Mould, or have
So gross a mind, as to partake of ought
That's yours without you——
But, oh thou too dear perjur'd man, I could
With thee prefer a dungeon, a low and loathsome dungeon
Before the stately guilded fretted Roofs,
The Pomp, the noise, the show, the revelling,
And all the glittering splendour of a Palace.
   Tim. I by resistless fate am hurry'd on——
   Evan. A vulgar, mean excuse for doing ill.
   Tim. If that were not, my honour is engag'd——
   Evan. It had a pre-engagement——
   Tim. All the great men of *Athens* urge me on
To marry and to preserve my Race.
   Evan. Suppose your Wife be false; (as 'tis not new
In *Athens*;) and suffer others to graft upon
Your stock; where is your Race? weak vulgar reason!
   Tim. Her honour will not suffer her.
   Evan. She may do it cunningly and keep her honour.
   Tim. Her love will then secure her; which is as fervent——
   Evan. As yours was once to me, and may continue
Perhaps as long, and yet you cannot know
She loves you. Since that base *Cecropian* Law
Made Love a merchandize, to traffick hearts
For marriage, and for Dowry, who's secure?
Now her great sign of Love is she's content
To bind you in the strongest chains, and to
A slavery, nought can manumize you from
But death: And I could be content to be
A slave to you, without those vile conditions——

Tim. Why are not our desires within our power?
Or why should we be punisht for obeying them?
But we cannot create our own affections;
They're mov'd by some invisible active Pow'r,
And we are only passive, and whatsoever
Of imperfection follows from th' obedience
To our desires, we suffer, not commit,
And 'tis a cruel and a hard decree,
That we must suffer first, and then be punish't for't.

    Evan. Your Philosophy is too subtle——but what
Security of Love from her can be like mine?
Is Marriage a bond of Truth, which does consist
Of a few trifling Ceremonies? Or are those
Charms or Philters? 'Tis true, my Lord, I was not
First lifted o're the Threshold, and then
Led by my Parents to *Minerva*'s Temple:
No young unyok'd Heifers blood was offer'd
To *Diana*; no invocation to *Juno*, or the *Parcæ*:
No Coachman drove me with a lighted torch;
Nor was your house adorn'd with Garlands then;
Nor had I Figs thrown on my head, or lighted
By my dear Mothers torches to your bed:
Are these slight things, the bonds of truth and constancy?
I came all Love into your arms, unmixt
With other aims; and you for this will cause
My death.

    Tim. I'de sooner seek my own, *Evandra*.

    Evan. Ah, my Lord, if that be true, then go not to *Melissa*,
For I shall die to see another have
Possession of all that e're I wisht for on earth.

    Tim. I would I had not seen *Melissa*:——

    Evan. Ah my dear Lord, there is some comfort left;
Cherish those noble thoughts, and they'l grow stronger,
Your lawful gratitude and Love will rise,
And quell the other rebel-passion in you;
Use all the endeavours which you can, and if
They fail in my relief, I'le die to make you happy.

    Tim. You have moved me to be womanish; pray retire,
I will love you.

    Evan. Oh happy word! Heav'n ever bless my Dear;

Farewell: but will you never see *Mellissa* more?

  Tim. Sweet Excellence! Retire.

  Evan. I will——will you remember your *Evandra*?

  Tim. Yes, I will.   [*Exit* Evandra.

How happy were Mankind in Constancy,

'Twould equal us with the Celestial Spirits!

O could we meet with the same tremblings still,

Those panting joyes, those furious desires,

Those happy trances which we found at first!

But, oh!

> *Unhappy man, whose most transporting joy*
> *Feeds on such luscious food as soon will cloy,*
> *And that which shou'd preserve, does it destroy.*

                              [*Exit* Timon.

[Act II, Scene i.]

Enter Melissa *and* Chloe.

  Mel. What think'st thou *Chloe*? will this dress become me?

  Chlo. Oh, most exceedingly! This pretty curle

Does give you such a killing Grace, I swear

That all the Youth at the Lord *Timon*'s Mask

Will die for you.

  Mel. No: But dost thou think so *Chloe*? I love

To make those Fellows die for me, and I

All the while look so scornfully, and then with my

Head on one side, with a languishing eye I do so

Kill 'em again: Prithee, what do they say of me,

Chloe?

  Chloe. Say! That you are the Queen of all their hearts,

Their Goddess, their Destiny, and talk of *Cupids* flames,

And darts, and Wounds! Oh the rarest language,

'Twould make one die to hear it; and ever now

And then steal some gold into my hand,

And then commend me too.

  Mel. Dear Soul, do they, and do they die for me?

  Chlo. Oh yes, the finest, properest Gentlemen——

  Mel. But there are not many that die for me? humh——

  Chlo. Oh yes, *Lamachus, Theodorus, Thessalus, Eumolpides,*

Memnon, and indeed all that see your Ladiship.

Mel. I'le swear! how is my complexion to day? ha, *Chloe*?

Chlo. O most fragrant! 'tis a rare white wash this!

Mel. I think it is the best I ever bought; had I not best
Lay on some more red, *Chloe*?

Chlo. A little more would do well; it makes you look
So pretty, and so plump, Madam.

Mel. I have been too long this morning in dressing.

Chlo. Oh no, I vow you have been but bare three hours.

Mel. No more? well, if I were sure to be thus pretty but seven
Years, I'de be content to die then on that condition.

Chlo. The gods forbid.

Mel. I'le swear I would; but dost thou think *Timon* will
Like me in this dress?

Chlo. Oh he dies for you in any dress, Madam!

Mel. Oh this vile tailor that brought me not home my new
Habit to day; he deserves the Ostracisme! a Villain,
To disorder me so; I am afraid it has done harm
To my complexion: I have dreamt of it these two nights,
And shall not recover it this week——

Chlo. Indeed Madam he deserves death from your eyes.

Mel. I think I look pretty well! will not *Timon*
Perceive my disorder?——hah——

Chlo. Oh no, but you speak as if you made this killing
Preparation for none but *Timon*.

Mel. O yes, *Chloe*, for every one, I love to have all the
Young Blades follow, kiss my hand, admire, adore me,
And die for me: but I must have but one favour'd
Servant; it is the game and not the quarry, I
Must look after it in the rest.

Chlo. Oh Lord, I would have as many admirers as I could.

Mel. Aye, so would I——but favour one alone.
No, I am resolv'd nothing shall corrupt my honesty;
Those admirers would make one a whore, *Chloe*,
And that undoes us; 'tis our interest to be honest.

Chlo. Would they? No I warrant you, I'de fain see
Any of those admirers make me a Whore.

Mel. *Timon* loves me honestly and is rich——

Chlo. You have forgot your *Alcibiades*:
He is the rarest person!

Mel. No, no, I could love him dearly: oh he was the beautiful'st man,

The finest wit in *Athens*, the best companion, fullest of mirth
And pleasure, and the prettiest wayes he had to please Ladies,
He would make his enemies rejoyce to see him.
   Chlo. Why? he is all this, and can do all this still.
   Mel. Ay, but he has been long banish'd for breaking *Mercuries*
Images, and profaning the mysteries of *Proserpine*;
Besides, the people took his Estate from him,
And I hate a poor Fellow, from my heart I swear.
I vow methinks I look so pretty to day, I could
Kiss my self, *Chloe*.
   Chloe. O dear Madam——I could look on you for ever: oh
What a world of murder you'l commit to day!
   Mel. Dost thou think so? ha! ha! no, no——

Enter a Servant.

   Serv. The Lord *Timon*'s come to wait on you, and begs
Admittance.
   Mel. Desire his presence.

Enter Timon.

   Tim. There is enchantment in her looks,   [*Aside.*
Afresh I am wounded every time I see her:
All happiness to beautiful *Melissa*.
   Mel. I shall want none in you my dearest Lord.
   Tim. Sweetest of Creatures, in whom all th' excellence
Of heav'nly Woman-kind is seen unmixt;
Nature has wrought thy mettle up without allay.
   Mel. I have no value, but my love of you,
And that I am sure has no allay, 'tis of
So strong a temper, neither time nor death,
Nor any change can break it——
   Tim. Dear charming sweet, thy value is so great,
No Kingdom upon Earth should buy thee from me:
But I have still an enemy with you,
That guards me from my happiness; a Vow
Against the Law of Nature, against Love,
The best of Nature, and the highest Law.
   Mel. It will be but a week in force.
   Tim. 'Tis a whole age: in all approaching joys,
The nearer they come to us, still the time

Seems longer to us: But my dear *Melissa*,
Why should we bind our selves with vows and oaths?
Alas, by Nature we are too much confin'd,
Our Liberties so narrow, that we need not
Find fetters for our selves: No, we should seize
On pleasure wheresoever we can find it,
Lest at another time we miss it there.

    Chlo. Madam, break your Vow, it was a rash one.

    Mel. Thou foolish Wench, I cannot get my things
In order till that time; dost think I will
Be marri'd like some vulgar Creature, which
Snatches at the first offer, as if she
Were desperate of having any other?

    Tim. Is there no hope that you will break your vow?

    Mel. If any thing, one word of yours wou'd do't:
But how can you be once secure, I'le keep
A vow to you, that would not to my self?

    Tim. Some dreadful accident may come, *Melissa*,
To interrupt our joyes; let us make sure
O'th' present minute, for the rest perhaps
May not be ours.

    Mel. It is not fit it shou'd, if I shou'd break a vow;
No, you shall never find a change in me,
All the fixt stars shall sooner stray
With an irregular motion, than I change:
This may assure you of my love, if not
Upon my knees I swear——
Were I the Queen of all the Universe,
And *Timon* were reduc'd to rags and misery,
I would not change my love to him.

    Tim. And here I vow,
Should all the frame of Nature be dissolv'd,
Should the firm Centre shake, should Earthquakes rage
With such a fury to disorder all
The peaceful and agreeing Elements,
Till they were huddled into their first Chaos,
As long as I could be, I'de be the same,
The same adorer of *Melissa*!

    Mel. This is so great a blessing Heav'n cann't add to it.

    Tim. Thou art my Heav'n, *Melissa*, the last mark

Of all my hopes and wishes, so I prize thee,
That I could die for thee.

Enter a Servant *of* Timons.

Serv. My Lord, your dinner's ready, and your Lordships
Guests wait your wisht presence: the Lord
Nicias is already there.
    Tim. Let's hast to wait on him, *Melissa.*
    Mel. It is my duty to my Father.   [*Exeunt.*

★   ★   ★

[Act II, Scene ii.] Timon's House.

★   ★   ★

[The Meat is serv'd up with Kettle Drums, and Trumpets.

★   ★   ★

    Apem. When I can find a man that's better than
A beast, I will fall down and worship him.
    Tim. Thou art an *Athenian*, and I bear with thee.
Is the Masque ready?
    Poet. 'Tis, my noble Lord.
    Apem. What odd and childish folly Slaves find out
To please and court all thy distemper'd Appetites!
They spend their flatteries to devour those men
Upon whose Age they'l void it up agen
With poysonous spite and envy.
Who lives that's not deprav'd, or else depraves?
Who die that bear not some spurns to their Graves
Of their friends giving? I should fear that those
Who now are going to dance before me,
Should one day stamp on me: it has been done.
    Tim. Nay, if you rail at all Society,
I'll hear no more—— be gone.
    Apem. Thou may'st be sure I will not stay to see
Thy folly any longer, fare thee well; remember
Thou would'st not hear me, thou wilt curse thy self for't.

217

Tim. I do not think so—— fare thee well.　　　*[Exit* Apemantus.

Enter Servant.

　Serv. My Lord, there are some Ladies masqu'd desire admittance.
　Tim. Have not my doors been always open to
Ev'ry *Athenian*? They do me honour,
Wait on 'em in, were I not bound to do
My duty here, I would.
　Chloe. I have not had the opportunity　　　*[To Melissa.*
To deliver this till now, it is a Letter
From *Alcibiades.*
　Mel. Dear *Alcibiades,* Oh how shall I love him,
When he's restor'd to his Estate and Country!
He will be richer far than *Timon* is,
And I shall chuse him first of any man;
How lucky 'tis I should put off my Wedding.

　　　　　　　[Enter Evandra *with Ladies masqu'd.*

　Tim. Ladies, you do my house and me great honour;
I should be glad you would unmask, that I
Might see to whom I owe the Obligation.
　1. Lad. We ask your pardon, we are stoln out upon
Curiosity, and dare not own it.
　Tim. Your pleasure Ladies, shall be mine.
　Evan. This is the fine gay thing so much admir'd,　　　*[Aside.*
That's born to rob me of my happiness,
And of my life; her face is not her own,
Nor is her love, nor speech, nor motion so:
Her smiles, her amorous looks, she puts on all,
There's nothing natural: She always acts
And never shews her self; How blind is Love
That cannot see this Vanity!

　　　　　　　[Masque begins.
Enter Shepherds *and* Nymphs.
　　　*A Symphony of Pipes imitating the chirping
　　　　　　of Birds.*

　1. Nymph. Hark how the Songsters of the Grove
　　　　　　Sing Anthems to the God of Love.
　　　　　　Hark how each am'rous winged pair,
　　　　　　With Loves great praises fill the Air.

Chorus.   On ev'ry side the charming sound
              Does from the hollow Woods rebound.

                                Retornella.

2. Nymph. Love in their little veins inspires
              Their cheerful Notes, their soft Desires:
              While Heat makes Buds or Blossoms spring,
              These pretty couples love and sing.
Chorus   But Winter puts out their desire,
with Flutes. And half the year they want Loves fire.

                                Retornella.

Full   {But Ah how much are our delights more dear,
Chorus. {For only Humane Kind love all the year.

Enter the Mænades *and* Ægipanes.

1. Bach.   Hence with your trifling Deitie
              A greater we adore,
            Bacchus, who always keeps us free
              From that blind childish power.

2. Bach.   Love makes you languish and look pale,
              And sneak, and sigh, and whine;
            But over us no griefs prevail,
              While we have lusty Wine.
Chorus {Then hang the dull Wretch who has care in his soul,
with   {Whom Love, or whom Tyrants, or Laws can controul,
Hout-boys{If within his right hand he can have a full Bowl.

1. Nymph. Go drivel and snore with your fat God of Wine,
              Your swell'd faces with Pimples adorning,
            Soak your Brains over night and your senses resign,
              And forget all you did the next Morning.

2. Nymph. With dull aking Noddles live on in a mist,
              And never discover true Joy:
            Would Love tempt with Beauty, you could not resist,
              The Empire he slights, he'd destroy.

1. Bach.   Better our heads, than hearts should ake,
              His childish Empire we despise;
            Good Wine of him a Slave can make,
              And force a Lover to be wise.
            Better, *&c.*

2. Bach.	Wine sweetens all the cares of Peace,
	And takes the Terrour off from War.
	To Loves affliction it gives ease,
	And to its Joy does best prepare.
	It sweetens, &c.

1. Nymph.	'Tis Love that makes great Monarchs fight,
	The end of Wealth and Power is Love;
	It makes the youthful Poets write,
	And does the Old to Youth improve.

Retornella of Hout-boys.

1. Bach.	'Tis Wine that Revels in their Veins,
	Makes Cowards valiant, Fools grow wise,
	Provokes low Pens to lofty strains,
	And makes the young Loves Chains despise.

Retornella.

Nymphs and
Shepherds. } Love rules the World.

Mænades and
Ægipanes. } 'Tis Wine, 'tis Wine.

Nymphs and
Shepherds. } 'Tis Love, 'tis Love.

Mænades and
Ægipanes. } 'Tis Wine, 'tis Wine.

Enter *Bacchus* and *Cupid.*

Bacchus. Hold, Hold, our Forces are combin'd,
And we together rule Mankind.

General
Chorus. { Then we with our Pipes, and our Voices will join
To sound the loud praises of Love and good Wine.
Wine gives vigour to Love, Love makes Wine go down.
And by Love and good Drinking, all the World is our own.

Tim. 'Tis well design'd, and well perform'd, and I'll
Reward you well: let us retire into my next
Apartment, where I've devis'd new pleasures for you,
And where I will distribute some small Presents,
To testifie my Love and Gratitude.
Phæax. A noble Lord!
Ælius. Bounty it self.

✳   ✳   ✳

[Act III, Scene iv.]

*   *   *

Timon. How much is a Dog more generous than a man;
Oblige him once, hee'l keep you Company,
Ev'n in your utmost want and misery.

Enter Ælius.

Who's that? *Ælius?* my Lord——*Ælius?*
Demetrius, go let him know *Timon* would speak
With him.——

Dem. goes to him, he turns back.

Do you not know me *Ælius?*
 Ælius. Not know my good Lord *Timon!*
 Tim. Think you I have the Plague?
 Ælius. No, my Lord.
 Tim. Why do you shun me then?
 Ælius. I shun you? I'd serve your Lordship with my life.
 Tim. I'll not believe, he who would refuse me money,
Wou'd venture his life for me.
 Ælius. I am very unfortunate not to have it in my Power
To supply you; but I am going to the *Forum,* to a Debter,
If I receive any, your Lordship shall command it. [*Ex.* Ælius.
 Tim. Had I so lately all the Caps and Knees of th' Athenians,
And is't come to this? Brains hold a little.

Enter Thrasillus.

 Thras. Who's there? *Timon?*   [*Runs back.*
 Tim. There's another Villain.

Enter Isander.

How is't *Isander?*
 Isand. Oh Heav'n! *Timon!*
 Tim. What, did I fright you? am I become so dreadful
An Object? is poverty contagious?
 Isand. Your Lordship ever shall be dear to me.
It makes me weep to think I cou'd not serve you
When you sent your Servant. I am expected at the Senate.

I humbly ask your pardon; I'll sell all I have
But I'll supply you soon.   [*Ex.* Isander.
 Tim. Smooth tongue, dissembling, weeping knave, farewel.
And farewel all Mankind! It shall be so——*Demetrius?*
Go to all these fellows. Tell 'em I'm supply'd, I have no
Need of 'em. Set out my condition to be as good
As formerly it has been, that this was but a Tryal,
And invite 'em all to Dinner.
 Dem. My Lord, there's nothing for 'em.
 Tim. I have taken order about that.
 Dem. What can this mean?   [*Ex.* Demetrius.
 Tim. I have one reserve can never fail me,
And while *Melissa*'s kind I can't be miserable;
She has a vast fortune in her own disposal.
The Sun will sooner leave his course than she
Desert me.

Enter first Servant.

Is *Melissa* at home?
 1 Serv. She is, my Lord; but will not see you.
 Tim. What does the Rascal say? Damn'd Villain
To bely her so?   [*Strikes him.*
 1 Serv. By Heav'n 'tis truth. She saies she will not see you.
Her woman told me first so. And when I would not
Believe her, she came and told me so her self;
That she had no business with you; desir'd you would
Not trouble her; she had affairs of consequence; &c.
 Tim. Now *Timon* thou art faln indeed; fallen from all thy
Hopes of happiness. Earth, open and swallow the
Most miserable wretch that thou did'st ever bear.
 1 Serv. My Lord! *Melissa*'s passing by.

Enter Melissa.

 Tim. Oh Dear *Melissa*!
 Mel. Is he here? what luck is this?
 Tim. Will you not look on me? not see your *Timon?*
And did not you send me word so?

Enter Evandra.

 Mel. I was very busy, and am so now; I must obey my

Father; I am going to him.

Tim. Was it not *Melissa* said, If *Timon* were reduc'd
To rags and misery, and she were Queen of all the Universe,
She would not change her love?

Mel. We can't command our wills;
Our fate must be obey'd.   [*Ex.* Mel.

Tim. Some Mountain cover me, and let my name,
My odious name be never heard of more.
O stragling Senses whither are you going?
Farewel, and may we never meet again.
Evandra! how does the sight of her perplex me!   [*Aside.*
I've been ungrateful to her, why should I
Blame Villains who are so to me?

Evan. Oh *Timon*! I have heard and felt all thy afflictions;
I thought I never shou'd have seen thee more;
Nor ever would, had'st thou continu'd prosperous.
Let false *Melissa* basely fly from thee,
Evandra is not made of that coarse stuff.

Tim. Oh turn thy eyes from an ungrateful man!

Evan. No, since I first beheld my ador'd *Timon*,
They have been fixt upon thee present, and when absent
I've each moment view'd thee in my mind,
And shall they now remove?

Tim. Wilt thou not fly a wretched Caitif? who
Has such a load of misery beyond
The strength of humane nature to support?

Evan. I am no base Athenian Parasite,
To fly from thy Calamities; I'll help to bear 'em.

Tim. Oh my *Evandra*, they're not to be born.
Accursed *Athens*! Forest of two-legg'd Beasts;
Plague, civil War, and famine, be thy lot:
Let propagation cease, that none of thy
Confounding spurious brood may spring
To infect and damn succeeding Generations;
May every Infant like the Viper gnaw
A passage through his mothers cursed Womb;
And kill the hag, or if they fail of it,
May then the Mothers like fell rav'nous Bitches
Devour their own base Whelps.

Evan. Timon! compose thy thoughts, I know thy wants,

223

And that thy Creditors like wild Beasts wait
To prey upon thee; and base *Athens* has
To its eternal Infamy deserted thee.
But thy unwearied bounty to *Evandra*
Has so enrich'd her, she in wealth can vie
With any of th' extorting Senators,
And comes to lay it all at thy feet.
    Tim. Thy most amazing generosity o'rewhelms me;
It covers me all o're with shame and blushes.
Thou hast oblig'd a wretch too much already,
And I have us'd thee ill for't; fly, fly, *Evandra*!
I have rage and madness, and I shall infect thee.
Earth! take me to thy Center; open quickly!
Oh that the World were all on fire!
    Evan. Oh my dear Lord! this sight will break my heart;
Take comfort to you, let your Creditors
Swallow their maws full; we have yet enough,
Let us retire together and live free
From all the smiles and frowns of humane kind;
I shall have all I wish for, having thee.
    Tim. My senses are not sound, I never can
Deserve thee: I've us'd thee scurvily.
    Evan. No, my dear *Timon*, thou hast not.
Comfort thy self, if thou hast been unkind,
Forgive thy self and I forgive thee for it.
    Tim. I never will.
Nor will I be oblig'd to one   [*Aside.*
I have treated so injuriously as her——
    Evan. Pray, my Lord, go home; strive to compose
Your self. All that I have was and is yours; I wish
It ne're had been, that yet I might have shewn
By stronger proofs how much I love my *Timon*.

*   *   *

[Act IV, Scene iii.]

Timon in the Woods digging.

    Tim. O blessed breeding Sun, draw from the Fens,
The Bogs and muddy Marishes, and from

Corrupted standing Lakes, rotten humidity
Enough to infect the Air with dire consuming Pestilence,
And let the poisonous exhalations fall
Down on th' *Athenians*; they're all flatterers,
And so is all mankind.
For every degree of fortune's smooth'd
And sooth'd by that below it; the learn'd pate
Ducks to the golden Fool; There's nothing level
In our conditions, but base Villany;
Therefore be abhor'd each man and all Society;
Earth yields me roots; thou common whore of mankind,
That put'st such odds amongst the rout of Nations;
I'll make thee do thy right office. Ha, what's here?
Gold, yellow, glittering precious gold! enough
To purchase my estate again: Let me see further;
What a vast mass of Treasure's here! There ly,
I will use none, 'twill bring me flatterers.
I'll send a pattern on't to the Athenians,
And let 'em know what a vast Mass I've found,
Which I'll keep from 'em. I think I see a Passenger
Not far off, I'll send it by him to the Senate.   [*Ex.* Timon.

[Act IV, Scene iv.]

Enter Evandra.

   Evan. How long shall I seek my unhappy Lord?
But I will find him or will lose my life.
Oh base and shameful Villany of man,
Amongst so many thousands he has oblig'd,
Not one would follow him in his afflictions!
Ha! here is a Spade! Sure this belongs to some one
Who's not far off, I will enquire of him.

Enter Timon.

   Tim. Who's there? what beast art thou that com'st
To trouble me?
   Evan. Pray do not hurt me. I am come to seek
The poor distressed *Timon*, did you see him?
   Tim. If thou be'st born of wicked humane race,

225

Why com'st thou hither to disturb his mind?
He has forsworn all Company!

Evan. Is this my Lord? oh dreadful transformation!
My dearest Lord, do you not know me?

Tim. Thou walk'st upon two legs, and hast a face
Erect towards Heav'n; and all such Animals
I have abjur'd; they are not honest,
Those Creatures that are so, walk on all four,
Prithee be gone.

Evan. He's much distracted, sure! Have you forgotten
Your poor *Evandra*?

Tim. No! I remember there was such a one,
Whom I us'd ill! why dost thou follow misery?
And add to it? prithee be gone.

Evan. These cruel words will break my heart. I come
Not to increase thy misery but mend it.
Ah, my dear *Timon*, why this Slave-like habit?
And why this Spade?

Tim. 'Tis to dig roots, and earn my dinner with.

Evan. I have converted part of my estate
To money and to Jewels, and have brought 'em
To lay 'em at thy feet, and the remainder
Thou soon shalt have.

Tim. I will not touch 'em; no, I shall be flatter'd.

Evan. Comfort thy self and quit this savage life;
We have enough in spite of all the baseness
Of th' *Athenians*, let not those Slaves
Triumph o're thy afflictions, wee'l live free.

Tim. If thou disswad'st me from this life, Thou hat'st me;
For all the Principalities on earth,
I would not change this Spade! prithee be gone,
Thou tempt'st me but in vain.

Evan. Be not so cruel.
Nothing but death shall ever take me from thee.

Tim. I'll never change my life: what would'st thou
Do with me?

Evan. I'd live the same: Is there a time or place,
A temper or condition I would leave
My *Timon* in?

Tim. You must not stay with me!

Evan. Oh too unkind!
I offer'd thee all my prosperity——
And thou most niggardly deniest me part
Of thy Afflictions.
   Tim. Ah soft *Evandra*! is not the bleak Air
Too boist'rous a Chamberlain for thee?
Or dost thou think these reverend trees that have
Outliv'd the Raven, will be Pages to thee?
And skip where thou appoint'st 'em? Will the Brook
Candid with Morning Ice, be Caudle to thee?
   Evan. Thou wilt be all to me.
   Tim. I am savage as a Satyr, and my temper
Is much unsound, my brain will be distracted.
   Evan. Thou wilt be *Timon* still, that's all I ask.
   Tim. It was a comfort to me when I thought
That thou wer't prosperous. Thou art too good
To suffer with me the rough boist'rous weather,
To mortifie thy self with roots and water,
'Twill kill thee. Prithee be gone.
   Evan. To Death if you command.
   Tim. I have forsworn all humane conversation.
   Evan. And so have I but thine.
   Tim. 'Twill then be misery indeed to see
Thee bear it.
   Evan. On my knees I beg it.
If thou refusest me, I'll kill my self.
I swear by all the Gods.
   Tim. Rise my *Evandra*!
I now pronounce to all the world, there is
One woman honest; if they ask me more
I will not grant it: Come, my dear *Evandra*,
I'll shew thee wealth enough I found with digging,
To purchase all my land again, which I
Will hide from all mankind.
   Evan. Put all my Gold and Jewels to't.
   Tim. Well said *Evandra*!

★   ★   ★

[Act IV, Scene v.]

Enter Poet, Painter *and* Musician.

Poet. As I took note o' the place it cannot be far off,
Where he abides.
Mus. Does the rumour hold for certain, that he's so full of Gold?
Poet. 'Tis true! H' has found an infinite store of Gold,
He has sent a Pattern of it to the Senate;
You will see him a Palm again in *Athens*,
And flourish with the highest of 'em all.
Therefore 'tis fit in this suppos'd distress,
We tender all our services to him——
Paint. If the report be true we shall succeed.
Mus. If we shou'd not——

Re-enter Timon *and* Evandra.

Poet. Wee'll venture our joint labours. Yon is he,
I know by the description.
Mus. Let's hide our selves and see how he will take it.

[*A Symphony.*

Evan. Here's Musick in the Woods, whence comes it?
Tim. From flattering Rogues who have heard that I
Have Gold; but that their disappointment would be greater,
In taking pains for nought, I'd send 'em back——
Poet. Hail worthy *Timon*——
Mus. Our most noble Master——
Paint. My most excellent Lord.
Tim. Have I once liv'd to see three honest men?
Poet. Having so often tasted of your bounty,
And hearing you were retir'd, your friends faln off,
For whose ungrateful natures we are griev'd,
We come to do you service.
Mus. We are not of so base a mold we should
Desert our noble Patron!
Tim. Most honest men! oh, how shall I requite you?
Can you eat roots, and drink cold water?
Poet. Whate're we can, we will to do you service.
Tim. Good men! come you are honest, you have heard
That I have gold enough! speak truth, y'are honest.
Poet. So it is said: but therefore came not we.

Mus. Not we my Lord.

Paint. We thought not of it.

Tim. You are good men, but have one monstrous fault.

Poet. I beseech your honour, what is it?

Tim. Each of you trusts a damn'd notorious Knave.

Paint. Who is that, my Lord?

Tim. Why one another, and each trusts himself.
Ye base Knaves, Tripartite! begone! make haste!
Or I will use you so like Knaves.   [*He stones 'em.*

  Poet. Fly, fly,——   [*All run out.*

  Tim. How sick am I of this false World! I'll now
Prepare my Grave, to lie where the light foam
Of the outragious Sea may wash my Corps.

  Evan. My dearest *Timon*, do not talk of Death;
My Life and thine together must determine.

  Tim. There is no rest without it; prithee leave
My wretched Fortune, and live long and happy,
Without thy *Timon*. There is wealth enough.

  Evan. I have no wealth but thee, let us lie down to rest;
I am very faint and heavy——   [*They lie down.*

Enter Melissa *and* Chloe.

  Mel. Let the Chariot stay there.
It is most certain he has found a Mass of money,
And he has sent word to the Senate he's richer than ever.

  Chlo. Sure were he rich, he would appear again.

  Mel. If he be, I doubt not but with my love I'll charm
Him back to *Athens*, 'twas my deserting him has
Made him thus Melancholy.

  Chlo. If he be not, you'l promise love in vain.

  Mel. If he be not, my promise shall be vain;
For I'll be sure to break it: Thus you saw
When *Alcibiades* was banish'd last,
I would not see him; I am always true
To interest and to my self. There Lord *Timon* lies!

  Tim. What wretch art thou come to disturb me?

  Mel. I am one that loves thee so, I cannot lose thee.
I am gotten from my Father and my Friends,
To call thee back to *Athens*, and her arms
Who cannot live without thee.

Evan. It is *Melissa*! prithee listen not
To her destructive *Syrens* voice.

Tim. Fear not.

Mel. Dost thou not know thy dear *Melissa*,
To whom thou mad'st such vows?

Tim. O yes, I know that piece of vanity,
That frail, proud, inconstant foolish thing.
I do remember once upon a time,
She swore eternal love to me, soon after
She would not see me, shun'd me, slighted me.

Mel. Ah now I see thou never lov'dst me *Timon*,
That was a tryal which I made of thee,
To find if thou didst love me, if thou hadst
Thou wouldst have born it: I lov'd thee then much more
Than all the World——but thou art false I see,
And any little change can drive thee from me,
And thou wilt leave me miserable.

Evan. Mind not that Crocodiles tears,
She would betray thee.

Mel. Is there no truth among Mankind? had I
So much ingratitude, I had left
Thy fallen fortune, and ne're seen thee more:
Ah *Timon*! could'st thou have been kind, I could
Rather have beg'd with thee, than have enjoy'd
With any other all the Pomp of *Greece*;
But thou art lost and hast forgotten all thy Oaths.

Evan. Why shou'd you strive to invade anothers right?
He's mine, for ever mine: These arms
Shall keep him from thee.

Mel. Thine! poor mean Fool! has marriage made him so?
No,——Thou art his Concubine, dishonest thing;
I would enjoy him honestly.

Tim. Peace, screech Owl: There is much more honesty
In this one woman than in all thy Sex
Blended together; our hearts are one;
And she is mine for ever: wert thou the Queen
Of all the Universe, I would not change her for thee.

Evan. Oh my dear Lord! this is a better Cordial
Than all the World can give.

Tim. False! proud! affected! vain fantastick thing;

Be gone, I would not see thee, unless I were
A Basilisk: thou boast'st that thou art honest of thy Body,
As if the Body made one honest: Thou hast a vile
Corrupted filthy mind——

    Mel. I am no Whore as she is.

    Tim. Thou ly'st, she's none: But thou art one in thy Soul:
Be gone, or thou'lt provoke me to do a thing unmanly,
And beat thee hence.

    Mel. Farewel Beast.——   [*Ex.* Mel. *and* Chlo.

    Evan. Let me kiss thy hand my dearest Lord,
If it were possible more dear than ever.

    Tim. Let's now go seek some rest within my Cave
        If any we can have without the Grave.   [*Exeunt.*

[Act V, Scene i.]

Enter Timon *and* Evandra.

    Tim. Now after all the follies of this life,
Timon has made his everlasting Mansion
Upon the beached Verge of the Salt Flood;
Where every day the swelling Surge shall wash him;
There he shall rest from all the Villainies,
Betraying smiles, or th'oppressing frowns
Of proud and impotent Man.

    Evan. Speak not of death, I cannot lose thee yet,
Throw off this dire consuming Melancholy.
Oh could'st thou love as I do, thou'd'st not have
Another wish but me. There is no state on Earth
Which I can envy while I've thee within
These Arms——take comfort to thee, think not yet
Of Death——leave not *Evandra* yet.

    Tim. Thinkst thou in Death we shall not think,
And know, and love, better than we can here?
Oh yes, *Evandra*! There our Happiness
Will be without a wish——I feel my long sickness
Of health and living now begin to mend,
And nothing will bring me all things: thou *Evandra*
Art the thing alone on Earth would make me wish
To play my part upon the troublesome Stage,
Where folly, madness, falshood, and cruelty,

Are the only actions represented.

    Evan. That I have lov'd my *Timon* faithfully
Without one erring thought, the Gods can witness;
And as my life was true my death shall be,
If I one minute after thee survive,
The scorn and infamy of all my Sex
Light on me, and may I live to be
Melissa's Slave.

    Tim. Oh my ador'd *Evandra!*
Thy kindness covers me with shame and grief,
I have deserv'd so little from thee;
Wer't not for thee I'd wish the World on Fire.

Enter Nicias, Phæax, Isidore, Isander, Cleon, Thrasillus, *and* Ælius.

More Plagues yet!

    Nici. How does the Worthy *Timon?*
It grieves our hearts to see thy low condition,
And we are come to mend it.

    Phæax. We and the *Athenians* cannot live without thee,
Cast from thee this sad grief, most noble *Timon,*
The Senators of *Athens* greet thee with
Their love, and do with one consenting voice
Intreat thee back to *Athens.*

    Tim. I thank 'em and would send 'em back the Plague,
Could I but catch it for 'em.

✶   ✶   ✶

[Act V, Scene iii.]

Enter Timon *and* Evandra *coming out of the Cave.*

    Evan. Oh my dear Lord! why do you stoop and bend
Like Flowers ore-charg'd with dew, whose yielding stalks
Cannot support 'em? I have a Cordial which
Will much revive thy Spirits.

    Tim. No, sweet *Evandra,*
I have taken the best Cordial, Death, which now
Kindly begins to work about my Vitals;
I feel him, he comforts me at heart.

    Evan. Oh my dear *Timon!* must we then part?

232

That I should live to see this fatal day!
Had death but seiz'd me first, I had been happy.
    Tim. My poor *Evandra*! lead me to my Grave!
Lest Death o'retake me——he pursues me hard:
He's close upon me. 'Tis the last office thou
Can'st do for *Timon*.
    Evan. Hard, stubborn Heart,
Wilt thou not break yet? Death, why art thou coy
To me that court thee?
    Tim. Lay me gently down
In my last tenement. Death's the truest Friend,
That will not flatter, but deals plainly with us.
So, now my weary Pilgrimage on Earth
Is almost finisht! Now my best *Evandra*
I charge thee, by our loves, our mutual loves,
Live! and live happy after me: and if
A thought of *Timon* comes into thy mind,
And brings a tear from thee, let some diversion
Banish it——quickly, strive to forget me.
    Evan. Oh! *Timon*! Thinkst thou I am such a Coward,
I will not keep my word? Death shall not part us.
    Tim. If thou'lt not promise me to live, I cannot
Resign my life in peace, I will be with thee
After my Death; my soul shall follow thee,
And hover still about thee, and guard thee from
All harm.
    Evan. Life is the greatest harm when thou art dead.
    Tim. Can'st thou forgive thy *Timon* who involv'd
Thee in his sad Calamities?
    Evan. It is a blessing to share any thing
With thee! oh thou look'st pale! thy countenance changes!
Oh whither art thou going?
    Tim. To my last home. I charge thee live, *Evandra*!
Thou lov'st me not, if thou wilt not obey me;
Thou only! dearest! kind! constant thing on earth,
Farewel.   [*Dies.*
    Evan. He's gone! he's gone! would all the world were so,
I must make haste, or I shall not o're-take
Him in his flight. *Timon*, I come, stay for me,
Farewel base World.   [*Stabs her self. Dies.*

[Act V, Scene iv.]

Enter Alcibiades, Phrinias, *and* Thais, *his Officers and Souldiers, and his Train, the Senators. The People by degrees assembling.*

Enter Melissa.

    Mel. My *Alcibiades*, welcome! doubly welcome!
The Joys of Love and Conquest ever bless thee.
Wonder and terrour of Mankind, and Joy
Of Woman-kind: now thy *Melissa*'s happy:
She has liv'd to see the utmost day she wisht for,
Her *Alcibiades* return with Conquest
O're this ungrateful City; and but that
I every day heard thou wert marching hither,
I had been with thee long ere this.
    Alcib. What gay, vain, prating thing is this?
    Mel. How my Lord! do you question who *Melissa* is?
And give her such foul Titles?
    Alcib. I know *Melissa*, and therefore give her such
Titles: for when the Senate banisht me
She would not see me, tho' upon her knees
Before she had sworn eternal love to me;
I see thy snares too plain to be caught now.
    Mel. I ne'r refus'd to see you, Heav'n can witness!
Who ever told you so, betray'd me basely:
Not see you! sure there's not a sight on earth
I'd chuse before you: You make me astonish'd!
    Alcib. All this you swore to *Timon*; and next day
Despis'd him——I have been inform'd
Of all your falsehood, and I hate thee for't;
I have Whores, good honest faithful Whores!
Good Antidotes against thy poison——Love;
Thy base false love; and tell me, is not one
Kind, faithful, loving Whore, better than
A thousand base, ill-natur'd honest Women?
    Mel. I never thought I should have liv'd to hear
This from my *Alcibiades*.
    Alcib. Do not weep,
Since I once lik'd thee, I'll do something for thee:
I have a Corporal that has serv'd me well,

I will prefer you to him.

    Mel. How have I merited this scorn——Farewel,
I'll never see you more.   [*Exit.*

    Alcib. I hope you will not.

★   ★   ★

Enter Nicias, Thrasillus, Phæax, Isidore, Isander, Ælius, *and* Cleon,
with Halters about their necks.

    Nicias. We come my noble Lord at thy Command,
And thus we humbly kneel before thy mercy.

    Phæ. Spare our lives, and wee'l employ 'em in
Thy service, worthy *Alcibiades.*

    Alcib. Do you acknowledge you are ungrateful Knaves?

    All. We do.

    Alcib. And that you have used me basely?

    All. We have, but we are very sorry.

    Alcib. I should do well to hang you for the Death
Of my brave Officer; but thousand such base lives
As yours would not weigh with his! go, ye have
Your liberty. And now the people are assembled,
I will declare my intentions towards them.

                          [*He ascends the Pulpit.*

My Fellow Citizens! I will not now upbraid
You for the unjust sentence past upon me,
In the return of which I have subdu'd
Your Enemies and all revolted places,
Made you Victorious both at Land and Sea,
And have with continual toil and numberless dangers
Stretcht out the bounds of your Dominions far
Above your hopes or expectations.
I will not recount the many enterprises,
No Grecian can be ignorant of. 'Tis enough
You know how I have serv'd you. Now it remains
I farther shou'd declare my self; I come
First to free you good Citizens of *Athens*
From the most insupportable yoaks
Of your four hundred Tyrants; and then next
To claim my own Estate which has unjustly
By them been kept from me that rais'd them.

235

I do confess, I in revenge of your decree
Against me, set up them, but never thought
They would have been such Cursed Tyrants to you,
Till now. They have gone on and fill'd the time
With most licentious acts; making their wills,
Their base corrupted wills, the scope of Justice,
While you in vain groan'd under all your suff'rings.
Thus when a few shall Lord it o're the rest,
They govern for themselves and not the People.
They rob and pill from them, from thence t' increase
Their private stores; but when the Government
Is in the Body of the People, they
Will do themselves no harm; therefore henceforth
I do pronounce the Government shall devolve upon the
People, and may Heav'n prosper 'em.

[*People shout and cry*, Alcibiades! Alcibiades! Long live
Alcibiades, Liberty, Liberty, &c. Alcib. *Descends.*

Enter Messenger.

Mes. My noble Lord! I went as you commanded,
And found Lord *Timon* dead, and his *Evandra*
Stab'd, and just by him lying in his Tomb,
On which was this Inscription.
    Alcib. I'll read it.
        Here lies a wretched Corse, of wretched Soul bereft,
        Timon *my name, a Plague consume you Caitiffs left.*
Poor *Timon*! I once knew thee the most flourishing man
Of all th' *Athenians*, and thou still hadst been so,
Had not these smiling, flattering Knaves devour'd thee,
And murder'd thee with base ingratitude.
His death pull'd on the poor *Evandra's* too;
That Miracle of Constancy in Love.
Now all repair to their respective homes,
Their several Trades, their bus'ness and diversions;
And whilst I guard you from your active Foes,
And fight your Battels, be you secure at home.
        May Athens *flourish with a lasting Peace;*
        And may its wealth and power ever increase.

[*All the People shout and cry*, Alcibiades! Alcibiades! Liberty, Liberty, &c.

EPILOGUE

If there were hopes that ancient solid Wit
Might please within our new fantastick Pit;
This Play might then support the Criticks shock,
This *Scion* grafted upon *Shakespeare*'s stock;
For join'd with his our Poets part might thrive,
Kept by the vertue of his sap alive.
Though now no more substantial English Playes,
Than good old Hospitality you praise;
The time shall come when true old sence shall rise
In Judgment over all your vanities.
Slight kickshaw Wit o'th' Stage, French meat at Feasts,
Now daily Tantalize the hungry Guests;
While the old English Chine us'd to remain,
And many hungry onsets would sustain.
At these thin Feasts each Morsel's swallow'd down,
And ev'ry thing but the Guests stomach's gone.
At these new fashion'd Feasts you have but a Tast,
With Meat or Wit you scarce can break a Fast.
This *Jantee* slightness to the French we owe,
And that makes all slight Wits admire 'em so.
They're of one Level, and with little pains
The Frothy Poet good reception gains;
But to hear English Wit there's use of brains.
Though Sparks to imitate the French think fit
In want of Learning, Affectation, Wit,
And which is most, in Cloaths, wee'l ne'r submit.
Their Ships or Plays o're ours shall ne're advance,
For our Third Rates shall match the First of *France*.
With English Judges this may bear the Test,
Who will for *Shakespeare*'s part forgive the rest.
The Sparks judge but as they hear others say,
They cannot think enough to mind the Play.
They to catch Ladies (which they dress at)
Or 'cause they cannot read or think at home;
Each here *deux yeux* and am'rous looks imparts,
Levells *Crevats* and *Perriwigs* at Hearts;
Yet they themselves more than the Ladies mind,
And but for vanity wou'd have 'em kind.

237

No passion——
But for their own Dear persons them can move,
Th' admire themselves too much to be in Love.
Nor Wit, nor Beauty, their hard Hearts can strike,
Who only their own sence or persons like.
But to the men of Wit our Poet flies,
To save him from Wits mortal Enemies.
Since for his Friends he has the best of those,
Guarded by them he fears not little Foes.
And with each Mistress we must favour find,⎤
They for *Evandra*'s sake will sure be kind; ⎬
At least all those to constant Love inclin'd. ⎦

18. Edward Ravenscroft, from his adaptation of *Titus Andronicus*

1678

From *Titus Andronicus, or The Rape of Lavinia . . . A Tragedy, Alter'd from Mr. Shakespeare's Works* (1687).

Edward Ravenscroft (*c.*1650–*c.*1700), a prolific dramatist, had his adaptation performed in the Autumn of 1678. He makes few changes until the final scene.

[Preface]

READER,

I Think it a greater theft to Rob the dead of their Praise than the Living of their Money: That I may not appear Guilty of such a Crime, 'tis necessary I should acquaint you, that there is a Play in Mr. *Shakespeare*'s Volume under the name of *Titus Andronicus*, from whence I drew part of this. I have been told by some anciently conversant with the Stage, that it was not Originally his, but brought by a private Author to be Acted, and he only gave some Master-touches to one or two of the Principal Parts or Characters; this I am apt to believe, because 'tis the most incorrect and indigested piece in all his Works; It seems rather a heap of Rubbish than a Structure.—However as if some great Building had been design'd, in the removal we found many Large and Square Stones both usefull and Ornamental to the Fabrick, as now Modell'd: Compare the Old Play with this, you'l finde that none in all that Authors Works ever receiv'd greater Alterations or Additions, the Language not only refin'd, but many Scenes entirely New: Besides most of the principal Characters heighten'd, and the Plot much encreas'd. The Success answer'd the Labour, tho' it first appear'd upon the Stage, at the beginning of the pretended Popish Plot, when neither Wit nor Honesty had Encouragement: Nor cou'd this expect favour since it shew'd the Treachery of Villains, and the Mischiefs carry'd on by Perjury, and False Evidence; and how Rogues may frame a Plot that shall deceive and destroy both the Honest and the Wise; which were the reasons why I did forward it at so unlucky a conjuncture, being content rather to lose the Profit, than not expose to the World the Picture of such Knaves and Rascals as then Reign'd in the opinion of the Foolish and Malicious part of the Nation: but it bore up against the Faction, and is confirm'd a Stock-Play. . . .

★　　★　　★

[Act V, Scene v.]

Enter Demetrius, Chiron, Junius, *in* Titus' *Garden.*

Demet. Now *Junius*, which is the place?
Jun. A little further.—— [*Walking forward.*
Chiron. Now shall that Wealth be our Easy purchase,
For which *Titus* sweat drops of Blood in War.
Jun. The place is cover'd close since I was here.
Lend me your Sword, my Lord, to pierce the ground,
And with the point find where the Gold does Lie.
Demet. Take mine. [Dem. *gives* Jun. *his naked Sword.*
Chi. Wherefore dost thou pause?
Jun. Why should this wound the Earth, that's innocent?
'Twere better run it in the Hearts of Villains,

Of Murderers and Ravishers.
    Dem. What means the Child?
    Jun. Thieves, Thieves!

Enter Titus *and Servants.*

    Chir. We are betray'd.
    Titus. There, Seize them, bind their hands, stop their Mouths.
    Dem. Villains forbear, we are the Empress Sons.
    Titus. Princes, and come to Rob an Old mans Orchard?
So: binde them fast. Oh my Little dear decoy,
Handsomly thou hast brought these Wild fowl to my Nets.

Enter Lavinia.

Come, come *Lavinia,* look, thy foes are bound.
Stop close their Mouths, let 'em not speak to me;
But let them hear what fearfull words I utter.
Oh Villains! *Chiron* and *Demetrius*!
Here stands the Spring whom you have stain'd with Mud;
This goodly Summer with your Winter mix'd.
You kill'd her Husband, and for that vile fault,
Two of her Brothers were Condemn'd to death,
My hand Cut off, and Subject made of Mirth.
Both her sweet Hands, her Tongue, and that more dear
Than Hands or Tongue, her spotless Chastity,
Inhumane Traytors, you constrain'd and forc'd.
Hark Villains, how I mean to Martyr you:
This one hand yet is left to Cut your Throats,
Whilst that *Lavinia* 'twixt her Stumps does hold
The Bason that receives your Guilty Blood.
Then shall your flesh be torn off with hot Pincers,
And your bones scrap'd 'till you are Skellitons.
For worse then *Philomel* you us'd my Daughter,
And worse then *Progne* I will be reveng'd.
Your Flesh shall be Cook'd for the Empress Pallate,
And your Blood mixt with all the Wine that's drunk.
Come bring them in, be every one officious,
To make this Banquet, which I wish may prove
More stern and Bloody than the *Centaurs* Feast.   [*Exeunt.*

[Act V, Scene vi.] Titus' house.

Enter Marcus, Lucius, Captains *and* Romans.

Mar. Wellcome worthy *Romans.*
Lucius. Wellcome, Valiant Friends.
Mar. All wellcome to the house of Old *Andronicus.*
A house of Woe and Sorrow, for nothing
But grief and Sad despair inhabit here.
And yet at sight of you the good Old man,
The Injur'd *Titus* will Even weep for Joy.

Enter Titus.

Lucius. See where he comes. But why dear aged Father
Dost thou appear thus like an Executioner?
Why is this Bloody Weapon in thy hand?
And why are these gray hairs sprinkl'd with blood?
Titus. 'Tis done, the bloody Act is done.
I have taken Vengeance on the Ravishers,
Chiron, Demetrius.——But I want the *Moor*,
The *Moor*, that dismall Fiend of darkness,
Those others, *Junius* and I entrap'd.——

Enter Goth *and Souldiers, with the* Moor *Bound.*

Goth. Bring in the Villain.
Titus. Ha the *Moor*!
Now would I clap my hands for Joy,
Were I not prevented by his Cruelty,
Which rob'd me of one.
Goth. Renowned *Roman*! Now Revenge that loss,
Revenge thy wrongs and mine.
Tit. Say *Goth*, for by thy habit *Goth* thou art,
Why hast thou done me this good turn?
Goth. I am a Soldier, and love not to speak but to the purpose.
Short then will be my speech and blunt.
Lucius. Say on.
Goth. Behold this *Moor* the Sire of this squob toad.
For this he and *Tamora* club'd together,
The Queen of *Goths* Tup'd by a Goat.
Tit. Ha! ha! ha!

Goth. The Nurse that only knew this secret deed—
This morning dy'd, but with her parting breath
Declar'd the secret to my Wife her frend.
And bid her bear this issue to the *Moor*—
Who wou'd reward her for't—and so he did:
For she no sooner had perform'd the trust,
But he his dagger struck into her heart,
And Bore away the Child in's Arms.——
I was not then far off, and knew it well.
And therefore follow'd him with these my friends.
Seiz'd him in flight, and bring him bound to you.

   Marc. Now Empress thy deeds of darkness come to light.

   Goth. If not concern'd for *Romes* dishonour
In a polluted Empress, Lustfull *Tamora,*
At least, incited by your private Wrongs,
Torment the Villain; Add to his pain one more
For murder of my wife.

   Tit. O worthy *Goth* be ever lov'd of us.
We will devise the Villains Punishment,
And thou shall be an Executioner.

   Luc. Say wall-Ey'd slave, whither would you convey
This growing Image of thy fiend-like face?
Why do'st not Speak? what, deaf, not a word!

   Tit. What! Monster art thou sullen?
But this and, *Moor,* much more thou shalt confess.
Drag him from hence, within there is a Rack,
Go bind him to't, that shall Extort from him
Each secret that lies hid in his dark soul.   { *Exeunt* Goth,

   Luc. Behold the Hellish Dog;   { Moor, *and Child.*
See how he Rowls his eyes and grins.

   Marc. The Trumpets sound, the Emperour is near,
Retire and lay your bloody weapon by.

   Tit. I'le fit my self for his reception.   [*Exit* Tit.

   Luc. Look out and give the word.
The Emperour shall hear our Musick too.

   Marc. See here he comes—see how the Tribunes croud above.

Enter Emperor, Tamora, Senators, *and others;* Marcus, Lucius, *and*
Captains *Range themselves on the other side.*

   Emp. What, hath the Firmament more Suns than one?

Luc. What dost avail to call thy self a Sun,
That art so muffl'd in black clouds,
The steams that rise from blood, hang round thee like a fog.
    Emp. See Empress I am brav'd already,
Came I to talk with Boys?
    Marc. Nephew, cease discourse,
This business must be quietly debated.
                        [Scene *draws and discovers a Banquett.*
Enter Titus, Junius, Lavinia *Vayl'd.*

    Marc. This great preparation by the carefull *Titus*
Was ordain'd to that Honourable End.
    Titus. With their presence let no'ne refuse to grace
The poor Table of *Andronicus.*——
First, I entreat that favour of the Emperour.
Next of his Empress.
    Tam. We are beholding to the good *Andronicus.*
    Titus. A poor Old man, but a well-meaning heart.
Give me a Bowl fill'd with *Falernian* Wine,
The like to every one——Health to the Emperour.
Madam, you'l pledge this Health.
    Tam. Ay, honest *Titus.*

            [*All drink, Trumpets sound on both sides.*

    Titus. Honest if you knew my thoughts.   [*Aside.*
    Emp. Why is that Lady Veil'd?
    Titus. My Lord the Emperour, resolve me this:
Was it well done of Old *Virginius*
To slay his Daughter with his own right hand
Because she had been Forc'd, Stain'd and Deflowr'd?
    Emp. It was, *Andronicus.*
    Titus. Your reason, mighty Emperour.
    Emp. Because she shou'd not then survive her shame,
And by her presence still renew his sorrows.
    Titus. A Reason weighty, strong and effectual,
A Pattern, Precedent, and lively warrant
For me most wretched to perform the like.
Dye, then, *Lavinia,* and thy shame with thee,
And with thy shame thy Fathers sorrow dye.   [*Kills* Lav.
    Emp. What hast thou done, unnatural and unkind?

Tam. Why hast thou slain thy only Daughter thus?

Tit. See there—no hands, no tongue is left, ⎰Titus *pulls off*
Nothing that could explain her Injuries, ⎱Lavinias *Veil.*
I am more wofull than *Virginius* was;
And had a thousand times more cause than he
To do this deed.

Emp. If she was Ravish'd, tell by whom?

Tit. That *Aron* best can tell.

Emp. The *Moor*!

Tam. Hear him not, he's Mad.

Emp. If it be not Frenzy, make it appear.

Tam. He cannot, 'tis perfect Madness.

Tit. I'le make both that and more appear.
A Child of darkness too is come to light.
Draw back that Screen.

[*The* Moor *discover'd on a Rack.*

Tam. *Aron* in Torment!

Tit. Empress keep your seat,
What here you see, is now beyond redress.
Moor, confess the Ravishers.

[Aron *shakes his head in sign he will not.*

No? Stretch him.——
By whom had'st thou this black brat,
This Babe of darkness?

[Aron *shakes his head again.*

Nor that neither? Disjoynt his Limbs.
Say now, did not *Chiron* and *Demetrius*
By thine and this Empress advice,
Wrong my *Lavinia*, and prompted
By you two, Murder *Bassianus*?

Aron. Ha—ha—ha——

Emp. Empress, what Crimes are these laid to your charge
And to your Sons——they Murder *Bassianus*?

Tam. All distraction still. They? Alas! no.
But *Demetrius*, *Chiron*, for you I fear;
Where are my Sons, if safe they would be here?

Tit. Reveal then what is yet unseen.

[*A Curtain drawn discovers the head and hands of* Dem. *and* Chir. *hanging up against the wall. Their bodies in Chairs in bloody Linnen.*

————Empress behold,
There are their heads, their hands, and mangl'd Truncks.

Tam. O dismall sight!

Tit. But here their hearts and Tongues.
No dish but holds some part of which y'ave fed.
And all the Wine y'ave drunk mixt with their blood.

Tam. Inhumane Villain!

Tit. Like the Earth thou hast swallow'd thy own encrease,
Thy self hast Eaten what thy self hast bred;
Thus cramm'd, thou'rt bravely faten'd up for Hell.
And thus to *Pluto* I do serve thee up.

[*Titus stabs the* Empress.

Emp. Dye frantick Wretch, for these effects of Madness.

[*Emp. stabs* Titus.

Luc. Can the sons eye behold the father bleed?
Thus quickly I revenge what thou hast done:
Dye unbelieving Tyrant.

[*Lucius stabs the* Emperor. *The* Sena. *and* Capt. *begin to move from above.*

Mar. Romans before you stir hear me a word;
I charge you hear me.

Emill. Speak *Marcus.*

Mar. Let any then forbear to move from's place
'Till we have heard the *Moors* confession.
Though he laughs upon the Wheel and mocks our torments,
Yet I will try another Experiment.
Give me the Hellish infant:

[*Marcus holds the Child as if he would Kill it.*

Moor, now speak
Or the young Kid goes after the Old Goat.

Aron. Save but the Child, I'le tell thee woundrous things,
That highly may advantage you to hear.

Tam. Moor, speak not a word against my honour
To save the World.

Aron. Yes, Empress, to save that childe I will.
The blow is given that will send you soon
Both from the shame and Punishment,
But all shall now be bury'd in my death,
Unless you swear to me that child shall Live.

Mar. Tell on thy Mind, thy child shall live.

Aron. Swear that it shall, and then I will begin.

Marc. Whom should we swear by? thou believ'st no God.

Moor. What if I do not? as indeed I do not,
Yet do I know you are Religious,
And have a thing within you called Conscience.
Therefore I urge your Oath for that I know
An Idiot holds his bauble for a God,
And keeps the Oath which by that god he swears.
Therefore I urge an Oath: swear then
To save my Boy, Nourish and bring him up,
Or else I will discover nought to thee.

Mar. By our Gods I swear.

Moor. And *Lucius* too, swear thou.

Lucius. I swear as *Marcus* did.

Moor. First know then I begot him on the *Empress*.

Emp. O Luxurious woman!

Aron. Nay this was but a deed of Charity
To that which you shall hear of me anon.
'Twas her two sons that Murder'd *Bassianus*.
They Cut *Lavinia*'s tongue and ravish'd her.

Mar. Barbarous Villains, like thy self!

Aron. Indeed I was their tutor to instruct them:
I train'd thy Nephews to that obscure hole,
I wrote the Letter which was found,
And hid the Gold within the Letter mention'd,
Confederate with the Queen and her two Sons.
I play'd the cheater for Old *Titus* hand.
For this device the *Empress* gave me twenty Kisses,
Sweet as were those I had in her Embraces,
When we were acting Pleasures, which produc'd
That Little thing where *Moor* and *Goths* combin'd,
And that is it which you have Sworn to save.

246

Emp. Stop the Villains Mouth, let him speak no more;
No more such words to my dishonour.
   Tam. I have now no other Son, and shou'd
Be kind to it in Death; let it approach me then,
That I may leave with it my parting Kiss.——

   [*The Child is brought to the* Empress, *she Stabs it.*

Dye thou off-spring of that Blab-tongu'd *Moor.*
   Aron. Accursed *Empress*!
   Tam. Accursed *Moor.*
May that breath be thy last as this is mine.   [*Dies.*
   Aron. She has out-done me in my own Art—
Out-done me in Murder— Kill'd her own Child.
Give it me— I'le eat it.
   Emp. If Spirits Live after our Bodies dye,
May the good Gods at distance far keep mine,
From that damn'd *Moors,* and *Empress* too from thine.
   Marcus. Romans, from what you have seen and heard.
Now Judge what cause had *Titus* to Revenge
These Wrongs unspeakable, past patience.
Have we done ought amiss, shew us wherein,
And from the highest Tower of this great Pile,
The poor remainder of *Andronici*
Will hand in hand all headlong cast us down,
And on the ragged Stones beat forth our Brains.
Speak *Romans* speak, and if you say we shall,
Lucius and I will thus Embracing fall.
   Emil. Worthy *Marcus,* and Valiant *Lucius* Live;
Lucius, Live Emperour of *Rome.*
I know it is the wish of all, then speak aloud.
   Omnes. Lucius, all hail, *Romes* Royall Emperour.
   Lucius. Thanks Noble *Romans.*

   [*All disappear from above.*

But worthy Friends, pray give me leave a while,
For Nature puts me to a heavy task,
At distance stand, but *Marcus* draw you near,
To shed obsequious tears upon this trunk.
O take this warm Kiss on thy pale cold Lips,
These sorrowfull drops upon thy bloud-stayn'd face;

247

The last true duty of thy pious Son.

    Marcus. Tear for Tear, and Loving Kiss,
Thy Brother *Marcus* tenders on thy Lips.

    Jun. Ah my poor dear Grandfather——
Father, I cannot speak more for tears.——

Enter All below.

    Emil. You sad *Andronici*, having done with grief,
Give Sentence on this execrable Wretch
That fill'd your House with all this Ruine.

    Lucius. It was decreed he should expire in flames,
Around him kindle streight his Funeral Fire.
The Matter is prepar'd, now let it blaze:

[The Fire flames about the Moor.

He shall at once be burnt and Rack'd to death.

    Aron. Wherefore shou'd Rage be mute and Fury dumb?
Ten thousand worser ills than e're I did
Would I perform if I might have my will.
If one good deed in all my Life I did
I now repent it from my very heart,
For proof I do, I'le Curse ye 'till I dye——
Vengeance and blewest Plagues consume ye all.

    Marcus. Snarle on, and like a Curs'd fell dog,
In howlings end thy Life.

[The Scene closes.

    Lucius. Now convey the Emp'rour to his Fathers Tomb;
As for that hatefull Tygress *Tamora*,
No Rights nor Funerall Ceremony.
My Noble Father and *Lavinia*
Shall be closed in our Houshold Monument,
Romans and Friends, assist ye all a while.
When these sad Ceremonies be perform'd,
Lead me to Empire, Crown me if you please,
But nothing this afflicted heart can ease.

19. John Dryden, from his adaptation of *Troilus and Cressida*

1679

From *Troilus and Cressida, Or, Truth Found too Late. A Tragedy ... To which is Prefix'd, A Preface Containing the Grounds of Criticism in Tragedy* (1679).

As Dryden explains in his preface, he has attempted to meet the neoclassic demands for poetic justice, unity of time and place, and a higher style for tragedy. The major alteration is in the character of Cressida, who is changed into a loyal and misunderstood heroine, gaining nobility in suicide. The play was performed some time before April 1679.

THE PREFACE TO THE PLAY.

The Poet *Æschylus* was held in the same veneration by the *Athenians* of after Ages as *Shakespeare* is by us; and *Longinus* has judg'd, in favour of him, that he had a noble boldnesse of expression, and that his imaginations were lofty and Heroick: but on the other side *Quintilian* affirms, that he was daring to extravagance. 'Tis certain, that he affected pompous words, and that his sence too often was obscur'd by Figures: Notwithstanding these imperfections, the value of his Writings after his decease was such, that his Countrymen ordain'd an equal reward to those Poets who could alter his Plays to be Acted on the Theater, with those whose productions were wholly new, and of their own. The case is not the same in *England*; though the difficulties of altering are greater, and our reverence for *Shakespeare* much more just, than that of the *Grecians* for *Æschylus*. In the Age of that Poet, the *Greek* tongue was arriv'd to its full perfection; they had then amongst them an exact Standard of Writing, and of Speaking: The *English* Language is not capable of such a certainty; and we are at present so far from it, that we are wanting in the very Foundation of it, a perfect Grammar. Yet it must be allow'd to the present Age, that the tongue in general is so much refin'd since *Shakespeare*'s time, that many of his words, and more of his Phrases, are scarce intelligible. And of those which we understand some are ungrammatical, others coarse; and his whole stile is so pester'd with Figurative expressions, that it is as affected as it is obscure. 'Tis true, that in his later Plays he had worn off somewhat of the rust; but the Tragedy which I have undertaken to correct, was, in all probability, one of his first endeavours on the Stage.

The Original story was Written by one *Lollius* a *Lombard*, in Latin verse, and Translated by *Chaucer* into English: intended I suppose a Satyr on the Inconstancy of Women: I find nothing of it among the Ancients; not so much as the name once *Cressida* mention'd. *Shakespeare*, (as I hinted) in the Aprenticeship of his Writing, model'd it into that Play, which is now call'd by the name of *Troilus and Cressida*; but so lamely is it left to us, that it is not divided into Acts: which fault I ascribe to the Actors, who Printed it after *Shakespeare*'s death; and that too, so carelessly, that a more uncorrect Copy I never saw. For the Play itself, the Author seems to have begun it with some fire; the Characters of *Pandarus* and *Thersites*, are promising enough; but as if he grew weary of his task, after an Entrance or two, he lets 'em fall: and the later part of the Tragedy is nothing but a confusion of Drums and Trumpets, Excursions and Alarms. The chief persons, who give name to the Tragedy, are left alive: *Cressida* is false, and is not punish'd. Yet after all, because the Play was *Shakespeare*'s, and that there appear'd in some places of it, the admirable Genius of the Author; I undertook to remove that heap of Rubbish, under which many excellent thoughts lay wholly bury'd. Accordingly, I new model'd the Plot; threw out many unnecessary persons; improv'd those Characters which were begun, and left unfinish'd: as *Hector*, *Troilus*, *Pandarus* and *Thersites*; and added that of *Andromache*. After this, I made with no small trouble, an Order and Connexion of all the Scenes; removing them from the places where they were inartificially set: and though it was impossible to keep 'em all unbroken, because the Scene must be sometimes in the City, and sometimes in the Camp, yet I have so order'd them that there is a coherence of 'em with one another, and a dependence on the main design: no leaping from *Troy* to the Grecian Tents, and thence back again in the same Act; but a due proportion of time allow'd for every motion. I need not say that I have refin'd his Language, which before was obsolete; but I am willing to acknowledg, that as I have often drawn his English nearer to our times, so I have somtimes conform'd my own to his: & consequently, the Language is not altogether so pure, as it is significant. The Scenes of *Pandarus* and *Cressida*, of *Troilus* and *Pandarus*, of *Andromache* with *Hector* and the Trojans, in the second Act, are wholly *New*: together with that of *Nestor* and *Ulysses* with *Thersites*; and that of *Thersites* with *Ajax* and *Achilles*. I will not weary my Reader with the Scenes which are added of *Pandarus* and the Lovers, in the Third; and those of *Thersites*, which are wholly alter'd: but I cannot omit the last Scene in it, which is almost half the Act, betwixt *Troilus* and *Hector*. The occasion of raising it was hinted to me by Mr. *Betterton*: the contrivance and working of it was my own. They who think to do me an injury, by saying that it is an imitation of the Scene betwixt *Brutus* and *Cassius*, do me an honour, by supposing I could imitate the incomparable *Shakespeare*: but let me add, that if *Shakespeare*'s Scene, or that faulty Copy of it in *Amintor* and *Melantius* had never been, yet *Euripides* had furnish'd me with an excellent example in his *Iphigenia*, between *Agamemnon* and *Menelaus*: and from thence indeed, the last turn of it is borrow'd. The occasion which *Shakespeare*, *Euripides*, and *Fletcher*, have all taken, is the same; grounded upon Friendship: and the quarrel of two virtuous men, rais'd by natural degrees, to the extremity of passion, is conducted in all three, to the declination of the same passion; and concludes with a warm renewing of their Friendship. But the particular groundwork which *Shakespeare* has taken, is incomparably the best: Because he has not only chosen two the greatest Heroes of their Age; but has likewise interested the Liberty of *Rome*, and their own honors, who were the redeemers of it, in this debate. And if he has made *Brutus* who was naturally a patient man, to fly into excess at first; let it be remembered in his defence, that just before, he has receiv'd the news of *Portia*'s death: whom the Poet, on purpose neglecting a little Chronology, supposes to have dy'd before *Brutus*, only to give him an occasion of being more easily exasperated. Add to this, that the injury he had receiv'd from *Cassius*, had long been brooding in his mind; and that a melancholy man, upon consideration of an affront, especially from a Friend, would be more eager in his passion, than he who had given it, though naturally more cholerick. . . .

I have been so tedious in three Acts, that I shall contract my self in the two last. The beginning Scenes of the fourth Act are either added, or chang'd wholly by me; the middle of it is *Shakespeare* alter'd, and mingled with my own, three or four of the last Scenes are altogether new. And the whole Fifth Act, both the Plot and the Writing are my own Additions.

But having written so much for imitation of what is excellent, in that part of the *Preface* which related only to myself; methinks it would neither be unprofitable nor unpleasant to enquire how far we ought to imitate our own Poets, *Shakespeare* and *Fletcher* in their Tragedies: And this will occasion another enquiry, how those two Writers differ between themselves: but since neither of these questions can be solv'd unless some measures be first taken, by which we may be enabled to judge truly of their Writings: I shall endeavour as briefly as I can, to discover the grounds and reason of all Criticism, applying them in this place only to Tragedy. *Aristotle* with his Interpreters, and *Horace*, and *Longinus*, are the Authors to whom I owe my lights; and what part soever of my own Plays, or of this, which no mending could make regular, shall fall under the condemnation of such Judges, it would be impudence in me to defend. I think it no shame to retract my errors, and am well pleas'd to suffer in the cause, if the Art may be improv'd at my expence: I therefore proceed to,

The Grounds of Criticism in Tragedy.

Tragedy is thus defined by *Aristotle*, (omiting what I thought unnecessary in his Definition.) 'Tis an imitation of one intire, great, and probable action; not told but represented, which by moving in us fear and pity, is conducive to the purging of those two passions in our minds. More largly thus, Tragedy describes or paints an Action, which Action must have all the proprieties above nam'd. First, it must be one or single, that is, it must not be a History of one Mans life: Suppose of *Alexander* the Great, or *Julius Cæsar*, but one single action of theirs. This condemns all *Shakespeare*'s Historical Plays, which are rather Chronicles represented, than Tragedies, and all double action of Plays. As to avoid a Satyr upon others, I will make bold with my own *Marriage-A-la-Mode*, where there are manifestly two Actions, not depending on one another: but in *Oedipus* there cannot properly be said to be two Actions, because the love of *Adrastus* and *Euridice* has a necessary dependance on the principal design, into which it is woven. The natural reason of this Rule is plain, for two different independant actions, distract the attention and concernment of the Audience, and consequently destroy the intention of the Poet: If his business be to move terror and pity, and one of his Actions be Comical, the other Tragical, the former will divert the people, and utterly make void his greater purpose. Therefore as in Perspective, so in Tragedy, there must be a point of sight in which all the lines terminate: Otherwise the eye wanders, and the work is false. This was the practice of the *Grecian* Stage. But *Terence* made an innovation in the *Roman*: all his Plays have double Actions; for it was his custome to Translate two Greek Comedies, and to weave them into one of his, yet so, that both the Actions were Comical; and one was principal, the other but secondary or subservient. And this has obtain'd on the *English* Stage, to give us the pleasure of variety.

As the Action ought to be one, it ought as such, to have Order in it, that is, to have a natural beginning, a middle, and an end: A natural beginning says *Aristotle*, is that which could not necessarily have been plac'd after another thing, and so of the rest. This consideration will arraign all Plays after the new model of *Spanish* Plots, where accident is heap'd upon accident, and that which is first might as reasonably be last: an inconvenience not to be remedyed, but by making one accident naturally produce another, otherwise 'tis a Farce, and not a Play. Of this nature, is the *Slighted Maid*; where there is no Scene in the first Act, which might not by as good reason be in the fifth. And if the Action ought to be one, the Tragedy ought likewise to conclude with the Action of it. Thus in *Mustapha*, the Play should naturally have ended with the death of *Zanger*, and not have given us the grace Cup after Dinner, of *Solyman*'s divorce from *Roxolana*.

The following properties of the Action are so easy, that they need not my explaining. It ought to be great, and to consist of great Persons, to distinguish it from Comedy; where the Action is trivial, and the persons of inferior rank. The last quality of the action is, that it ought to be probable, as well as admirable and great. 'Tis not necessary that there should be Historical truth in it; but always necessary that there should be a likeness of truth, something that is more than barely possible, probable being that which succeds or happens oftner than it misses. To invent therefore a probability, and to make it wonderfull, is the most difficult undertaking in the Art of Poetry: for that which is not wonderfull, is not great, and that which is not probable, will not delight a reasonable Audience. This action thus describ'd, must be represented and not told, to distinguish Dramatic Poetry from Epic: but I hasten to the end, or scope of Tragedy; which is to rectify or purge our passions, fear and pity.

To instruct delightfully is the general end of all Poetry: Philosophy instructs, but it performs its work by precept: which is not delightfull, or not so delightfull as Example. To purge the passions by Example, is therefore the particular instruction which belongs to Tragedy. *Rapin*, a judicious Critic, has observ'd from *Aristotle*, that pride and want of commiseration are the most predominant vices in Mankinde: therefore to cure us of these two, the inventors of Tragedy, have chosen to work upon two other passions, which are fear and pity. We are wrought to fear, by their seting before our eyes some terrible example of misfortune, which hapned to persons of the highest Quality; for such an action demonstrates to us, that no condition is privileg'd from the turns of Fortune: this must of necessity cause terror in us, and consequently abate our pride. But when we see that the most virtuous, as well as the greatest, are not exempt from such misfortunes, that consideration moves pity in us: and insensibly works us to be helpfull to, and tender over the distress'd, which is the noblest and most Godlike of moral virtues. Here 'tis observable, that it is absolutely necessary to make a man virtuous, if we desire he should be pity'd: We lament not, but detest a wicked man, we are glad when we behold his crimes are punish'd, and that Poetical justice is done upon him. *Euripides* was censur'd by the Critics of his time, for making his chief characters too wicked: for example, *Phædra*, though she loved her Son-in-law with reluctancy, and that it was a curse upon her Family for offending *Venus*, yet was thought too ill a pattern for the Stage. Shall we therefore banish all characters of villany? I confess I am not of that opinion; but it is necessary that the Hero of the Play be not a Villain: that is, the characters which should move our pity ought to have virtuous inclinations, and degrees of morall goodness in them. As for a perfect character of virtue, it never was in Nature; and therefore there can be no imitation of it: but there are allays of frailty to be allow'd for the chief Persons, yet so that the good which is in them, shall outweigh the bad; and consequently leave room for punishment on the one side, and pity on the other.

After all, if any one will ask me, whether a Tragedy cannot be made upon any other grounds, than those of exciting pity and terror in us? *Bossu*, the best of modern Critics, answers thus in general: That all excellent Arts, and particularly that of Poetry, have been invented and brought to perfection by men of a transcendent Genius; and that therefore they who practice afterwards the same Arts, are oblig'd to tread in their footsteps, and to search in their Writings the foundation of them: for it is not just that new Rules should destroy the authority of the old. But *Rapin* writes more particularly thus: That no passions in a story are so proper to move our concernment as Fear and Pity; and that it is from our concernment we receive our pleasure, is undoubted;

when the Soul becomes agitated with fear for one character, or hope for another; then it is that we are pleas'd in Tragedy, by the interest which we take in their adventures.

Here therefore the general answer may be given to the first question, how far we ought to imitate *Shakespeare* and *Fletcher* in their Plots; namely that we ought to follow them so far only, as they have Copy'd the excellencies of those who invented and brought to perfection Dramatic Poetry: those things only excepted which Religion, customs of Countries, Idioms of Languages, &c. have alter'd in the Super-structures, but not in the foundation of the design.

How defective *Shakespeare* and *Fletcher* have been in all their Plots, Mr. *Rymer* has discover'd in his *Criticisms*: neither can we, who follow them, be excus'd from the same or greater errors; which are the more unpardonable in us, because we want their beauties to counterveil our faults. The best of their designs, the most approaching to Antiquity, and the most conducing to move pity, is the *King and no King*; which if the Farce of *Bessus* were thrown away, is of that inferior sort of Trage-dies, which end with a prosperous event. 'Tis probably deriv'd from the story of *Œdipus*, with the character of *Alexander the Great*, in his extravagancies, given to *Arbaces*. The taking of this Play, amongst many others, I cannot wholly ascribe to the excellency of the action; for I finde it moving when it is read: 'tis true, the faults of the Plot are so evidently prov'd, that they can no longer be deny'd. The beauties of it must therefore lie either in the lively touches of the passions: or we must conclude, as I think we may, that even in imperfect Plots, there are less degrees of Nature, by which some faint emotions of pity and terror are rais'd in us: as a less Engine will raise a less proportion of weight, though not so much as one of *Archimedes* making; for nothing can move our nature, but by some natural reason, which works upon passions. And since we acknowledge the effect, there must be something in the cause.

The difference between *Shakespeare* and *Fletcher* in their Plotting seems to be this, that *Shakespeare* generally moves more terror, and *Fletcher* more compassion: For the first had a more Masculine, a bolder and more fiery Genius; the Second a more soft and Womanish. In the mechanic beauties of the Plot, which are the Observation of the three Unities, Time, Place, and Action, they are both deficient; but *Shake-speare* most. *Ben. Jonson* reform'd those errors in his Comedies, yet one of *Shakespeare*'s was Regular before him: which is, *The Merry Wives of Windsor*. For what remains concerning the design, you are to be refer'd to our English Critic. That method which he has prescrib'd to raise it from mistake, or ignorance of the crime, is certainly the best though 'tis not the only: for amongst all the Tragedies of *Sophocles*, there is but one, *Œdipus*, which is wholly built after that model.

After the Plot, which is the foundation of the Play, the next thing to which we ought to apply our Judgment is the manners, for now the Poet comes to work above ground: the ground-work indeed is that which is most necessary, as that upon which depends the firmness of the whole Fabric; yet it strikes not the eye so much, as the beauties or imperfections of the manners, the thoughts and the expressions.

The first Rule which *Bossu*, prescribes to the Writer of an Heroic Poem, and which holds too by the same reason in all Dramatic Poetry, is to make the moral of the work; that is, to lay down to your self what that precept of morality shall be, which you would insinuate into the people: as namely, *Homer*'s, (which I have Copy'd in my *Conquest of Granada*) was, that Union preserves a Common-wealth, and discord destroys it. *Sophocles*, in his *Œdipus*, that no man is to be accounted happy before his death. 'Tis the Moral that directs the whole action of the Play to one center; and that action or Fable, is the example built upon the moral, which confirms the truth of it to our experience: when the Fable is design'd, then and not before, the Persons are to be introduc'd with their manners, characters and passions.

The manners in a Poem, are understood to be those inclinations, whether natural or acquir'd, which move and carry us to actions, good, bad, or indifferent in a Play; or which incline the persons to such, or such actions: I have anticipated part of this discourse already, in declaring that a Poet ought not to make the manners perfectly good in his best persons, but neither are they to be more wicked in any of his characters, than necessity requires. To produce a Villain, without other reason than a natural inclination to villany, is in Poetry to produce an effect without a cause: and to make him more a Villain than he has just reason to be, is to make an effect which is stronger than the cause.

The manners arise from many causes: and are either distinguish'd by complexion, as choleric and phlegmatic, or by the differences of Age or Sex, of Climates, or Quality of the persons, or their present condition: they are likewise to be gather'd from the several Virtues, Vices, or Passions, and many other common-places which a Poet must be suppos'd to have learn'd from natural Philosophy, Ethics, and History; of all which whosoever is ignorant, does not deserve the Name of Poet.

But as the manners are usefull in this Art, they may be all compris'd under these general heads: First, they must be apparent, that is in every character of the Play, some inclinations of the Person must appear: and these are shown in the actions and discourse. Secondly the manners must be suitable or agreeing to the Persons; that is, to the Age, Sex, dignity, and the other general heads of Manners: thus when a Poet has given the Dignity of a King to one of his persons, in all his actions and speeches, that person must discover Majesty, Magnanimity, and jealousy of power; because these are suitable to the general manners of a King. The third property of manners is resemblance; and this is founded upon the particular characters of men, as we have them deliver'd to us by relation or History: that is, when a Poet has the known character of this or that man before him, he is bound to represent him such, at least not contrary to that which Fame has reported him to have been: thus it is not a Poets choice to make *Ulysses* choleric, or *Achilles* patient, because *Homer* has describ'd 'em quite otherwise. Yet this is a Rock, on which ignorant Writers daily split: and the absurdity is as monstrous, as if a Painter should draw a Coward running from a Battle, and tell us it was the Picture of *Alexander the Great*.

The last property of manners is, that they be constant, and equal, that is, maintain'd the same through the whole design: thus when *Virgil* had once given the name of *Pious* to *Æneas*, he was bound to show him such, in all his words and actions through the whole Poem. All these properties *Horace* has hinted to a judicious observer. 1. *Notandi sunt tibi mores*, 2. *aut famam sequere*, 3. *aut sibi convenientia finge*. 4. *Servetur ad imum, qualis ab incepto processerit, & sibi constet.*[1]

From the manners, the Characters of persons are deriv'd, for indeed the characters are no other than the inclinations, as they appear in the several persons of the Poem. A character being thus defin'd, that which distinguishes one man from another. Not to repeat the same things over again which have been said of the manners, I will only add what is necessary here. A character, or that which distinguishes one man from all others, cannot be suppos'd to consist of one particular Virtue, or Vice, or passion only; but 'tis a composition of qualities which are not contrary to one another in the same person: thus the same man may be liberal and valiant, but not liberal and covetous; so in a Comical character, or humour, (which is an inclination to this, or that par-

---

[1] Horace, *A.P.* 156, 119, 126–7: 'You must note the manners of each age . . .;' 'Either follow tradition or invent what is self-consistent'; '. . . have [the character] kept to the end even as it came forth at the first, and have it self-consistent.'

ticular folly) *Falstaff* is a lyar, and a coward, a Glutton, and a Buffoon, because all these qualities may agree in the same man; yet it is still to be observ'd, that one virtue, vice, and passion, ought to be shown in every man, as predominant over all the rest: as covetousness in *Crassus*, love of his Country in *Brutus*; and the same in characters which are feign'd.

The chief character or Hero in a Tragedy, as I have already shown, ought in prudence to be such a man, who has so much more in him of Virtue than of Vice, that he may be left amiable to the Audience, which otherwise cannot have any concernment for his sufferings: and 'tis on this one character that the pity and terror must be principally, if not wholly founded. A Rule which is extreamly necessary, and which none of the Critics that I know, have fully enough discover'd to us. For terror and compassion work but weakly, when they are divided into many persons. If *Creon* had been the chief character in *Œdipus*, there had neither been terror nor compassion mov'd; but only detestation of the man and joy for his punishment; if *Adrastus* and *Euridice* had been made more appearing characters, then the pity had been divided, and lessen'd on the part of *Œdipus*: but making *Œdipus* the best and bravest person, and even *Jocasta* but an underpart to him; his virtues and the punishment of his fatall crime, drew both the pity, and the terror to himself.

By what had been said of the manners, it will be easy for a reasonable man to judge, whether the characters be truly or falsely drawn in a Tragedy; for if there be no manners appearing in the characters, no concernment for the persons can be rais'd: no pity or horror can be mov'd, but by vice or virtue, therefore without them, no person can have any business in the Play. If the inclinations be obscure, 'tis a sign the Poet is in the dark, and knows not what manner of man he presents to you; and consequently you can have no Idea, or very imperfect, of that man: nor can judge what resolutions he ought to take; or what words or actions are proper for him: Most Comedies made up of accidents, or adventures, are liable to fall into this error: and Tragedies with many turns are subject to it: for the manners never can be evident, where the surprises of Fortune take up all the business of the Stage; and where the Poet is more in pain, to tell you what hapned to such a man, than what he was. 'Tis one of the excellencies of *Shakespeare*, that the manners of his persons are generally apparent; and you see their bent and inclinations. *Fletcher* comes far short of him in this, as indeed he does almost in every thing: there are but glimmerings of manners in most of his Comedies, which run upon adventures: and in his Tragedies, *Rollo, Otto,* the *King and No King, Melantius,* and many others of his best, are but Pictures shown you in the twi-light; you know not whether they resemble vice, or virtue, and they are either good, bad, or indifferent, as the present Scene requires it. But of all Poets, this commendation is to be given to *Ben. Jonson,* that the manners even of the most inconsiderable persons in his Plays are every where apparent.

By considering the Second quality of manners, which is that they be suitable to the Age, Quality, Country, Dignity, &c. of the character, we may likewise judge whether a Poet has follow'd Nature. In this kinde *Sophocles* and *Euripides,* have more excell'd among the Greeks than *Æschylus:* and *Terence,* more than *Plautus* among the Romans: Thus *Sophocles* gives to *Œdipus* the true qualities of a King, in both those Plays which bear his Name: but in the latter which is the *Œdipus Colonæus,* he lets fall on purpose his Tragic Stile, his Hero speaks not in the Arbitrary tone; but remembers in the softness of his complaints, that he is an unfortunate blind Old man, that he is banish'd from his Country, and persecuted by his next Relations. The present French Poets are generally accus'd, that wheresoever they lay the Scene, or in whatsoever Age, the manners of their Heroes are wholly French: *Racine*'s *Bajazet* is bred at *Constantinople*; but his civilities are convey'd to him by some secret passage, from *Versailles* into the *Seraglio.* But our *Shakespeare,* having ascrib'd to *Henry the Fourth* the character of a King, and of a Father, gives him the perfect manners of each Relation, when either he transacts with his Son, or with his Subjects. *Fletcher,* on the other side gives neither to *Arbaces,* nor to his King in the *Maids Tragedy,* the qualities which are suitable to a Monarch: though he may be excus'd a little in the latter; for the King there is not uppermost in the character; 'tis the Lover of *Evadne,* who is King only, in a second consideration; and though he be unjust, and has other faults which shall be nameless, yet he is not the Hero of the Play: 'tis true we finde him a lawfull Prince, (though I never heard of any King that was in *Rhodes*) and therefore Mr. *Rymer*'s Criticism stands good; that he should not be shown in so vicious a character. *Sophocles* has been more judicious in his *Antigone* for though he represent in *Creon* a bloody Prince, yet he makes him not a lawful King, but an Usurper, and *Antigone* her self is the Heroin of the Tragedy: But when *Philaster* wounds *Arethusa* and the Boy; and *Perigot* his Mistress, in *The Faithfull Shepherdess,* both these are contrary to the character of Manhood: Nor is *Valentinian* manag'd much better, for though *Fletcher* has taken his Picture truly, and shown him as he was, an effeminate voluptuous man, yet he has forgotten that he was an Emperor, and has given him none of those Royal marks, which ought to appear in a lawfull Successor of the Throne. If it be enquir'd, what *Fletcher* should have done on this occasion; ought he not to have represented *Valentinian* as he was? *Bossu* shall answer this question for me, by an instance of the like nature: *Mauritius* the Greek Emperor, was a Prince far surpassing *Valentinian*, for he was endued with many Kingly virtues; he was Religious, Mercifull, and Valiant, but withall he was noted of extream covetousness, a vice which is contrary to the character of a Hero, or a Prince: therefore says the Critic, that Emperor was no fit person to be represented in a Tragedy, unless his good qualities were only to be shown, and his covetousness (which sullyed them all) were slur'd over by the artifice of the Poet. To return once more to *Shakespeare*; no man ever drew so many characters, or generally distinguished 'em better from one another, excepting only *Jonson*: I will instance but in one, to show the copiousness of his Invention; 'tis that of *Calyban*, or the Monster in the *Tempest*. He seems there to have created a person which was not in Nature, a boldness which at first sight would appear intolerable: for he makes him a Species of himself, begotten by an *Incubus* on a *Witch*; but this as I have elsewhere prov'd, is not wholly beyond the bounds of credibility, at least the vulgar still believe it. We have the separated notions of a spirit, and of a Witch; (and Spirits according to *Plato*, are vested with a subtil body; according to some of his followers, have different Sexes) therefore as from the distinct apprehensions of a Horse, and of a Man, Imagination has form'd a *Centaur*, so from those of an *Incubus* and a *Sorceress*, *Shakespeare* has produc'd his Monster. Whether or no his Generation can be defended, I leave to Philosophy; but of this I am certain, that the Poet has most judiciously furnish'd him with a person, a Language, and a character, which will suit him, both by Fathers and Mothers side: he has all the discontents, and malice of a Witch, and of a Devil; besides a convenient proportion of the deadly sins; Gluttony, Sloth, and Lust, are manifest; the dejectedness of a slave is likewise given him, and the ignorance of one bred up in a Desart Island. His person is monstrous, as he is the product of unnatural Lust; and his language is as hobgoblin as his person: in all things he is distinguish'd from other mortals. The characters of *Fletcher* are poor & narrow, in comparison of *Shakespeare*'s; I remember not one which is not borrow'd from him; unless you will except that strange mixture of a man in the *King and no King*: So that in this part *Shakespeare* is generally worth our Imitation; and to imitate *Fletcher* is but to Copy after him who was a Copyer.

Under this general head of Manners, the passions are naturally included, as belonging to the Characters. I speak not of pity and of terror, which are to be mov'd in the Audience by the Plot; but of Anger, Hatred, Love, Ambition, Jealousy, Revenge, *&c.* as they are shown in this or that person of the Play. To describe these naturally, and to move then artfully, is one of the greatest commendations which can be given to a Poet: to write pathetically, says *Longinus*, cannot proceed but from a lofty *Genius*. A Poet must be born with this quality; yet, unless he help himself by an acquir'd knowledg of the Passions, what they are in their own nature, and by what springs they are to be mov'd, he will be subject either to raise them where they ought not to be rais'd, or not to raise them by the just degrees of Nature, or to amplify them beyond the natural bounds, or not to observe the crisis and turns of them, in their cooling and decay: all which errors proceed from want of Judgment in the Poet, and from being unskill'd in the Principles of Moral Philosophy. Nothing is more frequent in a Fanciful Writer, than to foil himself by not managing his strength: therefore, as in a Wrestler, there is first requir'd some measure of force, a well-knit body, and active Limbs, without which all instruction would be vain; yet, these being granted, if he want the skill which is necessary to a Wrestler, he shall make but small advantage of his natural robustuousness: So in a Poet, his inborn vehemence and force of spirit, will only run him out of breath the sooner, if it be not supported by the help of Art. The roar of passion indeed may please an Audience, three parts of which are ignorant enough to think all is moving which is noise, and it may stretch the lungs of an ambitious Actor, who will dye upon the spot for a thundring clap; but it will move no other passion than indignation and contempt from judicious men. *Longinus*, whom I have hitherto follow'd, continues thus: If the passions be Artfully employ'd, the discourse becomes vehement and lofty; if otherwise, there is nothing more ridiculous than a great passion out of season. . . . Thus then the Passions, as they are consider'd simply and in themselves, suffer violence when they are perpetually maintain'd at the same height; for what melody can be made on that Instrument all whose strings are screw'd up at first to their utmost stretch, and to the same sound? But this is not the worst; for the Characters likewise bear a part in the general calamity, if you consider the Passions as embody'd in them: for it follows of necessity, that no man can be distinguish'd from another by his discourse, when every man is ranting, swaggering, and exclaiming with the same excess: as if it were the only business of all the Characters to contend with each other for the prize at *Billingsgate*; or that the Scene of the Tragedy lay in *Bet'lem*. Suppose the Poet should intend this man to be Cholerick, and that man to be patient; yet when they are confounded in the Writing, you cannot distinguish them from one another: for the man who was call'd patient and tame, is only so before he speaks; but let his clack be set a going, and he shall tongue it as impetuously, and as loudly as the errantest Hero in the Play. By this means, the characters are only distinct in name; but in reality, all the men and women in the Play are the same person. No man should pretend to write, who cannot temper his fancy with his Judgment: nothing is more dangerous to a raw horseman, than a hot-mouth'd Jade without a curb.

'Tis necessary therefore for a Poet, who would concern an Audience by describing of a Passion, first to prepare it, and not to rush upon it all at once. *Ovid* has judiciously shown the difference of these two ways, in the speeches of *Ajax* and *Ulysses*: *Ajax* from the very beginning breaks out into his exclamations, and is swearing by his Maker.— '*Agimus, proh Jupiter*' inquit.[1] *Ulysses* on the contrary, prepares his Audience with all the submissiveness he can practice, & all the calmness of a reasonable man; he found his Judges in a tranquillity of spirit, and therefore set out leasurely and softly with 'em, till he had warm'd 'em by degrees; and then he began to mend his pace, and to draw them along with his own impetuousness: yet so managing his breath, that it might not fail him at his need, and reserving his utmost proofs of ability even to the last. The success you see was answerable; for the croud only applauded the speech of *Ajax*;——

> *Vulgique secutum ultima murmur erat:*—— [2]

But the Judges awarded the prize for which they contended to *Ulysses*.

> *Mota manus Procerum est, et quid facundia posset*
> *re patuit, fortisque viri arma Disertus.*[3]

The next necessary rule is to put nothing into the discourse which may hinder your moving of the passions. Too many accidents as I

[1] Ovid, *Metamorphoses* 13.5: 'By Jupiter! he cried.'

[2] *Ibid.*, 13.123f.: 'And the applause of the crowd followed his closing words.'

[3] *Ibid.*, 13.382f.: 'The company of chiefs was moved, and their decision proved the power of eloquence: to the eloquent man were given the brave man's arms.'

have said, incomber the Poet, as much as the Arms of *Saul* did *David*; for the variety of passions which they produce, are ever crossing and justling each other out of the way. He who treats of joy and grief together, is in a fair way of causing neither of those effects. There is yet another obstacle to be remov'd, which is pointed Wit, and Sentences affected out of season; these are nothing of kin to the violence of passion: no man is at leisure to make sentences and similes, when his soul is in an Agony. I the rather name this fault, that it may serve to mind me of my former errors; neither will I spare myself, but give an example of this kind from my *Indian Emperor: Montezuma*, pursu'd by his enemies, and seeking Sanctuary, stands parlying without the Fort, and describing his danger to *Cydaria*, in a simile of six lines;

> *As on the sands the frighted Traveller*
> *Sees the high Seas come rowling from afar*, &c.

My Indian Potentate was well skill'd in the Sea for an Inland Prince, and well improv'd since the first Act, when he sent his son to discover it. The Image had not been amiss from another man, at another time: *Sed nunc non erat his locus:*[1] he destroy'd the concernment which the Audience might otherwise have had for him; for they could not think the danger near, when he had the leisure to invent a Simile.

If *Shakespeare* be allow'd, as I think he must, to have made his Characters distinct, it will easily be infer'd that he understood the nature of the Passions: because it has been prov'd already, that confus'd passions make undistinguishable Characters: yet I cannot deny that he has his failings; but they are not so much in the passions themselves, as in his manner of expression: he often obscures his meaning by his words, and sometimes makes it unintelligible. I will not say of so great a Poet, that he distinguish'd not the blown puffy stile, from true sublimity; but I may venture to maintain that the fury of his fancy often transported him, beyond the bounds of Judgment, either in coyning of new words and phrases, or racking words which were in use, into the violence of a Catachresis: 'Tis not that I would explode the use of Metaphors from passions, for *Longinus* thinks 'em necessary to raise it; but to use 'em at every word, to say nothing without a Metaphor, a Simile, an Image, or description, is I doubt to smell a little too strongly of the Buskin. I must be forc'd to give an example of expressing passion figuratively; but that I may do it with respect to *Shakespeare*, it shall not

[1] Horace, *A.P.* 19: 'For such things there is a place, but not just now.'

be taken from any thing of his: 'tis an exclamation against Fortune, quoted in his *Hamlet*, but written by some other Poet.

> *Out, out, thou strumpet fortune; all you Gods,*
> *In general Synod, take away her Power,*
> *Break all the spokes and sallyes from her Wheel,*
> *And bowl the round Nave down the hill of Heav'n*
> *As low as to the Fiends.* [2.2.487ff.]

And immediately after, speaking of *Hecuba*, when *Priam* was kill'd before her eyes:

> *The mobbled Queen ran up and down,*
> *Threatning the flame with bisson rheum: a clout about that head,*
> *Where late the Diadem stood; and for a Robe*
> *About her lank and all o're-teemed loyns,*
> *A blanket in th' alarm of fear caught up.*
> *Who this had seen, with tongue in venom steep'd*
> *'Gainst Fortune's state would Treason have pronounc'd:*
> *But if the Gods themselves did see her then,*
> *When she saw* Pyrrhus *make malicious sport*
> *In mincing with his sword her Husband's Limbs,*
> *The instant burst of clamor that she made*
> *(Unless things mortal move them not at all)*
> *Would have made milch the burning eyes of Heav'n,*
> *And passion in the Gods.* [2.2.496ff.]

What a pudder is here kept in raising the expression of trifling thoughts. Would not a man have thought that the Poet had been bound Prentice to a Wheel-wright, for his first Rant? and had follow'd a Ragman, for the clout and blanket, in the second? Fortune is painted on a wheel; and therefore the writer in a rage, will have Poetical Justice done upon every member of that Engin: after this execution, he bowls the Nave downhill, from Heaven, to the Fiends: (an unreasonable long mark a man would think;) 'tis well there are no solid Orbs to stop it in the way, or no Element of fire to consume it: but when it came to the earth, it must be monstrous heavy, to break ground as low as to the Center. His making milch the burning eyes of Heaven, was a pretty tollerable flight too; and I think no man ever drew milk out of eyes before him: yet to make the wonder greater, these eyes were burning. Such a sight indeed were enough to have rais'd passion in the Gods, but to excuse the effects of it, he tells you perhaps they did not see it. Wise men would be glad to find a little sence couch'd under all those pompous words; for Bombast is commonly the delight of that Audience, which loves Poetry, but understands it not: and as commonly has been the practice of those Writers, who not being able to infuse a natural passion into the mind, have made it their business to ply the ears, and to stun their Judges by the noise. But *Shakespeare* does not often thus; for the passions in his Scene between *Brutus* and *Cassius* are extreamly natural, the thoughts are such as arise from the matter, and the expression of 'em not viciously figurative. I cannot leave this Subject before I do justice to that Divine Poet, by giving you one of his passionate descriptions: 'tis of *Richard* the Second when he was depos'd, and led in Triumph through the Streets of *London* by *Henry* of *Bullingbrook*: the painting of it is so lively, and the words so moving, that I have scarce read any thing comparable to it, in any other language. Suppose you have seen already the fortunate Usurper passing through the croud, and follow'd by the shouts and acclamations of the people; and now behold King *Richard* entring upon the Scene: consider the wretchedness of his condition, and his carriage in it; and refrain from pitty if you can.

> *As in a Theatre, the eyes of men*
> *After a well-grac'd Actor leaves the Stage,*
> *Are idly bent on him that enters next,*
> *Thinking his prattle to be tedious:*
> *Even so, or with much more contempt, mens eyes*
> *Did scowl on* Richard: *no man cry'd God save him:*
> *No joyful tongue gave him his welcom home,*
> *But dust was thrown upon his Sacred head,*
> *Which with such gentle sorrow he shook off,*
> *His face still combating with tears and smiles*
> *(The badges of his grief and patience)*
> *That had not God (for some strong purpose) steel'd*
> *The hearts of men, they must perforce have melted,*
> *And Barbarism it self have pity'd him.* [5.2.23ff.]

To speak justly of this whole matter; 'tis neither height of thought that is discommended, nor pathetic vehemence, nor any nobleness of expression in its proper place; but 'tis a false measure of all these, something which is like 'em, and is not them: 'tis the *Bristol-stone*, which appears like a Diamond; 'tis an extravagant thought, instead of a sublime one; 'tis roaring madness instead of vehemence; and a sound of words, instead of sence. If *Shakespeare* were stript of all the Bombast in his passions, and dress'd in the most vulgar words, we should find the beauties of his thoughts remaining; if his embroideries were burnt down, there would still be silver at the bottom of the melting-pot: but I fear (at least, let me fear it for myself) that we who Ape his sounding words, have nothing of his thoughts, but are all out-side; there is not so much as a dwarf within our Giants cloaths. Therefore, let not *Shakespeare* suffer for our sakes; 'tis our fault, who succeed him in an Age which is more refin'd, if we imitate him so ill, that we coppy his failings only, and make a virtue of that in our Writings, which in his was an imperfection.

For what remains, the excellency of that Poet was, as I have said, in the more manly passions; *Fletcher*'s in the softer: *Shakespeare* writ better betwixt man and man; *Fletcher*, betwixt man and woman: consequently, the one describ'd friendship better; the other love: yet *Shakespeare* taught *Fletcher* to write love; and *Juliet*, and *Desdemona*, are Originals. 'Tis true, the Scholar had the softer soul; but the Master had the kinder. Friendship is both a virtue, and a Passion essentially; love is a passion only in its nature, and is not a virtue but by Accident: good nature makes Friendship; but effeminacy Love. *Shakespeare* had an Universal mind, which comprehended all Characters and Passions; *Fletcher* a more confin'd, and limited: for though he treated love in perfection, yet Honour, Ambition, Revenge, and generally all the stronger Passions, he either touch'd not, or not Masterly. To conclude all; he was a Limb of *Shakespeare*.

I had intended to have proceeded to the last property of manners, which is, that they must be constant; and the characters maintain'd the same from the beginning to the end; and from thence to have proceeded to the thoughts and expressions suitable to a Tragedy: but I will first see how this will relish with the Age. 'Tis I confess but cursorily written; yet the Judgment which is given here, is generally founded upon Experience: But because many men are shock'd at the name of Rules, as if they were a kinde of Magisterial prescription upon Poets, I will conclude with the words of *Rapin*, in his reflections on *Aristotles* work of Poetry: If the Rules be well consider'd: we shall find them to be made only to reduce Nature into Method, to trace her step by step, and not to suffer the least mark of her to escape us: 'tis only by these, that probability in Fiction is maintain'd, which is the Soul of Poetry: they are founded upon good Sence, and Sound Reason, rather than on Authority; for, though *Aristotle* and *Horace* are produc'd, yet no man must argue, that what they write is true, because they writ it; but 'tis evident, by the ridiculous mistakes and gross absurdities, which have been made by those Poets who have taken their Fancy only for their guide, that if this Fancy be not regulated, 'tis a meer caprice, and utterly incapable to produce a reasonable and judicious Poem.

(Sig A$_2$^{v}–b$_3$^{v})

The Prologue Spoken by Mr. *Betterton*,
Representing the Ghost of *Shakespeare*.

See, my lov'd *Britons*, see your *Shakespeare* rise,
An awfull ghost confess'd to human eyes!
Unnam'd, methinks, distinguish'd I had been
From other shades, by this eternal green,
About whose wreaths the vulgar Poets strive,
And with a touch, their wither'd Bays revive.
Untaught, unpractis'd, in a barbarous Age,
I found not, but created first the Stage.
And, if I drain'd no *Greek* or *Latin* store,
'Twas, that my own abundance gave me more.
On foreign trade I needed not rely,
Like fruitfull *Britain*, rich without supply.
In this my rough-drawn Play, you shall behold
Some Master-strokes, so manly and so bold
That he, who meant to alter, found 'em such
He shook; and thought it Sacrilege to touch.
Now, where are the Successours to my name?
What bring they to fill out a Poets fame?
Weak, short-liv'd issues of a feeble Age;
Scarce living to be Christen'd on the Stage!
For Humour farce, for love they rhyme dispence,
That tolls the knell, for their departed sence.
Dulness might thrive in any trade but this:
'T wou'd recommend to some fat Benefice.
Dulness, that in a Playhouse meets disgrace
Might meet with Reverence, in its proper place.
The fulsome clench that nauseats the Town ⎫
Wou'd from a Judge or Alderman go down! ⎬
Such virtue is there in a Robe and gown! ⎭
And that insipid stuff which here you hate

Might somewhere else be call'd a grave debate:
Dulness is decent in the Church and State.
But I forget that still 'tis understood
Bad Plays are best decry'd by showing good:
Sit silent then, that my pleas'd Soul may see
A Judging Audience once, and worthy me:
My faithfull Scene from true Records shall tell
How *Trojan* valour did the *Greek* excell;
Your great forefathers shall their fame regain,
And *Homers* angry Ghost repine in vain.

[Act I, Scene i.] The Greek Camp.

Enter Agamemnon, Menelaus, Ulysses, Diomedes, Nestor.

Agam. Princes, it seems not strange to us nor new,
That after Nine years Seige *Troy* makes defence,
Since every Action of Recorded Fame
Has with long difficulties been involv'd,
Not Answering that Idea of the thought
Which gave it Birth. Why then you Grecian Chiefs,
With sickly Eyes do you behold our labours,
And think 'em our dishonour, which indeed,
Are the protractive Tryals of the Gods,
To prove heroique Constancy in Men?
    Nestor. With due observance of thy Soveraign Seat
Great *Agamemnon, Nestor* shall apply,
Thy well-weigh'd words: In struggling with misfortunes,
Lyes the true proof of Virtue: on smooth Seas,
How many bawble Boats dare set their Sails,
And make an equall way with firmer Vessels!
But let the Tempest once inrage that Sea,
And then behold the strong rib'd *Argosie*,
Bounding between the Ocean and the Ayr
Like *Perseus* mounted on his *Pegasus.*
Then where are those weak Rivals of the Maine?
Or to avoid the Tempest fled to Port,
Or made a Prey to *Neptune*: even thus
Do empty show, and true-priz'd worth divide
In storms of Fortune.
    Ulysses. Mighty *Agamemnon!*

Heart of our Body, Soul of our designs,
In whom the tempers, and the minds of all
Shou'd be inclos'd: hear what *Ulysses* speaks.
   Agam.——You have free leave.
   Ulysses. *Troy* had been down ere this, and *Hectors* Sword
Wanted a Master but for our disorders:
The observance due to rule has been neglected;
Observe how many *Grecian* Tents stand void
Upon this plain; so many hollow factions:
For when the General is not like the Hive
To whom the Foragers should all repair,
What Hony can our empty Combs expect?
O when Supremacy of Kings is shaken,
What can succeed: How cou'd communities
Or peacefull traffick from divided shores,
Prerogative of Age, Crowns, Scepters, Lawrells,
But by degree stand on their solid base!
Then every thing resolves to brutal force
And headlong force is led by hoodwink'd will,
For wild Ambition, like a ravenous Woolf,
Spurd on by will and seconded by power,
Must make an universal prey of all,
And last devour it self.
   Nest. Most prudently *Ulysses* has discover'd
The Malady whereof our state is sick.
   Diom. 'Tis truth he speaks, the General's disdain'd
By him one step beneath, he by the next:
That next by him below: So each degree
Spurns upward at Superiour eminence:
Thus our distempers are their sole support;
Troy in our weakness lives, not in her strength.
   Agam. The Nature of this sickness found, inform us
From whence it draws its birth?
   Ulysses. The great *Achilles* whom opinion crowns
The chief of all our Host——
Having his ears buzz'd with his noisy Fame
Disdains thy Sovereign charge, and in his Tent,
Lyes mocking our designes, with him *Patroclus*
Upon a lazy Bed, breaks scurril Jests
And with ridiculous and awkward action,

Which, slanderer, he imitation calls
Mimicks the Grecian chiefs.

    Agam. As how *Ulysses*?

    Ulysses. Ev'n thee the King of men he do's not spare
(The monkey Authour) but thy greatness Pageants
And makes of it Rehearsals: like a Player
Bellowing his Passion till he break the spring
And his rack'd Voice jar to his Audience;
So represents he Thee, though more unlike
Than *Vulcan* is to *Venus*.
And at this fulsome stuff, this wit of Apes,
The large *Achilles* on his prest Bed lolling,
From his deep Chest roars out a loud Applause,
Tickling his spleen, and laughing till he wheeze.

    Nestor. Nor are you spar'd *Ulysses*, but as you speak in Council
He hems ere he begins, then strokes his Beard,
Casts down his looks, and winks with half an Eye;
'Has every action, cadence, motion, tone,
All of you but the sence.

    Agam. Fortune was merry
When he was born, and plaid a trick on Nature
To make a mimick Prince: he ne're acts ill
But when he would seem wise:
For all he says or do's from serious thought
Appears so wretched that he mocks his title
And is his own Buffoon.

    Ulysses. In imitation of this scurril fool
Ajax is grown self-will'd as broad *Achilles*,
He keeps a Table too, makes Factious Feasts,
Rails on our State of War, and sets *Thirsites*
(A slanderous slave of an ore-flowing gall)
To level us with low Comparisons:
They tax our Policy with Cowardice
Count Wisdom of no moment in the War,
In brief, esteem no Act, but that of hand;
The still and thoughtful parts which move those hands
With them are but the tasks cut out by fear
To be perform'd by Valour.

    Agam. Let this be granted, and *Achilles* horse
Is more of use than he: but you grave pair

Like time and wisdome marching hand in hand
Must put a stop to these incroaching Ills:
To you we leave the care:
You who cou'd show whence the distemper springs
Must vindicate the Dignity of Kings.   [*Exeunt.*

*   *   *

[Act I, Scene ii.] Troy.

*   *   *

Enter Troilus *passing over.*

   Cressida. What sneaking fellow comes yonder?
   Pand. Where, yonder! that's *Deiphobus*: No I lye, I lye, that's
Troilus, there's a man Neece! hem! O brave *Troilus*! the Prince of
chivalry, and flower of fidelity!
   Cressi. Peace, for shame, peace.
   Pand. Nay but mark him then! O brave *Troilus*! there's a man of
men, Neece! look you how his Sword is bloody, and his Helmet more
hack'd than *Hectors*, and how he looks, and how he goes! O admirable
youth! he nere saw two and twenty. Go thy way *Troilus*, go thy way!
had I a sister were a grace, and a daughter a Goddesse, he shou'd take
his choice of 'em, O admirable man! *Paris*? *Paris* is dirt to him, and I
warrant *Hellen* to change wou'd give all the shooes in her shop to boot.

Enter Common Souldiers passing over.

   Cressi. Here come more.
   Pand. Asses, fools, dolts, dirt and dung, stuff and lumber: porredg
after meat! but I cou'd live and dye with *Troilus*. Nere look Neece,
nere look, the Lyons are gone; Apes and Monkeys, the fag end of the
creation. I had rather be such a man as *Troilus*, than *Agamemnon* and all
Greece.
   Cressi. There's *Achilles* among the Greeks, he's a brave man!
   Pand. Achilles! a Carman, a beast of burden; a very Camel, have
you any eyes Neece, do you know a man? is he to be compar'd with
Troilus?

Enter Page.

   Page. Sir, my Lord *Troilus* wou'd instantly speak with you.
   Pand. Where boy, where?

Page. At his own house, if you think convenient.

Pand. Good boy tell him I come instantly, I doubt he's wounded, farewell good Neece: But I'le be with you by and by.

Cressi. To bring me, Uncle?

Pand. Aye, a token from Prince *Troilus.*

Cressi. By the same token you are a procurer Uncle.

[*Exit* Pandarus.

Cressida *alone.*

A strange dissembling Sex we Women are,
Well may we men, when we our selves deceive.
Long has my secret Soul lov'd *Troilus.*
I drunk his praises from my Uncles mouth,
As if my ears cou'd nere be satisfi'd;
Why then, why said I not, I love this Prince?
How cou'd my tongue conspire against my heart,
To say I lov'd him not? O childish love!
'Tis like an Infant froward in his play,
And what he most desires, he throws away.

[*Exit* Cressida.

*   *   *

[Act II, Scene iii.] Troy.

*   *   *

Pand. Oh faint heart, faint heart! well, there's much good matter in these old proverbs! No, she'll not come I warrant her; she has no blood of mine in her, not so much as will fill a flea: but if she does not come, and come, and come with a swing into your arms, I say no more, but she has renounc'd all grace, and there's an end.

Troil. I will believe thee: go then, but be sure.

Pand. No, you wou'd not have me go; you are indifferent: shall I go say you: speak the word then:—yet I care not: you may stand in your own light; and lose a sweet young Ladies heart: well, I shall not go then!

Troil. Fly, fly, thou tortur'st me.

Pand. Do I so, do I so? do I torture you indeed? well I will go.

Troil. But yet thou dost not go!

Pand. I go immediately, directly, in a twinkling, with a thought. Yet you think a man never does enough for you: I have been labouring in your business like any Mole. I was with Prince *Paris* this morning, to make your excuse at night for not supping at Court: and I found him, faith how do you think I found him; it does my heart good to think how I found him: yet you think a man never does enough for you.

Troil. Will you go then, what's this to *Cressida*?

Pand. Why you will not hear a Man; what's this to *Cressida*? why I found him abed, abed with *Hellena* by my troth: 'tis a sweet Queen, a sweet Queen, a very sweet Queen;——but she's nothing to my Cousin *Cressida*; she's a blowse, a gipsie, a Tawney-moor to my Cousin *Cressida*: And she lay with one white arm underneath the whorsons neck: oh such a white, lilly-white, round, plump arm it was——and you must know it was stript up to th'elbows: and she did so kisse him, and so huggle him:——as who shou'd say——

Troil. But still thou stay'st: what's this to *Cressida*?

Pand. Why I made your excuse to your Brother *Paris*; that I think's to *Cressida*; but such an arm, such a hand, such taper fingers, t'other hand was under the bed-clouths, that I saw not, I confess, that hand I saw not.

Troil. Again thou tortur'st me.

Pand. Nay I was tortur'd too; old as I am, I was tortur'd too: but for all that, I cou'd make a shift, to make him, to make your excuse, to make your father;——by *Jove* when I think of that hand, I am so ravish'd, that I know not what I say: I was tortur'd too.

[*Troilus turns away discontented.*

Well I go, I go; I fetch her, I bring her, I conduct her: not come quoth a, and I her Uncle! [*Exit* Pandarus.

Troilus. I'm giddy; expectation whirls me round.

*   *   *

[Act II, Scene iii.] The Greek Camp.

Enter Nestor, Ulysses.

Ulyss. I have conceiv'd an embryo in my brain:
Be you my time to bring it to some shape.

Nest. What is't, *Ulysses*?

Ulyss. The seeded pride,
That has to this maturity blown up
In rank *Achilles*, must or now be cropt,
Or shedding, breed a nursery of like ill,
To overtop us all.

Nest. That's my opinion.

Uliss. This challenge which *Æneas* brings from *Hector*,
However it be spred in general terms,
Relates in purpose only to *Achilles*.
And will it wake him to the answer think you?

Nest. It ought to do: whom can we else oppose
Who cou'd from *Hector* bring his honour off,
If not *Achilles*? the Successe of this
Although particular, will give an Omen
Of good or bad, ev'n to the general cause.

Ulyss. Pardon me *Nestor*, if I contradict you.
Therefore 'tis fit *Achilles* meet not *Hector*.
Let us like Merchants show our coarsest wares,
And think perchance they'll sell: but if they do not,
The lustre of our better yet unshown
Will show the better; let us not consent
Our greatest warriour shou'd be match'd with *Hector*.
For both our honour and our shame in this,
Shall be attended with strange followers.

Nest. I see 'em not with my old eyes; what are they?

Ulyss. What glory our *Achilles* gains from *Hector*,
Were he not proud, we all should share with him:
But he already is too insolent:
And we had better parch in *Affrick* Sun
Than in his pride, shou'd he scape *Hector* fair.
But grant he shou'd be foyl'd
Why then our common reputation suffers,
In that of our best Man: No, make a Lottery;
And by device let blockish *Ajax* draw
The chance to fight with *Hector*: among our selves
Give him allowance as the braver Man;
For that will physick the great Myrmidon,
Who swells with loud applause; and make him fall
His Crest, if brainless *Ajax* come safe off.
If not, we yet preserve a fair opinion,
That we have better men.

Nest. Now I begin to relish thy advice:
Come let us go to *Agamemnon* straight,
T'inform him of our project.

Ulyss. 'Tis not ripe.

The skilfull Surgeon will not lance a sore
Till Nature has digested and prepar'd
The growing humours to his healing purpose.
Else must he often grieve the patients sence,
When one incision once well-time'd wou'd serve:
Are not *Achilles*, and dull *Ajax* friends?
   Nest. As much as fools can be.
   Ulyss. That knot of friendship first must be unty'd
Ere we can reach our ends; for while they love each other
Both hating us, will draw too strong a byasse,
And all the Camp will lean that way they draw:
For brutall courage is the Soldiers Idoll:
So, if one prove contemptuous, back'd by t'other,
'Twill give the law to cool and sober sence,
And place the power of war in Mad-mens hands.
   Nest. Now I conceive you; were they once divided,
And one of them made ours, that one would check
The others towring growth: and keep both low,
As Instruments, and not as Lords of war.
And this must be by secret coals of envy,
Blown in their brest: comparisons of worth;
Great actions weigh'd of each: and each the best,
As we shall give him voice.

Enter Thersites,

   Ulyss. Here comes *Thersites*,
Who feeds on *Ajax*: yet loves him not, because he cannot love.
But as a *Species*, differing from mankinde,
Hates all he sees; and rails at all he knows;
But hates them most, from whom he most receives,
Disdaining that his lot shou'd be so low,
That he shou'd want the kindeness which he takes.
   Nest. There's none so fit an Engine: Save ye *Thersites*.
   Ulyss. Hayl noble *Grecian*, Thou relief of toyls,
Soul of our mirth, and joy of sullen war.
In whose converse our winter-nights are short,
And Summer-days not tedious.
   Thers. Hang you both.
   Nest. How, hang us both?
   Thers. But hang thee first, thou very reverend fool!

Thou sapless Oke, that liv'st by wanting thought.
And now in thy three hundreth year repin'st
Thou should'st be fell'd: hanging's a civil death,
The death of men: thou canst not hang: thy trunk
Is only fit for gallows to hang others.

   Nest. A fine greeting.

   Thers. A fine old Dotard, to repine at hanging
At such an Age! what saw the Gods in thee
That a Cock-Sparrow shou'd but live three years,
And thou shoud'st last three Ages? He's thy better;
He uses life: he treads himself to death.
Thou hast forgot thy use some hundred years:
Thou stump of Man, thou worn-out broom: thou lumber.

   Nest. I'le hear no more of him, his poyson works;
What, curse me for my age!

   Ulyss. Hold, you mistake him, *Nestor*; 'tis his custome:
What malice is there in a mirthfull scene!
'Tis but a keen-edg'd Sword, spread o're with balme
To heal the wound it makes.

   Thers. Thou beg'st a curse!
May'st thou quit scores then, and be hang'd on *Nestor*,
Who hangs on thee: thou lead'st him by the nose:
Thou play'st him like a puppet; speak'st within him,
And when thou hast contriv'd some dark design
To loose a thousand *Greeks*; make dogs meat of us,
Thou layst thy Cuckows egg within his nest,
And mak'st him hatch it: teachest his remembrance
To lye; and say, the like of it was practis'd
Two hundred years ago; thou bring'st the brain
And he brings only beard to vouch thy plots.

   Nest. I'm no mans fool.

   Thers. Then be thy own, that's worse.

   Nest. He'll rail all day.

   Ulyss. Then we shall learn all day.
Who forms the body to a gracefull carriage
Must imitate our awkward motions first;
The same prescription does the wise *Thersites*
Apply to mend our minds. The same he uses
To *Ajax*, to *Achilles*; to the rest;
His Satyrs are the physick of the Camp.

Thers. Wou'd they were poyson to't, Rats-bane and Hemlock:
Nothing else can mend you and those two brawny fools.
    Ulyss. He hits 'em right:
Are they not such, my *Nestor?*
    Thers. Dolt-heads, Asses.
And beasts of burthen; *Ajax* and *Achilles!*
The pillars, no, the porters of the war.
Hard-headed Rogues! Engines, meer wooden Engines,
Push'd on to do your work.
    Nest. They are indeed.
    Thers. But what a Rogue art thou
To say they are indeed: Heaven made 'em horses
And thou put'st on their harnesse: rid'st and spur'st 'em:
Usurp'st upon heav'ns fools, and mak'st 'em thine.
    Nest. No: they are headstrong fools to be corrected
By none but by *Thersites*: thou alone
Canst tame, and train 'em to their proper use;
And doing this mayst claim a just reward
From *Greece*, and Royall *Agamemnons* hands.
    Thers. Ay, when you need a man, you talk of giving;
For wit's a dear commodity among you:
But when you do not want him, then stale porridge,
A starv'd dog wou'd not lap; and furrow water
Is all the wine we taste, give drabs and pimps:
I'le have no gifts with hooks at end of 'em.
    Ulyss. Is this a Man, O *Nestor*, to be bought?
Asia's not price enough! bid the world for him.
And shall this man, this *Hermes* this *Apollo*,
Sit lagg of *Ajax* table? almost minstrell,
And with his presence grace a brainless feast?

★   ★   ★

[Act IV, Scene i.] Troy.

★   ★   ★

    Cressi. And is it true, that I must go from *Troy?*
    Troil. A hatefull truth!
    Cressi. What, and from *Troilus* too?
    Troil. From *Troy* and *Troilus*: and suddenly.

277

So suddenly 'tis counted but by minutes.

   Cressi. What, not an hour allow'd for taking leave?

   Troil. Ev'n that's bereft us too: our envious fates

Justle betwixt, and part the dear adieus

Of meeting lips, clasp'd hands, and lock'd embraces.

Æneas within. My Lord, is the Lady ready yet?

   Troil. Hark, you are call'd: some say the Genius so

Cryes come, to him who instantly must dye.

   Pand. Where are my tears? some rain to'lay this wind:

Or my heart will be blown up by th' roots!

   Troil. Hear me my Love! be thou but true like me.

   Cressi. I, true! how now, what wicked thought is this?

   Troil. Nay, we must use expostulation kindly,

For it is parting from us:

I spoke not, be thou true, as fearing thee;

But be thou true, I said to introduce

My following protestation: be thou true,

And I will see thee.

   Cressi. You'll be expos'd to dangers.

   Troil. I, care not: but be true.

   Cressi. Be true again?

   Troil. Hear why I speak it love.

The *Grecian* Youths are full of *Grecian* Arts:

Alas a kind of holy jealousie

Which I beseech you call a vertuous sin,

Makes me afraid how far you may be tempted.

   Cressi. O Heavens, you love me not!

   Troil. Dye I a villain then!

In this I do not call your faith in question

But my own merit.

   Cressi. Fear not; I'le be true.

   Troil. Then fate thy worst; for I will see thee, love.

Not all the *Grecian* host shall keep me out,

Nor *Troy*, though wall'd with fire, shou'd hold me in.

Æneas within. My Lord, my Lord *Troilus*: I must call you.

   Pand. A mischief call him: nothing but Schreech-owls? do, do, call
again; you had best part 'em now in the sweetnesse of their love! I'le
be hang'd if this *Æneas* be the Son of *Venus*, for all his bragging.
Honest *Venus* was a Punk: wou'd she have parted Lovers. No he has not
a drop of *Venus*' blood in him: honest *Venus* was a Punk.

Troil. to Pand. Prithee go out; and gain one minute more.

Pand. Marry and I will: follow you your business; lose no time, 'tis very precious; go, bill again: I'le tell the Rogue his own I warrant him. 　　　　　　　　　　　　　　　　　　　[*Exit* Pandarus.

Cressi. What have we gain'd by this one minute more?

Troil. Only to wish another, and another
A longer struggling with the pangs of death.

Cressi. O those who do not know what parting is
Can never learn to dye!

Troil. When I but think this sight may be our last,
If *Jove* cou'd set me in the place of *Atlas*
And lay the weight of Heav'n and Gods upon me
He cou'd not presse me more.

Cressi. Oh let me go that I may know my grief;
Grief is but guess'd, while thou art standing by:
But I too soon shall know what absence is.

Troil. Why 'tis to be no more: another name for death.
'Tis the Sunn parting from the frozen North;
And I, me thinks, stand on some Icey cliff,
To watch the last low circles that he makes;
Till he sink down from Heav'n! O only *Cressida*,
If thou depart from me, I cannot live:
I have not soul enough to last for grief,
But thou shalt hear what grief has done with me.

Cressi. If I could live to hear it, I were false,
But as a careful traveller, who fearing
Assaults of Robbers, leaves his wealth behind,
I trust my heart with thee; and to the *Greeks*
Bear but an empty Casket.

Troil. Then, I will live; that I may keep that treasure:
And arm'd with this assurance, let thee go
Loose, yet secure as is the gentle Hawk
When whistled off she mounts into the wind:
Our loves, like Mountains high above the clouds,
Though winds and tempests beat their aged feet,
Their peaceful heads nor storm nor thunder know,
But scorn the threatning rack that roles below.

　　　　　　　　　　　　　　　　　　　[*Exeunt* Ambo.

★　　　★　　　★

[Act IV, Scene ii.] The Greek Camp.

Enter Hector, Ajax, Agamemnon, Diomede, Ulysses, Troilus, *going with torches over the stage.*

Agam. We go wrong; we go wrong.
Ajax. No, yonder 'tis; there where we see the light.
Hect. I trouble you.
Ajax. Not at all Cousin: Here comes *Achilles* himself to guide us.

Enter Achilles.

Achill. Welcome brave *Hector*, welcome princes all:
Agam. So now, brave Prince of *Troy*, I take my leave;
Ajax commands the guard, to wait on you.
Men. Good night my Lord!
Hect. Good night Sweet Lord *Menelaus*.
Thers. aside. Sweet quoth a! sweet Sink, sweet shore, sweet
Jakes!
Achill. Nestor will stay; and you Lord *Diomede*.
Keep *Hector* company an hour or two.
Diom. I cannot Sir: I have important business.
Achill. Enter my Lords.
Ulyss. to Troil. Follow his torch: he goes to *Calchas*'s tent.
                    [*Exeunt* Achill. Hect. Ajax *at one way*, Diomede,
                              another; and after him Ulyss. Troilus.
Thers. This *Diomede*'s a most false-hearted rogue, an unjust Knave:
I will no more trust him when he winks with one eye, than I will a
Serpent when he hisses. He will spend his mouth and promise, like
Brabbler the Hound: but when he performs, Astronomers set it down
for a prodigy. Though I long to see *Hector*, I cannot forbear dogging
him. They say a keeps a *Trojan* Drabb: and uses *Calchas* tent, that
fugitive Priest of *Troy*; that Canonical Rogue of our side. I'le after
him: nothing but whoring in this Age: all incontinent Rascalls!
                                                        [*Exit* Thersites.

Enter Calchas, Cressida.

Calch. O, what a blessing is a vertuous child!
Thou hast reclam'd my mind, and calm'd my passions
Of anger and revenge: my love to *Troy*
Revives within me, and my lost *Tyara*
No more disturbs my mind.

Cress. A vertuous conquest.

Calch. I have a womans longing to return
But yet which way without your ayd I know not.

Cress. Time must instruct us how.

Calch. You must dissemble love to *Diomede* still:
False *Diomede*, bred in *Ulysses* School
Can never be deceiv'd,
But by strong Arts and blandishments of love:
Put 'em in practice all; seem lost and won,
And draw him on, and give him line again.
This *Argus* then may close his hundred eyes
And leave our flight more easy.

Cress. How can I answer this to love and *Troilus*?

Calch. Why 'tis for him you do it: promise largely;
That Ring he saw you wear, he much suspects
Was given you by a Lover; let him have it.

Diom. within. Hoa; *Calchas, Calchas!*

Calch. Hark! I hear his voice.
Pursue your project: doubt not the success.

Cress. Heaven knows, against my will: and yet my hopes
This night to meet my *Troilus*, while 'tis truce,
Afford my minde some ease.

Calch. No more: retire.   [*Exit.* Cressida.

Enter Diomede; Troilus *and* Ulysses *appear listening at one door, and*
Thersites *watching at another.*

Diom. I came to see your Daughter, worthy *Calchas*.

Calch. My Lord I'le call her to you.   [*Exit* Calchas.

Ulysses to Troil. Stand where the torch may not discover us.

Enter Cressida.

Troil. Cressida comes forth to him!

Diom. How now my charge?

Cress. Now my sweet Guardian: hark a word with you.

                                        [*Whisper.*

Troil. Aye, so familiar?

Diom. Will you remember?

Cress. Remember: yes.

Troil. Heav'ns! what shou'd she remember! plague and mad-
nesse!

Ulysses. Prince, you are mov'd: let us depart in time
Lest your displeasure should enlarge it self
To wrathfull terms: this place is dangerous;
The time unfit: 'beseech you let us go.

   Troil. I pray you stay; by Hell, and by Hell torments
I will not speak a word.

   Diom. I'le hear no more: good night.

   Cress. Nay, but you part in anger!

   Troil. Does that grieve thee? O wither'd truth!

   Diom. Farewell Cousner.

   Cress. Indeed I am not: pray come back again.

   Ulyss. You shake, my Lord, at something: will you go?
You will break out.

   Troil. By all the Gods I will not.
There is between my will and all my actions,
A guard of patience! stay a little while.

   Thers. aside. How the devill luxury with his fat rump, and potato finger, tickles these together! put him off a little, you foolish Harlot! 'twill sharpen him the more.

   Diom. But will you then?

   Cressi. I will as soon as ere the War's concluded.

   Diom. Give me some token, for the surety of it:
The Ring I saw you wear.

   Cressi. Giving it. If you must have it.

   Troil. The Ring! nay then 'tis plain! O beauty, where's thy faith?

   Ulyss. You have sworn patience.

   Thersi. aside. That's well, that's well, the pledge is given, hold her to her word good Devil, and her soul's thine I warrant thee.

   Diom. Who's wast?

   Cressi. By all *Diana*'s waiting train of stars,
And by her self, I will not tell you whose.

   Diom. Why then thou lov'st him still, farewell for ever:
Thou never shalt mock *Diomede* again.

   Cressi. You shall not go, one cannot speak a word
But straight it starts you.

   Diom. I do not like this fooling.

   Thersi. aside. Nor I by *Pluto*: but that which likes not me, pleases me best.

   Diom. I shall expect your promise.

   Cressi. I'le perform it.

Not a word more, good night——I hope for ever: [*Aside.*
Thus to deceive deceivers is no fraud.
                              [*Exeunt* Diomede, Cressida *severally.*
    Ulyss. All's done my Lord.
    Troil. Is it?
    Ulyss. Pray let us go.
    Troil. Was *Cressida* here?
    Ulyss. I cannot conjure Trojan.
    Troil. She was not, sure, she was not!
Let it not be believ'd for womanhood:
Think we had Mothers, do not give advantage
To biting Satyr, apt without a theme
For defamation, to square all the sex
By *Cressid's* rule, rather think this not *Cressida.*
    Thersi. aside. Will he swagger himself out on's own eyes?
    Troil. This she! no this was *Diomedes Cressida.*
If beauty have a Soul, this is not she:
I cannot speak for rage, that Ring was mine,
By Heaven I gave it, in that point of time
When both our joys were fullest!——if he keeps it
Let dogs eat *Troilus.*
    Thersi. aside. He'll tickle it for his Concupy: this will be sport to see!
Patroclus will give me any thing for the intelligence of this whore;
a parrot will not do more for an almond, than he will for a com-
modious drab: I would I cou'd meet with this Rogue *Diomede* too;
I wou'd croke like a Raven to him; I wou'd bode: it shall go hard but
I'le find him out.   [*Exit* Thersites.

Enter Æneas.

    Æn. I have been seeking you this hour, my Lord:
Hector by this is arming him in *Troy.*
    Ulyss. Commend me, gallant *Troilus,* to your Brother:
Tell him I hope he shall not need to arm:
The fair *Polixena* has by a letter
Disarm'd our great *Achilles* of his rage.
    Troil. This I shall say to *Hector.*
    Ulyss. So I hope!
Pray Heaven *Thersites* have inform'd me true,——   [*Aside.*
    Troil. Good night, my Lord; accept distracted thanks.
                              [*Exit* Ulysses.

Enter Pandarus.

Pand. Hear ye, my Lord, hear ye; I have been seeing yon poor girl. There have been old doings there i'faith.

Troil. aside. Hold yet, my Spirits; let him powr it in: The poyson's kind: the more I drink of it The sooner 'twill dispatch me.

Æne. to Pand. Peace you babbler!

Pand. She has been mightily made on by the *Greeks*: she takes most wonderfully among 'em: *Achilles* kiss'd her, and *Patroclus* kiss'd her: Nay and old *Nestor* put aside his gray beard and brush'd her with his whiskers. Then comes me *Agamemnon* with his Generals Staff, diving with a low bow e'en to the ground, and rising again, just at her lips: And after him came *Ulysses*, and *Ajax*, and *Menelaus*: and they so pelted her i'faith: pitter patter, pitter patter, as thick as hayl-stones. And after that a whole rout of 'em: Never was woman in *Phrygia* better kiss'd.

Troil. aside. Hector said true: I finde, I finde it now!

Pand. And last of all comes me *Diomede* so demurely: that's a notable sly Rogue I warrant him! mercy upon us, how he layd her on upon the lips! for as I told you, she's most mightily made on among the *Greekes*. What, cheer up I say Man! she has every ones good word. I think in my conscience, she was born with a caull upon her head.

Troil. aside. Hell, death, confusion, how he tortures me!

Pand. And that Rogue-Priest my Brother, is so courted and treated for her sake: the young Sparks do so pull him about, and haul him by the Cassock: nothing but invitations to his Tent, and his Tent, and his Tent. Nay and one of 'em was so bold, as to ask him if she were a Virgin, and with that the Rogue my Brother, takes me up a little God in his hand, and kisses it; and swears devoutly that she was, then was I ready to burst my sides with laughing, to think what had pass'd betwixt you two.

Troil. O I can bear no more: she's falshood all: False by both kinds; for with her mothers milk She suck'd th'infusion of her Fathers Soul. She only wants an opportunity, Her Soul's a whore already.

Pand. What, wou'd you make a Monopoly of a womans lips? A little consolation or so, might be allow'd one wou'd think in a lovers absence!

Troil. Hence from my sight: let ignominy brand thy hated name:
Let Modest Matrons at thy mention start;
And blushing Virgins, when they read our Annals,
Skip o're the guilty page that holds thy Legend,
And blots the noble work.

Pand. O world, world; thou art an ungratefull patch of Earth!
Thus the poor Agent is despis'd! he labours painfully in his calling,
and trudges between parties: but when their turns are serv'd, come
out's too good for him. I am mighty melancholy: I'le e'en go home,
and shut up my doors; and dye o'th sullens like an old bird in a Cage!

[*Exit* Pandarus.

Enter Diomede *and* Thersites.

Thers. aside. There; there he is: now let it work: now play thy part
jealousy, and twinge 'em: put 'em between thy milstones, and grinde
the Rogues together.

Diom. My Lord I am by *Ajax* sent to inform you
This hour must end the truce.

Æneas to Troil. Contain your self;
Think where we are.

Diom. Your stay will be unsafe.

Troil. It may for those I hate.

Thers. aside. Well said *Trojan*: there's the first hit.

Diom. Beseech you Sir make haste, my own affairs
Call me another way.

Thers. aside. What affairs, what affairs? Demand that, Dolthead! the
Rogue will lose a quarrell for want of wit to ask that question.

Troil. May I enquire where your affairs conduct you?

Thers. aside. Well sayd again; I beg thy pardon.

Diom. Oh, it concerns you not.

Troil. Perhaps it does.

Diom. You are too inquisitive: nor am I bound
To satisfy an Enemies request.

Troil. You have a Ring upon your finger *Diomede*,
And given you by a Lady.

Diom. If it were; 'Twas given to one who can defend her gift.

Thers. aside. So, so; the boars begin to gruntle at one another: set
up your bristles now a'both sides: whet and foam, Rogues.

Troil. You must restore it, *Greek*, by Heaven you must:
No spoil of mine shall grace a Traitors hand.

And, with it, give me back the broken vows
Of my false fair; which, perjur'd as she is,
I never will resigne, but with my Soul.

    Diom. Then thou it seems art that forsaken fool
Who wanting merit to preserve her heart,
Repines in vain to see it better plac'd;
But know, (for now I take a pride to grieve thee)
Thou art so lost a thing in her esteem
I never heard thee nam'd but some scorn follow'd:
Thou wert our table talk for laughing meals:
Thy name our sportful theme for Evening walks:
And intermissive hours of cooler Love:
When hand in hand we went.

    Troil. Hell and furies!

    Thersi. aside. O well sung Scorpion! Now *Menelaus* his Greek horns
are out o' doors, there's a new Cuckold start up on the Trojan side.

    Troil. Yet this was she, ye Gods that very she,
Who in my arms lay melting all the Night;
Who kiss'd and sigh'd, and sigh'd, and kiss'd again,
As if her Soul flew upward to her lips,
To meet mine there, and panted at the passage.
Who loath to finde the breaking day, look'd out,
And shrunk into my bosome, there to make
A little longer darkness.

    Diom. Plagues and tortures!

    Thersi. aside. Good, good, by *Pluto*! their fool's mad to lose his har-
lot; and our fool's mad, that t'other fool had her first: if I sought peace
now, I cou'd tell 'em there's punk enough to satisfie 'em both: whore
sufficient! but let 'em worry one another, the foolish currs; they think
they can never have enough of carrion.

    Æneas. My Lords, this fury is not proper here,
In time of truce; if either side be injur'd
Tomorrow's Sun will rise apace, and then——

    Troil. And then! but why should I defer till then?
My blood calls now, there is no truce for Traytors.
My vengeance rowls within my breast, it must,
It will have vent.——   [*Draws.*

    Diom. Hinder us not *Æneas,*
My blood rides high as his, I trust thy honour;
And know thou art too brave a foe to break it.——   [*Draws.*

Thersi. aside. Now Moon! now shine sweet Moon! let 'em have just light enough to make their passes: and not light enough to ward 'em.

Æne. drawing too. By Heav'n he comes on this who strikes the first.
You both are mad! Is this like gallant men
To fight at midnight, at the Murderers hour?
When only guilt and rapine draws a Sword?
Let night enjoy her dues of soft repose;
But let the Sun behold the brave mans courage.
And this I dare engage for *Diomede*
Foe though I am, he shall not hide his head,
But meet you in the very face of danger.

Diom. putting up. Be't so: and were it on some precipice
High as *Olympus*, and a Sea beneath
Call when thou dar'st, just on the sharpest point
I'le meet, and tumble with thee to destruction.

Troil. A gnawing conscience haunts not guilty men
As I'le haunt thee, to summon thee to this,
Nay, should'st thou take the *Stygian lake* for refuge
I'le plunge in after, through the boiling flames
To push thee hissing down the vast Abysse.

Diom. Where shall we meet?

Troil. Before the Tent of *Calchas*:
Thither, through all your Troops, I'le fight my way;
And in the sight of perjur'd *Cressida*
Give death to her through thee.

Diom. Tis largely promis'd.
But I disdain to answer with a boast;
Be sure thou shalt be met.

Troil. And thou be found.   [*Exeunt* Troilus, Æneas, *one way:*
                                               Diomede *the other.*

Thers. Now the furies take *Æneas*, for letting 'em sleep upon their quarrell: who knows but rest may cool their brains, and make 'em rise maukish to mischief upon consideration? May each of 'em dream he sees his Cockatrice in t'others arms: and be stabbing one another in their sleep, to remember 'em of their business when they wake: let 'em be punctual to the point of honour; and if it were possible let both be first at the place of Execution. Let neither of 'em have cogitation enough, to consider 'tis a whore they fight for: and let 'em vallue their lives at as little as they are worth. And lastly let no succeeding fools take warning by 'em; but in imitation of them when a Strumpet is in question,

Let 'em beneath their feet all reason trample;
And think it great to perish by Example. [*Exit.*

*   *   *

[Act V, Scene ii.] The Greek Camp.

*   *   *

Troilus returning. What Prisoner have you there?

Hect. A gleaning of the war: a Rogue he says.

Troil. Dispatch him and away. [*Going to kill him.*

Thers. Hold, hold: what, is't no more but dispatch a man and away? I am in no such hast: I will not dye for *Greece*; I hate *Greece*, and by my good will wou'd nere have been born there; I was mistaken into that Country, and betray'd by my parents to be born there. And besides I have a mortal Enemy amongst the *Grecians*, one *Diomede* a damned villain, and cannot dye with a safe conscience till I have first murther'd him.

Troil. Shew me that *Diomede* and thou shalt live.

Thers. Come along with me and I'le conduct thee to *Calchas* his Tent, where I believe he's now making warre with the Priests daughter.

Hect. Here we must part, our destinies divide us;
Brother and friend, farewell.

Troil. When shall we meet?

Hect. When the Gods please: if not, we once must part.
Look; on yon hill their squander'd Troops unite.

Troil. If I mistake not, 'tis their last Reserve:
The storm's blown ore; and those but after-drops.

Hect. I wish our Men be not too far ingag'd:
For few we are and spent; as having borne
The burden of the Day: but hap what can
They shall be charg'd: *Achilles* must be there;
And him I seek, or death.
Divide our Troops; and take the fresher half.

Troil. O Brother—

Hect. No dispute of Ceremony!
These are enow for me; in faith enow:
Their bodies shall not flag while I can lead;

Nor wearied limbs confess mortality,
Before those Ants that blacken all yon hill
Are crept into their Earth: Farewell.   [*Exit* Hector.
　　Troil. Farewell; come Greek:
　　Thers. Now these Rival-rogues will clapperclaw one another, and
I shall have the sport on't.   [*Exit* Troil. *with* Thersites.

Enter Achilles *and* Myrmidons.

　　Achil. Which way went *Hector*?
　　Myrmyd. Up yon sandy hill:
You may discern 'em by their smoaking track;
A wavering body working with bent hams
Against the rising, spent with painfull march,
And by loose-footing cast on heaps together.
　　Achill. O thou art gone! thou sweetest, best of friends;
Why did I let thee tempt the shock of war
Ere yet thy tender nerves had strung thy limbs,
And knotted into strength? Yet, though too late,
I will, I will revenge thee, my *Patroclus*!
Nor shall thy Ghost thy Murtherer's long attend,
But thou shalt hear him calling *Charon* back,
Ere thou art wafted to the farther shore.
Make hast, my Soldiers: give me this days pains
For my dead friend: strike every hand with mine,
Till *Hector*, breathless, on the ground we lay!
Revenge is honour, the securest way.   [*Exit with* Myrmidons.

Enter Thersites, Troilus, Trojans.

　　Thers. That's *Calchas*' tent.
　　Troil. Then that one spot of Earth contains more falshood
Than all the Sun sees in his race beside.
That I shou'd trust the Daughter of a Priest!
Priesthood, that makes a Merchandise of Heaven!
Priesthood that sells even to their prayr's and blessings!
And forces us to pay for our own cousnage!
　　Thers. Nay cheats Heav'n too with entrails and with offals;
Gives it the garbidge of a Sacrifice
And keeps the best for private Luxury.
　　Troil. Thou hast deserv'd thy life, for cursing Priests:
Let me embrace thee; thou art beautifull:

That back, that nose; those eyes are beautiful:
Live, thou art honest; for thou hat'st a Priest.

Thers. aside. Farewell Trojan; if I scape with life, as I hope; and thou art knock'd o'th head, as I hope too; I shall be the first that ever scap'd the revenge of a Priest, after cursing him; and thou wilt not be the last, I Prophecy, that a Priest will bring to ruin.   [*Exit* Ther.

Troil. Me thinks my soul is rowz'd to her last work:
Has much to do, and little time to spare.
She starts within me, like a Traveller
Who sluggishly out-slept his morning hour
And mends his pace, to reach his Inn betimes.
                    Noise within, follow, follow.
A Noise of Arms! the Traitor may be there:
Or else, perhaps, that conscious scene of Love,
The Tent, may hold him, yet I dare not search
For oh I fear to find him in that place.   [*Exit* Troilus.

Enter Calchas, Cressida.

Cress. Where is he? I'le be justify'd or dye.
Calch. So quickly vanish'd! he was here but now:
He must be gone to search for *Diomede*,
For *Diomede* told me, here they were to fight.
Cress. Alas!
Calch. You must prevent, and not complain.
Cress. If *Troilus* dye, I have no share in life.
Calch. If *Diomede* sink beneath the sword of *Troilus*,
We lose not only a Protector here,
But are debard all future means of flight.
Cressi. What then remains?
Calch. To interpose betimes
Betwixt their swords; or if that cannot be
To intercede for him, who shall be vanquish'd,
Fate leaves no middle course.——   [*Exit* Calchas.
                    Clashing within.
Cressi. Ah me I hear 'em;
And fear 'tis past prevention.

Enter Diomede, *retiring before* Troilus, *and falling as he enters.*

Troil. Now beg thy life, or dye.
Diom. No: use thy fortune:

I loath the life, which thou canst give, or take.
 Troil. Scornst thou my mercy villain!——take thy wish.——
 Cressi. Hold, hold your hand my Lord, and hear me speak.

> Troilus *turns back: in which time* Diomede *rises: Trojans and Greeks*
> *enter, and rank themselves on both sides of their Captains.*

 Troil. Did I not hear the voice of perjur'd *Cressida?*
Com'st thou to give the last stab to my heart?
As if the proofs of all thy former falshood
Were not enough convincing, com'st thou now
To beg my Rivals life?
Whom, oh, if any spark of truth remain'd,
Thou coud'st not thus, ev'n to my face, prefer!
 Cressi. What shall I say? that you suspect me false
Has struck me dumb! but let him live, my *Troilus,*
By all our loves, by all our past endearments
I do adjure thee spare him.
 Troil. Hell and death!
 Cressi. If ever I had pow'r to bend your mind,
Believe me still your faithful *Cressida:*
And though my innocence appear like guilt,
Because I make his forfeit life my suit,
'Tis but for this, that my return to you
Wou'd be cut off for ever by his death:
My father, treated like a slave and scorn'd,
My self in hated bonds a Captive held.
 Troil. Cou'd I believe thee, cou'd I think thee true
In triumph wou'd I bear thee back to *Troy,*
Though *Greece* could rally all her shatter'd troops,
And stand embatteld to oppose my way.
But, Oh, thou Syren, I will stop my ears
To thy enchanting notes; the winds shall bear
Upon their wings thy words more light than they.
 Cressi. Alas I but dissembled love to him;
If ever he had any proof beyond
What modesty might give——
 Diom. No! witnesse this——[*the Ring shown.*]
There, take her Trojan; thou deserv'st her best,
You good, kind-natur'd, well-believing fools
Are treasures to a woman.

I was a jealous, hard vexatious Lover
And doubted ev'n this pledge till full possession:
But she was honourable to her word;
And I have no just reason to complain.

    Cressi. O, unexampled, frontlesse impudence!
    Troil. Hell show me such another tortur'd wretch as *Troilus*!
    Diom. Nay, grieve not: I resigne her freely up:
I'm satisfi'd: and dare engage for *Cressida*,
That if you have a promise of her person,
She shall be willing to come out of debt.

    Cressi. [*kneeling.*] My only Lord: by all those holy vows
Which if there be a pow'r above are binding,
Or, if there be a Hell below, are fearful,
May every imprecation, which your rage
Can wish on me, take place, if I am false.

    Diom. Nay, since you're so concern'd to be believ'd,
I'm sorry I have press'd my charge so far;
Be what you wou'd be thought: I can be grateful.

    Troil. Grateful! Oh torment! now hells blewest flames
Receive her quick; with all her crimes upon her,
Let her sink spotted down. Let the dark host
Make room; and point: and hisse her, as she goes.
Let the most branded Ghosts of all her Sex
Rejoyce, and cry, here comes a blacker fiend!
Let her——

    Cressi. Enough my Lord; you've said enough:
This faithlesse, perjur'd, hated *Cressida*,
Shall be no more the subject of your Curses:
Some few hours hence, and grief had done your work;
But then your eyes had miss'd the Satisfaction
Which thus I give you——thus—   [*She stabs her self;*
                                            they both run to her.

    Diom. Help, save her, help!
    Cressi. Stand off; and touch me not, thou Traitor, *Diomede*:
But you, my only *Troilus*, come near:
Trust me, the wound which I have giv'n this breast
Is far lesse painful, than the wound you gave it.
Oh, can you yet believe, that I am true?

    Troil. This were too much, ev'n if thou hadst been false!
But, Oh, thou purest, whitest innocence,

(For such I know thee now) too late I know it!
May all my curses, and ten thousand more
Heavier than they, fall back upon my head,
Pelion and *Ossa* from the Gyants graves,
Be torn by some avenging Deity,
And hurld at me, a bolder wretch than they,
Who durst invade the Skys!
   Cressi. Hear him not, Heavens!
But hear me bless him with my latest breath;
And since I question not your hard decree,
That doom'd my days unfortunate and few,
Add all to him you take away from me;
And I dye happy that he thinks me true.   *[Dyes.*
   Troil. She's gone for ever, and she blest me dying!
Cou'd she have curs'd me worse? She dy'd for me,
And like a woman, I lament for her:
Distraction pulls me several ways at once:
Here pity calls me to weep out my eyes;
Despair then turns me back upon my self,
And bids me seek no more, but finish here: *[Sword to his breast.*
Ha, smilst thou Traitor? Thou instruct'st me best,
And turn'st my just revenge to punish thee.
   Diom. Thy worst, for mine has been before hand with thee,
I triumph in thy vain credulity,
Which levels thy despairing state to mine:
But yet thy folly, to believe a foe,
Makes thine the sharper, and more shamefull loss.
   Troil. By my few moments of remaining life:
I did not hope for any future joy,
But thou hast given me pleasure ere I dye,
To punish such a Villain.——Fight apart.   *[To his Souldiers.*
For Heaven and hell have mark'd him out for me,
And I shou'd grudg ev'n his least drop of blood,
To any other hand.——

    [Troilus and Diomede *fight, and both parties engage at the same time.
The Trojans make the Greeks retire, and* Troilus *makes* Diomede
give ground, and hurts him. Trumpets sound; Achilles *Enters with
his Myrmidons, at the backs of the Trojans, who fight in a Ring
encompass'd round.* Troilus *singling* Diomede *gets him down and*

kills him: and Achilles *kills* Troilus *upon him. All the Trojans dye upon the place,* Troilus *last.*

Enter Agamemnon, Menelaus, Ulysses, Nestor, Ajax, *and Attendants.*

Achill. Our toyls are done, and those aspiring Walls
(The work of Gods, and almost mateing Heaven,)
Must crumble into rubbish on the plain.
Agam. When mighty *Hector* fell beneath thy Sword,
Their Old foundations shook, their nodding Towers
Threatned from high the amaz'd Inhabitants:
And Guardian Gods for fear forsook their fanes.
Achill. Patroclus, now be quiet: *Hector's* dead:
And as a second offring to thy Ghost,
Lyes *Troilus* high upon a heap of slain:
And noble *Diomede* beneath; whose death
This hand of mine reveng'd.
Ajax. Reveng'd it basely,
For *Troilus* fell by multitudes opprest;
And so fell *Hector*: but 'tis vain to talk.
Ulyss. Hayl *Agamemnon*! truly Victor now!
While secret envy, and while open pride,
Among thy factious Nobles discord threw;
While publique good was urg'd for private ends,
And those thought Patriots, who disturb'd it most;
Then like the headstrong horses of the Sun,
That light which shou'd have cheer'd the World, consum'd it:
Now peacefull order has resum'd the reynes,
Old time looks young, and Nature seems renew'd:
   Then, since from homebred Factions ruine springs,
   Let Subjects learn obedience to their Kings.

[*Exeunt Omnes.*

20. Thomas Otway, from his adaptation of *Romeo and Juliet*

1679

From *The History and Fall of Caius Marius* (1679).

Thomas Otway (1652–85) was one of the major Restoration dramatists, and as a tragedian was often compared to Shakespeare. His version of *Romeo and Juliet* was performed in September or October 1679, with repeated success on the stage as in print. Otway changes the setting of the play to Rome, and to the strife between Caius Marius and Metellus. In so far as Otway retains parts of Shakespeare, the characters' names correspond as follows: Caius Marius [Old Montague]; his son Marius Junior [Romeo]; Metellus [Old Capulet]; his daughter Lavinia [Juliet]; Sylla [Paris]; Granius, brother to Marius Junior [Benvolio]; Sulpitius [Mercutio]; Priest of Hymen [Friar Lawrence]. Otway's device of having Juliet awake before the death of Romeo was followed in the adaptations of *Romeo and Juliet* by Theophilus Cibber (1744) and Garrick (1748).

[PROLOGUE]

In Ages past, (when will those Times renew?)
When Empires flourisht, so did Poets too.
When Great *Augustus* the World's Empire held,
Horace and *Ovid*'s happy Verse excell'd.
Ovid's soft Genius and his tender Arts
Of moving Nature melted hardest Hearts.
It did th' Imperial Beauty *Julia* move
To listen to the Language of his Love.
Her Father honour'd him: and on her Breast,
With ravish'd sense in her Embraces prest,
He lay transported, fancy-full and blest.
Horace's lofty Genius boldlier rear'd

His manly head, and through all Nature steer'd;
Her richest Pleasures in his Verse refin'd,
And wrought 'em to the relish of the Mind.
He lasht with a true Poet's fearless Rage
The Villanies and Follies of the Age.
Therefore *Mæcenas* that great Fav'rite rais'd
Him high, and by him was he highly prais'd.
Our *Shakespeare* wrote too in an Age as blest,
The happiest Poet of his time and best.
A gracious Prince's Favour chear'd his Muse,
A constant Favour he ne'r fear'd to lose.
Therefore he wrote with Fancy unconfin'd,
And Thoughts that were Immortal as his Mind.
And from the Crop of his luxuriant Pen
E're since succeeding Poets humbly glean.
Though much the most unworthy of the Throng,
Our this-day's Poet fears h' has done him wrong:
Like greedy Beggars that steal Sheaves away,
You'll find h' has rifled him of half a Play.
Amidst this baser Dross you'll see it shine
Most beautifull, amazing, and Divine.
To such low Shifts of late are Poets worn,
Whilst we both Wit's and *Cæsar*'s Absence mourn.
Oh! when will He and Poetry return?
When shall we there again behold him sit
'Midst shining Boxes and a Courtly Pit,
The Lord of Hearts, and President of Wit?
When that blest Day (quick may it come) appears,
His Cares once banisht, and his Nation's Fears,
The joyfull Muses on their Hills shall sing
Triumphant Songs of *Britain*'s happy *King*.
Plenty and Peace shall flourish in our Isle,
And all things like the *English* Beauty smile.
You Criticks shall forget your nat'ral Spite,
And Poets with unbounded Fancy write.
Ev'n This-day's Poet shall be alter'd quite:
His Thoughts more loftily and freely flow;
And he himself, whilst you his Verse allow,
As much transported as he's humble now.

*   *   *

[Act II, Scene i.] A walled Garden belonging to *Metellus* house.

*   *   *

Enter Marius junior *in the Garden.*

Mar. jun. He laughs at Wounds that never felt their smart.
What Light is that which breaks through yonder Shade? ⎰Lavinia *in*
Oh! 'tis my Love!   ⎱*the Balcony.*
She seems to hang upon the cheek of Night,
Fairer than Snow upon the Raven's back,
Or a rich Jewel in an *Æthiop*'s ear.
Were she in yonder Sphear, she'd shine so bright,
That Birds would sing and think the Day were breaking.
Lavin. Ah me!
Mar. jun. She speaks.
Oh! speak agen, bright Angel: for thou art
As glorious to this Night, as Sun at Noon
To the admiring eyes of gazing Mortals,
When he bestrides the lazy puffing Clouds,
And sails upon the bosom of the Air.
Lavin. O *Marius, Marius*! wherefore art thou *Marius*?
Deny thy Family, renounce thy Name:
Or if thou wilt not, be but sworn my Love,
And I'll no longer call *Metellus* Parent.
Mar. jun. Shall I hear this, and yet keep silence?
Lavin. No.
'Tis but thy Name that is my Enemy.
Thou would'st be still thy self, though not a *Marius*,
Belov'd of me, and charming as thou art.
What's in a Name? that which we call a Rose,
By any other name wou'd smell as sweet.
So *Marius*, were he not *Marius* call'd,
Be still as dear to my desiring Eyes,
Without that Title. *Marius*, lose thy Name,
And for that Name, which is no part of Thee,
Take all *Lavinia*.
Mar. jun. aloud. At thy word I take thee.
Call me but Thine, and Joys will so transport me,
I shall forget my self, and quite be chang'd.

Lavin. Who art Thou, that thus hid and veil'd in Night
Hast overheard my Follies?

Mar. jun. By a Name
I know not how to tell thee who I am.
My Name, dear Creature,'s hatefull to my self,
Because it is an Enemy to Thee.

Lavin. Marius? how cam'st thou hither? tell, and why?
The Orchard-walls are high, and hard to climb,
And the place Death, consid'ring who thou art,
If any of our Family here find thee.
By whose Directions didst thou find this place?

Mar. jun. By Love, that first did prompt me to enquire.
He lent me Counsell, and I lent him Eyes.
I am no Pilot; yet wert thou as far
As the vast Shoar washt by the farthest Sea,
I'd hazard Ruine for a Prize so dear.——

Lavin. Oh *Marius!* vain are all such Hopes and Wishes.
The hand of Heav'n has thrown a Bar between us,
Our Houses Hatred and the Fate of *Rome,*
Where none but *Sylla* must be happy now.
All bring him Sacrifices of some sort,
And I must be a Victim to his Bed.
To night my Father broke the dreadfull news;
And when I urg'd him for the Right of Love,
He threaten'd me to banish me his House,
Naked and shiftless to the World. Would'st thou,
Marius, receive a Beggar to thy Bosom?

Mar. jun. Oh! were my Joys but fixt upon that point,
I'd then shake hands with Fortune and be friends;
Thus grasp my Happiness, embrace it thus,
And bless th'ill turn that gave thee to my Arms.

Lavin. Thou know'st the mark of Night is on my Face,
Else should I blush for what th' hast heard me speak.
Fain would I dwell on Form; fain, fain deny
The things I've said: but farewell all such Follies.
Dost thou then love? I know thou 'lt say thou dost;
And I must take thy word, though thou prove false.

Mar. jun. By yon bright *Cynthia*'s beams that shines above.

Lavin. Oh! swear not by the Moon, th' inconstant Moon,
That changes Monthly, and shines but by seasons,

Lest that thy Love prove variable too.

   Mar. jun. What shall I swear by?

   Lavin. Do not swear at all.

Or, if thou wilt, swear by thy gracious Self,

Who art the God of my Idolatry,

And I'll believe thee.

   Mar. jun. Witness, all ye Powr's.

   Lavin. Nay, do not swear: although my Joy be great,

I'm hardly satisfy'd with this night's Contract:

It seems too rash, too unadvis'd and sudden,

Too like the Lightning, which does cease to be

E're one can say it is. Therefore this time

Good night, my *Marius*: may a happier hour

Bring us to crown our Wishes.

   Mar. jun. Why wilt thou leave me so unsatisfy'd?

   Lavin. What wouldst thou have?

   Mar. jun. Th' Exchange of Love for mine.

   Lavin. I gave thee mine before thou didst request it;

And yet I wish I could retrieve it back.

   Mar. jun. Why?

   Lavin. But to be frank, and give it thee agen.

My Bounty is as boundless as the Sea,

My Love as deep: the more I give to Thee,

The more I have: for both are Infinite.

I hear a Noise within. Farewell, my *Marius*;

Or stay a little, and I'll come agen.

   Mar. jun. Stay? sure for ever.

   Lavin. Three words, and, *Marius*, then good night indeed.

If that thy Love be honourably meant,

Thy purpose Marriage, send me word to morrow,

And all my Fortunes at thy feet I'll lay.

   Nurse within. Madam!

   Lavin. I come anon. But if thou mean'st not well,

I do beseech thee—

   Nurse within. Madam! Madam!

   Lavin. By and by, I come—

To cease thy Suit, and leave me to my Griefs.

To morrow I will send.   *[Exit.*

   Mar. jun. So thrive my Soul. Is not all this a Dream,

Too lovely, sweet and flatt'ring, to be true?

Re-enter Lavinia.

   Lavin. Hist, *Marius*, hist. Oh for a Falkner's voice,
To Lure this Tassell-gentle back agen.
Restraint has Fears, and may not speak aloud:
Else would I tear the Cave where Echo lies,
With repetition of my *Marius*.
   Mar. jun. It is my Love that calls me back agen.
How sweetly Lovers voices sound by night!
Like softest Musick to attending ears.
   Lavin. Marius.
   Mar. jun. My dear.
   Lavin. What a clock to morrow?
   Mar. jun. At the hour of nine.
   Lavin. I will not fail: 'Tis twenty years till then.
Why did I call thee back?
   Mar. jun. Let me here stay till thou remember'st why.
   Lavin. The Morning's breaking, I wou'd have thee gone,
And yet no farther than a Wanton's Bird,
That lets it hop a little from his hand,
To pull it by its Fetters back agen.
   Mar. jun. Would I were thine.
   Lavin. Indeed and so would I.
Yet I should kill thee sure with too much cherishing.
No more . . . Good night.
   Mar. jun. There's such sweet Pain in parting,
That I could hang for ever on thy Arms,
And look away my life into thy Eyes.
   Lavin. To morrow will come.
   Mar. jun. So it will. Good night.
Heav'n be thy Guard, and all its Blessings wait thee.   [*Ex.* Lavin.

To morrow! 'tis no longer: but Desires
Are swift, and longing Love wou'd lavish time.
To morrow! oh to morrow! till that come,
The tedious Hours move heavily away,
And each long Minute seems a lazy Day.
Already Light is mounted in the Air,
Striking it self through every Element.
Our Party will by this time be abroad,
To try the Fate of *Marius* and *Rome*.

Love and Renown sure court me thus together.
Smile, smile, ye Gods, and give Success to both.   [*Exit.*

★   ★   ★

[Act IV, Scene i.]

SCENE *the Garden.*

Enter Lavinia *and* Marius junior.

Lavin. Wilt thou be gone? it is not yet near Day.
It was the Nightingale, and not the Lark,
That pierc'd the fearfull hollow of thy Ear.
Nightly on yon Pomegranate-tree she sings.
Believe me, Love, it was the Nightingale.
Mar. jun. Oh! 'twas the Lark, the Herald of the Morn,
No Nightingale. Look, Love, what envious Streaks
Of Light embroider all the cloudy East.
Night's Candles are burnt out, and jocund Day
Upon the Mountain-tops sits gaily drest,
Whilst all the Birds bring Musick to his Levy.
I must be gone and live, or stay and dy.
Lavin. Oh! oh! what wretched Fortune is my lot!
Sure, giving Thee, Heav'n grew too far in Debt
To pay, till Bankrupt-like it broke; whilst I,
A poor compounding Creditor, am forc'd
To take a Mite for endless Summs of Joy.
Mar. jun. Let me be taken, let me suffer Death,
I am content, so Thou wilt have it so.
By Heav'n, yon gray is not the Morning's Eye,
But the Reflexion of pale *Cynthia*'s Brightness.
Nor is 't the Lark we hear, whose Notes do beat
So high, and Echo in the Vault of Heav'n.
I'm all desire to stay, no will to go.
How is 't, my Soul? let's talk: it is not Day.
Lavin. Oh! it is, it is. Fly hence away, my *Marius.*
It is the Lark, and out of tune she sings,
With grating Discords and unpleasing Strainings.
Some say the Lark and loathsome Toad change Eyes:
Now I could wish they had chang'd Voices too;

301

Or that a Lethargy had seiz'd the Morning,
And she had slept, and never wak'd agen,
To part me from th' Embraces of my Love.
What shall become of Me, when Thou art gone?
   Mar. jun. The Gods that heard our Vows, and know our Loves,
Seing my Faith, and thy unspotted Truth,
Will sure take care, and let no Wrongs annoy thee.
Upon my Knees I'll ask 'em every day,
How my *Lavinia* does: and every night,
In the severe Distresses of my Fate,
As I perhaps shall wander through the Desart,
And want a place to rest my weary Head on,
I'll count the Stars, and bless 'em as they shine,
And court 'em all for my *Lavinia*'s Safety.
   Lavin. Oh Banishment! eternal Banishment!
Ne'r to return! must we ne'r meet agen?
My Heart will break, I cannot think that Thought
And live. Cou'd I but see to th' end of Woe,
There were some Comfort . . . but eternall Torment
Is even insupportable to Thought.
It cannot be that we shall part for ever.
   Mar. jun. No, for my Banishment may be recall'd;
My Father once more hold a Pow'r in *Rome*:
Then shall I boldly claim *Lavinia* mine,
Whilst happiest men shall envy at the Blessing,
And Poets write the Wonders of our Loves.
   Lavin. If by my Father's Cruelty I'm forc'd,
When left alone, to yield to *Sylla*'s Claim,
Defenseless as I am, and thou far from me;
If, as I must, I'd rather dy than suffer't,
What a sad Tale will that be when 'tis told thee?
I know not what to fear, or hope, or think,
Or say, or doe. I cannot let thee go.
   Mar. jun. A Thousand things would, to this purpose said,
But sharpen and add weight to parting Sorrow.
Oh my *Lavinia*! if my Heart e're stray,   *[Kneels.*
Or any other Beauty ever charm me,
If I live not entirely onely thine,
In that curst moment when my Soul forsakes thee,
May I be hither brought a Captive bound,

T'adorn the Triumph of my basest Foe.

    Lavin. And if I live not faithfull to the Lord
Of my first Vows, my dearest onely *Marius*,
May I be brought to Poverty and Scorn,
Hooted by Slaves forth from thy gates, O *Rome*,
Till flying to the Woods t' avoid my Shame,
Sharp Hunger, Cold, or some worse Fate destroy me;
And not one Tree vouchsafe a Leaf to hide me.

    Mar. jun. What needs all this?——

    Lavin. Oh! I could find out things
To talk to thee for ever.

    Mar. jun. Weep not; the time
We had to stay together has bin employ'd
In richest Love.

    Lavin. We ought to summon all
The spirit of soft Passion up, to chear
Our Hearts thus lab'ring with the pangs of Parting.
Oh my poor *Marius*!

    Mar. jun. Ah my kind *Lavinia*!

    Lavin. But dost thou think we e're shall meet agen?

    Mar. jun. I doubt it not, and all these Woes shall serve
For sweet Discourses in our time to come.

    Lavin. Alas! I have an ill-divining Soul;
Methinks I see thee, now thou 'rt from my Arms,
Like a stark Ghost with Horrour in thy Visage.
Either my Eye-sight fails, or thou look'st pale.

    Mar. jun. And trust me, Love, in my Eye so dost Thou.
Dry Sorrow drinks our Bloud. . . . Farewell.

    Lavin. Farewell then.   [*Ex.* Mar. jun.

    Nurse within. Madam!

    Lavin. My Nurse!

    Nurse within. Your Father's up, and Day-light broke abroad.
Be wary, look about you.

    Lavin. Hah! is he gone? My Lord, my Husband, Friend,
I must hear from thee every day i'th' hour:
For absent Minutes seem as many Days.
Oh! by this reck'ning I shall be most old,
E're I agen behold my *Marius*. Nay,
Gone too already? 'twas unkindly done,
I had not yet imparted half my Soul,

Not a third part of its fond jealous Fears.
But I'll pursue him for't, and be reveng'd;
Hang such a tender Tale about his Heart,
Shall make it tingle as his Life were stung.
Nay too—I'll love him; never, never leave him;
Fond as a Child, and resolute as Man.   [*Ex.* Lavin.

*   *   *

[Act IV, Scene iii.] The Country.

*   *   *

Enter Marius senior *and* Granius.

   Mar. sen. Where are we? are we yet not near *Salonium*?
Lead me to yonder shady Poplar, where
The poor old *Marius* a while may sit,
And joy in Rest. Oh my distemper'd Head!
The Sun has beat his Beams so hard upon me,
That my Brain's hot as molten Gold. My Skull!
Oh my tormented Skull! Oh *Rome! Rome! Rome!*
Hah! what are those?
   Gran. They seem, Sir, Rural Swains,
Who tend the Herds that graze beneath these Woods.
   Mar. sen. Who are you? to what Lord do ye belong?
   2. Herds. We did belong to *Caius Marius* once: but they say he's
gone a Journey: and now we belong to one another.
   Mar. sen. Have ye forgot me then? ungratefull Slaves!
Are you so willing to disown your Master?
Who would have thought t' have found such Baseness here,
Where Innocence seems seated by the Gods,
As in her Virgin-nakedness untainted?
Confusion on ye, ye sordid Earthlings.   [*Ex. all but one.*
   1. Herds. Oh fly, my Lord, your foes are thick abroad:
Just now a Troup of Murtherers past this way,
And ask'd with horrour for the Traitour *Marius*.
By this time at *Salonium*, at your House,
They are in search of you. Fly, fly, my Lord.   [*Exit.*
   Mar. sen. I shall be hounded up and down the World,
Now every Villain, that is Wretch enough

To take the price of Bloud, dreams of my Throat.
Help and support me till I reach the Wood,
Then go and find thy wretched Brother out.
Asunder we may dodge our Fate, and lose her.
In some old hollow Tree or o'regrown Brake
I'd rest my weary Lims, till Danger pass me.   [*Goes into the Wood.*

Enter Souldiers again.

   1. Sould. A thousand Crowns? 'tis a Reward might buy
As many Lives, for they are cheap in *Rome*;
And 'tis too much for one.

   2. Sould. Let's set this Wood
A flaming, if you think he's here, and then
Quickly you'll see th' old Droan crawl humming out.

   1. Sould. Thou always lov'st to ride full speed to Mischief. There's
no consideration in thee. Look you, when I cut a Throat, I love to doe
it with as much Deliberation and Decency as a Barber cuts a Beard.
I hate a slovenly Murther done hand over head: a man gets no credit
by it.

   3. Sould. The man that spoke last spoke well. Therefore let us to
yon adjacent Village, and sowce our selves in good *Falernum.*
                                                      [*Ex. Souldiers.*

   Mar. sen. O Villains! not a Slave of those
But has serv'd under me, has eat my Bread,
And felt my Bounty . . . Drought! parching Drought!
Was ever Lion thus by Dogs emboss'd?
Oh! I could swallow Rivers: Earth yield me Water;
Or swallow *Marius* down where Springs first flow.

Enter Marius junior *and* Granius.

   Mar. jun. My Father!
   Mar. sen. Oh my Sons!
   Mar. jun. Why thus forlorn? stretcht on the Earth?
   Mar. sen. Oh! get me some Refreshment, cooling Herbs,
And Water to allay my ravenous Thirst.
I would not trouble you if I had Strength:
But I'm so faint that all my Lims are useless.
Now have I not one *Drachma* to buy Food;
Must we then starve? no, sure the Birds will feed us.
   Mar. jun. There stands a House on yonder side o'th' Wood,

It seems the Mansion of some Man of note:
I'll go and turn a Beggar for my Father.
    Mar. sen. Oh my Soul's comfort! do. Indeed I want it.
I, who had once the plenty of the Earth,
Now want a Root and Water. Go, my Boy,
And see who'll give a Morsell to poor *Marius.*
Nay, I'll not starve: no, I will plunge in Riot,
Wallow in Plenty. Drink? I'll drink, I'll drink!
Give me that Goblet hither. . . . Here's a Health
To all the Knaves and Senators in *Rome.*
    Mar. jun. Repose your self a while, till we return.
    Mar. sen. I will, but prithee let me rave a little.
Go, prithee go, and do n't delay. I'll rest;   [*Ex.* Mar. jun.
As thou shalt, *Rome,* if e're my Fortune raise me.

Enter Lavinia.

Another Murth'rer? this brings smiling Fate:
A deadly Snake cloath'd in a dainty Skin.
    Lavin. I've wander'd up and down these Woods and Meadows,
Till I have lost my way.
Against a tall, young, slender, well-grown Oak
Leaning, I found *Lavinia* in the Bark.
My *Marius* should not be far hence.
    Mar. sen. What art Thou,
That dar'st to name that wretched Creature *Marius?*
    Lavin. Do not be angry, Sir, what e're thou art;
I am a poor unhappy Woman, driven
By Fortune to pursue my banish'd Lord.
    Mar. sen. By thy dissembling Tone thou shouldst be Woman,
And *Roman* too.
    Lavin. Indeed I am.
    Mar. sen. A *Roman?*
If thou art so, be gone, lest Rage with Strength
Assist my Vengeance, and I rise and kill thee.
    Lavin. My Father, is it you?
    Mar. sen. Now thou art Woman;
For Lies are in thee. I? am I thy Father?
I ne'r was yet so curst; none of thy Sex
E're sprung from me. My Offspring all are Males,
The Nobler sort of Beasts entit'led Men.

Lavin. I am your Daughter, if your Son's my Lord.
Have you ne'r heard *Lavinia's* name in *Rome*,
That wedded with the Son of *Marius*?
    Mar. sen. Hah!
Art thou that fond, that kind and doting thing,
That left her Father for a banisht Husband?
Come near——
And let me bless thee, though thy Name's my Foe.
    Lavin. Alas! my Father, you seem much opprest:
Your Lips are parcht, bloud-shot your Eyes and sunk.
Will you partake such Fruits as I have gather'd?
Taste, Sir, this Peach, and this Pomegranate; both are
Ripe and refreshing.
    Mar. sen. What? all this from Thee,
Thou Angel, whom the Gods have sent to aid me?
I do n't deserve thy Bounty.
    Lavin. Here, Sir,'s more.
I found a Crystall Spring too in the Wood,
And took some Water; 'tis most soft and cool.
    Mar. sen. An Emperour's Feast! but I shall rob thee.
    Lavin. No, I 've eat, and slak'd my Thirst. But where's my Lord,
My dearest *Marius*?
    Mar. sen. To th' neighbouring Village
He's gone, to beg his Father's Dinner, Daughter.
    Lavin. Will you then call me Daughter? will you own it?
I'm much o'repaid for all the Wrongs of Fortune.
But surely *Marius* can't be brought to want.
I've Gold and Jewels too, and they'l buy Food.

Enter Marius junior.

    Mar. sen. See here, my *Marius*, what the Gods have sent us.
See thy *Lavinia*.
    Mar. jun. Hah!   [*They run and embrace.*
    Mar. sen. What? dumb at meeting?
    Mar. jun. Why weeps my Love?
    Lavin. I cannot speak, Tears so obstruct my Words,
And choak me with unutterable Joy.
    Mar. jun. Oh my Heart's Joy!
    Lavin. My Soul!
    Mar. jun. But hast thou left

Thy Father's House, the Pomp and State of *Rome*,
To follow desart Misery?

   Lavin. I come
To bear a part in every thing that's thine,
Be 't Happiness or Sorrow. In these Woods,
Whilst from pursuing Enemies you 're safe,
I'll range about, and find the Fruits and Springs,
Gather cool Sedges, Daffadills and Lillies,
And softest Camomill to make us Beds,
Whereon my Love and I at night will sleep,
And dream of better Fortune.

Enter Granius *and Servant with Wine and Meat.*

   Mar. sen. Yet more Plenty?
Sure *Comus*, the God of Feasting, haunts these Woods,
And means to entertain us as his Guests.

   Servant. I am sent hither, *Marius*, from my Lord,
Sextilius the Prætor, to relieve thee,
And warn thee that thou straight depart this place,
Else he the Senate's Edict must obey,
And treat thee as the Foe of *Rome*.

   Mar. sen. But did he,
Did he, *Sextilius*, bid thee say all this?
Was he too proud to come and see his Master,
That rais'd him out of nothing? Was he not
My menial Servant once, and wip'd these Shoes,
Ran by my Chariot-wheels, my Pleasures watcht,
And fed upon the Voidings of my Table?
Durst he affront me with a sordid Alms?
And send a saucy Message by a Slave?
Hence with thy Scraps: back to thy Teeth I dash 'em.
Be gone whilst thou art safe. Hold, stay a little.

   Serv. What Answer would you have me carry back?

   Mar. sen. Go to *Sextilius*, tell him thou hast seen
Poor *Caius Marius* banish'd from his Country,
Sitting in Sorrow on the naked Earth,
Amidst an ample Fortune once his own,
Where now he cannot claim a Turf to sleep on.   [*Ex. Servant.*
How am I fallen!

                                    [*Soft Musick.*

Musick? sure, the Gods
Are mad, or have design'd to make me so.

Enter Martha.

Well, what art Thou?
   Marth. Am I a Stranger to thee?
Martha's my name, the *Syrian* Prophetess,
That us'd to wait upon thee with good Fortune;
Till banish'd out of *Rome* for serving Thee.
I've ever since inhabited these Woods,
And search'd the deepest Arts of wise Foreknowledge.
   Mar. sen. I know thee now most well. When thou wert gone,
All my good Fortune left me. My lov'd Vulturs,
That us'd to hover o're my happy Head,
And promise Honour in the day of Battel,
Have since bin seen no more. Ev'n Birds of prey
Forsake unhappy *Marius*: Men of prey
Pursue him still. Hast thou no Hopes in store?
   Marth. A hundred Spirits wait upon my will,
To bring me Tidings, from th'Earth's farthest Corners,
Of all that happens out in States and Councils.
I tell thee therefore, *Rome* is once more thine.
The Consuls have had Blows, and *Cinna*'s beaten,
Who with his Army comes to find thee out,
To lead him back with Terrour to that City.
   Mar. sen. Speak on.
   Marth. Nay, e're thou think'st it he will be with thee.
But let thy Sons and these fair Nymphs retire,
Whilst I relieve thy wearied Eyes with Sleep,
And chear thee in a Dream with promis'd Fate.
   Mar. jun. Come, my *Lavinia*, *Granius*, wee'll withdraw
To some cool Shade, and wonder at our Fortune.   [*Ex.*
           [Martha *waves her Wand. A Dance.*
   Mar. sen. O Rest, thou Stranger to my Senses, welcome.

*   *   *

309

[Act IV, Scene iv.] Metellus' house.

Enter Metellus, Lavinia, *Priest of* Hymen.

    Lavin. Nay, you have catcht me; you may kill me too:
But with my Cries I'll rend the Echoing Heav'ns,
Till all the Gods are Witness how you use me.
    Metell. What! like a Vagrant fly thy Father's House?
And follow fulsomely an exil'd Slave,
Disdain'd by all the World? But abject Thou,
Resolve to go, or bound be sent to *Sylla*,
With as much Scorn as thou hast done me Shame.
    Lavin. Do, bind me, kill me, rack these Lims: I'll bear it.
But, Sir, consider still I am your Daughter;
And one hour's Converse with this Holy man
May teach me to repent, shew Obedience.
    Metell. Think not t'evade me by protracting time:
For if thou dost not, may the Gods forsake me,
As I will Thee, if thou escape my Fury.   [*Ex.* Metell.
    Lavin. Oh! bid me leap (rather then go to *Sylla*)
From off the Battlements of any Tow'r,
Or walk in Thievish ways, or bid me lurk
Where Serpents are: chain me with roaring Bears;
Or hide me nightly in a Charnell-house
O're-cover'd quite with Dead mens rattling Bones,
With reeky Shanks, and yellow chapless Sculls:
Or bid me go into a new-made Grave,
And hide me with a Dead man in his Shrowd:
Things that to hear but told have made me tremble:
And I'll go through it without fear or doubting,
To keep my Vows unspotted to my Love.
    Priest. Take here this Vial then, and in this moment
Drink it, when straight through all thy Veins shall run
A cold and drowzy Humour more than Sleep:
And in Death's borrow'd likeness shalt thou lie
Two Summer-days, then wake as from a Slumber.
Till *Marius* by my Letters know what's past,
And come by stealth to *Rome*.
    Lavin. Give me; Oh! give me: tell me not of Fears.
    Priest. Farewell: be bold and prosp'rous.   [*Exit.*
    Lavin. Oh! farewell. . . .

Heav'n knows if ever we shall meet agen.
I have a faint cold Fear thrills through my Veins,
That almost freezes up the heat of Life.
I'll call him back agen to comfort me.
Stay, Holy man. But what should he doe here?
My dismall Scene 'tis fit I act alone.
What if this Mixture do not work at all?
Shall I to morrow then be sent to *Sylla*?
No, no . . . this shall forbid it; ly thou there. . . .   {*Lays down*
Or how, if, when I'm laid into the Tomb,   {*the Dagger.*
I wake before the time that *Marius* come
To my Relief? There, there's a fearfull Point.
Shall I not then be stifled in the Vault,
Where for these many hundred years the Bones
Of all my bury'd Ancestours are packt?
Where, as they say, Ghosts at some hours resort,
With Mandrakes shreeks, torn from the Earth's dark Womb,
That living Mortals hearing them run mad?
Or if I wake, shall I not be distracted,
Inviron'd round with all these hideous Fears,
And madly play with my Fore-fathers Joints;
Then in this Rage with some great Kinsman's Bones,
As with a Club, dash out my desp'rate Brains?
What? *Sylla*? get thee gone, thou meager Lover:
My Sense abhors thee. Do n't disturb my Draught;
'Tis to my Lord. [*Drinks.*] Oh *Marius! Marius! Marius!*   [*Exit.*

★   ★   ★

[Act V, Scene ii.] *Scene changes to the* Forum, *where is placed
the Consul's Tribunall.*

★   ★   ★

*Enter several Old men in black with Cypress Wreaths, leading Virgins in
white with Myrtle, who kneel before the Tribunal.*
    Then enters Marius senior *as Consul, Lictors,* Sulpitius, *and Guards.*

★   ★   ★

    Marius sen. Advance *Sulpitius*: old *Ancharius* there,
Who was so violent for my Destruction,

311

That his Beard brussled as his Face distorted:
Away with him. Dispatch these Triflers too.
But spare the Virgins, 'cause mine Eyes have seen 'em:
Or keep 'em for my Warriours to rejoice in.

   Anch. Thou who wert born to be the Plague of *Rome,*
What wouldst thou doe with me?

   Mar. sen. Dispose thee hence
Amongst the other Offall, for the jaws
Of hungry Death, till *Rome* be purg'd of Villains.
Thou dy'st for wronging *Marius.*——

   Child. Oh my Lord!
(For you must be a Lord, you are so angry),
For my sake spare his Life. I have no Friend
But him to guard my tender years from Wrongs.
When he is dead, what will become of me,
A poor and helpless Orphan, naked left
To all the Ills of the wide faithless world?

   Mar. sen. Take hence this Brat too; mount it on a Spear,
And let it sprawl to make the Grandsire sport.

   Child. Oh cruel man! I'll hang upon your Knees,
And with my little dying Hands implore you.
I may be fit to doe you some small pleasures:
I'll find a thousand tender ways to please you;
Smile when you rage, and stroak you into Mildness;
Play with your manly Neck, and call you Father:
For mine (alas!) the Gods have taken from me.

   Mar. sen. Young Crocodile! Thus from their Mothers Breasts
Are they instructed, bred and taught in *Rome.*
For that old Paralitick Slave, dispatch him:
Let me not know he breaths another moment.
But spare this, 'cause 't has learnt its Lesson well,
And I've a Softness in my heart pleads for him.

Enter Messenger.

Well now?

   Mess. Metellus.

   Mar. sen. Hah! *Metellus?* what?

   Mess. Is found.

   Mar. sen. Speak, where?

   Mess. In an old Suburb Cottage,

Upbraiding Heav'n, and cursing at your Fortune.
  Mar. sen. Haste, let him be preserv'd for my own Fury.
Clap, clap your hands for joy, ye Friends of *Marius.*
Ten thousand Talents for the news I'll give thee:
The Core and Bottom of my Torment's found;
And in a moment I shall be at ease.
Rome's Walls no more shall be besmear'd with Bloud,
But Peace and Gladness flourish in her Streets.
Lets go. *Metellus!* we have found *Metellus!*
Let every Tongue proclaim aloud *Metellus*;
Till I have dasht him on the Rock of Fate.
Then be his Name forgot, and heard no more.   *[Exeunt.*

[Act V, Scene iii.]

SCENE *a Church-yard.*

Enter Marius junior.

  Mar. jun. As I have wander'd musing to and fro,
Still am I brought to this unlucky place,
As I had business with the horrid Dead:
Though could I trust the flattery of Sleep,
My Dreams presage some joyfull news at hand.
My Bosome's Lord sits lightly on his Throne,
And all this day an unaccustom'd Spirit
Lifts me above the ground with chearfull thoughts.
I dream'd *Lavinia* came and found me dead,
And breath'd such Life with Kisses on my Lips,
That I reviv'd, and was an Emperour.

Enter Catulus.

  Catul. My Lord already here?
  Mar. jun. My trusty *Catulus,*
What News from my *Lavinia*? speak, and bless me.
  Catul. She's very well.
  Mar. jun. Then nothing can be ill.
Something thou seem'st to know that's terrible.
Out with it boldly, man, What canst thou say
Of my *Lavinia*?
  Catul. But one sad word, She's dead.

Here in her Kindreds Vault I've seen her laid,
And have bin searching you to tell the News.
  Mar. jun. Dead? is it so? then I deny you, Stars.
Go, hasten quickly, get me Ink and Paper.
'Tis done: I'll hence to night.
Hast thou no Letters to me from the Priest?
No matter, get thee gone.   [*Ex.* Catulus.
Lavinia! yet I'll ly with thee to night;
But, for the means. Oh Mischief! thou art swift
To catch the straggling Thoughts of Desp'rate men.
I do remember an Apothecary,
That dwelt about this Rendezvous of Death:
Meager and very rufull were his Looks;
Sharp Misery had worn him to the Bones;
And in his needy Shop a Tortoise hung,
An Allegator stufft, and other Skins
Of ill-shap'd Fishes: and about his Shelves
A beggarly account of empty Boxes,
Green earthen Pots, Bladders, and musty Seeds,
Remnants of Packthread, and old Cakes of Roses,
Were thinly scatter'd, to make up a Show.
Oh for a Poison now! his Need will sell it,
Though it be present Death by *Roman* Law.
As I remember this should be the House.
His Shop is shut: with Beggars all are Holydays.
Holla! Apothecary; hoa!

Enter Apothecary.

  Apoth. Who's there?
  Mar. jun. Come hither, man.
I see thou'rt very poor;
Thou mayst doe any thing. Here's fifty *Drachma's,*
Get me a Draught of that will soonest free
A Wretch from all his Cares: thou understand'st me.
  Apoth. Such mortal Drugs I have; but *Roman* Law
Speaks Death to any he that utters 'em.
  Mar. jun. Art thou so base and full of Wretchedness,
Yet fear'st to dy? Famine is in thy Cheeks,
Need and Oppression starveth in thy Eyes,
Contempt and Beggary hang on thy Back;

The World is not thy Friend, nor the World's Law;
The World affords no Law to make thee rich:
Then be not poor, but break it, and take this.
   Apoth. My Poverty, but not my Will consents.
                                [Goes in, fetches a Vial of Poison.
Take this and drink it off, the Work is done.
   Mar. jun. There is thy Gold, worse Poison to mens Souls,
Doing more Murthers in this loathsome world
Than these poor Compounds thou'rt forbid to sell.
I sell thee Poison, thou hast sold me none.
Farewell . . . buy Food . . . and get thy self in flesh.
Now for the Monument of the *Metelli.*   *[Exit.*
     [Scene draws off, and shews the Temple and Monument.
               Re-enters.
It should be here: the door is open too.
Th'insatiate mouth of Fate gapes wide for more.

Enter Priest, and Boy with a Mattock and Iron Crow.

   Priest. Give me the Mattock and the wrenching Iron:
Now take this Letter, with what haste thou canst
Find out young *Marius,* and deliver it.   *[Ex. Boy.*
Now must I to the Monument alone.
What Wretch is he that's entring into th' Tomb?
Some Villain come to rob and spoil the Dead.
Whoe're thou art, stop thy unhallowed purpose.
   Mar. jun. Whoe're thou art, I warn thee to be gone,
And do not interrupt my horrid purpose.
For else, by Heav'n, I'll tear thee joint by joint,
And strew this hungry Church-yard with thy Lims.
My Mind and its Intents are savage wild,
More fierce and more inexorable far
Than empty Tigers or the roaring Sea.
   Priest. Then as a sacrilegious Slave I charge thee,
Obey and go with me, or thou must dy.
   Mar. jun. I know I must, and therefore I came hither.
Good Reverence, do not tempt a desp'rate man.
By Heav'n, I love thee better then my self:
For I against my self come hither arm'd.
Stay not, be gone.—Live, and hereafter say,
A Mad-man's Mercy gave thee honest Counsell.

Priest. I do defy thy Mercy and thy Counsell,
And here will seize thee as a Thief and Robber.
    Mar. jun. Wilt thou provoke me? then here, take thy Wages.
                                                        [Kills him.
    Priest. I'm kill'd. Oh *Marius*! now too late I know thee.
Thou'st slain the onely man could doe thee good.
    Lavinia . . . oh! . . .   *[Dies.*
    Mar. jun. Let me peruse this Face.
It is the honest Priest that joyn'd our hands,
In a Disguize conceal'd. Give me thy Hand,
Since in ill Fate's black Roll with me thou 'rt writ,
I'll bury thee in a triumphant Grave.
Thou detestable Maw, thou Womb of Death,
Gorg'd with the dearest Morsell of the Earth,
Thus will I force thy rotten Jaws to open,
And spite of thee yet cram thee with more Food.

                                  [Pulls down the side of the Tomb.

Oh gorgeous Palace! oh my Love! my Wife!
Death has had yet no pow'r upon thy Beauty;
That is not conquer'd. Beauty's Ensign yet
Is Crimson in thy Lips and in thy Cheeks;
And the pale Flag is not advanc'd yet there.
Why art thou still so fair? shall I believe
That the lean Monster Death is amorous,
And keeps thee here in Darkness for his Paramour?
For fear of that, I'll stay with thee for ever.
Come, bitter Conduct, thou unsavoury Guide:
Here's to my Love!   *[Drinks the Poison.*
And now Eyes look your last.
Arms take your last Embrace, whilst on these Lips
I fix the Seal of an eternall Contract. . . .
She breaths and stirs!   *[Lavinia wakes.*
    Lavin. in the Tomb. Where am I? bless me, Heav'n!
'Tis very cold; and yet here's something warm.
    Mar. jun. She lives, and we shall both be made immortall.
Speak, my *Lavinia*, speak some heav'nly news,
And tell me how the Gods design to treat us.
    Lavin. Oh! I have slept a long Ten thousand years,
What have they done with me? I'll not be us'd thus;

I'll not wed *Sylla*. *Marius* is my Husband.
Is he not, Sir? Methinks you're very like him.
Be good as he is, and protect me.
    Mar. jun. Hah!
Wilt thou not own me? am I then but like him?
Much, much indeed I'm chang'd from what I was;
And ne'r shall be my self, if thou art lost.
    Lavin. The Gods have heard my Vows; it is my *Marius*.
Once more they have restor'd him to my Eyes.
Hadst thou not come, sure I had slept for ever.
But there's a soveraign Charm in thy Embraces,
That might doe Wonders, and revive the Dead.
    Mar. jun. Ill Fate no more, *Lavinia*, now shall part us,
Nor cruel Parents, nor oppressing Laws.
Did not Heav'n's Pow'rs all wonder at our Loves?
And when thou toldst the tale of thy Disasters,
Was there not Sadness and a Gloom amongst 'em?
I know there was: and they in pity sent thee,
Thus to redeem me from this vale of Torments,
And bear me with thee to those Hills of Joys.
This World's gross air grows burthensome already.
I'm all a God: such heav'nly Joys transport me,
That mortal Sense grows sick and faints with lasting.   *[Dies.*
    Lavin. Oh! to recount my Happiness to thee,
To open all the Treasure of my Soul,
And shew thee how 'tis fill'd, would waste more time
Than so impatient Love as mine can spare.
He's gone; he's dead; breathless: alas! my *Marius*!
A Vial too: here, here has bin his Bane.
Oh Churl! drink all? not leave one friendly Drop
For poor *Lavinia*? Yet I'll drain thy Lips.
Perhaps some welcom Poison may hang there,
To help me to o'retake thee on thy Journy.
Clammy and damp as Earth. Hah! stains of Bloud?
And a man murther'd? 'Tis th'unhappy *Flamen*.
Who fix their Joys on any thing that's Mortall,
Let 'em behold my Portion, and despair.
What shall I doe? how will the Gods dispose me?
Oh! I could rend these Walls with Lamentation,
Tear up the Dead from their corrupted Graves,

And dawb the face of Earth with her own Bowels.

Enter Marius senior, *and Guards driving in* Metellus.

    Mar. sen. Pursue the Slave; let not his Gods protect him.
    Lavin. More Mischiefs? hah! my Father?
    Metell. Oh! I am slain.   [*Falls down and dies.*
    Lavin. And murther'd too. When will my Woes have end?
Come, cruel Tyrant.
    Mar. sen. Sure I have known that Face.
    Lavin. And canst thou think of any one good Turn
That I have done thee, and not kill me for't?
    Mar. sen. Art thou not call'd *Lavinia*?
    Lavin. Once I was:
But by my Woes may now be better known.
    Mar. sen. I cannot see thy Face.
    Lavin. You must, and hear me.
By this, you must: nay, I will hold you fast.   [*Seizes his Sword.*
    Mar. sen. What wouldst thou say? where's all my Rage gone now?
    Lavin. I am *Lavinia*, born of Noble race.
My blooming Beauty conquer'd many Hearts,
But prov'd the greatest Torment of my own:
Though my Vows prosper'd, and my Love was answer'd
By *Marius*, the noblest, goodliest Youth
That Man e're envy'd at, or Virgin sigh'd for.
He was the Son of an unhappy Parent,
And banish'd with him when our Joys were young;
Scarce a night old.
    Mar. sen. I do remember't well,
And thou art She, that Wonder of thy kind,
That couldst be true to exil'd Misery,
And to and fro through barren Desarts range,
To find th'unhappy Wretch thy Soul was fond of.
    Lavin. Do you remember't well?
    Mar. sen. In every point.
    Lavin. You then were gentle, took me in your Arms,
Embrac'd me, blest me, us'd me like a Father.
And sure I was not thankless for the Bounty.
    Mar. sen. No; thou wert next the Gods my onely Comfort.
When I lay fainting on the dry parcht Earth,
Beneath the scorching heat of burning Noon,

Hungry and dry, no Food nor Friend to chear me:
Then Thou, as by the Gods some Angel sent,
Cam'st by, and in Compassion didst relieve me.
 Lavin. Did I all this?
 Mar. sen. Thou didst, thou sav'dst my Life.
Else I had sunk beneath the weight of Want,
And bin a Prey to my remorseless Foes.
 Lavin. And see how well I am at last rewarded!
All could not balance for the short-term'd Life
Of one Old man: You have my Father butcher'd,
The onely Comfort I had left on Earth.
The Gods have taken too my Husband from me.
See where he lies, your and my onely Joy.
This Sword yet reeking with my Father's Gore,
Plunge it into my Breast: plunge, plunge it thus.
And now let Rage, Distraction and Despair
Seize all Mankind, till they grow mad as I am.
       [*Stabs her self with his Sword.*
 Mar. sen. Nay, now thou hast outdone me much in Cruelty.
Be Nature's Light extinguisht; let the Sun
Withdraw his Beams, and put the world in Darkness,
Whilst here I howl away my Life in Sorrows!
Oh! let me bury Me and all my Sins
Here with this good Old man. Thus let me kiss
Thy pale sunk Cheeks, embalm thee with my Tears.
My Son, how cam'st thou by this wretched End?
We might have all bin Friends, and in one House
Enjoy'd the Blessings of eternal Peace.
But oh! my cruel Nature has undone me.

Enter Messenger.

 Mess. My Lord, I bring you most disastrous News.
Sylla's return'd: his Army's on their march
From *Capua*, and to morrow will reach *Rome*.
At which the Rabble are in new Rebellion,
And your *Sulpitius* mortally is wounded.

Enter Sulpitius (*led in by two of the Guards*) *and* Granius.

 Mar. sen. Oh! then I'm ruin'd from this very moment.
Has my good Genius left me? Hope forsakes me.

The Name of *Sylla*'s banefull to my Fortune.
Be warn'd by me, ye Great ones, how y'embroil
Your Country's Peace, and dip your Hands in Slaughter.
Ambition is a Lust that's never quencht,
Grows more inflam'd and madder by Enjoyment.
Bear me away, and lay me on my Bed,
A hopelesse Vessel bound for the dark Land
Of loathsome Death, and loaded deep with Sorrows.

[*He is led off.*

    Sulpit. A Curse on all Repentance! how I hate it!
I'd rather hear a Dog howl than a Man whine.
    Gran. You're wounded, Sir: I hope it is not much.
    Sulpit. No; 'tis not so deep as a Well, nor so wide as a Church-
door. But 'tis enough; 'twill serve; I am pepper'd, I warrant, for this
world. A Pox on all Mad-men hereafter. If I get a Monument, let this
be my Epitaph:

> Sulpitius *lies here, that troublesome Slave,*
> *That sent many honester men to the Grave,*
> *And dy'd like a Fool when h' had liv'd like a Knave.*

[*Ex. omnes.*

21. Nahum Tate, from his adaptation of *Richard II*

1680

From *The History of King Richard The Second. Acted. . . . Under the Name of the Sicilian Usurper. With a Prefatory Epistle in Vindication of the Author. Occasion'd by the Prohibition of this Play on the Stage* (1681).

Nahum Tate (1652–1715) ran into difficulties with the authorities due to the uncomfortable parallels between Shakespeare's play and the contemporary political situation. It was performed on about 11–13 December 1680, and was forbidden on 14 December; when the theatre revived it on 18–19 January 1681 under another title (*The Tyrant of Sicily*) the playhouse was shut down for ten days. Tate, following the neoclassical concept of types and decorum, is particularly concerned to make Richard a good king, and to give him a loving and pathetic wife as a proof of his goodness.

[Preface.] To My Esteemed Friend George Raynsford, Esq;

SIR,

I Wou'd not have you surpriz'd with this Address, though I gave you no warning of it. The Buisiness of this Epistle is more Vindication than Complement; and when we are to tell our Grievances 'tis most natural to betake our selves to a Friend. 'Twas thought perhaps that this unfortunate Offspring having been stifled on the *Stage*, shou'd have been buried in Oblivion; and so it might have happened had it drawn its Being from me Alone; but it still retains the immortal Spirit of its first-Father, and will survive in Print, though forbid to tread the *Stage*. They that have not seen it Acted, by its being silenc't, must suspect me to have Compil'd a Disloyal or Reflecting *Play*. But how far distant this was from my Design and Conduct in the Story will appear to him that reads with half an Eye. To form any Resemblance between the Times here written of, and the Present, had been un-pardonable Presumption in Me. If the Prohibiters conceive any such Notion I am not accountable for That. I fell upon the new-modelling of this Tragedy, (as I had just before done on the *History of King Lear*) charm'd with the many Beauties I discover'd in it, which I knew wou'd become the *Stage*; with as little design of Satyr on present Transactions, as *Shakespeare* himself that wrote this Story before this Age began. I am not ignorant of the posture of Affairs in King *Richard* the Second's Reign, how dissolute then the Age, and how corrupt the Court; a Season that beheld *Ignorance* and Infamy preferr'd to *Office* and *Pow'r*, exercis'd in Oppressing Learning and Merit; but why a History of those Times shou'd be supprest as a Libel upon Ours, is past my Understanding. 'Tis sure the worst *Complement* that ever was made to a Prince. . . .

Our *Shakespeare* in this Tragedy, bated none of his Characters an Ace of the Chronicle; he took care to shew 'em no worse Men than They were, but represents them never a jot better. His *Duke of York* after all his buisy pretended Loyalty, is found false to his Kinsman and Sovereign, and joyn'd with the *Conspirators*. His King *Richard* Himself is painted in the worst Colours of History, Dissolute, Unadviseable, devoted to Ease and Luxury. You find old *Gaunt* speaking of him in this Language

> ———*Then there are found*
> *Lascivious Meeters, to whose Venom sound*
> *The open Ear of Youth do's always Listen.*
> *Where doth the World thrust forth a Vanity,*
> *(So it be New, there's no respect how Vile)*
> *That is not quickly buzz'd into his Ear?*
> *That all too late comes Counsel to be heard.* [2.1.18ff.]

without the least palliating of his Miscarriages, which I have done in the new Draft, with such words as These.

> *Your Sycophants bred from your Child-hood with you,*
> *Have such Advantage had to work upon you,*
> *That scarce your Failings can be call'd your Faults.*

His Reply in *Shakespeare* to the blunt honest Adviser runs thus.

> *And Thou a Lunatick Lean-witted-fool, &c.*
> *Now by my Seat's right Royal Majesty,*
> *Wer't thou not Brother to great Edward's Son.*

The Tongue that runs thus roundly in thy Head
Shou'd run thy Head from thy unreverent Shoulders.

[2.1.115, 120ff.]

On the contrary (though I have made him express some Resentment)
yet he is neither enrag'd with the good Advice, nor deaf to it. He
answers Thus——

————*Gentle Unkle;*
Excuse the Sally's of my Youthfull Blood.
We shall not be unmindfull to redress
(However difficult) our States Corruptions,
And purge the Vanities that crowd our Court.

I have every where given him the Language of an Active, Prudent
Prince, Preferring the Good of his Subjects to his own private Pleasure.
On his *Irish* Expedition, you find him thus bespeak his Queen——

Though never vacant Swain in silent Bow'rs
Cou'd boast a Passion so sincere as Mine,
Yet where the Int'rest of the Subject calls
We wave the dearest Transports of our Love,
Flying from Beauties Arms to rugged War, &c.

Nor cou'd it suffice me to make him speak like a King (who as Mr.
Rymer says in his *Tragedies of the last Age considered*, are always in
Poëtry presum'd Heroes) but to *Act* so too, viz. with *Resolution* and
Justice. Resolute enough our *Shakespeare* (copying the History) has
made him, for concerning his seizing old *Gaunt*'s Revennues, he tells
the wise Diswaders,

Say what ye will, we seize into our Hands
His Plate, his Goods, his Money and his Lands.

[2.1.109f.]

But where was the Justice of this Action? This Passage I confess was so
material a Part of the Chronicle (being the very Basis of *Bullingbrook*'s
Usurpation) that I cou'd not in this new Model so far transgress Truth
as to make no mention of it; yet for the honour of my Heroe I suppose
the foresaid Revennues to be *Borrow'd* onely for the present Exigence,
not *Extorted.*

Be Heav'n our Judge, we mean him fair,
And shortly will with Interest restore
The Loan our suddain Streights make necessary.

My Design was to engage the pitty of the Audience for him in his Distresses, which I cou'd never have compass'd had I not before shewn him a Wise, Active and Just Prince. Detracting Language (if any where) had been excusable in the Mouths of the Conspirators: part of whose Dialogue runs thus in *Shakespeare*:

> North. *Now afore Heav'n 'tis shame such Wrongs are born*
> *In him a Royal Prince and many more*
> *Of noble Blood in this Declining Land:*
> *The King is not Himself, but basely led*
> *By Flatterers, &c.*
> Ross. *The Commons He has pil'd with grievous Taxes*
> *And lost their Hearts, &c.*
> Will. *And daily new Exactions are devis'd*
> *As Blanks, Benevolences, and I wot not what;*
> *But what o' Gods Name doth become of This?*
> North. *War hath not wasted it, for warr'd he has not;*
> *But basely yielded upon Comprimize.*
> *That which his Ancestours atchiev'd with Blows*
> *More has He spent in Peace than they in War, &c.* [2.1.238ff.]

with much more villifying Talk; but I wou'd not allow even Traytors and Conspirators thus to bespatter the Person whom I design'd to place in the Love and Compassion of the Audience. Ev'n this very Scene (as I have manag'd it) though it shew the Confederates to be Villains, yet it flings no Aspersion on my Prince.

Further, to Vindicate ev'n his *Magnanimity* in Regard of his Resigning the Crown, I have on purpose inserted an intirely new Scene between him and his Queen, wherein his Conduct is sufficiently excus'd by the Malignancy of his Fortune, which argues indeed Extremity of Distress, but Nothing of Weakness.

After this account it will be askt why this Play shou'd be supprest, first in its own Name, and after in Disguise? All that I can answer to this, is, That it was *Silenc'd on the Third Day*. I confess, I expected it wou'd have found Protection from whence it receiv'd Prohibition; and so questionless it wou'd, cou'd I have obtain'd my Petition to have it perus'd and dealt with according as the Contents Deserv'd; but a positive Doom of Suppression *without Examination* was all that I cou'd procure.

The Arbitrary Courtiers of the Reign here written, scarcely did more Violence to the Subjects of their Time, than I have done to

Truth, in disguising their foul Practices. Take ev'n the *Richard* of *Shakespeare* and History, you will find him Dissolute, Careless, and Unadvisable: peruse my Picture of him and you will say, as *Æneas* did of *Hector,* (though the Figure there was alter'd for the Worse and here for the Better) *Quantum mutatus ab illo!* And likewise for his chief Ministers of State, I have laid Vertues to their Charge of which they were not Guilty. Every Scene is full of Respect to Majesty and the dignity of Courts, not one alter'd Page but what breaths Loyalty; yet had this Play the hard fortune to receive its Prohibition from Court.

For the two days in which it was Acted, the Change of the Scene, Names of Persons, &c. was a great Disadvantage: many things were by this means render'd obscure and incoherent that in their native Dress had appear'd not only proper but gracefull. I call'd my Persons *Sicilians* but might as well have made 'em Inhabitants of the Isle of *Pines,* or, World in the *Moon,* for whom an Audience are like to have small Concern. Yet I took care from the Beginning to adorn my Prince with such heroick Vertues, as afterwards made his distrest Scenes of force to draw Tears from the Spectators; which, how much more touching they would have been had the Scene been laid at Home, let the Reader judge. The additional Comedy I judg'd necessary to help off the heaviness of the Tale, which Design, Sir, you will not only Pardon, but Approve. I have heard you commend this Method in Stage writing, though less agreeable to stricktness of Rule; and I find your Choice confirm'd by our *Laureat's* last Piece, who confesses himself to have broken a Rule for the Pleasure of

Variety. *The Audience* (says he) *are grown weary*   * Epist. Ded. to
of melancholly Scenes, and I dare prophesie that few   the *Span. Fryar.*
*Tragedies (except those in Verse) shall succeed in this
Age if they are not lightned with a course of Mirth. . . .*

Once more, Sir, I beg your Pardon for digressing, and dismiss you to the following Poem, in which you will find some Master Touches of our *Shakespeare,* that will Vie with the best Roman Poets, that have so deservedly your Veneration. If it yield you any Diversion I have my Desire, who covet all Opportunities of shewing my self gratefull for your Friendship to me, which I am proud of, and amongst the many whom your ingenious and obliging Temper has devoted to you, there is none that more prizes your Conversation, than

    Your obliged Friend and humble Servant,

N. Tate.

*   *   *

325

[Act II, Scene i.] A Chamber.

★   ★   ★

Enter King, Queen, Northumberland, Ross, Willoughby, Pierce, *&c.*
With Guards and Attendants.

 Queen. How fares our Noble Uncle *Lancaster?*
 King. How is't with aged *Gaunt?*
 Gaunt. Ag'd as your Highness says, and Gaunt indeed.
Gaunt, as a Grave whose Womb holds nought but Bones,
 King. Can sick men play so nicely with their Names?
 Gaunt. Since thou dost seek to kill my Name in me,
I mock my Name great King to flatter thee.
 King. Should dying men, then, flatter those that Live?
 Gaunt. No, no, Men living flatter those that dye.
 King. Thou now a dying sayst, thou flatter'st me.
 Gaunt. Oh! no, Thou dyest though I the sicker am.
 King. I am in health, breathe free but see thee ill.
 Gaunt. Now he that made me knows I see thee ill.
Thy death-bed is no less than the whole Land,
Whereon thou ly'st in Reputation sick.
Yet hurri'd on by a malignant fate
Commit'st thy annoynted Body to the Cure
Of those Physitians that first Poyson'd thee!
Upon thy Youth a Swarm of flatterers hang
And with their fulsome weight are daily found
To bend thy yielding Glories to the ground.
 King. Judge Heav'n how poor a thing is Majesty,
Be thou thy self the Judge, when thou sick *Wight*
Presuming on an Agues Priviledge
Dar'st with thy Frozen admonition,
Make pale our Cheek; but I excuse thy weakness.
 Gaunt. Think not the Ryot of your Court can last,
Tho fed with the dear Life blood of your Realms;
For vanity at last preys of it self.
This Earth of Majesty, this seat of *Mars,*
This Fortress built by Nature in the Floods,
Whose Rocky shores beat back the foaming Sedge,
This *England* Conqu'rour of the Neighbring Lands,
Makes now a shameful Conquest on it self.

York. Now will I stake (my Liege) my Soul upon't;
Old *Gaunt* is hearty in his wishes for you,
And what he speaks, is out of honest Zeal,
And tho thy Anger prove to me as Mortal,
As is to him this sickness, yet blunt *York*
Must Eccho to his words and cry,
Thou art abus'd and flatter'd.
    King. Gentle Uncle,
Excuse the sallies of my youthful Blood,
I know y'are Loyal both and mean us well,
Nor shall we be unmindful to redress,
(However difficult) our States corruption,
And purge the Vanities that Crown'd our Court.
    Gaunt. My gracious Liege your Pardon, this bold duty,
Was all that stood betwixt my Grave and me.
Your Sycophants bred from your Child-hood with you,
Have such advantage had to work upon you,
That scarce your failings can be call'd your faults;
Now to Heav'ns care and your own Piety,
I leave my sacred Lord, and may you have
In life that peace that waits me in the Grave.
    King. Thanks my good Uncle, bear him to his Bed.   [*Exit Gaunt.*
Attend him well, and if a Princes Prayers
Have more than common interest with Heav'n,
Our Realm shall yet enjoy his honest Councel.
And now my Souldiers for our Irish Wars,
We must suppress these rough prevailing Kerns,
That live like Venom, where no Venom else
But only they have priviledg to live.
But first our Uncle *Gaunt* being indispos'd,
We do create his Brother both in Blood
And Loyalty our Uncle *York*,
Lord Governour of *England*, in our absence.
Observe me Lords, and pay him that respect
You give our Royal Presence.

Enter Northumberland.

    North. My Liege old *Gaunt* commends him to your Highness.
    King. What says our Uncle?
    North. Nothing; all is said.

His Tongue is now a stringless instrument,
But call'd on your lov'd name and blest you dying.
   King. The ripest fruit falls first and so doe's He;
His course is done, our Pilgrimage to come.
So much for that; return we to our War.
And 'cause our Coffers with too great a Court
And liberal Largess, are grown somewhat Light:
Prest with this exigence, we for a time
Do seize on our dead Uncles large Revenues
In *Herford*'s absence.
   York. O my Liege, pardon me if you please;
If not, I please not to be pardon'd. Spare to seize
The Royalties and Rights of banisht *Herford*:
I fear already he's too apt t'engage
Against your Power, and these proceedings will give
Countenance and growth to his Designs.
Forbear to draw such Dangers on your Head.
   King. Be Heav'n our judge we mean him nothing fowl
But shortly will with interest restore
The Loan our sudden streights make necessary.——
Weep not my Love nor drown with boding Tears,
Our springing Conquest, bear our absence well,
Nor think that I have joy to part with Thee,
Tho never vacant Swain in silent Bowers,
Cou'd boast a passion so sincere as mine,
Yet where the int'rest of the Subject calls,
We wave the dearest Transports of our Love
Flying from Beauty's Arms to rugged War;
Conscience our first, and Thou our second Care.   [*Exeunt*.

★   ★   ★

[Act III, Scene iii.] A Heath.

★   ★   ★

   King . . . Some poyson'd by their Wives, some sleeping kill'd;
All murther'd: for within the hollow Crown
That rounds the mortal Temples of a King,
Keeps death his Court, and there the Antique sits,
Scoffing his State, and grinning at his Pomp!

Allowing him a short fictitious Scene,
To play the Prince, be fear'd, and kill with looks,
'Till swell'd with vain conceit the flatter'd thing
Believes himself immortal as a God;
Then to the train fate's Engineer sets fire,
Blows up his pageant Pride, and farewell King!
Cover your heads and mock not flesh and blood,
With solemn reverence; throw away Respect,
Obeysance, Form and Ceremonious Duty,
For you have but mistook me all this while,
I live with bread like you, feel Wants, tast Grief,
Therefore am I no King, or a King nothing.
   Aum. Give to the Foe my Lord, this cold despair,
No worse can come of Fight, of Death much better.
My Fathers Troops are firm let's joyn with them,
And manage wisely that last stake o'th' War,
Want's craft can make a body of a limb.
   King. You chide me well; proud *Bullingbrook* I come,   [*Rises.*
To change blows with thee for our day of Doom.
This Ague-fit of fear is overblown,
An easie task it is to win our own;
Say, *Scroop*, where lies our Uncle with his Pow'r?
My fir'd heart now longs for the fatal hour.
   Scroop. Men by the Skies complexion judge the day,
So may you by my dull and heavy eye,
Find that my tongue brings yet a heavier Tale,
I play the Torturer by small and small!
Your Uncle *York* treating with *Bullingbrook*,
Was seiz'd by him, and's still kept close Confin'd
So that the strength which he was must'ring up,
Is quast and come to nought.
   King. Thou hast said enough,
Beshrew thee Cousin that didst lead me forth
Of that sweet I was in to despair!
What say ye now? what comfort have ye now?
By Heav'n I'll hate him everlastingly,
That bids me be of comfort any more!

Enter Queen, Dutchess, Ladies *and Attendants.*

Now by despair my Queen and her fair train!

Come to congratulate our Victory,
And claim the triumph we at parting promis'd;
Go tell 'em Lords, what feats you have perform'd,
And if ye please tell my adventures too,
You know I was no Idler in the War.
Oh! torture, now I feel my miseries sting,
And this appearance strikes me dead with shame.
   Queen. Welcome my Lord,
This minute is our own, and I'll devote it all
To extasie; the Realm receives her King,
And I my Lover,——thou dost turn away!
Nor are they tears of joy which thou dost shed,
I give thee welcome, thou reply'st with sighs!
   King. What language shall my bankrupt fortunes find,
To greet such Heavenly excellence as thine?
I promiss'd thee success and bring thee Tears!
O couldst thou but devorce me from thy Heart!
But oh! I know thy virtue will undoe thee,
Thou wilt be still a faithful constant Wife,
Feel all my Wrongs and suffer in my Fall!
There is the sting and venom of my Fate,
When I shall think that I have ruin'd Thee.
   Queen. I ask no more my Lord, at Fortunes hands
Than priviledge to suffer for your sake!
Who wou'd not share your Grief to share your Love?
This Kingdom yet, which once you did prefer
To the worlds sway, this Beauty and this Heart
Is *Richards* still, millions of Loyal thoughts
Are always waiting there to pay you homage.
That glorious Empire yields to you alone,
No *Bullingbrook* can chase you from that Throne.
   King. We'll march no farther, lead to th' Castle here.

                                                           [*Exeunt.*

*   *   *

[Act IV, Scene i.] Before Parliament;
York, Aumarle *in their Parliament robes.*

*   *   *

   Aum. With such Malignant fortune he is prest,
As renders bravest Resolution vain;

330

By force and fraud reduc't to that Distress,
That ev'n i' th' best opinion of his Friends
He is advis'd to yield his Scepter up,
This poor reserve being all, to make that seem
As voluntary, which perforce must be;
But how resents the *Queen* this strange Oppression?
   Dutch. As yet the worst has been dissembled to her,
A slumber now has seiz'd her wakeful Lids:
But heere she comes, I must attend, Away.   [*Exit Aum.*

Enter Queen *supported by* Ladies.

   Qu. Convey me to my Lord, or bring him hither.
Fate labours in my Brest and frights my Dreams;
No sooner sleep can seize my weeping Eyes,
But boding Images of Death and Horrour
Affright the Infant slumber into Cries.
A Thousand forms of ruin strike my thoughts;
A Thousand various Scenes of Fate are shewn,
Which in their sad Catastrophe agree,
The Moral still concludes in *Richard*'s fall.
   Dutch. How shall we now dare to inform her Grief
Of the sad Scene the King must Act to day?
   Qu. Ev'n now amidst a *Chaos* of distraction,
A Towring Eagle wing'd his cloudy way,
Pursu'd by rav'nous Kites, and clamorous Daws,
That stript th' imperial Bird of all his Plumes,
And with their Numbers sunk him to the ground:
But as I nearer drew, the Figure chang'd,
My *Richard* there lay weltring in his gore!
So dreamt *Calphurnia*, and so fell *Cæsar*.

Enter a Lady

   Lad. Madam, the King is coming.
   Qu. Thou bring'st a welcom hearing, and already
I feel his powerful influence chase my fears,
For grief it self must smile when *Richard*'s by.

Enter King *in Mourning.*

Oh Heav'n is this, is this my promis'd joy?
Not all the terrours of my sleep presented

A Spectacle like this! O speak, my Lord!
The Blood starts back to my cold Heart; O speak!
What means this dark and mournful Pageantry,
This pomp of Death?
 King. Command your Waiters forth,
My space is short, and I have much to say.
 Qu. Are these the Robes of State? Th' imperial Garb,
In which the King should go to meet his Senate?
Was I not made to hope this Day shou'd be
Your second Coronation, second Birth
Of Empire, when our Civil Broils shou'd sleep,
For ever husht in deep Oblivion's Grave?
 King. O *Isabel*! This Pageantry suits best
With the black Day's more black Solemnity;
But 'tis not worth a Tear, for, say what part
Of Life's vain Fable can deserve a Tear,
A real Sorrow for a feign'd Distress?
My Coronation was (methinks) a Dream,
Think then my Resignation is no more.
 Qu. What Resignation? Mean you of the Crown?
Will *Richard* then against himself conspire?
Th'Usurper will have more excuse than he:
No, *Richard*, never tamely yield your Honours!
Yield me; yield if you must your precious Life,
But seize the Crown, and grasp your Scepter dying.
 King. Why dost thou fret a Lyon in the Toil
To Rage, that only makes his Hunters sport?
Permit me briefly to recount the steps,
By which my Fortune grew to this distress:
Then tell me, what cou'd *Alexander* do
Against a Fate so obstinate as mine?
 Qu. Oh Heav'n! Is awful Majesty no more?
 King. First, had I not bin absent when th' Invader
Set footing here; or if being then in *Ireland*,
The cross Winds not forbad the News to reach me;
Or when the shocking Tidings were arriv'd,
Had not the veering Winds agen obstructed
My passage back, 'till rumour of my Death
Disperst the Forces rais'd by *Salisbury*;
Or when these hopes were perisht, had not *Baggot*,

Bushie, and *Green,* by *Bullingbrook* been murder'd,
Old *York* himself (our last reserve) surpriz'd,
There were some scope for Resolution left.
But what curst Accident i'th' power of Chance,
That did not then befall to cross my Wishes?
And what strange hit could *Bullingbrook* desire,
That fell not out to push his Fortunes on?
Whatever outmost Fate cou'd do to blast
My hopes was done; what outmost Fate cou'd do
T'advance proud *Bullingbrooks* as sure befell.
Now which of these Misfortunes was my fault?
Or what cou'd I against resisting Heav'n?
    Qu. Oh my dear Lord, think not I meant t'upbraid
Your Misery——

                [*Weeps over him.*

Death seize my Youth, when any other passion
For injur'd *Richard* in my Brest finds room,
But tendrest Love and Pity of his Woes!
    King. That I resign the Crown with seeming will,
Is now the best my Friends can counsel me.
Th' usurping House decrees it must be done,
And therefore best that it seem Voluntary.
    Qu. Has Loyalty so quite renounc't the World,
That none will yet strike for an injur'd King?
    King. Alas! my sinking Barque shall wreck no more
My gen'rous Friends, let Crowns and Scepters go
Before I swim to 'em in Subjects blood.
The King in pity to his Subjects quits
His Right, that have no pity for their King!
Let me be blest with cool Retreat and thee,
Thou World of Beauty, and thou Heav'n of Love!
To *Bullingbrook* I yield the Toils of State:
And may the Crown sit lighter on his Head
Than e're it did on *Richard*'s.
    Qu. Destiny
Is Tyrant over Kings; Heav'n guard my Lord.
    King. Weep not my Love, each Tear thou shedst is Theft,
For know, thou robb'st the great ones of their due;
Of Pomp divested we shou'd now put off,

Its dull Companion Grief.——Farewel my Love:
Thy *Richard* shall return to thee again,
The King no more.

    Qu. In spight of me, my sorrow
In sad Prophetic Language do's reply
Nor *Richard*, nor the King.   *[Exeunt severally.*

★   ★   ★

[Act V, Scene ii.] Before the Tower.

Enter Queen *in Mourning attended.*

    Qu. This way the King will come; this is the way
To *Julius Cæsar's* ill erected Tow'r,
To whose flint Bosom my dear injur'd Lord
Is deem'd a Pris'ner by proud *Bullingbrook*!
Here let us rest, if this rebellious Earth
Have any resting for her true King's Queen.   *[Sits down.*
This Garb no less befits our present state,
Than richest Tissue did our Bridal day;
Thus dead in Honour, my Lord and I
Officiate at our own sad Funeral.

Enter King Richard *guarded, seeing the Queen, starts; she at the sight of*
him. After a pause he speaks.

    King. Give grief a Tongue, art thou not *Isabel*,
The faithful Wife of the unfortunate *Richard*?
    Qu. O! can I speak and live? Yet silence gives
More tort'ring Death! O thou King *Richard's* Tomb,
And not King *Richard*!—— On thy sacred Face
I see the shameful Marks of fowlest usage;
Thy Royal Cheeks soil'd and besmear'd with Dust,
Foul Rubbish lodg'd in thy anointed Locks;
O thou dishonour'd Flower of Majesty!
Lean on my Brest whilst I dissolve to Dew,
And wash thee fair agen with Tears of Love.
    King. Join not with Grief fair Innocence
To make my end more wretched; learn dear Saint
To think our former State a happy Dream,

334

From which we wake into this true distress!
Thou most distrest, most Virtuous of thy sex,
Go Cloyster thee in some Religious house,
This vicious World and I can nere deserve thee!
For Shrines and Altars keep those precious Tears,
Nor shed that heav'nly Dew on Land accurst.
   Lad. Never did sorrow triumph thus before.
   King. Convey thee hence to *France*,
Think I am Dead, and that ev'n now thou tak'st
As from my Death-bed the last living leave.
In Winters tedious Nights sit by the fire
With good Old Matrons, let them tell thee Tales
Of woful Ages long ago betide,
And ere thou bid good Night, to quit their Griefs,
Tell thou the lamentable fall of Me!
And send the Hearers weeping to their Beds.
   Qu. Rob not my Virtue of its dearest Triumph!
Love like the Dolphin shews it self in storms:
This is the Season for my Truth to prove,
That I was worthy to be *Richard*'s Wife!
And wou'd you now command me from your Presence,
Who then shall lull your raging Griefs asleep,
And wing the hours of dull Imprisonment?
   King. O my afflicted Heart!
   Qu. No, with my Lord i'll be a Pris'ner too,
Where my officious Love shall serve him with
Such ready care, that he shall think he has
His num'rous Train of waiters round him still;
With wond'rous Storys wee'll beguile the day,
Despise the World and Triumph over fortune,
Laugh at fantastic life and die together.
   King. Now Heaven I thank thee, all my Griefs are paid!
I've lost a single frail uncertain Crown,
And found a Virtue Richer than the World:
Yes, Bird of Paradise, wee'll pearch together,
Sing in our Cage, and make our Cell a Grove.

Enter Northumberland, *Guards.*

   North. My Lord, King *Bullingbrook* has chang'd his Orders,
You must to *Pomfrett* Castle, not to th' *Tower*;

And for you, Madam, he has given Command
That you be instantly convey'd to *France*.

    King. Must I to *Pomfrett*, and my Queen to *France*?
Patience is stale, and I am weary on't,
Blood, Fire, rank Leprosies and blewest Plagues!

    Qu. But This was wanting to compleat our Woe.

    King. Northumberland Thou Ladder by whose Aid
The mounting *Bullingbrook* ascends my Throne,
The Time shall come when foul Sin gath'ring Head
Shall break in to Corruption. Thou shalt think,
Tho he divide the Realm and give thee half,
It is too little, helping him to All:
He too shall think that thou which knewst the Way
To plant unrightful Kings, wilt know agen
To cast him from the Throne he has Usurpt:
The Love of wicked Friends converts to Fear,
That Fear to Hate, that still concludes in Death.

    North. My guilt be on my head, so to our business.
Take leave and part.

    King. Doubly Divorc't! foul Fiends ye violate
A two-fold Marriage, 'twixt my Crown and me,
And then betwixt me and my tender Wife;
Oh *Isabel*, oh my unfortunate Fair,
Let me unkiss the Oath that bound our Loves,
And yet not so, for with a Kiss 'twas made.
Part us *Northumberland*, me towards the *North*
Where shiv'ring Cold and Sickness pines the Clime;
My Queen to *France*, from whence set forth in Pomp
She hither came, deckt like the blooming *May*,
Sent back like weeping Winter stript and Bare.

    Qu. For ever will I clasp these sacred Knees,
Tear up my Brest and bind them to my Heart!
Northumberland allow me one short minute
To yield my Life and Woes in one Embrace.
One Minute will suffice.

    North. Force her away.

    King. Permit yet once our Death-cold Lips to joyn,
Permit a Kiss that must Divorce for ever.——
I'll ravish yet one more.—Farewell my Love!
My Royal Constant Dear, farewel for ever!

Give Sorrow Speech, and let thy Farewell come,
Mine speaks the Voice of Death, but Thine is Dumb.

[*Ex. Guarded several Ways.*]

*   *   *

[Act V, Scene iv.]

SCENE, *A Prison.*

King Richard, *Solus.*

Rich. I have bin studying how to compare
This lonesom Prison to the populous World.
The Paradox seems hard; but thus I'll prove it:
I'll call my Brain the Female to my Soul;
My Soul the Father, and these Two beget
A Generation of succeeding Thoughts,
Th'Inhabitants that stock this little World
In humours like the People of the World,
No Thought Contented: for the better sort,
As Thoughts of things Divine, are mixt with doubts
That set the Faith it self against the Faith;
Thoughts tending to Ambition, they are plotting
Unlikely Wonders, how these poor weak Hands
May force a passage through these stubborn flints;
And 'cause they cannot, Die in their own Pride.
Thoughts tending to Content are whispring to me,
That I am not the first of Fortunes Slaves,
And shall not be the Last; poor flatt'ring Comfort,
Thus I and every other Son of Earth
With nothing shall be pleas'd, till we be eas'd
With being nothing.

[*A Table and Provisions shewn.*]

What mean my Goalers by that plenteous Board?
For three days past I've fed upon my Sighs,
And drunk my Tears; rest, craving Nature, rest,
I'll humour thy dire Need and tast this food,
That only serves to make Misfortune Live.

[*Going to sit, the Table sinks down.*]

Thus *Tantalus* they say is us'd below;
But *Tantalus* his Guilt is then his Torture.

I smile at this fantastick Cruelty.
Ha, Musick too!—Ev'n what my Torturers please.

[*Song and soft Musick.*

I.

Retir'd from any Mortals sight
   The Pensive *Damon* lay,
He blest the discontented Night,
   And Curst the Smiling Day.
The tender sharers of his Pain,
   His Flocks, no longer Graze,
But sadly fixt around the Swain,
   Like silent Mourners gaze.

2.

He heard the Musick of the Wood,
   And with a sigh Reply'd,
He saw the Fish sport in the Flood,
   And wept a deeper Tyde.
In vain the Summers Bloom came on,
   For still the Drooping Swain
Like Autumn Winds was heard to Groan,
   Out-wept the Winters Rain.

3.

Some Ease (said he) some Respite give!
   Why, mighty Powrs, Ah why
Am I too much distrest to Live,
   And yet forbid to Dye?
Such Accents from the Shepherd flew
   Whilst on the Ground He lay;
At last so deep a Sigh he drew,
   As bore his Life away.

After which a Messenger enters, gives him Letters.

Mess. Hail Royal Sir, with dang'rous difficulty
I've enter'd here to bear These to your hand.—
O killing Spectacle!
   Rich. From whom?——my Queen,
My *Isabel*, my Royal wretched Wife?

O Sacred Character, oh Heav'n-born Saint!
Why! here are words wou'd charm the raging Sea,
Cure Lunaticks, dissolve the Wizzard's Spell,
Check baleful Planets, and make Winter bloom.
How fares my Angel, say, what Air's made rich
With her arrival, for she breathes the Spring;
What Land is by her presence priviledged.
From Heavn's ripe Vengeance? O my lab'ring Heart!
In, hide Thee, and prepare in short to Answer
To th'infinite Enquiries that my Love
Shall make of this dear Darling of my Soul.
Whilst undisturb'd I seize the present Minute
To answer the Contents of this blest Paper.   [Ex. Mess.

[Sits down to write, Enter Exton and Servants.

Furies! what means this Pageantry of Death?
Speak thou the foremost Murderer, thy own hand
Is arm'd with th'Instrument of thy own Slaughter,
Go Thou and fill a room in Hell,
Another Thou.
                                            [Kills 4 of them.
          [Exton here strikes him down.
That hand shall burn in never quenching Fire,
That staggers thus my Person, cruel Exton,
The blackest Fiend shall see thee lodg'd beneath him.
The Damn'd will shun the Villain whose curst Hand
Has with the King's blood stain'd the King's own Land.

                              [Dies.

   Ext. Hast and convey his Body to our Master
Before the very Rumour reach his Ear.
As full of Valour as of Royal Blood,
Both have I spilt, O that the Deed were Good.
Despair already seizes on my Soul;
Through my dark Brest Eternal Horrours roul:
Ev'n that false Fiend that told me I did well,
Cry's now, This Deed is Register'd in Hell.   [Exit.

[Act V, Scene v.]

SCENE *a Palace.* Bullingbrook, *Lords and Attendants.*

Bull. Our last Expresses speak the Rebels high,
Who have consum'd with Fire Our Town of *Gloster.*

Enter Northumberland *and* Pierce.

Welcome *Northumberland,* what News?
    North. Health to my Liege, I have to *London* sent
The Heads of *Spencer, Blunt* and *Salisbury.*
    Pierce. Broccas and *Scelye* too are headless Trunks,
The dang'rous Chiefs of that consorted Crew
That sought your Life at *Oxford.*
    Ross. Our Abbot, griev'd to see his Plott defeated,
Has yielded up his Body to the Grave.
But here's *Carlile* yet living to receive
Your Royal Doom.
    Bull. Carlile, I must confess,
Tho thou hast ever bin my Enemy,
Such sparks of Honour always shin'd in Thee,
As priviledg Thee from our Justice now;
Choose out some secret place, some reverend Cell,
There live in peace, and we shall not disturb
The Quiet of thy Death.——What suddain Damp
Congeals my Blood?——ha, *Exton?* then comes Mischief!

Enter Exton *and Servants bearing in a Coffin.*

    Ext. Great Sir, within this Coffin I present
Thy bury'd Fear, possess the Crown secure,
Which breathless *Richard* never more will claim.
    Bull. Exton I thank thee not, for thou hast wrought
A Deed of Slaughter fatal for my Peace,
Which Thou and I, and all the Land shall rue.
    Ext. From your own Mouth, my Lord, did I this Deed.
    Bull. They love not Poyson that have need of Poyson,
Nor do I Thee; I hate his Murderer,
Tho' I did wish him Dead: Hell thank thee for it,
And guilt of Royal Blood be thy Reward;
Cursing and Curst go wander through the World,
Branded like *Cain* for all Mankind to shun Thee.

Wake *Richard*, wake, give me my Peace agen,
And I will give Thee back thy ravisht Crown.
Come Lords prepare to pay your last Respects
To this great Hearse, and help a King to Mourn
A King's untimely Fall: O tort'ring Guilt!
In vain I wish The happy Change cou'd be,
That I slept There, and *Richard* Mourn'd for Me.

22. Nahum Tate on Shakespeare's learning

1680

From the preface to his tragedy *The Loyal General* (1680).

To Edward Tayler.

*　　*　　*

I cannot forget the strong desire I have heard you express to see the Common Places of our *Shakespeare*, compar'd with the most famous of the Ancients. This indeed were a Task worthy the greatest Critique. Our Learned *Hales* was wont to assert, That since the time of *Orpheus* and the Oldest Poets, no Common Place has been touch'd upon, where our Author has not perform'd as well. Our *Laureat* has thrown in his Testimony, and declar'd, That *Shakespeare* was a Man that of all Men had the largest and most comprehensive Soul.

What I have already asserted concerning the necessity of Learning to make a compleat Poet, may seem inconsistent with my reverence for our *Shakespeare*.

—*Cujus amor semper mihi crescit in Horas.*[1]

I confess I cou'd never yet get a true account of his Learning, and am

---

[1] Virgil, *Eclogue* 10.73: 'For whom my love grows greater all the time.'

apt to think it more than Common Report allows him. I am sure he never touches on a Roman Story, but the Persons, the Passages, the Manners, the Circumstances, the Ceremonies, all are Roman. And what Relishes yet of a more exact Knowledge, you do not only see a Roman in his Heroe, but the particular Genius of the Man, without the least mistake of his Character, given him by their best Historians. You find his *Antony* in all the Defects and Excellencies of his Mind, a Souldier, a Reveller, Amorous, sometimes Rash, sometimes Considerate, with all the various Emotions of his Mind. His *Brutus* agen has all the Constancy, Gravity, Morality, Generosity, Imaginable, without the least Mixture of private Interest or Irregular Passion. He is true to him, even in the imitation of his Oratory, the famous Speech which he makes him deliver, being exactly agreeable to his manner of expressing himself. . . .

But however it far'd with our Author for Book-Learning, 'tis evident that no man was better studied in Men and Things, the most useful Knowledge for a *Dramatic* Writer. He was a most diligent Spie upon Nature, trac'd her through her darkest Recesses, pictur'd her in her just Proportion and Colours; in which Variety 'tis impossible that all shou'd be equally pleasant, 'tis sufficient that all be proper.

Of his absolute Command of the Passions, and Mastery in distinguishing of Characters, you have a perfect Account in [Dryden's] most excellent Criticism before *Troilus and Cressida*: If any Man be a lover of *Shakespeare* and covet his Picture, there you have him drawn to the Life; but for the Eternal Plenty of his Wit on the same Theam, I will only detain you with a few instances of his Reflections on the Person, and Cruel Practices of *Richard* the Third. First of all *Henry* the Sixth bespeaks him in these words:

> *The owl shriekt at thy birth, an evil sign . . .*
> *Thy Mother felt more than a Mothers Pain,*
> *And yet brought forth less than a Mothers hope;*
> *An indigested Lump, &c.* [*3H6*, 5.6.44ff.]

Richard afterwards makes as bold with himself, where this is part of his Soliloque.

> *Cheated of Feature by dissembling Nature,*
> *Deform'd, unfinish'd, sent before my time*
> *Into this breathing world, scarce half made up.* . . .
> [*R3*, 1.1.19ff.]

Queen *Margaret* cannot hear him mention'd without a new stream of Satyr.

> *A Hell-hound that doth Hunt us all to Death,*
> *That Dog that had his Teeth before his Eyes,*
> *To worry Lambs and lap their gentle Blood, &c.*
>
> [R3, 4.4.48ff.]

And never meets him but she presents him with his Picture;

> *Hells black Intelligencer,*
> *Their Factour to buy Souls and send 'em thither.*
>
> [R3, 4.4.71f.]

And again,

> *Thou elfish markt abortive Monster,*
> *Thou that wast seal'd in thy Nativity,*
> *The Slave of Nature and the son of Hell.*
> *Thou slander of thy heavy Mothers Womb.*
>
> [R3, 1.3.228ff.]

With very many other Taunts to the same purpose.

It cannot be deny'd but he is often insipid where he is careless, many Things he wrote in hurry; but for his more elaborate Scenes, what *Cicero* spoke of the Writings of *Archias*, will hold good. *Quae vero accurate cogitateque scripsisset, ad veterum Scriptorem Laudem pervenerunt.*[1] (Sig. A₃–aᵛ.)

---

[1] *Pro Archia* 8, 18: 'To his finished and studied work I have known such approval accorded that his glory rivalled that of the great writers of antiquity.'

23. Nahum Tate, from his adaptation of *King Lear*

1681

From *The History of King Lear. . . . Reviv'd with Alterations* (1681).

Tate's *Lear* (performed in about March 1681) was an even more decisive expression of neoclassic taste than the Dryden–D'Avenant *Tempest*, and held the stage (with modifications by Garrick and Colman) until Macready's production of 1838. The Fool is omitted altogether; Lear and Cordelia are kept alive; Edgar marries Cordelia. Tate introduces Arante, a confidante for Cordelia, and also omits the King of France.

[Dedication]

To My Esteemed Friend Thomas Boteler, Esq;

Sir,

You have a natural Right to this Piece, since, by your Advice, I attempted the Revival of it with Alterations. Nothing but the Power of your Perswasion, and my Zeal for all the Remains of *Shakespeare*, cou'd have wrought me to so bold an Undertaking. I found that the New-modelling of this Story, wou'd force me sometimes on the difficult Task of making the chiefest Persons speak something like their Character, on Matter whereof I had no Ground in my Author. *Lear*'s real, and *Edgar*'s pretended Madness have so much of extravagant *Nature* (I know not how else to express it) as cou'd never have started but from our *Shakespeare*'s Creating Fancy. The Images and Language are so odd and surprizing, and yet so agreeable and proper, that whilst we grant that none but *Shakespeare* cou'd have form'd such Conceptions, yet we are satisfied that they were the only Things in the World that ought to be said on those Occasions. I found the whole to answer your Account of it, a Heap of Jewels, unstrung and unpolisht; yet so dazling in their Disorder, that I soon perceiv'd I had seiz'd a Treasure.

'Twas my good Fortune to light on one Expedient to rectifie what was wanting in the Regularity and Probability of the Tale, which was to run through the whole A *Love* betwixt *Edgar* and *Cordelia*, that never chang'd word with each other in the Original. This renders *Cordelia*'s Indifference and her Father's Passion in the first Scene probable. It likewise gives Countenance to *Edgar*'s Disguise, making that a generous Design that was before a poor Shift to save his Life. The Distress of the Story is evidently heightned by it; and it particularly gave Occasion of a New Scene or Two, of more Success (perhaps) than Merit. This Method necessarily threw me on making the Tale conclude in a Success to the innocent distrest Persons: Otherwise I must have incumbred the Stage with dead Bodies, which Conduct makes many Tragedies conclude with unseasonable Jests. Yet was I Rackt with no small Fears for so bold a Change, till I found it well receiv'd by my Audience; and if this will not satisfie the Reader, I can produce an Authority that questionless will. *Neither is it of so Trivial an Undertaking to make a Tragedy end happily, for 'tis more difficult to Save than 'tis to Kill: The Dagger and Cup of Poyson are alwaies in Readiness; but to bring the Action to the last Extremity, and then by probable Means to recover All, will require the Art and Judgment of a Writer, and cost him many a Pang in the Performance.* (Mr. *Dryd.* Pref. to the *Span. Fryar.*)

I have one thing more to Apologize for, which is, that I have us'd less Quaintness of Expression even in the newest Parts of this Play. I confess 'twas Design in me, partly to comply with my Author's Style to make the Scenes of a Piece, and partly to give it some Resemblance of the Time and Persons here Represented. This, Sir, I submit wholly to you, who are both a Judge and Master of Style. Nature had exempted you before you went Abroad from the Morose Saturnine Humour of our Country, and you brought home the Refinedness of Travel without the Affectation. Many Faults I see in the following Pages, and question not but you will discover more; yet I will presume so far on your Friendship, as to make the Whole a Present to you, and Subscribe my self

Your obliged Friend and humble Servant,

N. Tate.

PROLOGUE.

Since by Mistakes your best Delights are made,
(For ev'n your Wives can please in Masquerade)

'Twere worth our While t' have drawn you in this day
By a new Name to our old honest Play;
But he that did this Evenings Treat prepare ⎫
Bluntly resolv'd before-hand to declare ⎬
Your Entertainment should be most old Fare. ⎭
Yet hopes, since in rich *Shakespeare*'s soil it grew, ⎫
'Twill relish yet with those whose Tasts are True, ⎬
And his Ambition is to please a Few. ⎭
If then this Heap of Flow'rs shall chance to wear
Fresh Beauty in the Order they now bear,
Ev'n this [is] *Shakespeare*'s Praise; each Rustick knows
'Mongst plenteous Flow'rs a Garland to Compose,
Which strung by his coarse Hand may fairer Show,
But 'twas a Pow'r Divine first made 'em Grow.
Why shou'd these Scenes lie hid, in which we find
What may at Once divert and teach the Mind?
Morals were alwaies proper for the Stage,
But are ev'n necessary in this Age.
Poets must take the Churches Teaching Trade,
Since Priests their Province of Intrigue invade;
But We the worst in this Exchange have got,
In vain our Poets Preach, whilst Church-men Plot.

[Act I, Scene i.] Lear's Palace.

Enter Bastard *solus.*

   Bast. Thou Nature art my Goddess, to thy Law
My Services are bound; why am I then
Depriv'd of a Son's Right because I came not
In the dull Road that custom has prescrib'd?
Why Bastard, wherefore Base, when I can boast
A Mind as gen'rous and a Shape as true
As honest Madam's Issue? why are we
Held Base, who in the lusty stealth of Nature
Take fiercer Qualities than what compound
The scanted Births of the stale Marriage-bed?
Well then, legitimate *Edgar*, to thy right
Of Law I will oppose a Bastard's Cunning.
Our Father's Love is to the Bastard *Edmund*

As to Legitimate *Edgar*: with success
I've practis'd yet on both their easie Natures:
Here comes the old Man chas't with th' Information
Which last I forg'd against my Brother *Edgar*,
A Tale so plausible, so boldly utter'd
And heightned by such lucky Accidents,
That now the slightest circumstance confirms him,
And Base-born *Edmund* spight of Law inherits.

Enter Kent *and* Gloster.

   Glost. Nay, good my Lord, your Charity
O'reshoots it self to plead in his behalf;
You are your self a Father, and may feel
The sting of disobedience from a Son
First-born and best Belov'd: Oh Villain *Edgar*!
   Kent. Be not too rash, all may be forgery,
And time yet clear the Duty of your Son.
   Glost. Plead with the Seas, and reason down the Winds,
Yet shalt thou ne're convince me, I have seen
His foul Designs through all a Father's fondness:
But be this Light and Thou my Witnesses
That I discard him here from my Possessions,
Divorce him from my Heart, my Blood and Name.
   Bast. It works as I cou'd wish; I'll shew my self.   [*Aside.*
   Glost. Ha *Edmund*! welcome Boy; O *Kent* see here
Inverted Nature, *Gloster*'s Shame and Glory,
This By-born, the wild sally of my Youth,
Pursues me with all filial Offices,
Whilst *Edgar*, begg'd of Heaven and born in Honour,
Draws plagues on my white head that urge me still
To curse in Age the pleasure of my Youth.
Nay weep not, *Edmund*, for thy Brother's crimes;
O gen'rous Boy, thou shar'st but half his blood,
Yet lov'st beyond the kindness of a Brother.
But I'll reward thy Vertue. Follow me.
My Lord, you wait the King who comes resolv'd
To quit the Toils of Empire, and divide
His Realms amongst his Daughters. Heaven succeed it;
But much I fear the Change.
   Kent. I grieve to see him

With such wild starts of passion hourly seiz'd,
As renders Majesty beneath it self.

   Glost. Alas! 'tis the Infirmity of his Age,
Yet has his Temper ever been unfixt,
Chol'rick and suddain; hark, They approach.

                     [*Exeunt* Gloster *and* Bast.
Flourish. Enter Lear, Cornwall, Albany, Burgundy, Edgar, Gonerill,
Regan, Cordelia, Edgar *speaking to* Cordelia *at Entrance.*

   Edgar. Cordelia, royal Fair, turn yet once more,
And ere successfull *Burgundy* receive
The treasure of thy Beauties from the King,
Ere happy *Burgundy* for ever fold Thee,
Cast back one pitying Look on wretched *Edgar.*

   Cord. Alas what wou'd the wretched *Edgar* with
The more Unfortunate *Cordelia;*
Who in obedience to a Father's will
Flys from her *Edgar's* Arms to *Burgundy's?*

   Lear. Attend my Lords of *Albany* and *Cornwall*
With Princely *Burgundy?*

   Alb. We do, my Liege.

   Lear. Give me the Mapp.—Know, Lords, We have divided
In Three our Kingdom, having now resolved
To disengage from Our long Toil of State,
Conferring All upon your younger years;
You, *Burgundy, Cornwall* and *Albany*
Long in Our Court have made your amorous sojourn
And now are to be answer'd—tell me my Daughters
Which of you Loves Us most, that We may place
Our largest Bounty with the largest Merit.
Gonerill, Our Eldest-born, speak first.

   Gon. Sir, I do love You more than words can utter,
Beyond what can be valu'd, Rich or Rare,
Nor Liberty, nor Sight, Health, Fame, or Beauty
Are half so dear, my Life for you were vile,
As much as Child can love the best of Fathers.

   Lear. Of all these Bounds, ev'n from this Line to this
With shady Forests and wide-skirted Meads,
We make Thee Lady, to thine and *Albany's* Issue
Be this perpetual.—What says Our Second Daughter?

Reg. My Sister, Sir, in part exprest my Love,
For such as Hers, is mine, though more extended;
Sense has no other Joy that I can relish,
I have my All in my dear Lieges Love!

Lear. Therefore to thee and thine Hereditary
Remain this ample Third of our fair Kingdom.

Cord. Now comes my Trial, how am I distrest,   [*Aside.*
That must with cold speech tempt the chol'rick King
Rather to leave me Dowerless, than condemn me
To loath'd Embraces!

Lear. Speak now Our last, not least in Our dear Love,
So ends my Task of State,——*Cordelia* speak,
What canst Thou say to win a richer Third
Than what thy Sisters gain'd?

Cord. Now must my Love in words fall short of theirs   [*Aside.*
As much as it exceeds in Truth.—Nothing my Lord.

Lear. Nothing can come of Nothing, speak agen.

Cord. Unhappy am I that I can't dissemble,
Sir, as I ought, I love your Majesty,
No more nor less.

Lear. Take heed *Cordelia*,
Thy Fortunes are at stake, think better on't
And mend thy Speech a little.

Cord. O my Liege,
You gave me Being, Bred me, dearly Love me,
And I return my Duty as I ought,
Obey you, Love you, and most Honour you!
Why have my Sisters Husbands, if they love you All?
Happ'ly when I shall Wed, the Lord whose Hand
Shall take my Plight, will carry half my Love,
For I shall never marry, like my Sisters,
To Love my Father All.

Lear. And goes thy Heart with this?
'Tis said that I am Chol'rick, judge me Gods,
Is there not cause? now Minion I perceive
The Truth of what has been suggested to Us,
Thy Fondness for the Rebel Son of *Gloster*,
False to his Father, as Thou art to my Hopes:
And oh take heed, rash Girl, lest We comply
With thy fond wishes, which thou wilt too late

Repent, for know Our nature cannot brook
A Child so young and so Ungentle.
 Cord. So young my Lord and True.
 Lear. Thy Truth then be thy Dow'r,
For by the sacred Sun and solemn Night
I here disclaim all my paternal Care,
And from this minute hold thee as a Stranger
Both to my Blood and Favour.
 Kent. This is Frenzy.
Consider, good my Liege——
 Lear. Peace *Kent.*
Come not between a Dragon and his Rage.
I lov'd her most, and in her tender Trust
Design'd to have bestow'd my Age at Ease!
So be my Grave my Peace as here I give
My Heart from her, and with it all my Wealth:
My Lords of *Cornwall* and of *Albany,*
I do invest you jointly with full Right
In this fair Third, *Cordelia*'s forfeit Dow'r.
Mark me, My Lords, observe Our last Resolve,
Our Self attended with an hundred Knights
Will make Aboad with you in monthly Course.
The Name alone of King remain with me,
Yours be the Execution and Revenues,
This is Our final Will, and to confirm it
This Coronet part between you.
 Kent. Royal *Lear,*
Whom I have ever honour'd as my King,
Lov'd as my Father, as my Master follow'd,
And as my Patron thought on in my Pray'rs——
 Lear. Away, the Bow is bent, make from the Shaft!
 Kent. No, let it fall and drench within my Heart,
Be *Kent* unmannerly when *Lear* is mad:
Thy youngest Daughter——
 Lear. On thy Life no more.
 Kent. What wilt thou doe, old Man?
 Lear. Out of my sight!
 Kent. See better first.
 Lear. Now by the gods——
 Kent. Now by the gods, rash King, thou swear'st in vain.

Lear. Ha Traytour——

Kent. Do, kill thy Physician, *Lear,*
Strike through my Throat, yet with my latest Breath
I'll Thunder in thine Ear my just Complaint,
And tell Thee to thy Face that Thou dost ill.

Lear. Hear me rash Man, on thy Allegiance hear me;
Since thou hast striv'n to make Us break our Vow
And prest between our Sentence and our Pow'r,
Which nor our Nature nor our Place can bear,
We banish thee for ever from our Sight
And Kingdom; if when Three days are expir'd
Thy hated Trunk be found in our Dominions
That moment is thy Death; Away.

Kent. Why fare thee well, King, since thou art resolv'd,
I take thee at thy word, and will not stay
To see thy Fall: the gods protect the Maid
That truly thinks, and has most justly said.
Thus to new Climates my old Truth I bear,
Friendship lives Hence, and Banishment is Here.   [*Exit.*

Lear. Now *Burgundy,* you see her Price is faln,
Yet if the fondness of your Passion still
Affects her as she stands, Dow'rless, and lost
In our Esteem, she's yours, take her or leave her.

Burg. Pardon me, Royal *Lear,* I but demand
The Dow'r your Self propos'd, and here I take
Cordelia by the Hand Dutchess of *Burgundy.*

Lear. Then leave her Sir, for by a Father's rage
I tell you all her Wealth. Away.

Burg. Then Sir be pleas'd to charge the breach
Of our Alliance on your own Will
Not my Inconstancy.

[*Exeunt. Manent* Edgar *and* Cordelia.

Edg. Has Heaven then weigh'd the merit of my Love,
Or is't the raving of my sickly Thought?
Cou'd *Burgundy* forgoe so rich a Prize
And leave her to despairing *Edgar*'s Arms?
Have I thy Hand *Cordelia,* do I clasp it,
The Hand that was this minute to have join'd
My hated Rivals? do I kneel before thee

And offer at thy feet my panting Heart?
Smile, Princess, and convince me, for as yet
I doubt, and dare not trust the dazling Joy.

   Cord. Some Comfort yet that 'twas no vicious Blot
That has depriv'd me of a Father's Grace,
But meerly want of that that makes me rich
In wanting it, a smooth professing Tongue:
O Sisters, I am loth to call your fault
As it deserves; but use our Father well,
And wrong'd *Cordelia* never shall repine.

   Edg. O heav'nly Maid that art thy self thy Dow'r,
Richer in Vertue than the Stars in Light,
If *Edgar*'s humble fortunes may be grac't
With thy Acceptance, at thy feet he lays 'em.
Ha my *Cordelia*! dost thou turn away?
What have I done t'offend Thee?

   Cord. Talk't of Love.

   Edg. Then I've offended oft—*Cordelia* too
Has oft permitted me so to offend.

   Cord. When, *Edgar*, I permitted your Addresses,
I was the darling Daughter of a King,
Nor can I now forget my royal Birth,
And live dependent on my Lover's Fortune.
I cannot to so low a fate submit,
And therefore study to forget your Passion,
And trouble me upon this Theam no more.

   Edg. Thus Majesty takes most State in Distress!
How are we tost on Fortune's fickle flood!
The Wave that with surprising kindness brought
The dear Wreck to my Arms, has snatcht it back,
And left me mourning on the barren Shore.

   Cord. This Baseness of th' ignoble *Burgundy*   [*Aside.*
Draws just suspicion on the Race of Men,
His Love was Int'rest, so may *Edgar*'s be
And He but with more Complement dissemble;
If so, I shall oblige him by Denying:
But if his Love be fixt, such Constant flame
As warms our Breasts, if such I find his Passion,
My Heart as gratefull to his Truth shall be,
And Cold *Cordelia* prove as Kind as He.   [*Exit.*

Enter Bastard *hastily.*

   Bast. Brother, I've found you in a lucky minute,
Fly and be safe, some Villain has incens'd
Our Father against your Life.
   Edg. Distrest *Cordelia*! but oh! more Cruel!
   Bast. Hear me Sir, your Life, your Life's in Danger.
   Edg. A Resolve so sudden
And of such black Importance!
   Bast. 'Twas not sudden,
Some Villain has of long time laid the Train.
   Edg. And yet perhaps 'twas but pretended Coldness,
To try how far my passion would pursue.
   Bast. He hears me not; wake, wake Sir.
   Edg. Say ye Brother?——
No Tears good *Edmund*, if thou bringst me tidings
To strike me dead, for Charity delay not,
That present will befit so kind a Hand.
   Bast. Your danger Sir comes on so fast
That I want time t'inform you, but retire
Whilst I take care to turn the pressing Stream.
O gods! for Heav'ns sake Sir.
   Edg. Pardon me Sir, a serious Thought
Had seiz'd me, but I think you talkt of danger
And wisht me to Retire; must all our Vows
End thus!—Friend I obey you—O *Cordelia*!   [*Exit.*
   Bast. Ha, ha! fond Man, such credulous Honesty
Lessens the Glory of my Artifice;
His Nature is so far from doing wrongs
That he suspects none: if this Letter speed
And pass for *Edgar*'s, as himself wou'd own
The Counterfeit but for the foul Contents,
Then my designs are perfect—here comes *Gloster*.

Enter Gloster.

   Glost. Stay *Edmund*, turn, what paper were you reading?
   Bast. A Trifle Sir.
   Glost. What needed then that terrible dispatch of it
Into your Pocket? come produce it Sir.
   Bast. A Letter from my Brother Sir, I had

Just broke the Seal but knew not the Contents,
Yet fearing they might prove to blame
Endeavour'd to conceal it from your sight.

   Glost. 'Tis *Edgar*'s Character.   [*Reads.*

   This Policy of Fathers is intollerable that keeps our Fortunes from us till
     Age will not suffer us to enjoy 'em; I am weary of the Tyranny: Come
     to me that of this I may speak more: if our Father would sleep till I
     wak't him, you shou'd enjoy half his Possessions, and live beloved of
     your Brother

                                           Edgar.

Slept till I wake him, you shou'd enjoy
Half his possessions?—*Edgar* to write this
'Gainst his indulgent Father? Death and Hell!
Fly, *Edmund*, seek him out, wind me into him
That I may bite the Traytor's heart, and fold
His bleeding Entrals on my vengefull Arm.

   Bast. Perhaps 'twas writ, my Lord, to prove my Vertue.

   Glost. These late Eclipses of the Sun and Moon
Can bode no less; Love cools, and friendship fails,
In Cities mutiny, in Countrys discord,
The bond of Nature crack't 'twixt Son and Father:
Find out the Villain, do it carefully
And it shall lose thee nothing.   [*Exit.*

   Bast. So, now my project's firm, but to make sure
I'll throw in one proof more and that a bold one;
I'll place old *Gloster* where he shall o're-hear us
Confer of this design, whilst to his thinking,
Deluded *Edgar* shall accuse himself.
Be Honesty my Int'rest and I can
Be honest too, and what Saint so Divine
That will successfull Villany decline!   [*Exit.*

                   ★   ★   ★

             [Act II, Scene ii.] A Heath.

Enter Edgar.

   Edg. I heard my self proclaim'd,
And by the friendly Hollow of a Tree
Escapt the Hunt. No Port is free, no place
Where Guards and most unusual Vigilance

Do not attend to take me—how easie now
'Twere to defeat the malice of my Trale,
And leave my Griefs on my Sword's reeking point;
But Love detains me from Death's peacefull Cell,
Still whispering me *Cordelia*'s in distress;
Unkinde as she is I cannot see her wretched,
But must be neer to wait upon her Fortune.
Who knows but the white minute yet may come
When *Edgar* may do service to *Cordelia*!
That charming Hope still ties me to the Oar
Of painfull Life, and makes me too, submit
To th' humblest shifts to keep that Life a foot.
My Face I will besmear and knit my Locks,
The Country gives me proof and precedent
Of Bedlam Beggars, who with roaring Voices
Strike in their numm'd and mortify'd bare Arms
Pins, Iron-spikes, Thorns, sprigs of Rosemary,
And thus from Sheep-coats Villages and Mills,
Sometimes with Prayers, sometimes with Lunatick Banns
Enforce their Charity, poor *Tyrligod*, poor *Tom*.
That's something yet, *Edgar* I am no more.   [*Exit.*

[Act III, Scene i.]

SCENE, *A Desert Heath.*

Enter Lear *and* Kent *in the Storm.*

 Lear. Blow Winds and burst your Cheeks, rage louder yet,
Fantastick Lightning singe, singe my white Head;
Spout Cataracts, and Hurricanos fall
Till you have drown'd the Towns and Palaces
Of proud ingratefull Man.
 Kent. Not all my best intreaties can perswade him
Into some needfull shelter, or to 'bide
This poor slight Cov'ring on his aged Head
Expos'd to this wild war of Earth and Heav'n.
 Lear. Rumble thy fill, fight Whirlwind, Rain and Fire:
Not Fire, Wind, Rain or Thunder are my Daughters:
I tax not you ye Elements with unkindness;
I never gave you Kingdoms, call'd you Children,

You owe me no Obedience, then let fall
Your horrible pleasure, here I stand your Slave,
A poor, infirm, weak and despis'd old man;
Yet I will call you servile Ministers,
That have with two pernicious Daughters join'd
Their high-engendred Battle against a Head
So Old and White as mine, Oh! oh! 'tis Foul.

   Kent. Hard by, Sir, is a Hovel that will lend
Some shelter from this Tempest.

   Lear. I will forget my Nature! what, so kind a Father?
Aye, there's the point.

   Kent. Consider, good my Liege, Things that love Night
Love not such Nights as this; these wrathfull Skies
Frighten the very wanderers o'th' Dark,
And make 'em keep their Caves; such drenching Rain,
Such Sheets of Fire, such Claps of horrid Thunder,
Such Groans of roaring Winds have ne're been known.

   Lear. Let the Great Gods,
That keep this dreadfull pudder o're our Heads
Find out their Enemies now, tremble thou Wretch
That hast within thee undiscover'd Crimes;
Hide, thou bloody Hand.
Thou perjur'd Villain, holy, holy Hypocrite,
That drinkst the Widows Tears, sigh now and cry
These dreadfull Summoners Grace, I am a Man
More sin'd against than sinning.

   Kent. Good Sir, to th' Hovell.

   Lear. My wit begins to burn.
Come on my Boy, how dost my Boy? art Cold?
I'm cold my Self; shew me this Straw, my Fellow,
The Art of our Necessity is strange,
And can make vile things precious; my poor Knave,
Cold as I am at Heart, I've one place There   [*Loud Storm.*
That's sorry yet for Thee.   [*Exit.*

[Act III, Scene ii.]

Gloster's *Palace. Enter* Bastard.

   Bast. The Storm is in our louder Rev'lings drown'd.
Thus wou'd I Reign cou'd I but mount a Throne.

The Riots of these proud imperial Sisters
Already have impos'd the galling Yoke
Of Taxes, and hard Impositions on
The drudging Peasants Neck, who bellow out
Their loud Complaints in Vain—Triumphant Queens!
With what Assurance do they tread the Crowd.
O for a Tast of such Majestick Beauty,
Which none but my hot Veins are fit t' engage;
Nor are my Wishes desp'rate, for ev'n now
During the Banquet I observed their Glances
Shot thick at me, and as they left the Room
Each cast by stealth a kind inviting Smile,
The happy Earnest——ha!

Two Servants from several Entrances deliver him each a Letter, and Ex.

Where merit is so Transparent, not to behold it   [*Reads.*
Were Blindness, and not to reward it Ingratitude.
Gonerill.

Enough! Blind, and Ingratefull should I be
Not to Obey the Summons of This Oracle.
Now for a Second Letter.   [*Opens the other.*
   If Modesty be not your Enemy, doubt not to
   Find me your Friend.   Regan.

Excellent *Sybill*! O my glowing Blood!
I am already sick of expectation,
And pant for the Possession—here *Gloster* comes
With Bus'ness on his Brow; be husht my Joys.

Enter Gloster.

   Glost. I come to seek thee, *Edmund*, to impart
A business of Importance; I knew
Thy loyal Heart is toucht to see the Cruelty of
These ingrateful Daughters against our royal Master.
   Bast. Most Savage and Unnatural.
   Glost. This change in the State sits uneasie.
The Commons repine aloud at their female Tyrants,
Already they Cry out for the re-installment of
Their good old King, whose Injuries, I fear,
Will inflame 'em into Mutiny.

357

Bast. 'Tis to be hopt, not fear'd.

Glost. Thou hast it Boy, 'tis to be hopt indeed.
On me they cast their Eyes, and hourly Court me
To lead 'em on, and whilst this Head is Mine
I am Theirs. A little covert Craft, my Boy,
And then for open Action—'twill be Employment
Worthy such honest daring Souls as Thine.
Thou, *Edmund*, art my trusty Emissary,
Haste on the Spur at the first break of day   {*Gives him*
With these Dispatches to the Duke of *Combray*;   {*Letters.*
You know what mortal Feuds have alwaies flam'd
Between this Duke of *Cornwall*'s Family, and his
Full Twenty thousand Mountaners
Th' invetrate Prince will send to our Assistance.
Dispatch; Commend us to his Grace, and Prosper.

    Bast. Yes, credulous old Man,   [*Aside.*
I will commend you to his Grace,
His Grace the Duke of *Cornwall*—instantly
To shew him these Contents in thy own Character,
And Seal'd with thy own Signet; then forthwith
The Chol'rick Duke gives Sentence on thy Life;
And to my hand thy vast Revenues fall
To glut my Pleasure that till now has starv'd.

    [Gloster *going off is met by* Cordelia *entring* [*with her servant Arante*],
               Bastard *observing at a Distance.*

    Cord. Turn, *Gloster*, Turn, by all the sacred Pow'rs
I do conjure you give my Griefs a Hearing,
You must, you shall, nay I am sure you will,
For you were always stil'd the Just and Good.

    Glost. What wou'dst thou, Princess? rise and speak thy Griefs.

    Cord. Nay, you shall promise to redress 'em too,
Or here I'll kneel for ever; I intreat
Thy succour for a Father and a King,
An injur'd Father and an injur'd King.

    Bast. O charming Sorrow! how her Tears adorn her   [*Aside.*
Like Dew on Flow'rs; but she is Virtuous,
And I must quench this hopeless Fire i'th' Kindling.

    Glost. Consider, Princess,
For whom thou begg'st, 'tis for the King that wrong'd Thee.

Cord. O name not that; he did not, cou'd not wrong me.
Nay muse not, *Gloster*, for it is too likely
This injur'd King ere this is past your Aid,
And gone Distracted with his savage Wrongs.
    Bast. I'll gaze no more——and yet my Eyes are Charm'd.   [*Aside.*
    Cord. Or what if it be Worse? can there be Worse?
As 'tis too probable this furious Night
Has pierc'd his tender Body, the bleak Winds
And cold Rain chill'd, or Lightning struck him Dead;
If it be so your Promise is discharg'd,
And I have only one poor Boon to beg,
That you'd Convey me to his breathless Trunk,
With my torn Robes to wrap his hoary Head,
With my torn Hair to bind his Hands and Feet,
Then with a show'r of Tears
To wash his Clay-smear'd Cheeks, and Die beside him.
    Glost. Rise, fair *Cordelia*, thou hast Piety
Enough t'atone for both thy Sisters Crimes.
I have already plotted to restore
My injur'd Master, and thy Vertue tells me
We shall succeed, and suddenly.   [*Exit.*
    Cord. Dispatch, *Arante*,
Provide me a Disguise, we'll instantly
Go seek the King, and bring him some Relief.
    Ar. How, Madam? are you Ignorant
Of what your impious Sisters have decreed?
Immediate Death for any that relieve him.
    Cord. I cannot dread the Furies in this case.
    Ar. In such a Night as This? Consider, Madam,
For many Miles about there's scarce a Bush
To shelter in.
    Cord. Therefore no shelter for the King,
And more our Charity to find him out:
What have not Women dar'd for vicious Love,
And we'll be shining Proofs that they can dare
For Piety as much; blow Winds, and Lightnings fall,
Bold in my Virgin Innocence, I'll flie
My Royal Father to Relieve, or Die.   [*Exeunt.*
    Bast. Provide me a Disguise, we'll instantly
Go seek the King:——ha! ha! a lucky change,

That Vertue which I fear'd would be my hindrance
Has prov'd the Bond to my Design;
I'll bribe two Ruffians that shall at a distance follow,
And seise 'em in some desert Place, and there
Whilst one retains her t' other shall return
T' inform me where she's Lodg'd; I'll be disguis'd too.
Whilst they are poching for me I'll to the Duke
With these Dispatches, then to th'Field
Where like the vig'rous *Jove* I will enjoy
This Semele in a Storm, 'twill deaf her Cries
Like Drums in Battle, lest her Groans shou'd pierce
My pittying Ear, and make the amorous Fight less fierce.

[*Exit.*

★　　★　　★

[Act III, Scene iv.] The Heath.

Enter Cordelia *and* Arante.

Ar. Dear Madam, rest ye here, our search is Vain,
Look here's a shed, beseech ye, enter here.
Cord. Prethee go in thy self, seek thy own Ease,
Where the Mind's free, the Body's Delicate:
This Tempest but diverts me from the Thought
Of what wou'd hurt me more.

Enter Two Ruffians.

1 Ruff. We have dog'd 'em far enough, this Place is private.
I'll keep 'em Prisoners here within this Hovell,
Whilst you return and bring Lord *Edmund* Hither;
But help me first to House 'em.
2 Ruff. Nothing but this dear Devil　　　　　[*Shows Gold.*
Shou'd have drawn me through all this Tempest;
But to our Work.

[*They seize* Cordelia *and* Arante, *who Shriek out.*
Soft, Madam, we are Friends, dispatch, I say.
Cord. Help, Murder, help! Gods! some kind Thunderbolt
To strike me Dead.

Enter Edgar.

Edg. What Cry was That?—ha, Women seiz'd by Ruffians?

360

Is this a Place and Time for Villany?
Avaunt ye Bloud-hounds.   *[Drives 'em with his Quarter staff.*
  Both. The Devil, the Devil!   *[Run off.*
  Edg. O speak, what are ye that appear to be
O'th' tender Sex, and yet unguarded Wander
Through the dead Mazes of this dreadfull Night,
Where (tho' at full) the Clouded Moon scarce darts
Imperfect Glimmerings?
  Cord. First say what art thou
Our Guardian Angel, that wer't pleas'd t' assume
That horrid shape to fright the Ravishers?
We'll kneel to Thee.
  Edg. O my tumultuous Bloud!   *[Aside.*
By all my trembling Veins, *Cordelia*'s Voice!
'Tis she her self!——My Senses sure conform
To my wild Garb, and I am Mad indeed.
  Cord. Whate're thou art, befriend a wretched Virgin,
And if thou canst direct our weary search.
  Edg. Who relieves poor *Tom*, that sleeps on the Nettle, with the
Hedge-pig for his Pillow?
                Whilst Smug ply'd the Bellows
                She truckt with her Fellows,
                    The Freckle-fac't Mab
                    Was a Blouze and a Drab,
                Yet *Swithin* made *Oberon* jealous
——Oh, Torture!   *[Aside.*
  Ar. Alack, Madam, a poor wandring Lunatick.
  Cord. And yet his Language seem'd but now well temper'd.
Speak, Friend, to one more wretched than thy self,
And if thou hast one Interval of sense,
Inform us if thou canst where we may find
A poor old Man, who through this Heath has stray'd
The tedious Night.——Speak, sawest thou such a One?
  Edg. The King, her Father, whom she's come to seek   *[Aside.*
Through all the Terrors of this Night. O Gods!
That such amazing Piety, such Tenderness
Shou'd yet to me be Cruel——
Yes, Fair One, such a One was lately here,
And is convey'd by some that came to seek him,
T' a Neighb'ring Cottage; but distinctly where,

I know not.

 Cord. Blessings on 'em.

Let's find him out, *Arante*, for thou seest

We are in Heavens Protection.   [*Going off.*

 Edg. O *Cordelia!*

 Cord. Ha!——Thou knowst my Name.

 Edg. As you did once know *Edgar*'s.

 Cord. Edgar!

 Edg. The poor Remains of *Edgar*, what your Scorn

Has left him.

 Cord. Do we wake, *Arante?*

 Edg. My Father seeks my Life, which I preserv'd

In hopes of some blest Minute to oblidge

Distrest *Cordelia*, and the Gods have giv'n it;

That Thought alone prevail'd with me to take

This Frantick Dress, to make the Earth my Bed,

With these bare Limbs all change of Seasons bide,

Noons scorching Heat, and Midnights piercing Cold,

To feed on Offals, and to drink with Herds,

To Combat with the Winds, and be the Sport

Of Clowns, or what's more wretched yet, their Pity.

 Ar. Was ever Tale so full of Misery!

 Edg. But such a Fall as this I grant was due

To my aspiring Love, for 'twas presumptuous,

Though not presumptuously persu'd;

For well you know I wore my Flames conceal'd,

And silent as the Lamps that Burn in Tombs,

'Till you perceiv'd my Grief, with modest Grace

Drew forth the Secret, and then seal'd my Pardon.

 Cord. You had your Pardon, nor can you Challenge more.

 Edg. What do I Challenge more?

Such Vanity agrees not with these Rags;

When in my prosp'rous State rich *Gloster*'s Heir,

You silenc'd my Pretences, and enjoyn'd me

To trouble you upon that Theam no more;

Then what Reception must Love's Language find

From these bare Limbs and Beggers humble Weeds?

 Cord. Such as the Voice of Pardon to a Wretch Condemn'd;

Such as the Shouts

Of succ'ring Forces to a Town besieg'd.

Edg. Ah! what new Method now of Cruelty?

Cord. Come to my Arms, thou dearest, best of Men,
And take the kindest Vows that e're were spoke
By a protesting Maid.

Edg. Is't possible?

Cord. By the dear Vital Stream that baths my Heart,
These hallow'd Rags of Thine, and naked Vertue,
These abject Tassels, these fantastick Shreds,
(Ridiculous ev'n to the meanest Clown)
To me are dearer than the richest Pomp
Of purple Monarchs.

Edg. Generous charming Maid,
The Gods alone that made, can rate thy Worth!
This most amazing Excellence shall be
Fame's Triumph, in succeeding Ages, when
Thy bright Example shall adorn the Scene,
And teach the World Perfection.

Cord. Cold and weary,
We'll rest a while, *Arante*, on that Straw,
Then forward to find out the poor Old King.

Edg. Look I have Flint and Steel, the Implements
Of wandring Lunaticks, I'll strike a Light,
And make a Fire beneath this Shed, to dry
Thy Storm-drencht Garments, ere thou Lie to rest thee;
Then Fierce and Wakefull as th' *Hesperian* Dragon,
I'll watch beside thee to protect thy Sleep;
Mean while, the Stars shall dart their kindest Beams,
And Angels Visit my *Cordelia*'s Dreams.   [*Exeunt.*

[Act III, Scene v.]

SCENE, *The Palace.*

Enter Cornwall, Regan, Bastard, *Servants.* Cornwall *with* Gloster's *Letters.*

Duke. I will have my Revenge ere I depart his house.
Regan, see here, a Plot upon our State,
'Tis *Gloster*'s Character, that has betray'd
His double Trust of Subject, and of Ost.

Reg. Then double be our Vengeance, this confirms

Th' Intelligence that we [just] now receiv'd,
That he has been this Night to seek the King;
But who, Sir, was the kind Discoverer?

   Duke. Our Eagle, quick to spy, and fierce to seize,
Our trusty *Edmund.*

   Reg. 'Twas a noble Service;
O *Cornwall*, take him to thy deepest Trust,
And wear him as a Jewel at thy Heart.

   Bast. Think, Sir, how hard a Fortune I sustain,
That makes me thus repent of serving you!   [*Weeps.*
O that this Treason had not been, or I
Not the Discoverer.

   Duke. Edmund, Thou shalt find
A Father in our Love, and from this Minute
We call thee Earl of *Gloster*; but there yet
Remains another Justice to be done,
And that's to punish this discarded Traytor;
But least thy tender Nature shou'd relent
At his just Sufferings, nor brooke the Sight,
We wish thee to withdraw.

   Reg. The *Grotto*, Sir, within the lower Grove,   [*To* Edmund *Aside.*
Has Privacy to suit a Mourner's Thought.

   Bast. And there I may expect a Comforter,
Ha, Madam?

   Reg. What may happen, Sir, I know not,
But 'twas a Friends Advice.   [*Ex.* Bastard.

   Duke. Bring in the Traytour.
Gloster brought in.

Bind fast his Arms.

   Glost. What mean your Graces?
You are my Guests, pray do me no foul Play.

   Duke. Bind him, I say, hard, harder yet.

   Reg. Now, Traytor, thou shalt find——

   Duke. Speak, Rebel, where has thou sent the King,
Whom spight of our Decree thou saw'st last Night?

   Glost. I'm tide to th'Stake, and I must stand the Course.

   Reg. Say where, and why thou hast conceal'd him.

   Glost. Because I wou'd not see thy cruel Hands
Tear out his poor old Eyes, nor thy fierce Sister
Carve his anointed Flesh; but I shall see

The swift wing'd Vengeance overtake such Children.

   Duke. See't shalt thou never. Slaves perform your Work,
Out with those treacherous Eyes, dispatch, I say,
If thou seest Vengeance——

   Glost. He that will think to live 'till he be old,
Give me some help——O cruel! oh! ye Gods.

                                                     [They put out his Eyes.

   Serv. Hold, hold, my Lord, I bar your Cruelty,
I cannot love your safety and give way
To such a barbarous Practise.

   Duke. Ha, my Villain?

   Serv. I have been your Servant from my Infancy,
But better Service have I never done you
Then with this Boldness——

   Duke. Take thy Death, Slave!

   Serv. Nay, then Revenge whilst yet my Bloud is Warm!   *[Fight.*

   Reg. Help here—are you not hurt, my Lord?

   Glost. Edmund, enkindle all the sparks of Nature
To quit this horrid Act.

   Reg. Out, treacherous Villain,
Thou call'st on him that Hates thee, it was He
That broacht thy Treason, shew'd us thy Dispatches;
There—read, and save the *Cambrian* Prince a Labour.
If thy Eyes fail thee, call for Spectacles.

   Glost. O my Folly!
Then *Edgar* was abus'd, kind Gods forgive me that.

   Reg. How is't, my Lord?

   Duke. Turn out that Eye-less Villain, let him smell
His way to *Cambray*; throw this Slave upon a Dunghill.
Regan, I Bleed apace, give me your Arm.   *[Exeunt.*

   Glost. All Dark and Comfortless!
Where are those various Objects that but now
Employ'd my busie Eyes? where those Eyes?
Dead are their piercing Rays that lately shot
O're flowry Vales to distant Sunny Hills,
And drew with Joy the vast Horizon in.
These groping Hands are now my only Guids,
And Feeling all my Sight.

   O Misery! what words can sound my Grief?
Shut from the Living whilst among the Living;

Dark as the Grave amidst the bustling World.
At once from Business and from Pleasure bar'd;
No more to view the Beauty of the Spring,
Nor see the Face of Kindred, or of Friend.
Yet still one way th' extreamest Fate affords,
And ev'n the Blind can find the Way to Death.
Must I then tamely Die, and unreveng'd?
So *Lear* may fall: No, with these bleeding Rings
I will present me to the pittying Crowd,
And with the Rhetorick of these dropping Veins
Enflame 'em to Revenge their King and me;
Then when the Glorious Mischief is on Wing,
This Lumber from some Precipice I'll throw,
And dash it on the ragged Flint below;
Whence my freed Soul to her bright Sphear shall fly, ⎫
Through boundless Orbs, eternal Regions spy, ⎬
And like the Sun, be All one glorious Eye. ⎭

                                              [Exit.

[Act IV, Scene i.]

A Grotto.

Edmund *and* Regan *amorously Seated,* Listning *to* Musick.

   Bast. Why were those Beauties made Another's Right
Which None can prize like Me? charming Queen
Take all my blooming Youth, for ever fold me
In those soft Arms. Lull me in endless Sleep
That I may dream of pleasures too transporting
For Life to bear.
   Reg. Live, live, my *Gloster*,
And feel no Death but that of swooning joy,
I yield thee Blisses on no harder Terms
Than that thou continue to be Happy.
   Bast. This Jealousie is yet more kind, is't possible
That I should wander from a Paradise
To feed on sickly Weeds? such Sweets live here
That Constancy will be no Vertue in me.
And yet must I forthwith go meet her Sister,   *[Aside.*
To whom I must protest as much——

Suppose it be the same; why best of all,
And I have then my Lesson ready conn'd.
 Reg. Wear this Remembrance of me.   [*Gives him a Ring.*
           ——I dare now
Absent my self no longer from the Duke
Whose Wound grows Dangerous——I hope Mortal.
 Bast. And let this happy Image of your *Gloster*,
       [*Pulling out a Picture, drops a Note.*
Lodge in that Breast where all his Treasure lies.   [*Exit.*
 Reg. To this brave Youth a Womans blooming beauties
Are due: my Fool usurps my Bed——What's here?
Confusion on my Eyes.   [*Reads.*

Where Merit is so Transparent, not to behold it were Blindness, and not to
reward it, Ingratitude. Gonerill.

Vexatious Accident! yet Fortunate too:
My Jealousie's confirm'd, and I am taught
To cast for my Defence——

Enter an Officer.

Now, what mean those Shouts? and what thy hasty Entrance?
 Off. A most surprizing and a sudden Change,
The Peasants are all up in Mutiny,
And only want a Chief to lead 'em on
To Storm your Palace.
 Reg. On what Provocation?
 Off. At last day's publick Festival, to which
The Yeomen from all Quarters had repair'd,
Old *Gloster*, whom you late depriv'd of Sight,
(His Veins yet Streaming fresh) presents himself,
Proclaims your Cruelty, and their Oppression,
With the King's Injuries; which so enrag'd 'em,
That now that Mutiny which long had crept
Takes Wing, and threatens your Best Pow'rs.
 Reg. White-liver'd Slave!
Our Forces rais'd and led by Valiant *Edmund*,
Shall drive this Monster of Rebellion back
To her dark Cell; young *Gloster*'s Arm allays
The Storm, his Father's feeble Breath did Raise.   [*Exit.*

[Act IV, Scene ii.]

The Field SCENE; *Enter* Edgar.

Edg. The lowest and most abject Thing of Fortune
Stands still in Hope, and is secure from Fear.
The lamentable Change is from the Best,
The Worst returns to Better.

Enter Gloster, *led by an old Man.*

       ——Who comes here— [*Aside.*
My Father poorly led? depriv'd of Sight,
The precious Stones torn from their bleeding Rings!
Something I heard of this inhumane Deed
But disbeliev'd it, as an Act too horrid
For the hot Hell of a curst Woman's fury.
When will the measure of my woes be full?
 Glost. Revenge, thou art afoot, Success attend Thee!
Well have I sold my Eyes, if the Event
Prove happy for the injur'd King.
 Old M. O, my good Lord, I have been your Tenant, and your
Father's Tenant these Fourscore years.
 Glost. Away, get thee Away, good Friend, be gone,
Thy Comforts can do me no good at All,
Thee they may hurt.
 Old M. You cannot see your Way.
 Glost. I have no Way, and therefore want no Eyes.
I stumbled when I saw: O dear Son *Edgar,*
The Food of thy abused Father's Wrath,
Might I but live to see thee in my Touch
I'd say, I had Eyes agen.
 Edg. Alas, he's sensible that I was wrong'd, [*Aside.*
And shou'd I own my Self, his tender Heart
Would break betwixt th' extreams of Grief and Joy.
 Old M. How now, who's There?
 Edg. A Charity for poor *Tom.* Play fair, and defie the foul Fiend.
O Gods! and must I still persue this Trade, [*Aside.*
Trifling beneath such Loads of Misery?
 Old M. 'Tis poor mad *Tom.*
 Glost. In the late Storm I such a Fellow saw,
Which made me think a Man a Worm.

368

Where is the Lunatick?

Old M. Here, my Lord.

Glost. Get thee now away, if for my sake
Thou wilt o're-take us hence a Mile or Two
I' th' way tow'rd *Dover*, do't for ancient Love,
And bring some cov'ring for this naked Wretch
Whom I'll intreat to lead me.

Old M. Alack, my Lord, He's Mad.

Glost. 'Tis the Time's Plague when Mad-men lead the Blind.
Do as I bid thee.

Old M. I'll bring him the best 'Parrel that I have
Come on't what will.   [*Exit.*

Glost. Sirrah, naked Fellow.

Edg. Poor *Tom*'s a cold;——I cannot fool it longer,
And yet I must——bless thy sweet Eyes, they Bleed.
Believe't, poor *Tom* ev'n weeps his Blind to see 'em.

Glost. Know'st thou the way to *Dover*?

Edg. Both Stile and Gate, Horse-way and Foot-path, poor
Tom has been scar'd out of his good Wits; bless every true Man's
Son from the foul Fiend.

Glost. Here, take this Purse, that I am wretched
Makes thee the Happier, Heav'n deal so still.
Thus let the griping Userers Hoard be Scatter'd,
So Distribution shall undo Excess,
And each Man have enough. Dost thou know *Dover*?

Edg. Aye, Master.

Glost. There is a Cliff, whose high and bending Head
Looks dreadfully down on the roaring Deep.
Bring me but to the very Brink of it,
And I'll repair the Poverty thou bearst
With something Rich about me; from that Place
I shall no leading need.

Edg. Give me thy Arm: poor *Tom* shall guid thee.

Glost. Soft, for I hear the Tread of Passengers.

Enter Kent *and* Cordelia.

Cord. Ah me! your Fear's too true, it was the King;
I spoke but now with some that met him
As Mad as the vext Sea, Singing aloud,
Crown'd with rank Femiter and furrow Weeds,

369

With Berries, Burdocks, Violets, Dazies, Poppies,
And all the idle Flow'rs that grow
In our sustaining Corn. Conduct me to him
To prove my last Endeavours to restore him,
And Heav'n so prosper thee.

 Kent. I will, good Lady.
Ha, *Gloster* here!——turn, poor dark Man, and hear
A Friend's Condolement, who at Sight of thine
Forgets his own Distress, thy old true *Kent.*

 Glost. How, *Kent*? from whence return'd?

 Kent. I have not since my Banishment been absent,
But in Disguise follow'd the abandon'd King;
'Twas me thou saw'st with him in the late Storm.

 Glost. Let me embrace thee, had I Eyes I now
Should weep for Joy, but let this trickling Blood
Suffice instead of Tears.

 Cord. O misery!
To whom shall I complain, or in what Language?
Forgive, O wretched Man, th' impiety
That brought thee to this pass, 'twas I that caus'd it.
I cast me at thy Feet, and beg of thee
To crush these weeping Eyes to equal Darkness,
If that will give thee any Recompence.

 Edg. Was ever Season so distrest as This?   *[Aside.*

 Glost. I think *Cordelia*'s Voice! rise, pious Princess,
And take a dark Man's Blessing.

 Cord. O, my *Edgar,*   *[Aside.*
My Vertue's now grown Guilty, works the Bane
Of those that do befriend me, Heav'n forsakes me,
And when you look that Way, it is but just
That you shou'd hate me too.

 Edg. O waive this cutting Speech, and spare to wound *[Aside.*
A Heart that's on the Rack.

 Glost. No longer cloud thee, *Kent*, in that Disguise,
There's business for thee and of noblest weight;
Our injur'd Country is at length in Arms,
Urg'd by the King's inhumane Wrongs and Mine,
And only wants a Chief to lead 'em on.
That Task be Thine.

 Edg. Brave *Britains* then there's Life in't yet.   *[Aside.*

Kent. Then have we one cast for our Fortune yet.
Come, Princess, I'll bestow you with the King,
Then on the Spur to Head these Forces.
Farewell, good *Gloster*, to our Conduct trust.
　Glost. And be your Cause as Prosp'rous as tis Just.　　　　[*Exeunt.*

★　　★　　★

[Act IV, Scene v.]

A Chamber. Lear *a Sleep on a Couch;* Cordelia,
and Attendants standing by him.

　Cord. His Sleep is sound, and may have good Effect
To Cure his jarring Senses, and repair
This Breach of Nature.
　Phys. We have employ'd the utmost Pow'r of Art,
And this deep Rest will perfect our Design.
　Cord. O *Regan, Gonerill,* inhumane Sisters,
Had he not been your Father, these white Hairs
Had challeng'd sure some pity. Was this a Face
To be expos'd against the jarring Winds?
My Enemy's Dog though he had bit me shou'd
Have stood that Night against my Fire——he wakes, speak to him.
　Gent. Madam, do you, 'tis fittest.
　Cord. How do's my royal Lord? how fares your Majesty?
　Lear. You do me wrong to take me out o'th' Grave.
Ha! is this too a World of Cruelty?
I know my Priviledge, think not that I will
Be us'd still like a wretched Mortal, no,
No more of That.
　Cord. Speak to me, Sir, who am I?
　Lear. You are a Soul in Bliss, but I am bound
Upon a wheel of Fire, which my own Tears
Do scald like Molten Lead.
　Cord. Sir, do you know me?
　Lear. You are a Spirit, I know, where did you Die?
　Cord. Still, still, far wide.
　Phys. Madam, he's scarce awake; he'll soon grow more compos'd.
　Lear. Where have I been? where am I? fair Day-light!
I am mightily abus'd, I shou'd ev'n Die with pity

371

To see Another thus. I will not swear
These are my Hands.

    Cord. O look upon me, Sir,
And hold your Hands in Blessing o're me, nay,
You must not kneel.

    Lear. Pray do not mock me.
I am a very foolish fond Old Man,
Fourscore and upward, and to deal plainly with you,
I fear I am not in my perfect Mind.

    Cord. Nay, then farewell to patience; witness for me
Ye mighty Pow'rs, I ne're complain'd till now!

    Lear. Methinks I shou'd know you, and know this Man,
Yet I am Doubtfull, for I am mainly Ignorant
What Place this is, and all the skill I have
Remembers not these Garments, nor do I know
Where I did Sleep last Night——pray do not mock me——
For, as I am a Man, I think that Lady
To be my Child *Cordelia.*

    Cord. O my dear, dear Father!

    Lear. Be your Tears wet? yes faith; pray do not weep,
I know I have giv'n thee Cause, and am so humbled
With Crosses since, that I cou'd ask
Forgiveness of thee, were it possible
That thou cou'dst grant it; but I'm well assur'd
Thou canst not; therefore I do stand thy Justice.
If thou hast Poyson for me I will Drink it,
Bless thee and Die.

    Cord. O pity, Sir, a bleeding Heart, and cease
This killing Language.

    Lear. Tell me, Friends, where am I?

    Gent. In your own Kingdom, Sir.

    Lear. Do not Abuse me.

    Gent. Be comforted, good Madam, for the Violence
Of his Distemper's past; we'll lead him in
Nor trouble him, till he is better Setled.
Wilt please you, Sir, walk into freer Air?

    Lear. You must bear with me, I am Old and Foolish.

                                [They lead him off.

    Cord. The Gods restore you—heark, I hear afar
The beaten Drum, Old *Kent*'s a Man of's Word.

O for an Arm
Like the fierce Thunderer's, when th' earth-born Sons
Storm'd Heav'n, to fight this injur'd Father's Battle.
That I cou'd shift my Sex, and dye me deep
In his Opposer's Blood, but as I may
With Womens Weapons, Piety and Pray'rs,
I'll aid his Cause.———You never-erring Gods
Fight on his side, and Thunder on his Foes
Such Tempest as his poor ag'd Head sustain'd;
Your Image suffers when a Monarch bleeds.
'Tis your own Cause, for that your Succours bring,
Revenge your Selves, and right an injur'd King.

[Act V, Scene i.]

SCENE, *A Camp.*

Enter Gonerill *and Attendants.*

 Gon. Our Sisters Pow'rs already are arriv'd,
And She her self has promis'd to prevent
The Night with her Approach: have you provided
The Banquet I bespoke for her Reception
At my Tent?
 Att. So please your Grace, we have.
 Gon. But thou, my Poysner, must prepare the Bowl
That Crowns this Banquet, when our Mirth is high,
The Trumpets sounding and the Flutes replying,
Then is the Time to give this fatal Draught
To this imperious Sister; if then our Arms succeed,
Edmund more dear than Victory is mine.
But if Defeat or Death it self attend me,
'Twill charm my Ghost to think I've left behind me   [*Trumpet.*
No happy Rival: heark, she comes.   [*Exeunt.*

[Act V, Scene ii.]

Enter Bastard *in his Tent.*

 Bast. To both these Sisters have I sworn my Love,
Each jealous of the other, as the Stung
Are of the Adder; neither can be held

If both remain Alive; where shall I fix?
Cornwall is Dead, and *Regan's* empty Bed
Seems cast by Fortune for me, but already
I have enjoy'd her, and bright *Gonerill*
With equal Charms brings dear variety,
And yet untasted Beauty: I will use
Her Husband's Countenance for the Battail, then
Usurp at once his Bed and Throne.

Enter Officers.

My trusty Scouts y' are well return'd, have ye descry'd
The Strength and Posture of the Enemy?
    Off. We have, and were surpriz'd to find
The banisht *Kent* return'd, and at their Head;
Your Brother *Edgar* on the Rear; Old *Gloster*
(A moving Spectacle) led through their Ranks,
Whose pow'rfull Tongue, and more prevailing Wrongs,
Have so enrag'd their rustick Spirits, that with
Th' approaching Dawn we must expect their Battle.
    Bast. You bring a welcome Hearing; Each to his Charge.
Line well your Ranks and stand on your Award,
To Night repose you, and i'th' Morn we'll give
The Sun a Sight that shall be worth his Rising.   [*Exeunt.*

[Act V, Scene iii.]

SCENE, *A Valley near the Camp.*

Enter Edgar *and* Gloster.

    Edg. Here, Sir, take you the shadow of this Tree
For your good Host, pray that the Right may thrive:
If ever I return to you again
I'll bring you Comfort.   [*Exit.*
    Glost. Thanks, friendly Sir;
The Fortune your good Cause deserves betide you.

An Alarum, after which Gloster *speaks.*

The Fight grows hot; the whole War's now at Work,
And the goar'd Battle bleeds in every Vein,
Whilst Drums and Trumpets drown loud Slaughter's Roar:

Where's *Gloster* now that us'd to head the Fray,
And scour the Ranks where deadliest Danger lay?
Here like a Shepherd in a lonely Shade,
Idle, unarm'd, and listning to the Fight.
Yet the disabled Courser, Maim'd and Blind,
When to his Stall he hears the ratling War,
Foaming with Rage tears up the batter'd Ground,
And tugs for Liberty.
No more of Shelter, thou blind Worm, but forth
To th' open Field; the War may come this way
And crush thee into Rest.——Here lay thee down
And tear the Earth, that work befits a Mole.
O dark Despair! when, *Edgar*, wilt thou come
To pardon and dismiss me to the Grave?   [*A Retreat sounded.*
Heark! a Retreat, the King has Lost or Won.

Re-enter Edgar, *bloody.*

 Edg. Away, old Man, give me your Hand, away!
King *Lear* has lost, He and his Daughter tane,
And this, ye Gods, is all that I can save
Of this most precious Wreck: give me your Hand.
 Glost. No farther, Sir, a Man may Rot even here.
 Edg. What? in ill Thoughts again? Men must endure
Their going hence ev'n as their coming hither.
 Glost. And that's true too.   [*Exeunt.*

[Act V, Scene iv.]

Flourish. Enter in Conquest, Albany, Gonerill, Regan, Bastard.—Lear,
   Kent, Cordelia *Prisoners.*

 Alb. It is enough to have Conquer'd, Cruelty
Shou'd ne're survive the Fight. Captain o'th' Guards
Treat well your royal Prisoners till you have
Our further Orders, as you hold our Pleasure.
 Gon. Heark, Sir, not as you hold our Husbands pleasure
            [*To the Captain aside.*
But as you hold your Life, dispatch your Pris'ners.
Our Empire can have no sure Settlement
But in their Death, the Earth that covers them
Binds fast our Throne. Let me hear they are Dead.

Capt. I shall obey your Orders.

Bast. Sir, I approve it safest to pronounce
Sentence of Death upon this wretched King,
Whose Age has Charms in it, his Title more,
To draw the Commons once more to his Side,
'Twere best prevent——

Alb. Sir, by your Favour,
I hold you but a Subject of this War,
Not as a Brother.

Reg. That's as we list to Grace him.
Have you forgot that He did lead our Pow'rs?
Bore the Commission of our Place and Person?
And that Authority may well stand up
And call it self your Brother.

Gon. Not so hot,
In his own Merits he exalts himself
More than in your Addition.

Enter Edgar, *disguised.*

Alb. What art Thou?

Edg. Pardon me, Sir, that I presume to stop
A Prince and Conquerour, yet ere you Triumph,
Give Ear to what a Stranger can deliver
Of what concerns you more than Triumph can.
I do impeach your General there of Treason,
Lord *Edmund,* that usurps the Name of *Gloster,*
Of fowlest Practice 'gainst your Life and Honour;
This Charge is True, and wretched though I seem
I can produce a Champion that will prove
In single Combat what I do avouch;
If *Edmund* dares but trust his Cause and Sword.

Bast. What will not *Edmund* dare? My Lord, I beg
The favour that you'd instantly appoint
The Place where I may meet this Challenger,
Whom I will sacrifice to my wrong'd Fame.
Remember, Sir, that injur'd Honour's nice
And cannot brook delay.

Alb. Anon, before our Tent, i'th' Army's view,
There let the Herald cry.

Edg. I thank your Highness in my Champion's Name,

He'll wait your Trumpet's call.
    Alb. Lead.   [*Exeunt.*

            Manent Lear, Kent, Cordelia, *guarded.*

    Lear. O *Kent, Cordelia*!
You are the onely Pair that I e'er wrong'd,
And the just Gods have made you Witnesses
Of my Disgrace, the very shame of Fortune,
To see me chain'd and shackled at these years!
Yet were you but Spectatours of my Woes,
Not fellow-sufferers, all were well!
    Cord. This language, Sir, adds yet to our Affliction.
    Lear. Thou, *Kent*, didst head the Troops that fought my Battel,
Expos'd thy Life and Fortunes for a Master
That had (as I remember) banisht Thee.
    Kent. Pardon me, Sir, that once I broke your Orders.
Banisht by you, I kept me here disguis'd
To watch your Fortunes, and protect your Person,
You know you entertain'd a rough blunt Fellow,
One *Caius*, and you thought he did you Service.
    Lear. My trusty *Caius*, I have lost him too!   [*Weeps.*
'Twas a rough Honesty.
    Kent. I was that *Caius*,
Disguis'd in that coarse Dress to follow you.
    Lear. My *Caius* too! wer't thou my trusty *Caius*,
Enough, enough——
    Cord. Ah me, he faints! his Blood forsakes his Cheek,
Help, *Kent*——
    Lear. No, no, they shall not see us weep,
We'll see them rot first.—Guards, lead away to Prison.
Come, *Kent, Cordelia* come,
We Two will sit alone, like Birds i'th Cage,
When Thou dost ask me Blessing, I'll kneel down
And ask of Thee Forgiveness; Thus we'll live,
And Pray, and Sing, and tell old Tales, and Laugh
At gilded Butter-flies, hear Sycophants
Talk of Court News, and we'll talk with them too,
Who loses, and who wins, who's in, who's out,
And take upon us the Mystery of Things
As if we were Heav'ns Spies.

Cord. Upon such Sacrifices
The Gods themselves throw Incense.
 Lear. Have I caught ye?
He that parts us must bring a Brand from Heav'n.
Together we'll out-toil the spight of Hell,
And Die the Wonders of the World; Away.   [*Exeunt, guarded.*

[Act V, Scene v.]

Flourish: Enter before the Tents, Albany, Gonerill, Regan, *Guards and Attendants;* Gonerill *speaking apart to the Captain of the Guards entring.*

 Gon. Here's Gold for Thee, Thou knowst our late Command
Upon your Pris'ners Lives, about it streight, and at
Our Ev'ning Banquet let it raise our Mirth
To hear that They are Dead.
 Capt. I shall not fail your Orders.   [*Exit.*

Albany, Gon. Reg. *take their Seats.*

 Alb. Now, *Gloster,* trust to thy single Vertue, for thy Souldiers,
All levied in my Name, have in my Name
Took their Discharge; now let our Trumpets speak,
And Herald read out This.
         [*Herald Reads.*
If any Man of Quality, within the Lists of the Army, will maintain upon Edmund, *suppos'd Earl of* Gloster, *that he is a manifold Traytour, let him appear by the third sound of the Trumpet; He is bold in his Defence.——* Agen, Agen.
        [*Trumpet Answers from within.*
Enter Edgar, *Arm'd.*

 Alb. Lord *Edgar!*
 Bast. Ha! my Brother!
This is the onely Combatant that I cou'd fear;
For in my Breast Guilt Duels on his side.
But, Conscience, what have I to do with Thee?
Awe Thou thy dull Legitimate Slaves, but I
Was born a Libertine, and so I keep me.
 Edg. My noble Prince, a word—ere we engage,   [*Aside.*
Into your Highness's Hands I give this Paper,
It will the truth of my Impeachment prove
Whatever be my fortune in the Fight.

Alb. We shall peruse it.

Edg. Now, *Edmund*, draw thy Sword,
That if my Speech has wrong'd a noble Heart,
Thy Arm may doe thee Justice: here i'th' presence
Of this high Prince, these Queens, and this crown'd List,
I brand thee with the spotted name of Traytour,
False to thy Gods, thy Father and thy Brother,
And what is more, thy Friend; false to this Prince:
If then Thou shar'st a spark of *Gloster*'s Vertue,
Acquit thy self, or if Thou shar'st his Courage,
Meet this Defiance bravely.

Bast. And dares *Edgar*,
The beaten routed *Edgar*, brave his Conquerour?
From all thy Troops and Thee, I forc't the Field,
Thou hast lost the gen'ral Stake, and art Thou now
Come with thy petty single Stock to play
This after-Game?

Edg. Half-blooded Man,
Thy Father's Sin first, then his Punishment,
The dark and vicious Place where he begot thee
Cost him his Eyes: from thy licentious Mother
Thou draw'st thy Villany; but for thy part
Of *Gloster*'s Blood, I hold thee worth my Sword.

Bast. Thou bear'st thee on thy Mother's Piety,
Which I despise; thy Mother being chaste
Thou art assur'd Thou art but *Gloster*'s Son,
But mine, disdaining Constancy, leaves me
To hope that I am sprung from nobler Blood,
And possibly a King might be my Sire:
But be my Birth's uncertain Chance as 'twill,
Who 'twas that had the hit to Father me
I know not; 'tis enough that I am I:
Of this one thing I'm certain——that I have
A daring Soul, and so have at thy Heart.
Sound Trumpet!

[*Fight*, Bastard *falls*.

Gon. and *Reg.* Save him, save him.

Gon. This was Practice, *Gloster*,
Thou won'st the Field, and wast not bound to Fight
A vanquisht Enemy, Thou art not Conquer'd

379

But couz'ned and betray'd.

 Alb. Shut your Mouth, Lady,
Or with this Paper I shall stop it——hold, Sir,
Thou worse than any Name, reade thy own evil;
No Tearing, Lady, I perceive you know it.

 Gon. Say if I do, who shall arraign me for't?
The Laws are Mine, not Thine.

 Alb. Most monstrous! ha, Thou know'st it too.

 Bast. Ask me not what I know,
I have not Breath to Answer idle Questions.

 Alb. I have resolv'd.   [*To* Edgar
   —Your Right, brave Sir, has conquer'd.
Along with me, I must consult your Father.

         [*Ex.* Albany *and* Edgar.

 Reg. Help every Hand to save a noble Life;
My half o'th' Kingdom for a Man of Skill
To stop this precious stream.

 Bast. Away ye Empericks,
Torment me not with your vain Offices:
The Sword has pierc't too far; *Legitimacy*
At last has got it.

 Reg. The Pride of Nature Dies.

 Gon. Away, the minutes are too precious,
Disturb us not with thy impertinent Sorrow.

 Reg. Art Thou my Rival then profest?

 Gon. Why, was our Love a Secret? cou'd there be
Beauty like Mine, and Gallantry like His
And not a mutual Love? just Nature then
Had err'd: behold that Copy of Perfection,
That Youth whose Story will have no foul Page
But where it says he stoopt to *Regan*'s Arms:
Which yet was but Compliance, not Affection;
A Charity to begging, ruin'd Beauty!

 Reg. Who begg'd when *Gonerill* writ That?

        [*Throws her a Letter.*
      Expose it

And let it be your Army's mirth, as 'twas
This charming Youth's and mine, when in the Bow'r
He breath'd the warmest ecstasies of Love,
Then panting on my Breast, cry'd matchless *Regan*

That *Gonerill* and Thou shou'd e'er be Kin!

 Gon. Die, *Circe*, for thy Charms are at an End,
Expire before my Face, and let me see
How well that boasted Beauty will become
Congealing Blood and Death's convulsive Pangs.
Die and be husht, for at my Tent last Night
Thou drank'st thy Bane, amidst thy rev'ling Bowls:
Ha! dost thou Smile? is then thy Death thy Sport
Or has the trusty Potion made thee Mad?

 Reg. Thou com'st as short of me in thy Revenge
As in my *Gloster*'s Love, my Jealousie
Inspir'd me to prevent thy feeble Malice
And Poison Thee at thy own Banquet.

 Gon. Ha!

 Bast. No more, my Queens, of this untimely Strife,
You both deserv'd my Love and both possest it.
Come, Souldiers, bear me in; and let
Your royal Presence grace my last minutes:
Now, *Edgar*, thy proud Conquest I forgive;
Who wou'd not choose, like me, to yield his Breath
T' have Rival Queens contend for him in Death?

            [*Exeunt.*

[Act V, Scene vi.]

SCENE, *A Prison.*

Lear *asleep, with his Head on* Cordelia's *Lap.*

 Cord. What Toils, thou wretched King, hast Thou endur'd
To make thee draw, in Chains, a Sleep so sound?
Thy better Angel charm thy ravisht Mind
With fancy'd Freedom! Peace is us'd to lodge
On Cottage Straw. Thou hast the Begger's Bed,
Therefore shou'dst have the Begger's careless Thought.
And now, my *Edgar*, I remember Thee,
What Fate has seiz'd Thee in this general Wreck
I know not, but I know thou must be wretched
Because *Cordelia* holds Thee Dear.
O Gods! a suddain Gloom o'er-whelms me, and the Image
Of Death o'er-spreads the Place.——Ha! who are These?

Enter Captain *and* Officers *with Cords.*

Capt. Now, Sirs, dispatch, already you are paid
In part, the best of your Reward's to come.
Lear. Charge, charge upon their Flank, their last Wing haults;
Push, push the Battel, and the Day's our own!
Their Ranks are broke, down, down with *Albany*!
Who holds my Hands?——O thou deceiving Sleep,
I was this very Minute on the Chace;
And now a Prisoner here.——What mean the Slaves?
You will not Murder me?
Cord. Help, Earth and Heaven!
For your Souls sake's, dear Sirs, and for the Gods.
Offic. No Tears, good Lady, no pleading against
Gold and Preferment. Come, Sirs, make
Ready your Cords.
Cord.   You, Sir, I'll seize,
You have a humane Form, and if no Pray'rs
Can touch your Soul to spare a poor King's Life,
If there be any Thing that you hold dear,
By That I beg you to dispatch me First.
Capt. Comply with her Request, dispatch her First.
Lear. Off Hell-hounds, by the Gods I charge you spare her;
'Tis my *Cordelia*, my true pious Daughter:
No Pity?——Nay then take an old Man's Vengeance.

Snatches a Partizan, and strikes down two of them; the rest quit Cordelia,
and turn upon him. Enter Edgar *and* Albany.

Edg. Death! Hell! Ye Vultures hold your impious Hands,
Or take a speedier Death than you wou'd give.
Capt. By whose Command?
Edg. Behold the Duke your Lord.
Alb. Guards, seize those Instruments of Cruelty.
Cord. My *Edgar*, Oh!
Edg. My dear *Cordelia*, Lucky was the Minute
Of our Approach, the Gods have weigh'd our Suffrings;
W' are past the Fire, and now must shine to Ages.
Gent. Look here, my Lord, see where the generous King
Has slain Two of 'em.
Lear. Did I not, Fellow?

I've seen the Day, with my good biting Faulchion
I cou'd have made 'em skip; I am Old now,
And these vile Crosses spoil me; Out of Breath!
Fie, Oh! quite out of Breath and spent.

   Alb. Bring in old *Kent*, and, *Edgar*, guide you hither
Your Father, whom you said was near,   [*Ex.* Edgar.
He may be an Ear-witness at the least
Of our Proceedings.

                                [Kent *brought in here.*

   Lear. Who are you?
My Eyes are none o' th' best, I'll tell you streight;
Oh *Albany*! Well, Sir, we are your Captives,
And you are come to see Death pass upon us.
Why this Delay?—or is't your Highness pleasure
To give us first the Torture? Say ye so?
Why here's old *Kent* and I, as tough a Pair
As e'er bore Tyrant's Stroke:—but my *Cordelia*,
My poor *Cordelia* here, O pitty!——

   Alb. Take off their Chains—Thou injur'd Majesty,
The Wheel of Fortune now has made her Circle,
And Blessings yet stand 'twixt thy Grave and Thee.

   Lear. Com'st Thou, inhumane Lord, to sooth us back
To a Fool's Paradise of Hope, to make
Our Doom more wretched? go too, we are too well
Acquainted with Misfortune to be gull'd
With Lying Hope; No, we will hope no more.

   Alb. I have a Tale t' unfold so full of Wonder
As cannot meet an easy Faith;
But by that Royal injur'd Head 'tis True.

   Kent. What wou'd your Highness?

   Alb. Know the noble *Edgar*
Impeacht Lord *Edmund*, since the Fight, of Treason,
And dar'd him for the Proof to single Combat,
In which the Gods confirm'd his Charge by Conquest;
I left ev'n now the Traytor wounded Mortally.

   Lear. And whither tends this Story?

   Alb. Ere they fought
Lord *Edgar* gave into my Hands this Paper,
A blacker Scrowl of Treason, and of Lust
Than can be found in the Records of Hell;

There, Sacred Sir, behold the Character
Of *Gonerill* the worst of Daughters, but
More Vicious Wife.

   Cord. Cou'd there be yet Addition to their Guilt?
What will not They that wrong a Father doe?

   Alb. Since then my Injuries, *Lear*, fall in with Thine:
I have resolv'd the same Redress for Both.

   Kent. What says my Lord?

   Cord. Speak, for me thought I heard
The charming Voice of a descending God.

   Alb. The Troops by *Edmund* rais'd, I have disbanded;
Those that remain are under my Command.
What Comfort may be brought to cheer your Age
And heal your savage Wrongs, shall be apply'd;
For to your Majesty we do Resign
Your Kingdom, save what Part your Self conferr'd
On Us in Marriage.

   Kent. Hear you that, my Liege?

   Cord. Then there are Gods, and Vertue is their Care.

   Lear. Is't Possible?
Let the Spheres stop their Course, the Sun make Hault,
The Winds be husht, the Seas and Fountains Rest;
All Nature pause, and listen to the Change.
Where is my *Kent*, my *Caius*?

   Kent. Here, my Liege.

   Lear. Why I have News that will recall thy Youth;
Ha! Didst Thou hear't, or did th' inspiring Gods
Whisper to me Alone? Old *Lear* shall be
A King again.

   Kent. The Prince, that like a God has Pow'r, has said it.

   Lear. Cordelia then shall be a Queen, mark that:
Cordelia shall be Queen; Winds catch the Sound
And bear it on your rosie Wings to Heav'n.
Cordelia is a Queen.

Re-enter Edgar *with* Gloster.

   Alb. Look, Sir, where pious *Edgar* comes
Leading his Eye-less Father: O my Liege!
His wondrous Story will deserve your Leisure:
What He has done and suffer'd for your Sake,

What for the Fair *Cordelia*'s.

   Glost. Where is my Liege? Conduct me to his Knees to hail
His second Birth of Empire; my dear *Edgar*
Has, with himself, reveal'd the King's blest Restauration.

   Lear. My poor dark *Gloster*!

   Glost. O let me kiss that once more sceptred Hand!

   Lear. Hold, Thou mistak'st the Majesty, kneel here;
Cordelia has our Pow'r, *Cordelia*'s Queen.
Speak, is not that the noble Suffring *Edgar*?

   Glost. My pious Son, more dear than my lost Eyes.

   Lear. I wrong'd Him too, but here's the fair Amends.

   Edg. Your leave, my Liege, for an unwelcome Message.
Edmund (but that's a Trifle) is expir'd;
What more will touch you, your imperious Daughters
Gonerill and haughty *Regan*, both are Dead,
Each by the other poison'd at a Banquet;
This, Dying, they confest.

   Cord. O fatal Period of ill-govern'd Life!

   Lear. Ingratefull as they were, my Heart feels yet
A Pang of Nature for their wretched Fall;——
But, *Edgar*, I defer thy Joys too long:
Thou serv'dst distrest *Cordelia*; take her Crown'd:
Th' imperial Grace fresh Blooming on her Brow;
Nay, *Gloster*, Thou hast here a Father's Right;
Thy helping Hand t' heap Blessings on their Head.

   Kent. Old *Kent* throws in his hearty Wishes too.

   Edg. The Gods and You too largely recompence
What I have done; the Gift strikes Merit Dumb.

   Cord. Nor do I blush to own my Self o'er-paid
For all my Suffrings past.

   Glost. Now, gentle Gods, give *Gloster* his Discharge.

   Lear. No, *Gloster*, Thou hast Business yet for Life;
Thou, *Kent* and I, retir'd to some cool Cell
Will gently pass our short reserves of Time
In calm Reflections on our Fortunes past,
Cheer'd with relation of the prosperous Reign
Of this celestial Pair; Thus our Remains
Shall in an even Course of Thought be past,
Enjoy the present Hour, nor fear the Last.

   Edg. Our drooping Country now erects her Head,

Peace spreads her balmy Wings, and Plenty Blooms.
Divine *Cordelia*, all the Gods can witness
How much thy Love to Empire I prefer!
Thy bright Example shall convince the World
(Whatever Storms of Fortune are decreed)
That Truth and Vertue shall at last succeed.

[*Ex. Omnes.*

24. Nahum Tate, from his adaptation of *Coriolanus*

1682

From *The Ingratitude of a Common-Wealth: Or, the Fall of Caius Martius Coriolanus* (1682).

This adaptation seems to have been performed in January 1682 (but possibly in the previous month). As with Tate's other versions the simultaneous desires for pathos and violence (rape, murder and suicide on-stage) produces a result which is closer to the tragedies of Webster and Fletcher.

[Dedication]

To the Right Honourable Charles, Lord Herbert. . . .

My Lord,

Your Lordship's favour for Learning in General, has encourag'd me to begg your Patronage of the following Sheets, which contain a remarkable piece of Roman History, though form'd into [a] Play. I have yet another Plea for Pardon, since I impose not on your Lordship's Protection a work meerly of my own Compiling; having in this Adventure Launcht out in *Shakespeare*'s Bottom. Much of what is offered here, is Fruit that grew in the Richness of his Soil; and whatever the Superstructure prove, it was my good fortune to build upon a Rock. Upon a close view of this Story, there appear'd in some Passages, no small Resemblance with the busie *Faction* of our own time. And I confess, I chose rather to set the *Parallel* nearer to Sight, than to throw it off at further Distance. Yet there are none that can apply any Part (as Satyr) on themselves, whose Designs and Practises are not of the same Cast. What offence to any good Subject in Stygmatizing on the Stage, those *Troublers* of the State that out of private Interest or Mallice Seduce the Multitude to *Ingratitude*, against Persons that are not only plac't in Rightful Power above them but also the Heroes and Defenders of their Country?

Where is the harm of letting the People see what Miseries *Common-Wealths* have been involv'd in, by a blind Compliance with their popular Misleaders? Nor may it be altogether amiss, to give these Projecters themselves, examples how wretched their dependence is on the uncertain Crowd. Faction is a Monster that often makes the slaughter 'twas designed for; and as often turns its fury on those that hatcht it. The Moral therefore of these Scenes being to Recommend Submission and Adherence to Establisht Lawful Power, which in a word, is *Loyalty*; They have so far a natural Claim to your Lordship's Acceptance: This Virtue seeming Inheritance in Your Lordship, and deriv'd from your Ancestours with Your Blood.

*   *   *

PROLOGUE

Written by Sir *George Raynsford*.

Our Author do's with modesty submit,
To all the Loyal Criticks of the Pit;
Not to the Wit-dissenters of the Age,
Who in a Civil War do still Engage,
The antient fundamental Laws o'th' Stage:
Such who have common Places got, by stealth,
From the Sedition of Wits Common-Wealth.
From Kings presented, They may well detract,
Who will not suffer Kings Themselves to Act.
   Yet he presumes we may be safe to Day,
Since *Shakespeare* gave Foundation to the Play:

'Tis Alter'd—and his sacred Ghost appeas'd;
I wish you All as easily were Pleas'd:
He only ventures to make Gold from Ore,
And turn to Money, what lay dead before.

*   *   *

[Act III, Scene ii.] Rome. A Street.

Enter *Volumnia*, met by *Valeria*, passing by in a Chair.

Val. Hold, hold, set me down—I Swear Madam, I had almost overseen my good Fortune, and past by your Ladyship.

Vol. Your Ladyships most humble Servant.

Val. And upon my Honour, Madam, my Hast is so Violent, and Affairs so Important, that nothing, but the Sight of your Ladyship, shou'd have Stop me: Well, I hear my Lord *Coriolanus* continues Obstinate; I Love an Obstinate Man most inordinately! Do's your Ladyship know, Madam, that I am the greatest Rabble-Hater of my Sex? I think 'em the common Nuisance of the World; there's no Thought, no Science, no Eloquence, no Breeding amongst 'em; and therefore your Ladyship must know, They are my Aversion: For, as to all these Particulars, and to every one of 'em, the Envy of the World must Grant—and your Ladyship knows, the World is most Malicious —I say, the Envy of the World must Grant—O *Jupiter*! What was I saying, Madam?

Vol. I beg your Ladyships Pardon, that——

Val. Then Madam, there's such Mistery in my Dress! the Wits see Poetry in it, the Souldiers Spirit and Courage, the Mathematicians describe the Spheres in't, and your Geographers, the *Terra Incognita*: and yet your Ladyship sees 'tis as plain as Nature; no Trim, no Ornament: There's my Lady *Galatea*, such a fantastical, fulsome Figure, all Curls and Feathers! And besides Madam, she's such an Eternal Talker! Her Tongue's the perpetual Motion, and she affects such hard Words, such an obdurate Phrase, that she exposes her self a publick Ludibry to the Universe.

Vol. Nay, now *Valeria*——

[*Here one of the Pages whisper* Valeria.

Val. How's that? *Titus Decius, Caius Proculus, Marcus Flavius, Publius Cotta*; All to Wait on me since I came Forth? Are they not all Banish't Men? Have I not Refus'd, incontinently, to see 'em these

three Days together; nay, though they came upon State Affairs? O
the Impudence of Man-kind! I Swear, a Lady had need look to her
Circumstances! Well, I'll to *Athens* agen, incontinently! Boy, tell em
I shall return at Six precisely—I Swear, Madam, this Love's my Aversion of all things in the World; and yet for the speculative part, I
presume, I understand it most Unmeasurably: Trust me, I cou'd Write
the Art of Love.

Vol. Think you so Madam?

Val. As thus; Sometimes to seem, inordinately, Jealous of them;
sometimes to make them, inordinately, Jealous of mee: to seem Merry
when I am Sad; Sad when I am Merry; to Rail at the Dress that
becomes me best, and Swear I put it on in Contradiction to Them.

Vol. Indeed Madam?

Val. O *Jupiter*! How insensibly the Time runs, whilst your Ladyship
is Discoursing; I cou'd hear your Ladyship Discourse all Day—but
this Business is the most uncivil Thing—but your Ladyship, and I,
shall take a Time: Your Ladyship will excuse my Hast; for I Swear,
I am in Hast most inordinately.   [*Exit.*

★   ★   ★

[Act IV, Scene iii.] Corioles.

Enter Aufidius *and* Nigridius.

Nigr. What Circe Sir, has wrought you to this Change?
By Hell I rather shou'd have thought to have seen,
Serpents with Doves embrac't, than this Agreement;
Call but to Mind your Mornings Wiser Thoughts:
Where is that fiery Resolution vanisht?
Have you, My Lord, forgot your Mornings Vow?
It seem'd the Voice of Fate.

Auf. Nigridius, No,
The Accents still are fresh upon my Mind;
I Swore, and call'd the Elements to Witness,
If I, and *Caius Martius* met once more,
That teeming Hour, *Corioles* or *Rome*,
In him or me shou'd Perish.

Nigr. Such a Sound,
And Utter'd, with so stern a Brow, shot Terror,
And to our View, Confest a flaming *Mars*;

But now (forgive me Sir) you seem reduc'd
To Less than Man, the Shaddow of your self:
What Witchcraft drew your Mind to this Alliance
With him, whose only *Genius* of the World,
Had Pow'r to Vie with yours?

    Auf. He bears himself more Proudly,
Ev'n to my Person, than I thought he wou'd,
When late I did embrace him; but his Nature
In that's no Changeling, and I must excuse
What cannot be Amended.

    Nigr. Yet I wish
You had not took this joynt Commission with him;
But either born the Action all your self,
Or left it whole to him.

    Auf. I understand Thee——
But spare to Fret a Lyon in the Toil.

    Nigr. The Palsy *Senate* lay their Fears aside,
And rest on his Protection as a *Gods*:
Your Souldiers use him as their Grace 'fore Meat:
Their Talk at Table, and their Thanks when done:
What Estimation shall your Foes take for you,
When you are lost, and darkn'd to your own?   [*Shout here.*
Heark in what Notes the very Rabble greet him.

    Auf. Death! Hell! This Infamy enflames my Brest,
Makes Emulation higher boyl than ever;
I'll sink *Corioles*, but I'll yet break with him;
And wreck the State, rather than want a Quarrel.   [*Exeunt.*

[Act IV, Scene iv.] Rome. A Street.

*   *   *

    Bru. Now good *Menenius*, if you Love your Country,
Or Pitty Her Distress, become Her Pleader;
Your pow'rful Tongue may be of force to stop him,
More than the instant Army we can Raise.

    Men. No, I'll not meddle.

    Sic. Pray go to him.

    Men. What shou'd I do?

    Bru. Only make tryal what your Love can work
For *Rome*, with *Martius*.

All Cit. Kneeling. Beseech you most Noble *Menenius.*

Men. Well, I will under-take't, and think he'll hear me,
Though much discourag'd with *Cominius* Treatment;
Yet I will prove him with my ablest Speed.

1 Cit. The *Gods* preserve you Sir, Commend my hearty Affections
to him; and if it stand with his good liking, we'll hang up our *Tribunes*,
and send him them for a Token.

Com. He'll never hear him;
I tell you, he sits Thron'd in Gold, his Eye
All Red, as 'twou'd Burn *Rome*; his Injury
The Jayler to his Pitty; I kneel'd to him,
'Twas very faintly he said Rise; dismist me
Thus with his speechless Hand; what he resolv'd,
He sent in Writing after me, and that
Most Fatal. Therefore curse your Crime, and Perish.

[*Exit.*

1 Cit. Some comfort yet, that we have these Vipers to *Carbinado*;
Come Neighbours, we'll see them smoak before us. Away, away with
'em.   [*Exeunt, Haling and Dragging off the* Tribunes.

[Act IV, Scene v.] Outside Rome.

Scene *Opening, shews* Coriolanus *seated in State, in a rich* Pavilion, *his
Guards and Souldiers with lighted Torches, as ready to set Fire on* Rome;
Petitioners as from the Citty *offer him Papers, which he scornfully throws
by: At length* Menenius *comes forward, and speaks to him:* Aufidius *with*
Nigridius, *making Remarks on 'em.*

Men. Now may the *Gods* in hourly Councel sit,
For thy Prosperity, and Love Thee,
As thy old Father *Menenius* do's:
O Son! my Son, What Fury sways thy Breast?
Thou art preparing Fire for us; look here,
Here's Water for the Flames:
Most hardly was I wrought to come to Thee;
But being assur'd none but my self cou'd move Thee;
I come, blown out from *Rome* with gales of Sighs.

Cor. Away.

Men. How?

Cor. No words Friend: Mother, Wife, or Child, I know not;
I'm not my own, but servanted to others;

391

Mine was the Injury, but the Remission
Lies not with me, but in the *Volsces* Breast;
And *Rome* must stand to them for their Account.
That we were Friends, forgetfulness must blot,
Ere lawless Pitty move: Therefore be gone,
My Ears against your Pray'rs are stronger, than
Your Gates against my Arms: Yet 'cause I Lov'd Thee,
Take this with thee; I Writ it for thy Sake,
And meant t'have sent it: Another word, *Menenius*,
I must not hear Thee speak: This Man, *Aufidius*,
Was my best Lov'd in *Rome*; yet thou beholdst——
   Auf. You bear a constant Temper.
   Cor. His Love to me,
Was much beyond the Kindness of a Father;
And I return'd him more than filial Duty;
Their latest Refuge was to send him to me.
   Auf. You are too Rigorous.
   Nigr. Fasten but that upon him, and you Gain
The Point we wish.
   Cor. Now plant our Fires against the Gates of *Rome*:
Bid all *Trumpets* Sound;
They shall have Musick to their flaming Citty.

As they Advance with their Lights, Enter from the other side, Volumnia,
Virgilia, *and Young* Martius, *with the rest of the* Roman *Ladies all in
Mourning.*

   Cor. Look there, my Mother, Wife, and little Darling,
Are come to Meet our Triumph on its way,
And be Spectators of our keen Revenge,
On this ingrateful Town.
   Virg. My dearest Lord!
   Vol. My First-born only Son.
   Cor. Life of my Life, Fly to me? O a Kiss,
Long as my Exile, Sweet as my Revenge;
And thou my *Turtle*, Nest Thee in my Heart: [*To the Boy.*
Forgive me *Gods*, that any dearest Transport,
Shou'd make my charm'd Scuse, unsaluted, leave
The Noblest Mother—sink my Knee in Earth,
Of deepest Duty more Impression shew,
Than that of common Sons.

Nigr. Observe you this?

Cor. What means this Silence? What, these sable Weeds?
This Troop of Stars beset with darkest Night?
O Mother, Wife! Too deeply you have took
My Banishment, and I must chide your Sorrow.
This Sadness for my Absence shew'd Dispair
Of Injur'd *Martius* Virtue, call'd in Question
The Justice of the *Gods* for my Revenge;
Virgilia speak, speak Mother; at your Feet
Behold a kneeling Conqueror: Answer to me.

Vol. Rise *Martius*, up, *Coriolanus* rise;
Whilst with no softer Cushion than these Flints
I Kneel to thee, and with this new Submission,
Shew Duty as mistaken all this while,
Between the Son and Parent.

Cor. What's this? Your Knees to me?
Then let the Pibbles of the Hungry Beach
Change Station with the Stars; the Mutinous Winds
Snatch Mountain-Oaks, and hurl 'em at the Sun;
Let all Impossibilities have Being,
And Nature fall as Giddy with the Round.

Vol. My Fire-Ey'd Warrior, Do you know this Lady?

Cor. The Noble Sister of *Publicola*,
The Moon of *Rome*, Chast as the frozen Snow,
That hangs on *Diana*'s Temple.

Vol. And this divine Epitome of yours;
This little *Martius* whom full Time shall ripen
Into your perfect self.

Cor. The *God* of Battles,
With the Consent of fav'ring *Jove* inspire
Thy Thoughts with Nobleness; that thou mayst prove,
The Wars proud *Standard* fixt in Tides of Blood;
Like a tall Sea-mark o're the dashing Waves,
And saving those that view Thee.

Vol. Your Knee, Sirrah.
Ev'n He, your Wife, these Ladies, and my Self,
Are humble Suitors——

Cor. Oh my boding Heart!

Vol. This Liv'ry was not for your Absence worn;
So dear we knew your safety to the *Gods*:

393

But now put on as funeral Robes, and Mourning
For our expiring *Rome*. O spare thy Country,
And do not Murder Nature.

   Cor. Witness for me
You conqu'ring Host, and Thou my valiant Partner;
What Tenderness and Duty I have shewn
These Ladies, whilst they did converse with me
As Wife and Mother: but since they exceed
The Bounds of Kindred, and encroach upon
Affairs of State, I as the *Volsces* General,
Support their Dignity, and take my Pomp.

                         [Ascends his Throne.

Yet Nature shall to any suit, unlock
Our yielding Ear, that do's not tend to Save
The *Roman* State, and Barring our Revenge;
In that particular, I shall forget
All enter-course of Blood;
Standing as Man were Author of himself,
And knew no other Kin.

   Vol. No more, no more;
You have said you will not grant us any thing,
For we have nothing else to ask, but that
Which you deny already—yet we'll speak.

   Cor. Aufidius, and you *Volsces,* mark, for we
Hear nought from *Rome* in private—your request:
What seeks that lovely Tempter, whose Dove's Eyes
Cou'd make the *Gods* forsworn—but shake not me?

   Virg. Think with your self my once indulgent Lord,
How more unhappy than all living Women,
Are we come hither, since thy sight, that shou'd
Make our Eyes flow with Joy, strikes Terrour through us;
Forcing the Mother, Wife, and Child, to see
The Son, the Husband, and the Father, tearing
His Countries Bowels with unnatural Rage,
Whilst frighted Destiny disowns the Deed,
And Hell is struck with Horrour.

   Vol. Thou debarr'st us
Ev'n of our Prayr's to th' *Gods,* and to this Hour,
No Wretchedness was e're deny'd that help:

How shall we ask the Death of *Rome*, or thee,
Oppos'd in fatal War; and one must fall?
Most wretched *Martius*, thou bleed'st ev'ry way;
For know 'tis sworn betwixt thy Wife and me,
In that curst hour that Thou despoilst our Citty,
Thou tread'st upon thy Mother's Earth.

    Virg. And mine; and this sweet smiling Flow'r.

    Boy. He shall not tread on me, I'll run away till I am bigger;
but then I'll Fight.

    Cor. Not to be struck with Woman's tenderness,
Requires, nor Child's, nor Woman's Face to see.
I have sate too long.   [*Descends.*

    Virg. Nay, go not from us thus:
If it were so, that our Request did tend
To Save the *Romans*, thereby to Destroy
The *Volsces*, whom you serve, you might condemn us,
As Poys'ners of your Honour: No, our suit
Is but to Reconcile 'em, that the *Volsces*
May say, This Mercy we have shewn the *Romans*;
This we receiv'd, whilst either Party gives
The Praise to Thee, and bless thy Memory,
For making this dear Peace.

    Vol. Thou know'st my Son,
Th' event of War's uncertain; but 'tis certain,
That if thou Conquer *Rome*, the Benefit
That thou shalt reap from thence, is such a Name,
As always shall be mention'd with a Curse:
Thy Chronicle writ thus; *The Man was Noble,*
But with his last performance stain'd his Glory,
And left his Rowl of Fame, but one foul Blot.
Pause, and reply to this.

★   ★   ★

[Act V, Scene i.] Rome. A Street.

★   ★   ★

    Virg. O my boding fear!   [*Shewing the Letter.*
Amidst this general Joy begins our Sorrow;
This Mourning we put on for *Rome*, must now

395

Become the Dress of our own private sorrow.

   Com. What mean those doleful Accents?

   Virg. False *Nigridius,*
(Disbanded for his Villany by *Martius*)
Is busy for Revenge; and hourly plots
Against his precious Life: The industry
Of good *Menenius* sends this information;
Whilst *Martius,* confident in Innocence,
Is obstinately blind to all his dangers;
Though in the Walls of an offended Citty,
Whose Streets yet mourn the Slaughter he has made.

   Vol. The *Gods* provide us then more noble Work,
To give our Virtues, yet a brighter Ray:
Come my *Virgilia;* with our ablest speed,
We will betake us to *Corioles.*

   Com. Consider Madam, what th' event may be;
Your Aid uncertain, but your Danger sure.

   Virg. Needful Suspition, necessary Caution,
He reckons only better terms for fear;
His Life is therefore any Villains Prize:
And he that dares not face a waking *Eunuch,*
May kill a sleeping *Gyant.*

   Boy. Shall not I go too? My Father promis'd to teach me to Fight:
I wou'd fain learn; and if any body hurts him, I'll kill their Boys now;
and them, when I am bigger.

   Vol. Hear'st thou *Virgilia?* All thy *Martius* Fire
Lies shrouded in this little Frame, and shall
With Time, break forth into as full a Blaze:
O we delay our Enterprize too long,
And seem ingrateful to the indulgent Pow'rs,
That have decreed our Names, the immortal Glory,
To Save *Rome* first, and then *Coriolanus.*

   Com. The *Gods,* whose Temples you preserv'd, protect you.

                                 [*Exeunt.*

[Act V, Scene ii.] Corioles.

Enter Aufidius, *and* Nigridius.

   Nigr. Compose this Fury, and recall your Reason.

   Auf. Preach Patience to the Winds, bid Tempests Sleep.

The golden Opportunity is lost,
And I cou'd curse my self as heartily
As ever I did *Martius*: O *Nigridius*,
I am a lazy Trifler, and unworthy
To be possest o'th' Beauty that I Love,
Or be reveng'd upon the Man I hate:
Why forc't I not my passage to his Heart,
Then pamper'd in the Banquet of his Blood,
Flown hot, as flame-born *Pluto*, to the Rape;
And quench't the Fevour in *Virgilia's* Arms?
  Nigr. Give o're this Frenzy.
  Auf. Now each Minute wrecks me,
With the Remembrance of my former Pangs,
Which War had almost hush't, and Blood wash't out.
Her Dove-like Sorrow, when she begg'd for *Rome*,
(With Eyes Tear-charg'd, yet sparkling through the Dew,
Whilst charming Pitty dimpled each soft Cheek)
Call'd back the Scene of my expecting Youth
When with vain promises of Joys to come,
I wak'd the Night, and watch't the Stars away;
So was I wrapt anew i'th' dazling Dream;
Believ'd her yet unwed; believ'd my self
The happy Youth design'd to Reap her Sweets;
To Lock the tender Beauty in my Arms;
Blushing, yet Granting; Trembling, and yet Embracing.
I shall go Mad with the Imagination.
  Nigr. Wake, wake my Lord from this fantastick Maze,
Return her Scorn upon your Rival's head,
And make at least a Mistress of Revenge:
Ev'n now he makes his Entrance at our Gates;
Presuming with a smooth and specious Tale,
To Acquit himself before the credulous People.

Enter an Officer *of* Aufidius *Party.*

  Off. Our Lords o'th' Citty, Noble *Tullus*,
Are met in Councel at your Pallace, where
They crave your Presence, having Summon'd thither
Your Partner *Caius Martius*, to give in
Th' Account of his Proceedings in this War;

And t' Answer at his Peril all Miscarriage.

Auf. Go, tell 'em I'll attend 'em instantly;
Deliver 'em this Paper, the Contents
Of what I have to Charge on *Martius*,
And shall make good to his Face.   [*Ex. Officer.*

Nigr. Now Sir, How fares it with you?

Auf. As with a Man by his own Alms empoyson'd.

Nigr. You hold your last Resolve.

Auf. I cannot tell;
We must proceed in't, as we find the People.

Nigr. The People will remain uncertain, whilst
You stand Competitors; but eithers fall,
Leaves th' other Heir to All.

Auf. I rais'd him, pawn'd my Honour for his **Truth**,
Whilst the sly Flatterer seduc'd my Friends,
Softning his Nature, never known before:
So base a Grain of *Cynick* obstinacy.
Banish't from *Rome*, I furnish't him with Pow'r;
Made him joynt Partner with me, gave him way
In all his own desires; nay, took some Pride
To do my self this wrong, till at the last,
I seem'd his Follower, not his Patron.

Nigr. True,
Our Army wonder'd at it, and at last,
When he had carry'd *Rome*, and that we look't
For no less Spoil, than Glory——

Auf. O there's it!
For which my Sinews shall be stretch't upon him.

Nigr. Your Native-Town you enter'd like a Pilgrim,
And had no welcome Home; whilst he return'd,
Tortring the Air with Noise; and patient Fools,
Whose Children he had Slaughter'd, tore their Throats,
With shouting his Applause.

Auf. Wreck me no more,
His Tryumphs sleep this Day; then shalt thou see,
Thy *Tullus* Glories bloom a second Spring:
I shall be yet the Wonder of the Crowd,
When this Controller of my Fate is gone:
'Tis Odds our *Senate* doom him; but if not,
I'll have my Party planted near.

Enter the Officer.

——Thy News?

Off. My Lord, the Councel have perus'd your Paper,
And summon your Appearance instantly.
What will surprize you more: I met ev'n now
Volumnia with *Virgilia*, and young *Martius*,
Just enter'd our *Corioles*,
And hastily enquiring for your Palace;
Menenius at that instant passing by.

Auf. Thou tell'st me Wonders, but I know thy Truth.
Nigridius, help me now to play this Game,
And draw at once our Net o're the whole Covey:
They have not yet seen *Martius*?

Off. No,—*Menenius* off'ring to Conduct 'em to him,
They grew divided in their Resolutions;
Virgilia held it best to seek out you,
Presuming on her former Pow'r with you;
But what they did determine on——

Auf. No more.
Nigridius, take our Guard along with you,
Whilst I attend the Councel; Seize 'em All,
Before they can attain to speak with *Martius*;
Dispose 'em privately within our Palace;
Virgilia by her self; you know my drift:
For soon as I've secur'd my Rivals Life,
All stain'd i'th' Husbands Blood, I'll Force the Wife.   [*Exeunt*

[Act V, Scene iii.]

SCENE, *A Palace.*

The Lords *of* Corioles, *as set in Councel.*

1 Lord. Let Justice, Lords, reward his Services,
Far as his Conduct shall be worthy found:
'Tis not unknown what Deeds he has perform'd,
Since first he had the Leading of our Pow'rs;
Molesting hourly *Romes* confed'rate Citties;
Restoring our lost Fields made rich with Blood;
Our burden'd Souldiers groan'd beneath the Spoil:
Yet—there to make a Hault in's Action,

Where most his Resolution was requir'd;
To flinch our Service at the Gates of *Rome*,
And make a Treaty where he shou'd have Storm'd;
Admits of no excuse, and I propose it
To your impartial Censures.—See he comes.

Enter Coriolanus; Aufidius *on the other side.*

Cor. Hail Lords, I am return'd your Souldier;
No more infected with my Countries Love,
Than when I parted hence: be pleas'd to know,
That prosperously I have attempted, and
With bloody passage Led your War,
Ev'n to the Gates of *Rome*; our Spoils brought home,
Ten times o're pay the Charges of the Action:
The Peace which with the *Romans* we have made,
Brings no less honour to *Corioles*,
Than shame to *Rome*. Behold their *Consul's* Hand,
With the *Patricians*, and the Seal o'th' *Senate*
To Composition, such as ne're was gain'd
By proudest Conquerour from the pettyest State:
Peruse it, and approve my Services.
   Auf. Ha! that again: Lords, heard you what he said?
   Cor. I say, I'll have my Services approv'd.
   Auf. Wrong not so much your Patience Lords, to Read
That fabulous Commentary, but forthwith
Give Sentence on his most apparent——
   Cor. Ha!
May I believe my Sense? Down, swelling Heart,
Thou wert my Partner, *Tullus*; but take heed,
No more I say, and thank me for this warning.
   Auf. O Vanity!
   Cor. I say let me be Calm.
   Auf. Out Blast—Read not the Paper, Lords,
But tell the Traytor——
   Cor. Traytor!
   Auf. That, *Martius.*
   Cor. Martius?
   Auf. Aye, *Martius, Caius Martius*! Dost thou think,
I'll grace thee with thy Robbery, thy stoln Name——
Coriolanus in *Corioles?*

Most awful Lords o'th' State, perfidiously
He has betray'd your Business, and giv'n up,
(For certain drops of Dew) your Citty *Rome*;
I say your Citty to his Wife and Mother,
Breaking his Oath of Service; call'd no Councel
Of War on This; but at his Nurses Tears,
He whin'd and roar'd away your Victory:
For a few Tears, sold all our Blood and Labour,
Whilst Pages blush't at him, and Men of heart,
Look't wond'ring at each other.

   Cor. Hear'st thou, *Mars*?
   Auf. Name not the fiery *God*, thou Boy of Tears.
   Cor. Scorpions and *Basilisks*!
   All Lords. Silence on your Lives.
   Cor. Measureless Lyar, thou hast made my Heart
Too big for what contains it. Boy? Oh Slave!
Carrion-breed, creeping Insect: Lords your Pardon;
'Tis the first time I e're was forc't to Brawl,
But your grave Judgment will consent with me,
To give this Fiend the Lye: Nay, his own Brawn,
That wears my Stripes, his Vassal Body, that
Must bear my Beatings with it to the Grave——
Cut me to pieces *Volsces*, Pound, Calcine me,
And throw my Dust to the Wind; yet when yo've done;
If you have Writ your Annals true, 'tis there,
There Registred to all Posterity,
That, as an Eagle in a Dove-coat, so
Was *Martius* Slaught'ring in *Corioles*.
   Auf. Dye Insolent.

Stamps with his Foot, the Conspirators Enter, and help him to Wound
Martius, *who kills some, and hurts* Aufidius. *The Lords rise, and come
forward.*

   1 Lord. Guards, Guards, secure 'em both.
Tread not upon him; off:
O *Tullus*, thou hast done a deed at which
Valour will Weep.
   Auf. Pray give me hearing,

                     [*A confus'd Noise heard from abroad.*

   2 Lord. Heark what Confusion storms without.

Enter Nigridius *hastily.*

Nigr. Hast, hast my Lords, disperse to every Quarter,
Our City's up in Arms, *Aufidius* Legions
Oppos'd by those were led by *Caius Martius.*
Prepare for dreadful Battle in our Streets,
Unless your speedy presence quell their Fury.

1 Lord. Disperse my Lords, each to a several Quarter,
With your best skill, to quench these threatning Flames.

[*Exeunt Lords severally.*

Nigr. Curst chance! Why bought you your Revenge so dear?
Auf. There's Blood upon thee.
Nigr. Blood long Thirsted for.   [*The Noise continues.*
Cor. 'Tis just you *Gods*, to give my Death this Pomp;
'Tis fit, that when *Coriolanus* Dies,
Corioles shall fall their Sacrifice;
Ev'n thou my Bond-slave follow'st in the Tryumph;
Hast then, and wait me to the nether World.
Auf. No, I have yet a pleasant Scene to Act;
My Bliss; but Fiend, thy Hell; bring in *Virgilia.*
Cor. Virgilia?
Auf. Yes, she's here, here in the Palace;
Out of her *Roman* Virtue come to seek you,
And spy those dangers out, which you were blind to;
Thou'lt not believe thy Foe, but heark, she comes;
I charge thee Dye not yet, till thou hast seen
Our Scene of Pleasures; to thy Face I'll Force her;
Glut my last Minuits with a double Ryot;
And in Revenges Sweets and Loves, Expire.

Virgilia *brought in Wounded.*

In Blood? *Nigridius* look! Behold a sight,
Wou'd turn the *Gorgon*-Snakes—my Rage is gone,
And I am touch't with Sorrow—my faint Nerves
Refuse my Weight, and hasty Death invades
At ev'ry Pore.——Oh Dark! dark! O, O.   [*Dies.*
Virg. Betray me not thou sluggish Blood, stream faster,
Aye, now the stubborn Heart resigns, and takes
The proud Destroyer to her inmost Courts.
Cor. O Heav'n!
Virg. 'Tis near, for that was *Martius* Voice;

My Eyes are dim; but that dear Sound agen;
O where, my dear Lord? Speak!
   Cor. If I do wake,
And that bright dismal Object be *Virgilia*,
Tell me what Sacrilegious Hand has stain'd
The whitest Innocence that Heav'n e're form'd:
What Rage cou'd hurt a Gentleness like thine,
Whose tender Soul cou'd weep
O're dying Roses, and at Blossoms fall?
Tell me thou Turtle, ruffled in a Storm;
What chance seduc'd thee to these Caves of Slaughter?
What means that purple Dew upon thy Breast?
   Virg. My Noble *Martius*, 'tis a *Roman* Wound,
Giv'n by *Virgilia*'s Hand, that rather chose
To sink this Vessel in a Sea of Blood,
Than suffer its chast Treasure, to become
Th' unhallowed *Pyrates* Prize; but Oh the *Gods*,
The indulgent *Gods* have lodg'd it in thy Bosome!
The Port, and Harbour of eternal Calms:
O Seal with thy dear Hand these dying Eyes;
To these cold Cheeks lay thine; and to thy Breast
Take my unspotted Soul, in this last Sigh.   *[Dyes.*
   Cor. Make way ye Stars, a nobler Brightness comes:
Ariadne shall to thee resign her Crown;
Yet my *Virgilia* mount not to thy Merit,
But grace the Orb thy *Martius* shall attain:
My Grief talks Idly.—Cold, my Love? She's gone;
And on her Cheeks a scatter'd Purple smiles,
Like streaks of Sun-shine from a setting Day:
But Oh my Heart! My Fears expire not here!
Volumnia, and my little darling *Boy*;
Where are they? Some kind *God* descend t' inform me.
   Nigr. Trouble not Heav'n for your Intelligence.
   Cor. Nigridius here? Then Heav'n indeed is distant!
   Nigr. With silent Transport, *Martius*, I have stood
To see thy Pangs; to have hasten'd on thy Death,
Had been too poor Revenge; remember *Martius*,
The Stripes, and foul disgrace thou laid'st upon me,
When once I bare Commission under thee:
Thou mad'st me pass the Fork before my Souldiers,

Discarded, Branded, Hooted from the Camp.

Cor. I do remember thy unequall'd Villany:
Had exemplary Punishment.

Nigr. That day
Thou drew'st this Blood from thy own Vitals, *Martius*:
'Tis thy young Boy, whom I this Hour have Mangled,
Gash't, Rack't, Distorted.

Cor. O this Tale of Horrour,
Wou'd rouse the sleeping Father from his Grave!
Yet Strength forsakes me for the dear Revenge.
Well, *Cerberus*, How then didst thou dispose him?
Didst eat him?

Nigr. Having kill'd your old *Menenius*,
Off'ring his feeble Vengeance, streight I threw
The Tortur'd Brat, with Limbs all broke (yet living
In quickest Sense of Pain) I say, I threw him
Into *Volumnia*'s Arms, who still retain'd
Her *Roman* Temper; till with bitter Language,
And most insulting, added to her Suff'rings,
I rous'd her silent Grief, to loud Disorder;
Then left her to the Tempest of her Fury,
To Act my Part, and be her own Tormenter.

Cor. Convultions! Feavers! blewest Pestilence!
Sleep on *Virgilia*, Wake not to a Story,
Whose Horrour wou'd exceed the Force of Death,
And turn thee into Stone.

Enter Volumnia *Distracted, with young* Martius *under her Arm.*

Vol. Soft, soft; steal but the Watch-word whilst they Sleep,
And we pass Free.

Cor. Furies! The Fiend spoke Truth.
O my poor Boy! Most wretched Mother, Oh!

Vol. Strike, strike your Torches, bid the Stars descend!
We wander in the Dark.
Heark! *Boreas* musters up his roaring Crew;
My Wings, and I'll among 'em; wreath my Head
With flaming *Meteors*; load my Arm with Thunder;
Which as I nimbly cut my cloudy Way,
I'll hurl on the ingrateful Earth, and laugh
To hear the Mortals Yelling.

Nigr. Mark you this?

Vol. Aye, there's th' *Hesperian* Dragon, I must pass him,
Before I reach the golden Bough; there *Cerberus*,
Gorge thy curst Maw with that, and cease thy Barking;
'Tis a delicious Morsel.

 Cor. Earth and Heav'n!
Is this *Volumnia*? *Martius* awful Mother,
And *Romes* Minerva?

 Boy. Dear Sir speak to my Grand-Mother,
Perhaps she'll answer you.

 Vol. Ha! What a merry World is this *Elizium*!
See how the youthful Sheepherds trip to the Pipe,
And fat *Silenus* waddles in the Round.
Beware thy Horns, *Pan, Cupids* with their Bow-strings
Have ty'd 'em fast to th' Tree! Ah, ha! ha! ha!
What's that?——a Summons to me from the *Gods*?
Back *Mercury*, and tell 'em I'll appear.
All Heav'n shall know how much I have been wrong'd:
They tore my little *Martius* from my Arms;
Broke all his innocent Limbs before my Face.
Indeed I never did deserve this usage;
For I was always Kind and Charitable;
For Virtue fam'd; and as I do remember,
'Twas I sav'd *Rome*, preserv'd ten thousand Infants,
From being Massacred like my poor Boy!
How? *Juno* dead! The Thunderer then is mine,
And I'll have more than *Juno*'s priviledge:
See how the *Æther* smoaks, the *Christaline*
Falls clatt'ring down! This giddy *Phaeton*
Will set the World on Fire! Down with him *Jove*:
Wilt thou not Bolt him?—Then I'll Act thy Part,
Force from thy slothful Hand the flaming Dart;
And thus I strike my Thunder through his Heart.

>   *Snatches a* Partizan *from the foremost of the Guards, and*
>   *strikes* Nigridius *through, as she runs off.*

 Cor. There struck the *Gods*.

 Boy. Look where my Mother sleeps, pray wake her Sir;
I have heard my Nurse speak of a dying Child,
And fancy it is now just so with me;

I fain wou'd hear my Mother bless me first.

 Cor. My pretty Innocence, she do's not sleep.

 Boy. Perhaps then I have done some Fault, makes her
Not speak to me.

 Cor. O *Gods*! may this be borne?

 Boy. I fain wou'd clasp you too; but when I try
To lift my Arms up to your Neck,
There's something holds 'em.

 Cor. Thy Torturers my Boy have crippled 'em,
And gash't thy pretty Cheeks.

 Boy. I know you Lov'd 'em;
But truly 'twas no fault of mine; they did it
Because I wou'd not cry; and I have heard
My Grand-Mother say, a *Roman* General's Son
Shou'd never cry.

 Cor. O Nature! A true Breed!

 Boy. 'Tis grown all Dark o'th sudden, and we sink
I know not whether; good Sir hold me fast.   [*Dies.*

 Cor. Fast as the Arms of Death: Now come my Pangs,
The chilling Damp prevails upon my Heart.
Thus, as th' Inhabitant of some sack't Town,
The Flames grown near, and Foe hard pressing on,
In hast lays hold on his most precious Store:
Then to some peaceful Country takes his Flight:
So, grasping in each Arm my Treasure, I
Pleas'd with the Prize, to Deaths calm Region Fly.   [*Dies.*

25. Thomas D'Urfey, from his adaptation of *Cymbeline*

1682

From *The Injured Princess, or the Fatal Wager* (1682).

Thomas D'Urfey (1653–1723), poet, dramatist and song-writer, added a parallel sub-plot and some modish violence to his version of *Cymbeline* (published in the spring of 1682). I have included the song (replacing 'Hark, hark the lark') which was printed separately in D'Urfey's *A New Collection of Songs & Poems* (1683). The characters' names correspond as follows: Ursaces [Posthumus]; Eugenia [Imogen]; Shatillion [Iachimo]. Pisanio is an old man who has a daughter Clarina, confidante to Eugenia and heroine of the rape scene; the name Iachimo is retained for the would-be rapist, a drunken companion of Cloten.

      ✱   ✱   ✱

[Act III, Scene i.] Lud's Town, alias London.
The Royal Palace; Eugenia's bedchamber

The Scene Discovers Eugenia *in Bed; a Lady waiting; a Chest standing by.*

Eugen. Who's there—*Clarina?*
Clarin. Yes, Madam.
Eugen. What hour is't my Dear?
Clarin. Past Twelve above a quarter.
Eugen. I have read three hours then.
My Eyes are weak; pray then go to Bed:
Indeed I trouble you; but leave the Candle burning,
And if thou think'st on't, bid my Woman call me
At five a Clock: Good night, Sleep seizes me;   [*Exit.* Clar.
To thy protection I commend me Heaven.   [*Sleeps.*

Enter Shattillion *from the Chest; a Table-book.*

   Shatt. All's still as Death, and hush'd as Midnight silence:
Now the Crickets sing, and mortal wearied Sense
Repairs it self by rest. Lewd *Tarquin* thus
Did softly tread and tremble, ere he wak'ned
The Chastity he wounded. Oh Soul of Beauty!
Sure none but I cou'd see thee thus, and leave thee
Thus in this lovely posture. But no more;
I've other business. Chill all my Bloud,
Ye Powers, and make me cold to her Allurements:
This is no loving minute; Come, to my design:
To note the Chamber: Here I'le write all down;
Such and such Pictures; there the Window; such
The adornment of her Bed; the Arras Figures:
Why such, and such, and the Contents o'th' Story.
Aye, but some natural Notes about her Body,
Above ten thousand meaner Witnesses,
Wou'd testifie to enrich my Inventory.
What's there, a Bracelet on her Arm? 'Tis so.

She stirs, and he starts back.

Now sleep thou Ape of Death, lye dull upon her;
And be her Sense but as a Monument,
Thus in a Chappel lying. Fortune befriend me;
'Tis mine, and this will witness outwardly,
As strongly as the Conscience does within,
To th' torture of her Lord: On her left Breast,
A Mole Cinque-spotted like the Crimson drops
In the bottom of a Cowslip: Here's a Voucher
Stronger than ever Law cou'd make; this Secret
Will force him think I've pick'd the Lock, and stoll'n
The Treasure of her Honour. No, now I have enough:
To th' Chest agen.
Swift, swift ye Dragons of the Night; lov'd *Phospher,*
Return the welcome day, I lodge in fear,
Tho' there's a heavenly Angel, Hell is here.   [*Gets into the Chest.*

Enter Cloten, *Gentlemen,* Silvio, *Musicians and Dancers.*

   Clot. I' Gad this damn'd Armour is plaguy troublesom: Does it
become [me,] *Florio?* Hah! Do I look like one that cou'd slay my ten

thousand in a morning, and never sweat for't? Have I the sow'r Look of a Heroe?

Silvio. Your Look will cause more wonder than fear, my Lord; you are too young to be very terrible.

Clot. Nay I know I shou'd look more like a Warrier, if I were not so handsom; Pox on't, I have look'd so clear ever since I took Physick last, that Gad I'me afraid people begin to think I paint.

Silvo. They often look smiling on you, I confess.

Clot. Come, begin then, first play and then sing; you shall charm her with your Fingers, and you with your Tongue, whilst I, God *Mars*, brandish my Weapon; and if tonguing, fingering and fighting, don't please her, the Devil's in her.

Flutes and a Song here

The Larks awake the drouzy morn,
   My dearest lovely *Chloe* rise,
And with thy dazling Rays adorn
   The Ample World and Azure Skies:
Each eye of thine out-shines the Sun,
   Tho' deck'd in all his light;
As much as he excells the Moon,
Or each small twinkling Star at Noon,
   Or Meteor of the Night.

Look down and see your Beauty's power,
   See, see the heart in which you raign;
No Conquer'd slave in Triumph bore
   Did ever wear so strong a Chain:
Feed me with Smiles that I may live,
   I'll ne'er wish to be free;
Nor ever hope for kind Reprieve,
Or Loves grateful bondage leave
   For Immortality.

[A Lady looks out.

Lelia. My Lady is rising Sir, she hears your Musick.

Clot. Ud so, she peeps through the Window yonder now.
The Dance, the Dance. *[Dance.*

Enter Eugenia *and* Clarina.

She comes; away all and leave me to her. *[Exeunt.*

Good morrow to the radiant Queen of Beauty!
Fierce *Mars* in Field
With Sword and Shield
Yields thee the time o'th' day.

Eugen. I am covetous of thanks Sir, and scarce can spare 'um.

Clot. Gad that's a little morose tho', to a Deity of my Valour and Quality.

Eugen. It suits my Humour Sir: but pray why thus in Armour? You amongst all men in my opinion, need not Burlesque your self.

Clot. Burlesque? Now she mauls me with her hard words. [*Aside.* Madam, I love and honour you in plain terms; pray give your consent, and let's be married; your Heroes hate delays.

Eugen. Married, what to such a Figure?

Clot. Figure? Why I'me a Lord, and the Queen's my Mother, as inconsiderable a Figure as you make me; Gads, that's more than a banish'd Fellow of your Acquaintance can pretend to, since you go to that.

Eugen. That banish'd Fellow is a God, when ballanc'd
With your weak merit; I swear his meanest
Garment that ever touch'd his Body, is more dear to me
Than the life's service of a hundred *Cloten's.*

Clot. His Garment? A Plague! what, his Shirt?

*   *   *

[Act IV, Scene i.] The Palace.

Enter Queen, Cloten, Clarina, Iachimo, Aurelia, *and Attendants.*

Queen. Thou seed of Mischief, young Practitioner
In th' Art of Treachery, how didst thou dare
To conceal this devilish Secret,
No less than the disturbance of a Nation?
But in thy death I'le strait revenge th' Affront.

Clar. Oh do not fright me with the name of Death!
But look with pity, Madam, on my tears,
And see a wretched Virgin beg for Life:
So may your Raign be prosp'rous, so your Beauty
Still fresh and heavenly, as your mercy flows
In showers of tender pity on my youth.

Cloten. Pity? Aye, let me have her, I'le show pity on her **Youth**;

Gad, I'le first make my Footman ravish her, and then have her hang'd.

Iachimo. And why your Footman, my Lord? I hope you have other Friends about you that will do her that kindness.

Queen. I have consider'd now she shall not die so well, But banish'd, live to prolong her misery, And none shall help her, upon pain of Death. My Lord *Iachimo*, to you I give the Wretch, Use her as she deserves: Hence hated Harpey.

Clar. Nay kill me now, and I will think you kind, Let me not be a prey to his wild Lust.

Queen. Away with her, I will not hear a word.

Iachimo. You'l like me better in the Countrey, Madam. Come, come, there's no remedy.   [*Drags her out.*

Clar. No spark of Pity; help, help.

Cloten. Stop her Mouth, away with her; I'le go and dispatch a small Affair, and follow thee.——   [*Exit.*

★ ★ ★

[Act IV, Scene iii.] A Rocky Cave.

Enter Pisanio.

Pisan. My Heart throbbs still, my Senses are disturb'd too, And since I left the Princess in yon Court, I have not been at rest; sure she's innocent And I and her rash Lord have been abus'd. I'le seek her out, And comfort her, for I believe she's innocent.   [*Exit.*

Enter Cloten *in* Ursaces *Cloaths, and* Iachimo *dragging in* Clarina *in a mean Habit.*

Clar. Look on my tears, and let them melt your heart, Your rocky hearts, yet harder far than Stone; For Stones melt, when relenting Heavens weeps, But you grow more obdurate with my tears.

Iachimo. Tears? Why thou canst not oblige me more than to weep soundly; it makes the flame of Love more vigorous; Oh I like a passionate Woman in that Business extreamly! she has the finest ways with her.

411

Clar. Think you not on your Souls? Alas, when I am dead,
As I will ne're outlive so black a Villany,
My Ghost will fright you, your wounded Consciences
Lash and torment you like a thousand Furies.

Clot. Ghost? A pox o'thy Ghost: Prithee art thou such a Fool to
think we fear the Devil? *Iachmio*, show her the contrary, rowze her,
towze her, Boy, I'le do thee an honourable kindness, and pimp for
thee, for fear of disturbance.

Iachimo. A very friendly part, faith, my Lord: Come, Madam, you
and I must be more familiar; nay, nay, no struling, my heart's a flame,
and you must quench the fire.

Clar. Rather be burn'd to ashes, barbarous Wretch!
Help, help! Oh Heaven, send down thy Thunder,
Dash me to the Earth, Rather than suffer this:
Help, help!

Enter Pisanio.

Pisan. What pitious Cry was that? sure 'twas a Woman's voice
By the shrill sound. Good Gods, what's this I see?
My Daughter here?

Clarin. Mercy—unlook'd for: 'Tis he, Oh my dear Father,
In a bless'd minute are you come to save me!

[*Runs and embraces him.*

Pisan. Ha! Lord *Cloten* too?
Then all's discover'd, and I'me lost.

Cloten. See *Iachimo*, yonder's that old Traitor too luckily faln into
our snare: Go, go, take his Daughter from him, and ravish her before
his face.

Iachimo. With all my heart; I'le not lose for a million.

Pisan. He comes upon his death that touches her:
Base men, have you no humane Nature?

Cloten. Does he expostulate? Kill, kill the Slave.

Pisan. I first shall see thy death.

Cloten. No, Thou shalt never see agen; for when I have conquer'd
thee,
With my Sword's point, I'le dig out both thy eyes,
Then drag thee to my Mother to be tortur'd.

Iachimo. I'le do his business presently.   [*Fight,* Pisanio *wounded.*

Pisan. Fly Daughter, fly, whilst my remains of Life
I render for thy safety.

412

Clarin. Oh save my Father! Heaven save him, save him.   [*Exit.*
          [*Fight still,* Pisanio *kills* Iachimo, *then falls down
                    with him, and* Cloten *disarms him.*

Pisan. Thou hast it now, I think.

Iachimo. A Plague on him, he has kill'd me. Oh——   [*Dyes.*

Cloten. Curs'd Misfortune! He's dead; but I'me resolv'd to be thy true Prophet however, thou shalt not see my death, unless with other eyes.   [*Puts out his eyes.*

Pisan. Hell-born Fury! Oh——

Cloten. So, now smell thy way out of the Wood, whilst I follow thy Daughter, find her, and cut her piece-meal: I'le sacrifice her to the Ghost of *Iachimo.*   [*Exit.*

Pisan. All dismal, dark as Night, or lowest Shades,
The Regions of the Dead, or endless Horror;
The Sun with all his light now gives me none,
But spreads his beamy Influence in vain,
And lends no Glimpse to light my Land of darkness.
Sure near this Place there lyes a Sword, [*Crawls about to find his Sword.*
I'le try if I can find it. Pitiless Fate,
Wilt thou not guide my hand? My Wound's not mortal,
And I shall yet live Ages: True sign of Grief,
When we do wish to die before our time.
I'le crawl into some Bush and hide my self,
Till Fate's at leisure; there
To the dumb Grove recount my Miseries,
Weep Tears of bloud from Wounds instead of Eyes.   [*Crawls out.*

★　★　★

26. Robert Gould, from *The Play-House.*
A Satyr

1685

From the expanded version in his *Works*, 1709.

Gould (d. 1709), a minor poet and dramatist, was a servant of Charles, Earl of Dorset and Middlesex, who attempted a literary career (mostly as satirist) without much success.

★   ★   ★

But if with *Profit* you wou'd reap *Delight*,
Lay *Shakespeare*, *Ben*, and *Fletcher* in Your sight:
Where Human Actions are with Life express'd,
Vertue advanc'd, and *Vice* as much depress'd.
There the kind Lovers with such Zeal complain,
You in their Eyes behold their inmost Pain,
And pray such Truth may not be Plac'd in vain.
There *Nature*'s secret Springs may all be view'd,
And, when she doubles, how to be pursu'd.
There *Art*, in all her subtle Shifts display'd,
There ev'ry *Humour* You may see pourtray'd,
From *Legislative Fops* down to the *Slaves of Trade*.
There all the *Passions*, weak, you'll first espy,
Hate, *Envy*, *Fear*, *Revenge* and *Jealousy*;
And by what Fewel fed to flame at last so high.
While *Wit* attending You'll for ever see,
Faithful amidst this vast Variety;
Like *Proteus*, but affording Nobler Game,
She ev'ry Shape assumes, and yet Remains the same.
In short, none ever Wrote or will again
So useful things in such a Heav'nly strain!

When e'er I *Hamlet* or *Othello* read,
My Hair starts up, and my Nerves shrink with dread!
Pity and *Terrour* raise my Wonder high'r,
'Till betwixt both I'm ready to expire!
When curs'd *Iago* cruelly I see
Work up the Noble *Moor* to *Jealousy*,
How cunningly the Villain weaves his Sin,
And how the other takes the Poison in;
Or when I hear his Godlike *Romans* rage,
And by what just degrees He does Asswage
Their Angry Mood, and by a Secret Art
Return the mutual Union back to either Heart;
When these and other such-like *Scenes* I scan,
'Tis then, Great Soul, I think thee more than Man!
Homer was Blind, yet cou'd all Nature see;
THOU wert unlearn'd, yet knew as much as He!
In *Timon*, *Lear*, the *Tempest*, we may find
Vast Images of thy Unbounded Mind:
These have been alter'd by our *Poets* now,
And with Success, too, that we must allow:
Third Days they get when *Part of THEE* is shown,
Which they but Seldom do when *All*'s their own.

*   *   *

Hail Sacred *Bards*! Hail ye Immortal *Three*!
The *British Muses* Great *Triumviri*!
Secure of Fame, You on the *Stage* will live
Whilst we have *Wits* to hear, and they have *Praise* to give.
'Tis some where said our *Courtiers* speak more *Wit*,
In *Conversation* than these *Poets* Writ:
Unjust Detraction! like it's *Author*, base;
And it shall here stand Branded with Disgrace.
Not but they had their Failings too;—but then
They were such Faults as only spoke 'em Men;
Errors which Human Frailty must admit,
The Wanton Rovings of Luxurious Wit.
To the Judicious plainly it appears,
Their Slips were more the Age's Fault than theirs:
Scarce had they ever struck upon the Shelves,

If not oblig'd to stoop beneath themselves:
Where *Fletcher's* loose, 'twas Writ to serve the *Stage*;
And *Shakespeare* play'd with Words to please a Quibbling Age.

    If *Plays* you love let these Your thoughts employ;
When *Wit* is read by *Wit* 'twill never cloy.
No other *Poets* so sublimely tell
The useful, happy Art of *Living Well*:
All strew'd with *Morals*, thick in ev'ry *Page*
Alike Instructive both to Youth and Age.
'Tis certain on a *Mistress* and a *Friend*
The chiefest Blessings of our Lives depend;
And by their *Draughts* we may exactly find
If that be Faithful, or if this be kind.
There You may breath the Air of ev'ry Clime
And make Remarks on *Custom*, *Place* and *Time*.
Thro' ev'ry Stage of Life You there may View ⎫
What Ills t'avoid, what Vertues to pursue; ⎬
And so with *Pleasure* reap *Advantage* too. ⎭
Unlike the *Authors* that have lately writ,
Who in their *Plays* such *Characters* admit,
So Lewd and Impious, they shou'd Punish'd be
Almost as much as *Oates* for Perjury:
With equal Scandal both supply the Age;
He has disgrac'd the *Gown*, and they the *Stage*.

★   ★   ★

27. Gerard Langbaine, from *An Account of the English Dramatick Poets*

1691

Gerard Langbaine the younger (1656–1692) is the first English theatre-historian. In 1680 he published *An exact catalogue of all the comedies that were ever printed or published*; in 1688 he issued *Momus Triumphans: or the plagiaries of the English stage expos'd* . . . a list of the sources of a great number of plays. His final work of reference gives a biography for each dramatist and a list of their plays with sources. As the only serious scholar in this field for many years Langbaine's work was frequently absorbed and enlarged by later historians.

[From the *Life* of D'Avenant]

[Sir Wm. Davenant's] *Law against Lovers*, a Tragi-Comedy made up of two Plays written by Mr. *Shakespeare*, viz. *Measure for Measure*, and *Much Ado about Nothing*. Tho' not only the Characters, but the Language of the whole Play almost, be borrow'd from Shakespeare: yet where the Language is rough or obsolete, our Author has taken care to polish it: as to give, instead of many, one Instance. *Shakespeare's* Duke of Vienna says thus;

> ———I love the People;
> But do not like to Stage me to their Eyes:
> Though it do well, I do not relish well
> Their loud Applause, and Aves vehement:
> Nor do I think the Man of safe discretion,
> That does affect it. [*MM*, 1.1.69ff.]

In Sr. William's Play the Duke speaks as follows;

> ———I love the People;
> But would not on the Stage salute the Croud.

I never relisht their Applause; nor think
The Prince has true discretion who affects it.
(108-9).

*   *   *

[From the *Life* of Dryden]

... To conclude, if Mr. *Shakespeare*'s Plots are more irregular than those of Mr. *Dryden*'s (which by some will not be allow'd) 'tis because he never read *Aristotle*, or *Rapin*. . . . (142)

... As to his Reflections on this Triumvirate [Shakespeare, Fletcher, Jonson] in general: I might easily prove, that [Dryden's] Improprieties in Grammar are equal to theirs: and that He himself has been guilty of Solecisms in Speech, and Flaws in Sence, as well as *Shakespeare*, *Fletcher*, and *Jonson*: but this would be to wast Paper and Time. (150)

[On *Troilus and Cressida*] This Play was likewise first written by *Shakespeare*, and revis'd by Mr. *Dryden*, to which he added several new Scenes, and even cultivated and improv'd what he borrow'd from the Original. The last scene in the third Act is a Masterpiece, and whether it be copied from *Shakespeare*, *Fletcher*, or *Euripides*, or all of them, I think it justly deserves Commendation. The Plot of this Play was taken by Mr. *Shakespeare* from Chaucer's *Troilus and Cressida*. . . . (173)

*   *   *

William SHAKESPEARE

One of the most Eminent Poets of his Time; he was born at *Stratford* upon *Avon* in *Warwickshire*; and flourished in the Reigns of Queen *Elizabeth*, and King *James* the First. His Natural Genius to *Poetry* was so excellent, that like those Diamonds,* which are found in *Cornwall*, Nature had little, or no occasion for the Assistance of Art to polish it. The Truth is, 'tis agreed on by most, that his Learning was not extraordinary; and I am apt to believe, that his Skill in the *French* and *Italian* Tongues, exceeded his knowledge in the *Roman* Language: for we find him not only beholding to *Cynthio Giraldi* and *Bandello*, for his Plots, but likewise a Scene in *Henry* the Fifth, written in *French*, between the Princess *Catherine* and her *Governante*: Besides *Italian*

---

* Dr. *Fuller* in his Account of *Shakespeare*.

Proverbs scatter'd up and down in his Writings. Few Persons that are acquainted with *Dramatick Poetry*, but are convinced of the Excellency of his Compositions, in all kinds of it: and as it would be superfluous in me to endeavour to particularise what most deserves praise in him, after so many Great Men that have given him their several Testimonials of his Merit; so I should think I were guilty of an Injury beyond pardon to his Memory, should I so far disparage it, as to bring his Wit in competition with any of our Age. . . . I shall . . . take the Liberty to speak my Opinion, as my predecessors have done, of [Shakespeare's] Works; which is this, That I esteem his Plays beyond any that have ever been published in our Language: and tho' I extreamly admire *Jonson*, and *Fletcher*; yet I must still aver, that when in competition with *Shakespeare*, I must apply to them what *Justus Lipsius* writ in his Letter to *Andraeas Schottus*, concerning *Terence* and *Plautus* when compar'd; *Terentium amo, admiror, sed Plautum magis.* . . . (453–4)

* * *

All's well that ends well; a Comedy. This Play is founded on a Novel written by Jean Boccaccio; See his Nov. Day the 3 Nov. the 9 concerning *Juliet* of *Narbona*, and *Bertrand* Count of *Rossilion*. . . . (455)

Comedy of Errors. This Play is founded on *Plautus* his *Menaechmi*: and if it be not a just Translation, 'tis at least a Paraphrase: and I think far beyond the Translation, called *Menechmus*, which was printed 4° *Lond.* 1595. . . . (455)

Cymbeline his Tragedy. This Play, tho' the Title bear the Name of a King of *Brute*'s Linage; yet I think ows little to the Chronicles of those Times, as far as I can collect, from *Grafton*, *Stow*, *Milton*, &c. But the Subject is rather built upon a Novel in *Boccace*, *viz.* Day 2. Nov. 9. This Play was reviv'd by *Durfey* about seven Years since, under the Title of *The Injured Princess*, or *The Fatal Wager*.

Henry the Fourth, the First part; with the Life of *Henry Percy*, sirnamed *Hot-spur*. This Play is built upon our *English* History: see the four former Years of his Reign, in *Harding*, *Buchanan*, *Caxton*, *Walsingham*, *Fabian*, *Polydore Virgil*, *Hall*, *Grafton*, *Hollingshead*, *Heyward*, *Trussel*, *Martin*, *Stow*, *Speed*, *Baker*, &c. As to the Comical part, 'tis certainly our Author's own Invention; and the Character of Sir *John Falstaff*, is owned by Mr. *Dryden*, to be the best of Comical Characters: and the Author himself had so good an Opinion of it, that he continued it in no less than four Plays. This part used to be play'd by Mr. *Lacy*, and never fail'd of universal applause.

Henry the Fourth, the Second part; containing his Death, and the Coronation of King *Henry* the Fifth. For the Historical part, consult the fore-mentioned Authors. The Epilogue to this Play is writ in Prose, and shews that 'twas writ in the Time of Q. *Elizabeth*.

Henry the Fifth his Life. This Play is likewise writ and founded on History, with a Mixture of Comedy. The Play is continued from the beginning of his Reign, to his Marriage with *Katherine* of *France*. For Historians, see as before, *Harding, Caxton, Walsingham, &c.* This Play was writ during the time that *Essex* was General in *Ireland*, as you may see in the beginning of the first Act; where our Poet by a pretty Turn, compliments *Essex*, and seems to foretell Victory to Her Majesties Forces against the Rebels.

Henry the Sixth, the First part.

Henry the Sixth, the Second part, with the Death of the Good Duke *Humphrey.*

Henry the Sixth, the Third part, with the Death of the Duke of *York.* These three Plays contain the whole length of this Kings Reign, *viz.* Thirty eight Years, six Weeks, and four Days. Altho' this be contrary to the strict Rules of *Dramatick Poetry*; yet it must be own'd, even by Mr. *Dryden* himself, That this Picture in *Miniature*, has many Features, which excell even several of his more exact Strokes of Symmetry, and Proportion. For the Story, consult the Writers of those Times, *viz. Caxton, Fabian, Pol. Virgil, Hall, Hollingshead, Grafton, Stow, Speed, &c.* (456–7)

*   *   *

Hamlet, Prince of *Denmark*, his Tragedy. I know not whether this Story be true or false; but I cannot find in the List given by Dr. *Heylin*, such a King of *Denmark*, as *Claudius*. All that I can inform the Reader, is the Names of those Authors that have written of the Affairs of *Denmark* and *Norway*; and must leave it to their further search: such are *Saxo-Grammaticus, Idacius, Crantzius, Pontanus, &c.* This Play was not many Years ago printed in quarto; all being mark'd, according to the Custom of the Stage, which was cut out in the Action. (457–8)

*   *   *

Lear King of *England*, his Tragedy. This Play is founded on History;

see such Authors as have written concerning *Brutes* History, as *Leland*, *Glocester*, *Huntingdon*, *Monmouth*, &c. But the Subject of this Story may be read succinctly in *Milton's* History of *England*, 4°. Book 1, p. 17. &c. This Play about eight Years since was reviv'd with Alterations, by Mr. *Tate*. (458)

*   *   *

Loves Labour's lost, a Comedy: the Story of which I can give no Account of.

Measure for Measure, a Comedy, founded on a Novel in *Cynthio Giraldi: viz. Deca Ottava, Novella* 5. The like Story is in *Goulart's Histoires Admirables de nôtre temps, Tome* 1. *page* 216. and in *Lipsii Monita* L.2. C.9. p. 125. This Play, as I have observed, was made use of with the Comedy *Much ado about nothing*, by Sir *William D'Avenant*, in his *Law against Lovers*.

Merry Wives of Windsor, a Comedy; which Mr. *Dryden* allows to be exactly form'd; and it was regular before any of *Ben. Jonson's*. This is not wholly without the Assistance of Novels; witness Mrs. *Ford's* conveying out Sir *John Falstaff* in the Basket of Foul Clothes; and his declaring all the Intrigue to her Husband, under the Name of Mr. *Broom*; which Story is related in the first Novel of *The Fortunate Deceived, and Unfortunate Lovers*: which Book, tho' written since *Shakespeare's* Time, I am able to prove several of those Novels are translated out of *Cynthio Giraldi*, others from *Mallespini*; and I believe the whole to be a Collection from old Novelists.

Macbeth, a Tragedy; which was reviv'd by the Dukes Company, and re-printed with Alterations, and New Songs, 4°. *Lond.* 1674. The Play is founded on the History of *Scotland*. The Reader may consult these Writers for the Story: *viz. Hector Boetius, Buchanan, Du chesne, Hollingshead*, &c. The same Story is succinctly related in Verse, in *Heywood's Hierarchy of Angels*, B. 1. p. 508. and in Prose in *Heylin's* Cosmography, Book 1. in the Hist. of *Brittain*, where he may read the Story at large. At the Acting of this Tragedy, on the Stage, I saw a real one acted in the Pit; I mean the Death of Mr. *Scroop*, who received his death's wound from the late Sir *Thomas Armstrong*, and died presently after he was remov'd to a House opposite to the Theatre, in *Dorset-Garden*.

Midsummer Nights Dream, a Comedy. The Comical part of this Play, is printed separately in 4°. and used to be acted at *Bartholomew* Fair, and other Markets in the Country by Strolers, under the Title of *Bottom the Weaver*.

Much ado about nothing, a Comedy. I have already spoke of Sir *William D'Avenant's* making use of this Comedy. All that I have to remark is, That the contrivance of *Borachio*, in behalf of *John* the Bastard to make *Claudio* jealous of *Hero*, by the Assistance of her Waiting-Woman *Margaret*, is borrowed from *Ariosto's Orlando Furioso*: see Book the fifth in the Story of *Lurcanio, and Geneuza*: the like Story is in *Spenser's Fairy Queen*, Book 2. Canto 4. (459–61)

★   ★   ★

Othello, *the Moor of* Venice *his Tragedy*. This is reckoned an Admirable Tragedy; and was reprinted 4°. *Lond.* 1680. and is still an Entertainment at the Theatre-Royal. Our Author borrowed the Story from *Cynthio's* Novels, Dec. 3. Nov. 7. . . . Mr. *Dryden* says, That most of *Shakespeare's* Plots, he means the Story of them, are to be found in this Author. I must confess, that having with great difficulty obtained the Book from *London*, I have found but two of those mentioned by him, tho' I have read the Book carefully over. (461)

★   ★   ★

Richard the Second his Life and Death; a Tragedy, which is extreamly commended even by Mr. *Dryden*, in his 'Grounds of Criticisme in Tragedy', printed before *Troilus and Cressida*: and Mr. *Tate*, who altered this Play in 1681. says, That there are some Master-touches in this Play, that will vye with the best *Roman* Poets. For the Plot, consult the Chronicles of *Harding, Caxton, Walsingham, Fabian, Pol. Virgil, Grafton, Hollingshead, Stow, Speed, &c.* (462).

★   ★   ★

Romeo and Juliet, a Tragedy. This Play is accounted amongst the best of our Author's Works. Mr. *Dryden* says, That he has read the Story of it in the Novels of *Cynthio*; which as yet I cannot find, but set it down in my former Catalogue, relying upon his Knowledge. But I have since read it in *French*, translated by M. *Pierre Boisteau*, whose Sir-name was *Launay*; who says it was writ by *Bandello*; but not having as yet met with *Bandello* in the Original, I must acquiesce in his Word.

The *French* Reader may peruse it in the first Tome of *Les Histoires Tragicques, extraictes des œuvres Italiennes de Bandello, imprimé* 8°. *à Turin* 1570.

Taming of the Shrew, a very diverting Comedy. The Story of the *Tinker*, is related by *Pontus Heuteras, Rerum Burdicarum, lib.* 4. and by *Goulart*, in his *Hist. Admirables*, Tom. 1. p. 360.

Tempest, a Comedy. How much this Play is now in Esteem, tho' the Foundation were *Shakespeare*'s, all People know. How it took at the *Black-fryars*, let Mr. *Dryden*'s Preface speak. For his Opinion of *Caliban*, the Monster's Character, let his Preface to *Troilus and Cressida* explain. 'No Man except *Shakespeare*, ever drew so many Charactars, or generally distinguish'd them better from one another, except only *Jonson*: I will instance but in one, to shew the copiousness of his Invention; 'tis that of *Caliban*, or the Monster in the *Tempest*: He seems here to have created a Person, which was not in Nature; . . .' As to the Foundation of this Comedy, I am ignorant whether it be the Author's own Contrivance, or a Novel built up into a Play. (462–4)

★   ★   ★

Twelfth-Night, or *What you will*; a Comedy. I know not whence this Play was taken; but the Resemblance of *Sebastian* to his Sister *Viola*, and her change of Habit, occasioning so many mistakes, was doubtless first borrowed (not only by *Shakespeare*, but all our succeeding Poets) from *Plautus*, who has made use of it in several Plays, as *Amphitruo*, *Mænechmi, &c.* . . .

Winter's Tale, a Tragi-comedy. The Plot of this Play may be read in a little Stitcht-pamphlet, which is call'd, as I remember, *The Delectable History of* Dorastus *and* Fawnia; printed 4°. *Lond.* (466)

28. Elkanah Settle?, from the operatic adaptation of *A Midsummer Night's Dream*

1692

From *The Fairy-Queen: an Opera* (1692).

Performed 2 May 1692, with music by Purcell, *The Fairy-Queen* is little more than a series of masques performed between the acts, with a grand finale. The ascription to Settle (1648–1724), made by F. C. Brown (*Elkanah Settle* (Chicago, 1910) p. 96), is not certain.

The Names of the Persons.

[Gives the *dramatis personae* of *A Midsummer Night's Dream*, omitting Hippolyta; then]

Singers and Dancers in the Second Act.

Fairy-Spirits, Night, Mistery, Secresie,
Sleep, and their Attendants, Singers, and Dancers.

Singers in the Third Act.

Nymphs, *Coridon*, and *Mopsa*; with a Chorus of *Fawns*, and *Naiads*, with *Woodmen*, and *Hay-makers* Dancers.

Singers and Dancers in the Fourth Act.

Spring, Summer, Autumn, Winter, and their Attendants. *Phœbus*: A Dance of the four Seasons.

Singers and Dancers in the Fifth Act.

Juno, Chinese Men and Women.
A Chorus of *Chineses.*
A Dance of 6 Monkeys.
An Entry of a *Chinese* Man and Woman.
A Grand Dance of 24 *Chineses.*

[Act I, Scene i.] A Palace.

*   *   *

Du. 'Tis true, *Lysander*, I have heard as much.
Hermia, resolve to be obedient.

Or, as the Law ordains it, you must take
An everlasting Farewel of the World.
To Morrow in the Morning give your answer: so farewell.

[*Ex. all but* Her. *and* Ly.

   Ly. O my true *Hermia*! I have never found
By Observation, nor by History,
That Lovers run a smooth, and even course:
Either they are unequal in their Birth——
   Her. O cross too high to be impos'd on Love!
   Ly. Or if there be a Simpathy in choice,
War, Sickness, or pale Death lay Siege to it,
Making it momentary as a sound,
Swift as the Lightning in the blackest night;
That at one Instant shews both Heav'n and Earth.
Yet ere a man can say, behold the Flame,
The jaws of darkness have devour'd it up;
So quick even brightest things run to Confusion.
   Her. If then true Lovers have been ever cross'd,
It stands as a Decree in Destiny.
Then let us teach each other Patience,
Because it is a customary thing.
   Ly. 'Tis well advis'd, my *Hermia*,
Pray hear me. I have an Aunt, a Widow,
She has no Child, and is extreamly rich. . . .

       ★   ★   ★

[Act II, Scene ii.] A Wood, by Moon-light.

Enter Titania, *and her Train.*

   Tit. Take Hands, and trip it in a round,
While I Consecrate the ground.
All shall change at my Command,
All shall turn to *Fairy-Land.*

The Scene changes to a Prospect of Grotto's, Arbors, and delightful Walks:
   The Arbors are Adorn'd with all variety of Flowers, the Grotto's supported
   by Terms, these lead to two Arbors on either side of the Scene, of a great

*length, whose prospect runs toward the two Angles of the House. Between
these two Arbors is the great Grotto, which is continued by several Arches,
to the farther end of the House.*

Now *Fairies* search, search every where,
Let no Unclean thing be near.
Nothing Venomous, or Foul,
No *Raven, Bat,* or hooting *Owle.*
No *Toad,* nor *Elf,* nor *Blind-worm*'s Sting.
No Poisonous Herb in this place Spring.
Have you search'd? is no ill near?
　　All. Nothing, nothing; all is clear.
　　Tit. Let your Revels now begin,
Some shall Dance, and some shall Sing.
All Delights this place surround,
Every sweet Harmonious Sound,
That e're Charm'd a skilful Ear,
Meet, and Entertain us here.
Let Eccho's plac'd in every Grot,
Catch, and repeat each Dying Note.

A PRELUDE.

Then the First *SONG.*

Come all ye Songsters of the Sky,
Wake, and Assemble in this Wood;
But no ill-boding Bird be nigh,
None but the Harmless and the Good.
　　May the God of Wit inspire,
　　　　The Sacred Nine to bear a part;
　　And the Blessed Heavenly Quire,
　　　　Shew the utmost of their Art.
　　While Eccho shall in sounds remote,
　　　　Repeat each Note,
　　　　　　Each Note, each Note.

Chorus.

May the God, *&c.*

Now joyn your Warbling Voices all,
Sing while we trip it on the Green;

But no ill Vapours rise or fall,
Nothing offend our *Fairy* Queen.

Chorus.

Sing while we trip, *&c.*

At the end of the first Stanza a Composition of Instrumental
Musick, in imitation of an Eccho. Then a Fairy Dance.

Tit. Come *Elves,* another Dance, and *Fairy* Song;
Then hence, and leave me for a while alone.
Some to kill *Kankers* in the *Musk-Rose-Buds*;
Some War with *Rere-mice* for their Leathern Wings,
To make my small *Elves* Coats. And some keep back
The clamarous Owl, that hoots, and wonders at us.
Each knows her Office. Sing me now to Sleep;
And let the Sentinels their Watches keep.   [*She lyes down.*

2. *SONG.*

Enter Night, Mystery, Secresie, Sleep; *and their Attendants.*

Night *Sings.*

Ni. See, even *Night* her self is here,
       To favour your Design;
   And all her Peaceful Train is near,
       That Men to Sleep incline.
         Let Noise and Care,
         Doubt and Despair,
       Envy and Spight,
       (The Fiends delight)
     Be ever Banish'd hence.
       Let soft Repose,
       Her Eye-lids close;
       And murmuring Streams,
       Bring pleasing Dreams;
   Let nothing stay to give offence.

See, even *Night, &c.*

Mys. I am come to lock all fast,
       Love without me cannot last.

427

Love, like Counsels of the Wise,
Must be hid from Vulgar Eyes.
'Tis holy, and we must conceal it,
They profane it, who reveal it.

I am come, &c.

Se. One charming Night
 Gives more delight,
Than a hundred lucky Days.
 Night and I improve the tast,
 Make the pleasure longer last,
A thousand thousand several ways.

Make the pleasure, &c.

Sl. Hush, no more, be silent all,
Sweet Repose has clos'd her Eyes.
Soft as feather'd Snow does fall!
 Softly, softly, steal from hence.
 No noise disturb her sleeping sence.
Rest till the Rosie Morn's uprise.

Chorus. Hush, no more, &c.

A Dance of the Followers of Night.

Enter Oberon.

Ob. What thou seest when thou dost wake,
For thy Lover thou must take,
Sigh, and Languish, for his sake.
Be it Ounce, or Wolf, or Bear,
Pard, or Boar with bristel'd Hair,
In thy Eye what first appear,
Make that Beastly thing thy Dear,
Wake, when some vile Creature's near.   [*Ex. Ob.*

  ★ ★ ★

[Act III, Scene v.]

Enter Titania, Bottom, *and Fairies.*

Tit. Come, lovely Youth, sit on this flowry Bed,
While I thy amiable looks survey;

428

Garlands of Roses shall adorn thy Head,
  A thousand Sweets shall melt themselves away,
To charm my Lover till the break of day.
Shall we have Musick sweet?
  Bot. Yes, if you please.
  Tit. Away, my Elves; prepare a Fairy Mask
To entertain my Love; and change this place
To my Enchanted Lake.

*The Scene changes to a great Wood; a long row of large Trees on each side:
A River in the middle: Two rows of lesser Trees of a different kind just on
the side of the River, which meet in the middle, and make so many Arches:
Two great Dragons make a Bridge over the River; their Bodies form two
Arches, through which two Swans are seen in the River at a great distance.*

Enter a Troop of Fawns, Dryades and Naiades.

A Song in two Parts.

If Love's a Sweet Passion, why does it torment?
If a Bitter, oh tell me whence comes my content?
Since I suffer with pleasure, why should I complain,
Or grieve at my Fate, when I know 'tis in vain?
  Yet so pleasing the Pain is, so soft is the Dart,
  That at once it both wounds me, and tickles my Heart.

I press her Hand gently, look Languishing down,
And by Passionate Silence I make my Love known.
But oh! how I'm Blest when so kind she does prove,
By some willing mistake to discover her Love.
  When in striving to hide, she reveals all her Flame,
  And our Eyes tell each other, what neither dares Name.

*While a Symphany's Playing, the two Swans come Swimming on through
the Arches to the bank of the River, as if they would Land; there turn
themselves into Fairies, and Dance; at the same time the Bridge vanishes,
and the Trees that were Arch'd, raise themselves upright.*

Four Savages Enter, fright the Fairies away, and Dance an Entry.

Enter Coridon, *and* Mopsa.

  Co. Now the Maids and the Men are making of Hay,
    We have left the dull Fools, and are stol'n away.

429

Then *Mopsa* no more
Be Coy as before,
But let us merrily, merrily Play,
And Kiss, and Kiss, the sweet time away.

Mo. Why how now, Sir *Clown*, how came you so bold?
I'd have you to know I'm not made of that mold.
I tell you again,
Maids must Kiss no Men.
No, no; no, no; no Kissing at all;
I'le not Kiss, till I Kiss you for good and all.

Co. No, no.

Mo. No, no.

Co. Not Kiss you at all.

Mo. Not Kiss, till you Kiss me for good and all.
Not Kiss, *&c.*

Co. Should you give me a score,
'Twould not lessen the store,
Then bid me chearfully, chearfully Kiss,
And take, and take, my fill of your Bliss.

Mo. I'le not trust you so far, I know you too well;
Should I give you an Inch, you'd take a whole Ell.
Then Lordlike you Rule,
And laugh at the Fool.
No, no, *&c.*

A Song by a Nymph.

When I have often heard young Maids complaining,
   That when Men promise most they most deceive,
Then I thought none of them worthy my gaining;
   And what they Swore, resolv'd ne're to believe.

But when so humbly he made his Addresses,
   With Looks so soft, and with Language so kind,
I thought it Sin to refuse his Caresses;
   Nature o'recame, and I soon chang'd my Mind.

Should he employ all his wit in deceiving,
   Stretch his Invention, and artfully feign;
I find such Charms, such true Joy in believing,
   I'll have the Pleasure, let him have the pain.

If he proves Perjur'd, I shall not be Cheated,
He may deceive himself, but never me;
'Tis what I look for, and shan't be defeated,
For I'll be as false and inconstant as he.

A DANCE of Hay-Makers.

After the DANCE

Chorus.

A Thousand Thousand ways we'll find,
To Entertain the Hours;
No Two shall e're be known so kind,
No Life so Blest as ours.

Tit. Now I will Feast the Pallate of my Love,
The Sea, the Air, the Earth I'll ransack for thee.
Name all that Art or Nature e're produc'd,
My Sprights shall fetch it instantly: O say
What will you have to Eat?

Bo. A Peck of Provender, if your Honour please; I could munch
some good dry Oats very heartily; I have a great exposition of Sleep
upon me; would some of your Attendants would shew me a necessary
place for that same purpose.

Tit. I'll lead thee to a Bank strew'd o'er with Violets,
With Jessamine, and cooling Orange Flowers,
There I will fold thee in my tender Arms,
As the sweet Woodbine, or the Female Ivy,
Circles the Barky Body of the Elm.
We'll Sport away the remnant of the Night,
And all the World shall envy my Delight.   [*Exeunt.*

[Act IV, Scene i.]

*   *   *

Enter Oberon.

Ob. Thou hast perform'd exactly each Command.
Titania too has given me the sweet Boy.
And now I have him, I will straight undo
The hated imperfection of her Eyes.
And gentle Puck, take thou the Asses Head,

431

From the transform'd Clown she doated on.
That he awaking when the others do,
May with his Fellows to their Homes repair.
And think no more of this Night's Accidents,
Than of the fierce vexation of a Dream,
But first, I will release the *Fairy Queen*.

> *Be, as thou wert wont to be;*
> *See, as thou wert wont to see.*
> *Cinthia's Bud, and Cupid's Flow'r,*
> *Has such force, and Blessed Pow'r.*

Now my *Titania*, wake.   [*She rises.*

Tit. My *Oberon*! What Visions have I seen?
Methought I was enamour'd of an Ass.

Ob. There lies your Love.

Tit. How came these things to pass?
How I detest that hateful Visage now!

Ob. Robin, take from the Fool the Ass's head.

Rob. Hark, thou King of Shadows, hark!
Sure I hear the morning Lark.

Ob. Let him warble on, I'll stay,
And bless these Lover's Nuptial Day.
Sleep, happy Lovers, for some Moments, sleep.

Rob. So, when thou wak'st with thy own Fools Eyes, peep.

[*He takes off the Ass's Head.*

Ob. Titania, call for Musick.

Tit. Let us have all Variety of Musick,
All that should welcome up the rising Sun.

The Scene changes to a Garden of Fountains. A Sonata plays while the Sun rises, it appears red through the Mist, as it ascends it dissipates the Vapours, and is seen in its full Lustre; then the Scene is perfectly discovered, the Fountains enrich'd with gilding, and adorn'd with Statues: The view is terminated by a Walk of Cypress Trees which lead to a delightful Bower. Before the Trees stand rows of Marble Columns, which support many Walks which rise by Stairs to the top of the House; the Stairs are adorn'd with Figures on Pedestals, and Rails; and Balasters on each side of 'em. Near the top, vast Quantities of Water break out of the Hills, and fall in mighty Cascade's to the bottom of the Scene, to feed the Fountains which are on each side. In the middle of the Stage is a very large Fountain, where the Water rises about twelve Foot.

Then the 4 Seasons enter, with their several Attendants.

One of the Attendants begins.

Now the Night is chac'd away,
    All salute the rising Sun;
'Tis the happy, happy Day,
    The Birth-Day of King *Oberon.*

Two others sing in Parts.

Let the Fifes, and the Clarions, and shrill Trumpets sound,
And the Arch of high Heav'n the Clangor resound.

A Machine appears, the Clouds break from before it, and Phœbus *appears
in a Chariot drawn by four Horses; and Sings.*

When a cruel long Winter has frozen the Earth,
    And Nature Imprison'd seeks in vain to be free;
I dart forth my Beams, to give all things a Birth,
    Making Spring for the Plants, every flower, and each Tree.

'Tis I who give Life, Warmth, and Being to all,
    Even Love who rules all things in Earth, Air, and Sea;
Would languish, and fade, and to nothing would fall,
    The World to its Chaos would return, but for me.

Chorus.

Hail! *Great Parent of us all,*
    Light and Comfort of the Earth;
Before thy Shrine the Seasons fall,
    Thou who givest all Beings Birth.

Spring.

Thus the ever Grateful Spring,
    Does her yearly Tribute bring;
All your Sweets before him lay,
    Then round his Altar Sing, and Play.

Summer.

Here's the *Summer,* Sprightly, Gay,
    Smiling, Wanton, Fresh, and Fair;
Adorn'd with all the Flowers of *May,*
    Whose various Sweets perfume the Air.

433

Autumn.

See my many Colour'd Fields,
    And loaded Trees my Will obey;
All the Fruit that Autumn yields,
    I offer to the God of Day.

Winter.

Now Winter comes Slowly, Pale, Meager, and Old,
First trembling with Age, and then quiv'ring with Cold;
Benum'd with hard Frosts, and with Snow cover'd o're,
Prays the S U N to Restore him, and Sings as before.

Chorus.

Hail Great Parent, &c.

A D A N C E of the Four Seasons.

*   *   *

[Act V, Scene i.]

*   *   *

*A Composition in imitation of Hunting, at the end of it a Shout, the Lovers
wake.*

*   *   *

[Act V, Scene iii.]

Enter Duke, Egeus, *Lovers, and Attendants.*

  Eg. Are not these Stories strange, my Gracious Lord?
  Du. More strange than true. I never could believe,
These Antick Fables, nor these Fairy toys.
Lovers, and Lunaticks have pregnant brains.
They in a moment by strong fancy see
More than cool reason e're could comprehend.
The Poet, with the mad-man may be joyn'd.

434

He's of imagination all made up,
And sees more Devils, than all Hell can hold.
Can make a *Venus* of an *Ethiop*.
And as imagination rolls about,
He gives the airy Fantasms of his Brain,
A Local habitation, and a name.
And so these Lovers, wandring in the night,
Through unfrequented ways, brim full of fear,
How easie is a Bush suppos'd a Bear!
       [*While a short Simphony Plays,* Enter Oberon, Titania,
                Robin-Good-fellow, *and all the Fayries.*
I hear strange Musick warbling in the Air.
   Ob. 'Tis Fairy Musick, sent by me;
To cure your Incredulity.
All was true the Lovers told,
You shall stranger things behold.
Mark the wonders shall appear,
While I feast your eye and ear.
   Du. Where am I? does my sence inform me right?
Or is my hearing better than my sight?
   Tit. When to Parlors we retire,
And Dance before a dying fire;
   Ob. Or when by night near Woods, or Streams,
We wanton by the Moons pale beams;
Then gross shades, and twinkling light,
Expose our Shapes to mortal sight.
But in the bright and open day,
When in *Sol's* Glorious beams we play,
Our bodies are, in that fierce light,
Too thin and pure for humane sight.
   Tit. Sir, then cast your eyes above:
See the Wife of mighty *Jove.*
            Juno *appears in a Machine drawn by Peacocks.*
   Ob. Juno, who does still preside,
Over the Sacred Nuptial Bed:
Comes to bless their days and nights,
With all true joys, and chaste delights.

*While a Symphony Plays, the Machine moves forward, and the Peacocks
spread their Tails, and fill the middle of the Theater.*

JUNO *Sings.*

Thrice happy Lovers, may you be
    For ever, ever free,
From that tormenting Devil, Jealousie.
    From all that anxious Care and Strife.
    That attends a married Life:
    Be to one another true,
    Kind to her as she to you.
And since the Errors of this Night are past,
May he be ever Constant, she be ever Chast.

The Machine ascends.

Ob. Now my gentle *Puck*, away,
Haste, and over-cast the Day.
Let thick Darkness all around,
Cover that Spot of Fairy Ground;
That so the gloomy Shades of Night
May usher in a glorious Light.

While the Scene is darken'd, a single Entry is danced; Then a Symphony is play'd; after that the Scene is suddainly Illuminated, and discovers a transparent Prospect of a Chinese Garden, *the Architecture, the Trees, the Plants, the Fruits, the Birds, the Beasts, quite different from what we have in this part of the World. It is terminated by an Arch, through which is seen other Arches with close Arbors, and a row of Trees to the end of the View. Over it is a hanging Garden, which rises by several ascents to the top of the House; it is bounded on either side with pleasant Bowers, various Trees, and numbers of strange Birds flying in the Air. On the Top of a Platform is a Fountain, throwing up Water, which falls into a large Basin.*

A Chinese *Enters and Sings.*

Thus the gloomy World
At first began to shine,
And from the Power Divine
A Glory round it hurl'd;
Which made it bright,
And gave it Birth in light.
Then were all Minds as pure,
As those Etherial Streams;

In Innocence secure,
Not Subject to Extreams.
There was no Room for empty Fame,
No cause for Pride, Ambition wanted aim.

A Chinese *Woman Sings.*

Thus Happy and Free,
Thus treated are we
With Nature's chiefest Delights,

Chorus. Thus happy, *&c.*

We never cloy
But renew our Joy,
And one Bliss another Invites.

Chorus. We never, *&c.*

Thus wildly we live,
Thus freely we give,
What Heaven as freely bestows.

Chorus. Thus wildly, *&c.*

We were not made
For Labour and Trade,
Which Fools on each other impose.

Chorus. We were not *&c.*

A Chinese *Man Sings.*

Yes, *Xansi,* in your Looks I find
    The Charms by which my Heart's betray'd;
Then let not your Disdain unbind
    The Prisoner that your Eyes have made.

She that in Love makes least Defence,
    Wounds ever with the surest Dart;
Beauty may captivate the Sence,
    But Kindness only gains the Heart.

Six Monkeys come from between the Trees, and Dance.

437

Two Women Sing in Parts.

1 Wo. *Hark how all Things with one Sound rejoyce,*
   And the World seems to have one Voice.
2 Wo. *Hark how the Echoing Air a Triumph Sings,*
   And all around pleas'd Cupids clap their Wings.
1 Wo. *Sure the dull God of Marriage does not hear;*
   We'll rouse him with a Charm. Hymen *appear!*
Chorus. *Appear!* Hymen *appear!*
Both. *Our Queen of Night commands you not to stay.*
Chorus. *Our Queen, &c.*

Enter Hymen.

Hy.   *See, see, I obey.*
   My Torch has long been out, I hate
   On loose dissembled Vows to wait.
   Where hardly, Love out-lives the Wedding-Night,
   False Flames, Love's Meteors, yield my Torch no Light.

Six Pedestals of China-*work rise from under the Stage; they support six large Vases of Porcelain, in which are six* China-Orange-trees.

Both Wo. *Turn then thy Eyes upon those Glories there,*
   And Catching Flames will on thy Torch appear.
Hy.   *My Torch, indeed, will from such Brightness shine:*
   Love ne'er had yet such Altars, so divine.

The Pedestals move toward the Front of the Stage, and the Grand Dance begins of Twenty four Persons; then Hymen *and the Two Women sing together.*

   They shall be as happy as they're fair;
   Love shall fill all the Places of Care:
   And every time the Sun shall display
      His Rising Light,
   It shall be to them a new Wedding-Day;
   And when he sets, a new Nuptial-Night.

A Chinese *Man and Woman dance.*

The Grand Cho. *They shall be, &c.*

All the Dancers join in it.

438

Ob. At Dead of Night we'll to the Bride-bed come,
And sprinkle hallow'd Dew-drops round the Room.
    Tit. We'll drive the Fume about, about,
To keep all Noxious Spirits out:
That the Issue they create,
May be ever fortunate.
    Ob. Stay; let us not, like very foolish Elves,
Take care of others, and neglect our selves.
If these should be offended, we are lost;
And all our Hopes, and future Fortunes cross'd.
    Tit. It is below the Fairy-Queen to fear.
Look there: Can there be any Danger near.
When Conquering Beauty fills that Heavenly Sphear?
    Ob. But here are Wits, and Criticks! and 'tis said,
Their Adders Tongues can sting, or hit us dead.
    Tit. Away: Let not the Name of Wits alarm us;
They are so very few, they cannot harm us.
    Ob. Consider: Sharpers, Beau's, the very Cits.
All either are, or else they would be Wits.
    Tit. Well, let 'em all be Wits; and if they shou'd
Blast us, or nip us in the very Bud,
The Loss will be their own another Day.
Are we not in a very hopeful Way
To make 'em all amends—if they will stay?
    Ob. They are impatient, and their Stomachs keen;
They will not be post-pon'd, 'tis you're Fifteen.
    Tit. Well, if their Appetites so fiercely crave,
We'll give 'em all the Ready that we have.
First, Losing Gamesters, Poets, Railing Wits;
Some Basset-Ladies, and all Broken Cits;
(Who live by what from others they purloyn)
We'll lend 'em mighty Sums—in Fairy-Coin.
    Ob. Ladies in Dreams shall have their Fortunes told;
The Young shall dream of Husbands, and the Old
Their Youthful Pleasures shall each Night repeat.
    Tit. Green-Sickness Girls, who nautiate wholesom Meat,
How they their Parents, and themselves may cheat.
    Ob. Widows, who were by former Husbands vex'd,
Shall dream how they may over-reach the next.
    Tit. Each separate Lady, to supply her Want,

Shall every Night dream of a new Gallant.
 Ob. Those Beau's, who were, at Nurse, chang'd by my Elves,
 Tit. Shall dream of nothing, but their pretty selves.
 Ob. We'll try a Thousand charming Ways to win ye.
 Tit. If all this will not do, the Devil's in ye.

A Select Bibliography of
Shakespeare Criticism, to 1692

No satisfactory bibliography of Shakespeare criticism in this or any other period has yet been produced: each student must assemble his own. This is a listing of the more general items only; for further information see:

EBISCH, W., and SCHÜCKING, L. L., *A Shakespeare Bibliography* (Oxford, 1931).
EBISCH, W., and SCHÜCKING, L. L., *Supplement for the Years 1930–1935* (Oxford, 1937).
SMITH, G. R., *A Classified Shakespeare Bibliography, 1936–1958* (Pennsylvania, 1963).

For work published since then the annual bibliographies may be consulted, of which the most useful is that in *Shakespeare Quarterly.*

(A) COLLECTIONS OF CRITICISM AND ALLUSIONS
The Shakespeare Allusion-Book: A Collection of Allusions to Shakespeare From 1591 to 1700. . . . Edited J. Munro (1909), and with a new preface by E. K. Chambers (Oxford, 1932), 2 vols. This is the fullest collection; an up-to-date edition of it is urgently needed.
THORN-DRURY, G., *Some 17th century allusions to Shakespeare.* . . . (1920).
THORN-DRURY, G., *More Seventeenth Century Allusions to Shakespeare* (1924).
SPINGARN, J. (ed.), *Critical Essays of the Seventeenth Century* (Oxford, 1908, 1957).
ADAMS, H. H., and HATHAWAY, B. (ed.), *Dramatic Essays of the Neoclassic Age* (1950).
HUGHES, C. E. (ed.), *The Praise of Shakespeare* (1904).
KERMODE, F. (ed.), *Four Centuries of Shakespearian Criticism* (New York, 1965; Harmondsworth, 1970).
SMITH, D. N. (ed.), *Shakespeare Criticism, 1623 to 1840* (1916; World's Classics series).
WILLIAMSON, C. (ed.), *Readings on the Character of Hamlet 1661–1947* (1950).

(B) INDIVIDUAL CRITICS: MODERN EDITIONS

PEPYS, SAMUEL, *Diary*, ed. H. B. Wheatley (1913), 8 vols; ed. R. C. Latham and W. Matthews (1970–).

DRYDEN, JOHN, *Of Dramatic Poesy and Other Critical Essays*, ed. G. G. Watson (1962), 2 vols.

DRYDEN, JOHN, *Prose 1668–1691. An Essay of Dramatick Poesie and shorter works*, ed. S. H. Monk *et al.* (Berkeley, Los Angeles and London, 1971): vol. XVII of the California *Works of John Dryden*.

The Critical Works of Thomas Rymer, ed. C. A. Zimansky (New Haven and London, 1956).

(C) HISTORIES OF LITERARY CRITICISM

RALLI, A., *A History of Shakespearian Criticism* (1932), 2 vols. A rather wooden survey, with the emphasis on summary rather than analysis.

EASTMAN, A. M., *A Short History of Shakespeare Criticism* (New York, 1968); mainly on critics since Coleridge.

BROWN, I., and FEARON, G., *Amazing Monument: A Short History of the Shakespeare Industry* (1939).

MARDER, L., *His Exits and Entrances: The Story of Shakespeare's Reputation* (Philadelphia, 1963); a lively and wide-ranging study, but spoiled by inadequate documentation.

CONKLIN, P. S., *A History of 'Hamlet' Criticism, 1601–1821* (New York, 1947, 1957).

(D) TEXTUAL STUDIES

BLACK, M. W., and SHAABER, M. A., *Shakespeare's Seventeenth Century Editors, 1632–85* (New York, 1937).

(E) THEATRICAL HISTORY, ADAPTATIONS

The London Stage, 1660–1800. Part 1, 1660–1700 ed. W. Van Lennep, with a Critical Introduction by E. L. Avery and A. H. Scouten (Carbondale, Ill., 1965). Lists all known productions of Shakespeare's plays (whether originals or adaptations) in the period, together with details of casts, takings, etc.

ODELL, G. C. D., *Shakespeare From Betterton to Irving* (New York, 1920), 2 vols.

SPENCER, H., *Shakespeare Improved. The Restoration Versions in Quarto and on the Stage* (Cambridge, Mass., 1927).

SPENCER, C. (ed.), *Davenant's 'Macbeth' from the Yale Manuscript* (New

Haven, 1961); *Five Restoration Adaptations of Shakespeare* (Urbana, Ill., 1965).

SORELIUS, G., '*The Giant Race Before the Flood*'. *Pre-Restoration Drama on the Stage and in the Criticism of the Restoration* (Uppsala, 1966).

ARNOTT, J. F., and ROBINSON, J. W., *English Theatrical Literature 1559– 1900, A Bibliography* (1970).

Index

The index is arranged in three parts: I. Shakespeare's works; II. Shakespearian characters; III. General index. Adaptations are indexed under the adapter's name, in III below. References to individual characters listed in II are not repeated under the relevant plays.

II SHAKESPEARIAN CHARACTERS

III GENERAL INDEX

THE CRITICAL HERITAGE SERIES

GENERAL EDITOR: B. C. SOUTHAM

Volumes published and forthcoming

Continued